PROTECTING INFORMATION

For many everyday transmissions, it is essential to protect digital information from noise or eavesdropping. This undergraduate introduction to error correction and cryptography is unique in devoting several chapters to quantum cryptography and quantum computing, thus providing a context in which ideas from mathematics and physics meet. By covering such topics as Shor's quantum factoring algorithm, this text informs the reader about current thinking in quantum information theory and encourages an appreciation of the connections between mathematics and science.

Of particular interest are the potential impacts of quantum physics: (i) a quantum computer, if built, could crack our currently used public-key cryptosystems; and (ii) quantum cryptography promises to provide an alternative to these cryptosystems, basing its security on the laws of nature rather than on computational complexity.

No prior knowledge of quantum mechanics is assumed, but students should have a basic knowledge of complex numbers, vectors, and matrices.

Susan Loepp is an Associate Professor of Mathematics in the Department of Mathematics and Statistics at Williams College. Her research is in commutative algebra, focusing on completions of local rings.

William K. Wootters, a Fellow of the American Physical Society, is the Barclay Jermain Professor of Natural Philosophy in the Department of Physics at Williams College. He does research on quantum entanglement and other aspects of quantum information theory.

"The authors have combined the two 'hot' subjects of cryptography and coding, looking at each with regard to both classical and quantum models of computing and communication. These exciting topics are unified through the steady, consistent development of algebraic structures and techniques. Students who read this book will walk away with a broad exposure to both the theory and the concrete application of groups, finite fields, and vector spaces."

– Ben Lotto, *Vassar College*

Protecting Information

*From Classical Error Correction to
Quantum Cryptography*

SUSAN LOEPP
Williams College

WILLIAM K. WOOTTERS
Williams College

CAMBRIDGE UNIVERSITY PRESS
Cambridge, New York, Melbourne, Madrid, Cape Town, Singapore, São Paulo

Cambridge University Press
32 Avenue of the Americas, New York, NY 10013-2473, USA

www.cambridge.org
Information on this title: www.cambridge.org/9780521827409

First published 2006

Printed in the United States of America

A catalog record for this publication is available from the British Library.

Library of Congress Cataloging in Publication Data

Loepp, Susan.
Protecting information : from classical error correction to quantum cryptography /
Susan Loepp, William K. Wootters.
    p.   cm.
Includes bibliographical references and index.
ISBN-13: 978-0-521-82740-9 (hardback)
ISBN-10: 0-521-82740-X (hardback)
ISBN-13: 978-0-521-53476-5 (pbk.)
ISBN-10: 0-521-53476-3 (pbk.)
1. Quantum computers.   2. Computer security.   I. Wootters, William Kent.   II. Title.
QA76.889.L64   2006
004.1 – dc22   2006002404

ISBN-13   978-0-521-82740-9 hardback
ISBN-10   0-521-82740-X hardback

ISBN-13   978-0-521-53476-5 paperback
ISBN-10   0-521-53476-3 paperback

Dedicated to
Leona and Franzie,
Dorothy and Franzie,
and Adrienne, Mary, and Nate

Contents

Preface

In these early decades of the information age, the flow of information is becoming more and more central to our daily lives. It has therefore become important that information transmission be protected against eavesdropping (as, for example, when one sends credit card information over the Internet) and against noise (which might occur in a cell phone transmission, or when a compact disk is accidentally scratched). Though most of us depend on schemes that protect information in these ways, most of us also have a rather limited understanding of how this protection is done. Part of the aim of this book is to introduce the basic concepts underlying this endeavor.

Besides its practical significance, it happens that the subject of protecting information is intimately related to a number of central ideas in mathematics and computer science, and also, perhaps surprisingly, in physics. Thus in addition to its significance for society, the subject provides an ideal context for bringing ideas from these disciplines together. This interdisciplinarity is part of what has attracted us to the subject, and we hope it will appeal to the reader as well.

Among undergraduate texts on coding or cryptography, this book is unusual in its inclusion of quantum physics and the emerging technology of quantum information. Quantum cryptography, in which an eavesdropper is detected by his or her unavoidable disturbance of delicate quantum signals, was proposed in the 1980s and since then has been investigated and developed in a number of laboratories around the world. Though it is still a technology of the future, that future may not be far from us. Indeed some companies are already selling quantum cryptographic systems for a limited range of applications. The other major potential quantum information technology, quantum computation, is further from realization – most experts agree that full-scale quantum computation is at least a few decades away – but it is being vigorously pursued by researchers because of its tremendous potential. Most notably, a quantum computer would render useless all the standard public key cryptosystems such as those used in Internet communications. Indeed, the very possibility of quantum computation is part of the motivation for developing quantum cryptography.

Thus this book pivots around two binary oppositions. First, there are the two reasons for protecting information: against eavesdropping and against noise. Second, there are two arenas in which one can work: the classical and the quantum. Most of the chapters lie primarily on one side or the other of each of these oppositions, but the book is constructed with the intention that these different facets complement and reinforce each other. Thus the mathematics and physics are to some extent interwoven, not necessarily seamlessly but in such a way as to make use of the connections.

The book has grown out of a one-semester course we have taught a few times now to upper-level undergraduates, mostly in mathematics, physics, and computer science. A student in this course needs to have a certain level of mathematical sophistication – linear algebra is particularly helpful though not absolutely required – but the physics is supposed to be self-contained. Partly because of the intended audience, we focus more on the mathematical structure of quantum mechanics than on its connections with other parts of physics, though a few terms such as "electric field" and "quark" do make cameo appearances. Most of the problems at the ends of the sections have been used in our course and seem to be about the right level of difficulty. There are a few, though, that have not been so tested. Let the teacher and student be warned!

We begin in Chapter 1 with a selected survey of ideas in cryptography. The chapter introduces modular arithmetic, first at an elementary level but building to a more sophisticated understanding. The chapter finishes with ideas from group theory and the theory of elliptic curves. The next logical step would be to take up the subject of quantum cryptography, but this requires some background in quantum physics, which is provided in

Chapter 2. Rather than keeping the quantum mechanics entirely formal, we ground it by imagining simple experiments involving the polarization of photons. The chapter develops the theory far enough that the ideas can be used not only for quantum cryptography but also, later, for quantum computation and basic quantum error correction. (The final section of the chapter can be omitted if one also chooses to omit the section on quantum error correction.)

With the quantum bases covered, we proceed in Chapter 3 to quantum cryptography, focusing on the most widely studied quantum strategy for distributing a secret key. Quantum key distribution motivates two other subjects in quantum mechanics, the no-cloning theorem and quantum teleportation, which are therefore also included in Chapter 3. But the full protocol for quantum key distribution cannot quite be discussed until we make further progress on the classical front, and this provides one motivation for Chapter 4 on classical error-correcting codes. The main mathematical ideas in this chapter revolve around vector spaces over $\mathbb{Z}_p$, where p is a prime number, as the main mathematical ideas of Chapter 2 revolved around vector spaces over the complex numbers. Armed with generator matrices, check matrices, and syndrome decoding, we return in Chapter 5 to quantum key distribution to flesh out the protocol. We then use $\mathbb{Z}_p$ and other finite fields in Chapter 6 to study generalized Reed-Solomon codes.

The final chapter belongs to the quantum world. First we develop enough of the theory of quantum computation to outline the quantum factoring algorithm, which threatens the public key cryptography introduced in Chapter 1. And the last section shows how in principle one can protect *quantum* information against noise.

It would be easy to make a long list of relevant topics that we do not cover in this book. Of particular note is the whole theory of information and entropy, including, for example, the fundamental limits on error correction. There are many excellent books on this subject, and we can imagine using such a book in conjunction with this one. (In our own experience we have found that the topics covered here give students more than enough to chew on.) While we have not attempted to give a complete bibliography such as one would find in a review article, we have tried, via footnotes, to give students enough entries into the literature to allow them to study in more depth any of the topics we have covered. Moreover, the book should supply the conceptual background needed to approach these sources.

We hope that it will also encourage an appreciation of the connections between mathematics and physics and the role that both of these disciplines play in current and future information technology.

Acknowledgments

This book has benefited from the comments and suggestions of many students who have taken our course in this subject over the last several years. We especially thank those who suffered through the first version, in which the students themselves were responsible for producing and sharing class notes. Some of these notes have, in some form, found their way into this book. Two recent students, Evan Miller and Evan Couzo, contributed especially valuable suggestions to a later draft. Besides those who took the course, there are other students who were tremendously helpful as teaching assistants. Among these, we particularly want to thank Kevin O'Connor, Teodora Ivanova, and Philippa Charters whose computer programs added much to the course and significantly influenced its content. The development of our course, the computer programs, and this book were generously supported by Williams College and a grant from the National Science Foundation.

We are grateful to Jon Hall of Michigan State University for sharing his expert knowledge, suggestions, and advice. Two colleagues at other institutions, Ben Lotto of Vassar College and Mike Westmoreland of Denison University, have both taught courses based on early, sketchy versions of this book, and we have learned much from their experiences and have incorporated their comments. Mike and Ben, along with Duane Bailey, Charles Bennett, Richard Jozsa, and Perry Susskind, have generously shared their suggestions on more recent versions as well. Obviously, they are not responsible for the remaining faults! Those are all to be blamed on the Berkshire hills that surround us here, whose colors have distracted us from our work.

1 Cryptography: An Overview

1.1 Elementary Ciphers

Cryptography is the design and use of communication schemes aimed at hiding the meaning of the message from everyone except the intended receiver. *Cryptanalysis* is the effort to foil an encryption system, to crack the code. The study of cryptography and cryptanalysis is called *cryptology* and is the focus of this chapter.[1] Later we will study some fairly sophisticated cryptographic systems, but we begin with a few elementary examples.

1.1.1 Substitution ciphers

Substitution ciphers are the familiar sort of encryption that one finds in Sunday newspaper puzzles, in which each letter of the alphabet stands for another letter. A special case is the *Caesar cipher*, in which the alphabet is simply shifted by some number of places. In the version used by Julius Caesar, the alphabet is shifted forward by three places. For example, if a letter of the original message, or *plaintext*, is A, the corresponding letter of the encrypted message, or *cyphertext*, is D, and so on as indicated here:

$$\text{plaintext: } A \; B \; C \ldots X \; Y \; Z$$

$$\text{ciphertext: } D \; E \; F \ldots A \; B \; C$$

---

[1] For a compact overview of cryptography and cryptanalysis, including many practical issues, see Piper and Murphy (2002). A more mathematical information-theoretic approach is given in Welsh (1988). A popular historical account can be found in Singh (1999). For a more thorough treatment of the history, see Kahn (1967).

We can express this cipher mathematically by assigning a number to each letter: $A \rightarrow 0$, $B \rightarrow 1, \ldots$, $Z \rightarrow 25$. Then if x represents a letter of the plaintext and y the corresponding letter of the ciphertext, Julius Caesar's cipher can be expressed as

$$y = x + 3 \ (\text{mod } 26),$$

where "(mod 26)" means that one takes the remainder upon dividing by 26. (Much more on modular arithmetic in later sections of this chapter.) If you are adept at cracking the substitution ciphers of the Sunday paper, you may find it surprising that Caesar was able to keep any messages secret with this simple strategy, but evidently it worked well enough.

A simple generalization of the Caesar cipher is expressed by the equation $y = ax + b$ (mod 26), where a and b are integers.[2] It is interesting to ask whether some values of a and b are better than others, and indeed this question is the subject of one of the exercises below. A further generalization is to use an arbitrary permutation of the alphabet.

How does one go about cracking a substitution cipher? The standard technique, which is well known today but was not known in Roman times, is *frequency analysis*. Let us assume that the cryptanalyst knows what language the plaintext is expressed in; suppose it is English. In typical English text, each letter occurs with a certain frequency. The most common letter in English is E: if you blindly point to a letter on a page in a novel, the probability that the letter will be E is around 12.7%. The following table gives the frequencies of all the letters, as computed from a sample of over 300,000 characters taken from newspapers and novels.[3]

E	12.7%	D	4.2%	P	1.9%
T	9.0%	L	4.0%	B	1.5%
A	8.2%	U	2.8%	V	1.0%
O	7.5%	C	2.8%	K	0.8%
I	7.0%	M	2.4%	Q	0.1%
N	6.7%	W	2.4%	X	0.1%
S	6.3%	F	2.2%	J	0.1%
H	6.1%	G	2.0%	Z	0.1%
R	6.0%	Y	2.0%		

---

[2] The special case with $a = 1$ and $b = 13$, called "ROT13," is used nowadays in online settings to hide such things as joke punchlines and puzzle solutions.

[3] Piper and Murphy (2002). The authors write that the table is based on one originally compiled by H. J. Beker and F. C. Piper.

We can use this table to crack a substitution cipher as follows. Given the ciphertext, we count how many times each letter appears. If the message is long enough, the frequencies of occurrence will help us guess how each letter should be decrypted. For example, if v occurs around 13% of the time, we guess that v represents the letter e. Once we have correctly guessed a few of the letters, we look for familiar words and so on. A related technique is to look for *pairs* of letters that occur frequently together. Some of the exercises at the end of this section will give you practice with frequency analysis.

1.1.2 Vigenère ciphers

We now consider a cipher that is more sophisticated than simple substitution. It was invented by Giovan Batista Belaso in the sixteenth century but later incorrectly attributed to Blaise de Vigenère and given his name. (Vigenère devised a more powerful variation on this cipher, in which the message itself was used to generate the key.)[4] The secret key in this case is a word or phrase. It is easiest to explain the cipher by giving an example; in the following example the message is "Meet me at midnight," and the key is "quantum." (Not a key that Belaso or Vigenère is likely to have used.)

```
PLAINTEXT:   M E E T M E A T M I D N I G H T

KEY:         Q U A N T U M Q U A N T U M Q U

CIPHERTEXT: C Y E G F Y M J G I Q G C S X N
```

To generate the ciphertext, we have associated an integer with each letter as before: A$\to$ 0, B$\to$ 1, etc.; in each column above we have added, mod 26, the numbers corresponding to the given letters of the plaintext and the key. For example, the first letter of the ciphertext is obtained as follows:

$$M + Q \; \to \; 12 + 16 \; (mod \; 26) = 2 \to C$$

In other words, each letter is encrypted with a Caesar cipher – the encryption is a cyclic shifting of the alphabet – but different letters can be shifted by different amounts. In the above example, six distinct Caesar ciphers

---

[4] Belaso's cipher is closely related to ciphers devised by others in the preceding century. A full account can be found in Kahn (1967).

are used in a pattern that repeats after seven letters. The intended recipient should know the key and can recover the plaintext by subtracting from each letter of the ciphertext the corresponding letter of the key.

Notice how this cipher improves on the simple substitution scheme. The letter M appears three times in our plaintext, and each time it is encrypted differently. Conversely, the letter G appears three times in the ciphertext, and each time it stands for a different letter of the plaintext. Thus a straightforward frequency analysis will not be nearly as effective as it is against a substitution cipher.

However, one can still use frequency analysis to crack the cipher if the message is long enough. Suppose that the cryptanalyst can somehow figure out the length of the repeated key. Let us say that the length is 7 as in the above example. Then every seventh letter is encrypted with the same Caesar cipher, which can be cracked by doing a frequency analysis on just those entries of the ciphertext. So the problem is not hard once we know the length of the key. But how might the cryptanalyst guess the length of the key? One method is to look for repeated strings of letters. For example, in a long message it is quite likely that the word "the" will be encrypted in the same way several times and will thus produce the same three-letter sequence several times. So if the cryptanalyst sees, for example, three instances of "rqv," the second instance displaced from the first by 21 steps and the third displaced from the second by 56 steps, he or she could reasonably guess that the repeated key is seven letters long, since 7 is the only positive integer (other than 1) that divides both 21 and 56. Of course such a guess becomes more trustworthy if more repetitions are discovered, since it is always possible for a string of letters of the ciphertext to be repeated by chance. This method of cracking the Vigenère cipher was discovered in the nineteenth century by Friedrich Kasiski.

An alternative version of the Vigenère cipher replaces the repeated key with a "running key," usually an easily accessible text that is at least as long as the message. For example, we might use as the key the Constitution of the United States, beginning with the preamble. Then our encryption of "Meet me at midnight" would look like this:

```
PLAINTEXT:  M E E T M E A T M I D N I G H T

KEY:        W E T H E P E O P L E O F T H E

CIPHERTEXT: I I X A Q T E H B T H B N Z O X
```

The recipient, knowing the key, again simply subtracts it, letter by letter, from the ciphertext to recover the original message.

Clearly the cryptanalytic method we just described will not work against this encryption scheme, because the key is no longer periodic. But the key does have some structure, and a cryptanalyst can use this structure to get a foothold on the plaintext. For example, if the cryptanalyst suspects that the key is a piece of English text, she can guess that the word "the" appears in it frequently. She can then try "the" as part of the key in various positions along the ciphertext and see if the resulting plaintext is plausible as part of the message. Let us try this in the above example, applying THE at each position of the ciphertext.

Trigram in ciphertext	Trigram minus THE
IIX	PBT
IXA	PQW
XAQ	ETM
AQT	HJP
⋮	⋮
ZOX	GHT

Most of the trigrams on the right-hand side of the table could not possibly be part of a message written in English. In fact the only plausible candidates are ETM and GHT. The latter is particularly helpful, because there are only a few combinations of letters that are likely to precede GHT in English. The cryptanalyst might try a few of these, to see what they would imply about the key. Here is a table showing what he or she would find:

Guess at plaintext	Ciphertext minus plaintext = key
OUGHT	NTTHE
NIGHT	OFTHE
FIGHT	WFTHE
RIGHT	KFTHE
LIGHT	QFTHE
EIGHT	XFTHE

Of these, only the first two make any sense as part of a passage in English, and of these the second is more likely. So the cryptanalyst might tentatively guess that NIGHT is part of the plaintext and OFTHE part of the key. Continuing in this way, working back and forth between the unknown plaintext and the unknown key, he or she has a reasonable chance of cracking the cipher.

1.1.3 One-time pad

What makes the Vigenère cipher insecure, even with the running key of the last example, is that the key has some structure that can be exploited by the cryptanalyst: the key is a piece of English text, and English definitely has some structure. The natural way to avoid this problem is to use a running key consisting of purely random letters. The key used in the following example was generated, literally, by tossing coins.

```
PLAINTEXT:   M  E  E  T  M  E  A  T  M  I  D  N  I  G  H  T

KEY:         P  O  V  N  H  U  J  B  K  R  C  J  D  C  O  F

CIPHERTEXT:  B  S  Z  G  T  Y  J  U  W  Z  F  W  L  I  V  Y
```

Of course the intended recipient must also have a copy of the random key.

In this example, even though there is plenty of structure in the plaintext, the randomness of the key – if it is truly random – guarantees that there will be no structure whatsoever in the ciphertext. This cryptographic scheme can therefore not be broken by cryptanalysis.[5] (An eavesdropper could try other attacks such as intercepting the secret key on its way to the intended recipient.) We are assuming here that the random key is at least as long as the message, so that it will not have to be repeated. Also, for complete security it is important that the key be used only once. If it is used twice, an eavesdropper could compare the two ciphertexts and look for patterns. This method of encryption – a random key used only once – is known as a *one-time pad*, suggesting that the key might be copied on a pad of paper, delivered to the intended recipient, used once, and then destroyed.

Nowadays much of the information that is conveyed from place to place is in digital form and can be expressed as a sequence of zeros and

---

[5] A precise statement of this claim was proved by Shannon (1949).

ones. A one-time pad works fine for such an application, the key in this case being a random binary string. For example, one might see the following encryption of a rather uninteresting message. (Here again the key was generated by tossing a fair coin, despite what you may think.)

```
PLAINTEXT:   0 1 0 1 0 1 0 1 0 1 0 1 0 1 0 1 0 1

KEY:         1 0 0 1 0 0 1 0 0 1 0 0 0 0 1 1

CIPHERTEXT:  1 1 0 0 0 1 1 1 0 0 0 1 0 1 1 0
```

In each column the two entries, one from the plaintext and one from the key, have been added mod 2: that is, the ordinary sum is replaced by its remainder upon division by 2, so that $1 + 1 \pmod{2} = 0$.

Though the one-time pad is perfectly secure against cryptanalysis, it is by no means the most widely used form of cryptography. The problem with the scheme is that the random key has to be generated and delivered securely to the intended recipient at a rate equal to or exceeding the rate at which messages are to be conveyed. If this rate is large, one might have to employ an army of trusted couriers to transport the key.

Later in this book we consider in some detail a recently invented scheme, quantum key distribution, that could potentially solve this problem by relying not on mathematics but on the laws of nature. But our study of quantum key distribution will have to wait until we have introduced the relevant laws in Chapter 2.

EXERCISES

Problem 1. We mentioned a substitution cipher in which each plaintext letter, represented by an integer x, is replaced by the letter corresponding to the integer $y = ax + b \pmod{26}$, where a and b are integers. If the alphabet we are using has n letters, where n is not necessarily 26, we can generalize this rule to $y = ax + b \pmod{n}$, where "mod n" means that we take the remainder upon division by n. In answering the following questions, assume that the integers a and b are restricted to the values $0, \ldots, n - 1$.

(a) Suppose that n has the value 26, as it does if the plaintext is in English and we do not encrypt spaces or punctuation marks. Is there a reason not to use certain values of the constant a or of the constant b? If so, which values are the bad ones and what makes them bad?

(b) If we also count "space" as a character to be encrypted, we have $n = 27$. Now what, if any, are the bad values of a? Of b?

(c) For a general n, make a conjecture as to what will be the bad values of a and b, if there are any.

Problem 2. The following ciphertext was encrypted by a simple shift of the alphabet. All spaces and punctuation marks were first deleted from the plaintext, which was then arbitrarily broken into five-letter blocks. Find the original plaintext.

```
VQFGE  KRJGT  VJKUU  GPVGP  EGUJK  HVGCE  JNGVV  GTDCE
MYCTF  DAVYQ  UVGRU
```

Problem 3. The following ciphertext was generated by a Vigenère cipher with a repeating key. All spaces and punctuation marks were removed from the plaintext, and the resulting ciphertext was broken into six-letter blocks.

```
NRUATW  YAHJSE  DIODII  TLWCIJ  DOIPRA  DPANTO  EOOPEG
TNCWAS  DOBYAP  FRALLW  HSQNHW  DTDPIJ  GENDEO  BUWCEH
LWKQGN  LVEEYZ  ZEOYOP  XAGPIP  DEHQOX  GIKFSE  YTDPOX
DENGEZ  AHAYOI  PNWZNA  SAOEOH  ZOGQON  AAPEEN  YSWYDB
TNZEHA  SIZOEJ  ZRZPRX  FTPSEN  PIOLNE  XPKCTW  YTZTFB
PRAYCA  MEPHEA  YTDPSA  EWKAUN  DUEESE  YCNJPP  LNWWYO
TSKYEG  YOSDTD  LTPSED  TDZPNK  CDACWW  DCKYSP  CUYEEZ
MYDFMW  YIJEEH  WICPNY  PWDPRA  LSPSEK  CDACOB  YAPFRA
LPLLRA  YTHJCK  XEOQRK  XAOZUN  NEKFTO  TDAZFK  FROPLR
PSWYDE  DMKCEI  JSPPRE  ZUO
```

(a) Look for strings of three or more letters that are repeated in the ciphertext. From the separations of different instances of the same string, try to infer the length of the key.

(b) Using frequency analysis or any other means, try to find the key and the plaintext. (You might find Section A.3 of the Appendix helpful.)

1.2 Enigma

Though our review of cryptography is by no means exhaustive, there is one historical example that we cannot pass by, namely, the Enigma cipher used by the German military before and during World War II.[6]

The Enigma cipher is more complex than the ciphers we have considered so far. Though it can be described in purely mathematical terms and could in principle be implemented by hand, the cipher is intimately tied to a mechanical device, the Enigma machine. In this section we describe a slightly simplified version of the Enigma machine and the cipher it generates.[7]

1.2.1 The Enigma cipher

The main cryptographic components of the machine are (i) the plugboard, (ii) the rotors, and (iii) the reflector. Each of these parts has the effect of permuting the alphabet, and in each case the permutation is achieved by electrical wires that we can imagine connecting the input letter to the output letter. The net effect of all the parts is obtained by following the wires through the machine, from the original input letter, typed on a keyboard, to the output letter, indicated by the lighting of a lightbulb labeled with that letter. We now describe briefly each of the components.

The *plugboard* includes an array of 26 jacks, one for each letter, and six electrical cables, each of which can be plugged into two of the jacks so as to interchange those two letters.[8] All the letters that are not part of such interchanges are left unchanged. Let us call the plugboard's permutation A; it is a function that maps the alphabet to itself. If x is an input letter, we will write Ax (without parentheses) to indicate the plugboard's output. Notice that the inverse function A^{-1}, which takes a given output of the plugboard to the corresponding input, is the same as A itself. This fact will be important in what follows.

---

[6] For more on the Enigma cipher, see for example Sebag-Montefiore (2000).
[7] Our main simplification is to avoid discussing the "rings," a feature of the Enigma machine that added some security but did not constitute one of the main cryptanalytic challenges.
[8] Each jack actually consists of a *pair* of holes – an input and an output – and each electrical cable consists of a pair of wires: if one wire sends the letter B to the letter J, for example, its companion wire sends J to B.

Each *rotor* is a disk, with 26 input locations arranged in a circle on one side, and 26 output locations arranged in an identical circle on the other side. Inside the rotor, a wire runs from each of the input locations to one of the output locations, and together, the 26 wires implement a complicated permutation with no special symmetries. The output of the plugboard becomes the input to the first rotor, the output of the first rotor becomes the input to the second rotor, and so on. In the original Enigma machine used by the German army, there were three standard rotors, each embodying a different permutation.

The *reflector* acts on the output of the last rotor and effects a permutation that, like that of the plugboard, simply interchanges letters in pairs. Unlike the permutation of the plugboard, the reflector's permutation is fixed and cannot be changed by the operator of the machine, at least not in the simple version of Enigma that we are considering here. (There were other versions allowing some freedom to adjust the reflector.) Also the permutation is not limited to six pairs of letters: *every* letter is sent to a different letter. We will call the reflector's permutation B, and we note that $B^{-1} = B$.

Let us now follow the path by which the input letter leads to a particular output letter. As we have implied above, the input letter first encounters the plugboard permutation, then each of the rotor permutations in turn, and then the reflector permutation. After that, the path goes *backwards* through the rotors (in reverse order) and finally through the plugboard again before the output is indicated by a labeled light-bulb. The whole path is diagrammed for a simplified alphabet in Fig. 1.1.[9] Notice that because the reflector leaves no letter unchanged, neither does the Enigma machine as a whole: it never encodes a letter as itself.

The most characteristic and subtle feature of the Enigma machine is this: though each rotor has a fixed permutation wired into it, its *orientation* with respect to the other rotors and with respect to the other components can change from one keystroke to the next. There is one special orientation of each rotor which we call the "standard" orientation. Let R_i be the permutation executed by the ith rotor when it is in its standard orientation. Then, if the rotor's orientation is rotated from its standard

---

[9] This figure and Fig. 1.2 were inspired by similar figures in Singh (1999).

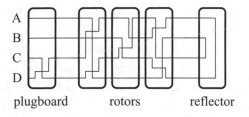

Figure 1.1: Schematic illustration of the main cryptographic elements of the Enigma machine for an alphabet of four letters. Here the letter A is encrypted as C. (The specific jigs and jags within each rotor have no special significance. All that matters in each rotor is the mapping between the left side and the right side.)

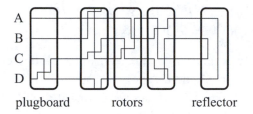

Figure 1.2: This is the same as Fig. 1.1 except that the first rotor (the one on the left) has advanced by one step. Now the letter A is encrypted as D. Circuit paths that seem to be heading off the top of the first rotor are continued at the bottom.

orientation by one "step," that is, by one 1/26 of a complete cycle, it is as if the permutation R_i were applied to an alphabet that had been shifted by one letter. In effect – and this statement defines the direction of the rotation – the rotor now implements the permutation $S^{-1}R_i S$, where S is the simple permutation A $\rightarrow$ B $\rightarrow$ $\cdots$ $\rightarrow$ Z $\rightarrow$ A, and S^{-1} is its inverse. (Here the order of operations is from right to left, so that the forward shift is applied first.) The effect of a one-step rotation is illustrated in Fig. 1.2. If the rotor has been rotated by n steps from its standard orientation (in the same direction as before), the permutation it executes is

$$S^{-n}R_i S^n, \tag{1.1}$$

where $S^{-n} = (S^{-1})^n$; that is, S^{-n} is the inverse of S applied n times.

At any given keystroke, each rotor has a specific orientation that is expressed in the value of n in Eq. (1.1). If there are three rotors, there are three such indices n_1, n_2, and n_3, each of which takes values from 0 to 25. At the next keystroke, the values will be different. Typically the difference is only in n_1, which is advanced by one unit mod 26. But when n_1 changes from 25 to 0, n_2 is advanced by one unit. (This is what is special about the "standard" orientation of the first rotor.) Similarly, n_3 is advanced by one unit only when n_2 changes from 25 to 0. Thus the number of keystrokes required before all the rotors return to their original orientations is $26^3 = 17576$.

Let us put all these pieces together to write down the mapping that the machine implements in a given keystroke (again, the expression should be read from right to left):

$$A(S^{-n_1}R_1S^{n_1})^{-1}(S^{-n_2}R_2S^{n_2})^{-1}(S^{-n_3}R_3S^{n_3})^{-1}B$$
$$(S^{-n_3}R_3S^{n_3})(S^{-n_2}R_2S^{n_2})(S^{-n_1}R_1S^{n_1})A \tag{1.2}$$

Recall that A and B are the permutations effected by the plugboard and the reflector respectively. We can simplify this expression a little by writing out the inverses of the products. One can verify that if C and D are invertible functions defined on the same set, the inverse of the product CD is the product of the inverses in reverse order; that is, $(CD)^{-1} = D^{-1}C^{-1}$. (To see this, note that $D^{-1}C^{-1}CD$ is the identity function.) Thus, for example, we can write $(S^{-n_1}R_1S^{n_1})^{-1} = (S^{n_1})^{-1}R_1^{-1}(S^{-n_1})^{-1} = S^{-n_1}R_1^{-1}S^{n_1}$. Applying this fact and combining factors when possible, we find that the mapping of Eq. (1.2) can be rewritten as

$$AS^{-n_1}R_1^{-1}S^{(n_1-n_2)}R_2^{-1}S^{(n_2-n_3)}R_3^{-1}S^{n_3}BS^{-n_3}R_3S^{(n_3-n_2)}R_2S^{(n_2-n_1)}R_1S^{n_1}A \tag{1.3}$$

In an actual Enigma machine, the *order* of the three rotors is adjustable; that is, each rotor can be taken out and put into a different rotor-slot. Thus the order in which the permutations R_1, R_2, and R_3 act need not be the same as in Eq. (1.3).

In Problem 3 at the end of this section, you are asked to show that the permutation given by Eq. (1.3) is its own inverse. This is no accident. The Enigma machine was designed so that the procedure for decryption is exactly the same as the procedure for encryption. Of course, in order for this to work, it is necessary that the person doing the decryption start the machine with all the same settings as the person who encrypted the message: the same plugboard permutation, the same order of the rotors, and the same initial orientation of each rotor. Any other setting would most likely produce a nonsensical string of letters.

This brings us to the protocol under which the German military used the Enigma machine, at least in the years leading up to World War II. Each message was encrypted with two secret keys: the *daily key* and the *message key*. Every person authorized to use the machine was given, each month, a codebook containing all the daily keys for that month. Each daily key consisted of three items:

1. The order of the three rotors. (There are six possible orders.)
2. The initial orientations of the rotors. (There are $26^3 = 17576$ such orientations.)
3. The plugboard settings. (There are about 10^{11} possible settings. See Problem 1.)

Altogether the number of possible daily keys is around 10^{16}. The *message key* was a sequence of three letters, chosen at random by the operator of the machine, specifying new orientations of the three rotors for a particular message. For example, the message key AAA would indicate that each rotor was to be set in its standard orientation, whereas AAB would mean that the last rotor should be rotated by one step. The number of possible message keys is $26^3 = 17576$.

Here is the protocol for sending a message:

1. Set the machine according to the daily key.
2. Type in the randomly chosen message key *twice*, and send the resulting six letters as encrypted by the machine.
3. Reset the rotor orientations according to the message key.
4. Type in the message itself and send the ciphertext generated by the machine.

Thus the protocol for deciphering a message is as follows:

1. Set the machine according to the daily key.
2. Type in the first six letters of the ciphertext to read the message key. (The result should be two copies of the message key, e.g., GPZGPZ.)
3. Reset the rotor orientations according to the message key.
4. Type in the rest of the ciphertext and read out the plaintext.

Clearly the Enigma cipher is complex and not a cipher that is easily cracked. And yet it was cracked by Polish cryptanalysts, years before the war started. The full story of this cryptanalysis is quite a long one. In the next section we outline just one piece of the story, but a piece that is particularly interesting mathematically.

Cracking Enigma

First, by a combination of methods, including the use of material originally obtained by French intelligence from a German informant, the Poles managed to figure out the basic structure of the machine and even the permutations embodied in the three rotors. With this information they were able to build several copies of the machine. But this was not enough to allow them to read encrypted messages. Indeed, the machine was so designed that even someone who had a copy of the machine could not decipher messages without knowing the key, and the Poles did not have the daily keys. As we have said, there are 10^{16} such keys possible; one could never hope to find the right key by trial and error. What was needed was a clever idea, and this was provided by the cryptanalyst Marian Rejewski.

To set the stage for his idea, let us imagine a set of intercepted messages, all from the same day, and consider just the first six letters of each message, that is, the letters that would have encoded the message keys. The messages might be as follows:

```
1ST MESSAGE:    Q Z A E L L ...
2ND MESSAGE:    R S Z J J Q ...
3RD MESSAGE:    E X T S I N ...
4TH MESSAGE:    S R W Q Y K ...
5TH MESSAGE:    Q P C E B D ...
6TH MESSAGE:    J P T R B N ...
```

You might have expected that the last three letters of each group of six would be the same as the first three, since the message key, which these letters encode, was typed in twice. But recall that after each letter is typed in, at least one of the rotors changes its orientation, so that the overall permutation effected by the machine is different. Thus the E in the first message encodes the same letter as the Q, but the encoding permutation has changed.

Indeed it is precisely this fact that was exploited by Rejewski. Let us focus on the change that takes place in the machine's permutation upon typing in three letters, starting from the setting determined by the particular daily key by which all of the above messages were encoded. Evidently, as we see from the first message printed above, whatever letter was sent to Q by the original permutation was sent to E by the three-keystrokes-later permutation. We will say that Q "evolves" into E. Similarly, by looking at the third message, we can see that E evolves into S, and from the fourth message we learn that S evolves into Q. Thus this "evolution" includes the following cycle: Q → E → S → Q. From the second and sixth messages we similarly obtain the cycle R → J → R. In the same way, given enough messages, all encrypted with the same daily key, one could write down all other cycles of this evolution. Rejewski recognized that the *lengths* of these cycles contained a crucial clue to the daily key. The reason is that these lengths *do not depend on the plugboard settings*. Recall that the largest contribution to the number 10^{16} of possible daily keys came from the 10^{11} plugboard settings. By finding a property of the messages that separates the rotor part of the daily key from the plugboard part, one could make the decryption manageable.

Indeed, the Poles, who possessed copies of the machine, could, by actually setting the rotors in all possible ways, make a detailed catalogue connecting the rotor portion of the daily key to a set of cycle lengths. Note, by the way, that in addition to the "evolution" we discussed above, which relates the initial keystroke to the fourth keystroke, there is also an evolution, typically with different cycle lengths, relating the second keystroke to the fifth, and another relating the third to the sixth. So the catalogue might include the following entry:

Rotor part of daily key		Lengths of cycles
1-3-2 AXK	1st → 4th:	2-cycle, 2-cycle, 11-cycle, 11-cycle
	2nd → 5th:	13-cycle, 13-cycle
	3rd → 6th:	1-cycle, 1-cycle, 5-cycle, 5-cycle, 7-cycle, 7-cycle

Here the "1-3-2" refers to the order of the rotors, and the letters AXK specify their orientations. The number of combinations for the rotor part of the daily key is $6 \times 26^3 \approx 100,000$, so the complete table would have to have about 100,000 entries. This is a large number, but with the help of a specially constructed device and with more than a year's work, the catalogue could be, and indeed was, constructed.

How could the catalogue be used to read encrypted messages? First, one would analyze the initial six letters of many messages from the same day to determine the cycle lengths for that day. Then one would find this set of cycle lengths in the table – it helps to organize the catalogue by cycle lengths rather than by rotor settings – and read off the rotor portion of the daily key. Now one can set the rotors accordingly and let the machine decrypt several messages. The results will not be immediately comprehensible, because the plugboard settings are still unknown. However, at this point the only thing standing in the way of the plaintext is the plugboard permutation, which does not change from one keystroke to the next. The resulting cryptanalytic problem is not as simple as a substitution cipher, since the electrical path inside the machine passes through the plugboard twice. Nevertheless, with the rotors set to the correct orientations, the Polish team was able to finish cracking the cipher relatively easily.

In this way and by other techniques, the standard Enigma cipher was rendered transparent years before the outbreak of World War II. However, in 1938 the Germans increased the complexity of the machine, and the Poles' catalogue was no longer directly applicable. Moreover the Polish cryptanalysts did not have enough computing power to crack the more complex version. Realizing that the Germans were likely to invade Poland soon, they passed their knowledge to French and British cryptanalysts. The British group, which eventually employed relatively sophisticated computing machines, was quite successful and was largely able to keep up with subsequent refinements of the Enigma cipher.

EXERCISES

Problem 1. This is a counting problem focusing on the Enigma plugboard. Recall that the plugboard permutation interchanges some of the letters in pairs. For example, A and F might be interchanged, and M and X might be interchanged.

(a) Suppose that only one pair of letters are interchanged and the other 24 letters are left unchanged. How many ways are there of choosing the special pair?

(b) In the standard Enigma machine, six pairs of letters were swapped. How many ways are there of choosing these six pairs? Does you answer agree with our rough estimate 10^{11}?

Problem 2. We said that if the ith rotor has advanced by one step from its standard orientation, it executes the permutation $S^{-1}R_i S$. Show that this statement is consistent with Figs. 1.1 and 1.2.

Problem 3. Show that the permutation given in Eq. (1.3) is its own inverse.

Problem 4. Consider the notion of "evolution" that we introduced in this section. We can formulate this notion mathematically as follows. For a given initial setting of the machine, as determined, for example, by the daily key, let P_m be the permutation executed by the machine after m keystrokes. We considered a case in which, for some unknown letter x, $P_0 x = Q$ and $P_3 x = E$. This is what we meant by saying that Q "evolves" into E. Evidently the permutation that expresses this evolution is $P_3 P_0^{-1}$. (Applying P_0^{-1} to Q gives x, and then applying P_3 gives E.) Show that the *cycle lengths* of the "evolution" $P_3 P_0^{-1}$ are indeed independent of the plugboard permutation A, as was noted by Rejewski. (Note that the permutation P_m is given by Eq. (1.3) with appropriate values of n_1, n_2, and n_3.)

Problem 5. Consider the Enigma machine with a certain initial setting of the rotors and plugboard. With this initial setting, let P_0 be the permutation the machine applies to the first letter of the plaintext, and let P_3 be the permutation that it applies to the fourth letter of the plaintext. Recall the following two facts about the permutations P_0 and P_3: (i) $P_0^{-1} = P_0$ and $P_3^{-1} = P_3$; (ii) P_0 does not send any letter to itself, and neither does P_3. These facts will be useful in this problem.

We have seen how cryptanalysts were able to crack Enigma by considering the lengths of the cycles of the permutation $P_3 P_0^{-1}$. Let $y_1, y_2, \ldots, y_m$ be a cycle of this permutation. That is, the y_i's are m distinct letters of the alphabet, and $P_3 P_0^{-1} y_1 = y_2$, $P_3 P_0^{-1} y_2 = y_3, \ldots, P_3 P_0^{-1} y_m = y_1$.

(a) Show that $P_0 y_m, P_0 y_{m-1}, \ldots, P_0 y_1$ is also a cycle of $P_3 P_0^{-1}$.

(b) Show that the cycle defined in part (a) consists entirely of letters that do not appear in the original cycle $y_1, y_2, \ldots, y_m$. It follows that the cycle lengths always come in matching pairs.

1.3   A Review of Modular Arithmetic and $\mathbb{Z}_n$

As we saw in Section 1.1, doing arithmetic modulo 26 is used frequently in classical cryptography. It turns out that arithmetic modulo other numbers also proves to be very useful. In this section, we review modular arithmetic in general and define $\mathbb{Z}_n$, which is a set with a modular arithmetic.[10] We start with two definitions.

Definition. Let a be an integer and n a nonzero integer. We say that n *divides a* if there is an integer m such that $nm = a$. If n divides a, we will write $n|a$. If n does not divide a, we write $n \nmid a$.

Definition. Let a and b be integers and n a positive integer. If $n|(a-b)$, we say that *a is congruent to b modulo n* and we write $a \equiv b(\bmod n)$.

Examples:
1. $4 \equiv 1(\bmod 3)$
2. $-3 \equiv -1(\bmod 2)$
3. $14 \equiv -2(\bmod 4)$
4. $14 \equiv 2(\bmod 4)$
5. If b is an integer and r is its remainder upon division by n, then $b \equiv r(\bmod n)$.

Definition. Let n be a positive integer. We define $\mathbb{Z}_n$ to be the set

$$\{0, 1, 2, \ldots, (n-1)\}$$

along with the two operations of addition modulo n and multiplication modulo n so that when we perform these operations we choose our answer to be a member of the set $\mathbb{Z}_n$.

Suppose $n = 6$. Then it is true that $4 + 5 \equiv 9(\bmod 6)$. However, when doing arithmetic in $\mathbb{Z}_6$, we require that all answers be in the set $\{0, 1, 2, 3, 4, 5\}$. So in $\mathbb{Z}_6$ we have that $4 + 5 = 3$ since $4 + 5 \equiv 3(\bmod 6)$ and 3 is in the set $\{0, 1, 2, 3, 4, 5\}$. Sometimes we will indicate that we are

---

[10] For more details on modular arithmetic and $\mathbb{Z}_n$ see, for example, Gallian (2006) or Stark (1970).

in $\mathbb{Z}_n$ by writing an expression like "$a + b$ (mod n)." Thus $4 + 5$ (mod 6) has the value 3.

We first examine $\mathbb{Z}_2$. The elements of $\mathbb{Z}_2$ are 0 and 1 and below are the addition and multiplication tables for $\mathbb{Z}_2$:

+	0	1
0	0	1
1	1	0

×	0	1
0	0	0
1	0	1

Notice that $\mathbb{Z}_2$ is pleasingly easy. Because of that, one may conjecture that it is relatively useless. But in fact, $\mathbb{Z}_2$ is one of the stars of protecting information. Not only is it incredibly important in cryptography, but it is also invaluable for the theory of correcting errors.

As two more examples, we now write out tables for $\mathbb{Z}_5$ and $\mathbb{Z}_6$

The tables for $\mathbb{Z}_5$

+	0	1	2	3	4
0	0	1	2	3	4
1	1	2	3	4	0
2	2	3	4	0	1
3	3	4	0	1	2
4	4	0	1	2	3

×	0	1	2	3	4
0	0	0	0	0	0
1	0	1	2	3	4
2	0	2	4	1	3
3	0	3	1	4	2
4	0	4	3	2	1

The tables for $\mathbb{Z}_6$

+	0	1	2	3	4	5
0	0	1	2	3	4	5
1	1	2	3	4	5	0
2	2	3	4	5	0	1
3	3	4	5	0	1	2
4	4	5	0	1	2	3
5	5	0	1	2	3	4

×	0	1	2	3	4	5
0	0	0	0	0	0	0
1	0	1	2	3	4	5
2	0	2	4	0	2	4
3	0	3	0	3	0	3
4	0	4	2	0	4	2
5	0	5	4	3	2	1

The addition tables for $\mathbb{Z}_5$, $\mathbb{Z}_6$, and, as you can imagine, $\mathbb{Z}_n$, where n is any positive integer, are very predictable. The multiplication tables, however, are a bit more mysterious. As an example, note that in the multiplication table for $\mathbb{Z}_5$, except for the first row, all elements of

$\mathbb{Z}_5$ appear in each row. This, however, is not true for $\mathbb{Z}_6$. Can you make a conjecture about what has to be true about the integer n so that in the multiplication table for $\mathbb{Z}_n$, except for the first row, all elements of $\mathbb{Z}_n$ appear in each row? (See Problem 2 at the end of this section.)

If we examine the multiplication table for $\mathbb{Z}_6$, we see that $2 \times 3 = 0$. Now, this might seem a bit distressing. This is an example of two nonzero elements whose product is zero. Students of linear algebra will recall that this happens with matrices also! But this does not happen in $\mathbb{Z}_5$. Can you determine for what n there are two nonzero elements in $\mathbb{Z}_n$ such that when you multiply them together, you get zero? (See Problem 3 at the end of this section.) Also, notice that in $\mathbb{Z}_6$, we have $3 \times 3 = 3 \times 1$, but $3 \neq 1$. In other words, we cannot cancel the left-hand 3 on both sides of the equation. So be careful when doing arithmetic in $\mathbb{Z}_n$ – not all rules we are used to will hold!

EXERCISES

Problem 1. Write out the addition and multiplication tables for $\mathbb{Z}_3$, $\mathbb{Z}_4$, and $\mathbb{Z}_7$.

Problem 2

(a) Let $a \in \mathbb{Z}_n$. Show that a and n are relatively prime (the only common divisor of both a and n is 1) if and only if there exists an element $b \in \mathbb{Z}_n$ such that $ab = 1$.

(b) Let $a \in \mathbb{Z}_n$. Show that a and n are relatively prime if and only if a's row in the multiplication table of $\mathbb{Z}_n$ contains every element of $\mathbb{Z}_n$.

(c) Show that n is a prime number if and only if in the multiplication table for $\mathbb{Z}_n$, except for the first row, all elements of $\mathbb{Z}_n$ appear in each row.

Problem 3

(a) Show that n is a prime number if and only if whenever $a, b \in \mathbb{Z}_n$ with $ab = 0$, we must have that $a = 0$ or $b = 0$.

(b) Show that n is a prime number if and only if for every $a, b, c \in \mathbb{Z}_n$ satisfying $a \neq 0$ and $ab = ac$, we have that $b = c$.

Problem 4. Show that addition and multiplication modulo n are well defined. In other words, show that if $a \equiv b(\text{mod } n)$ and $c \equiv d(\text{mod } n)$, then $a + c \equiv b + d(\text{mod } n)$ and $ac \equiv bd(\text{mod } n)$.

1.4 The Hill Cipher

So far in this chapter, we have discussed ciphers that substitute a single letter for a single letter. Of course, if we substituted blocks of letters for blocks of letters, the cipher would be more complicated and therefore harder for an adversary to break. For example, if we decided to use blocks of two, we would break the plaintext into blocks of two and then substitute according to a predetermined key. We could agree that every time we see *AA*, we substitute *UX*, every time we see *AB*, we substitute *HR*, etc. Note that there are $26 \times 26 = 676$ possible pairs of letters, so two people wanting to send secret messages to each other would have to agree on and record all 676 substitutions. If we used blocks of three, then there would be $26^3 = 17576$ substitutions. As we increase our block size, there are more possibilities that an adversary needs to check, but unfortunately, as we increase the block size, we also increase the number of substitutions that the two parties must agree on and record. The Hill cipher[11] provides us with a more concise description of a way to substitute blocks of letters for other blocks of letters.

In this chapter, we consider only the case where the block size is 2. But the method can be generalized to any block size. We note here that the Hill cipher is easily cracked using today's computers, but we discuss it to illustrate an elegant historical block cipher.

We start with a 2×2 key matrix, K, whose entries are elements of $\mathbb{Z}_{26}$. This matrix will serve as the key to our cipher and must not fall into the hands of an adversary or the cipher will be trivially broken. Suppose we choose

$$K = \begin{pmatrix} 4 & 3 \\ 1 & 2 \end{pmatrix}.$$

---

[11] For more details on the Hill cipher, see Stinson (2002).

Now, if the sender, whom we call Alice, wants to send the message *SNOW* to the legitimate recipient, Bob, she first breaks up the message into blocks of two: the first block is *SN* and the second is *OW*. Then she transforms each block into a two-dimensional vector with entries in $\mathbb{Z}_{26}$ according to the rule that 0 represents *A*, 1 represents *B*, ..., 25 represents *Z*. Call the vector representing the *i*th block $\vec{x}_i$, so that the vector representing *SN* is $\vec{x}_1 = \binom{18}{13}$ and the vector representing *OW* is $\vec{x}_2 = \binom{14}{22}$. To get the ciphertext, we compute $\vec{y}_i = K\vec{x}_i$ for every *i*, where all arithmetic is done in $\mathbb{Z}_{26}$, and convert these vectors back to letters. For our example,

$$\vec{y}_1 = K\vec{x}_1 = \begin{pmatrix} 4 & 3 \\ 1 & 2 \end{pmatrix} \begin{pmatrix} 18 \\ 13 \end{pmatrix} = \begin{pmatrix} (4(18) + 3(13)) \bmod 26 \\ (1(18) + 2(13)) \bmod 26 \end{pmatrix} = \begin{pmatrix} 7 \\ 18 \end{pmatrix}$$

$$\vec{y}_2 = K\vec{x}_2 = \begin{pmatrix} 4 & 3 \\ 1 & 2 \end{pmatrix} \begin{pmatrix} 14 \\ 22 \end{pmatrix} = \begin{pmatrix} (4(14) + 3(22)) \bmod 26 \\ (1(14) + 2(22)) \bmod 26 \end{pmatrix} = \begin{pmatrix} 18 \\ 6 \end{pmatrix}$$

The reader might find the tables in Section A.3 of the Appendix useful for these computations. Now, the number 7 represents the letter *H*, 18 represents *S*, and 6 represents *G*, so the ciphertext is *HSSG*. Notice that this method substitutes blocks of two letters for blocks of two letters as we originally desired, but the advantage is that instead of recording all 676 substitutions, all Alice and Bob need to know is the matrix *K*.

How does Bob find the plaintext given the ciphertext? Bob knows *K* and $\vec{y}_i$ for all *i*. He wants to find $\vec{x}_i$ for all *i*. In other words, he wants to solve the equation $\vec{y}_i = K\vec{x}_i$ for $\vec{x}_i$. Suppose we could find a matrix *B* with entries in $\mathbb{Z}_{26}$ such that $BK = \begin{pmatrix} 1 & 0 \\ 0 & 1 \end{pmatrix}$ with all arithmetic done in $\mathbb{Z}_{26}$. Then $\vec{y}_i = K\vec{x}_i$ implies $B\vec{y}_i = BK\vec{x}_i$, so $B\vec{y}_i = \begin{pmatrix} 1 & 0 \\ 0 & 1 \end{pmatrix}\vec{x}_i = \vec{x}_i$. We have thus reduced the problem to finding such a matrix *B*. Now, recall from linear algebra that if *A* is a square matrix with real numbers as entries, then there exists a matrix *C* with real numbers as entries such that $CA = I$ if and only if the determinant of *A* is not zero. Here *I* denotes the identity matrix – the matrix with ones on the main diagonal and zeros everywhere else. But be careful here ... the arithmetic used in standard linear algebra is not the same as we are using here. After all, we are doing all of our arithmetic modulo 26. But should that make a difference? Consider the following example:

Example 1.4.1. Suppose $K = \begin{pmatrix} 3 & 1 \\ 1 & 1 \end{pmatrix}$. Then the determinant of K is $2 \neq 0$. But if there were a matrix B such that $BK = I$ where all arithmetic is done modulo 26, then we would have

$$\begin{pmatrix} a & b \\ c & d \end{pmatrix}\begin{pmatrix} 3 & 1 \\ 1 & 1 \end{pmatrix} = \begin{pmatrix} 1 & 0 \\ 0 & 1 \end{pmatrix}.$$

So,

$$\begin{pmatrix} 3a+b & a+b \\ 3c+d & c+d \end{pmatrix} = \begin{pmatrix} 1 & 0 \\ 0 & 1 \end{pmatrix}.$$

Therefore, we must have that in $\mathbb{Z}_{26}$, $3a + b = 1$, $a + b = 0$, $3c + d = 0$, and $c + d = 1$. Now, solving the second equation for b and plugging the result into the first equation, we get $2a = 1$. But there is no element a of $\mathbb{Z}_{26}$ satisfying this equation. It follows that no such B exists.

We now point out another troubling property of the above matrix K. Suppose Alice were to use K to send encrypted messages to Bob. If a block of plaintext were AA, to find the corresponding ciphertext, Alice would compute

$$\begin{pmatrix} 3 & 1 \\ 1 & 1 \end{pmatrix}\begin{pmatrix} 0 \\ 0 \end{pmatrix} = \begin{pmatrix} 0 \\ 0 \end{pmatrix},$$

arriving at the corresponding ciphertext AA. But suppose that part of the plaintext were NN. In that case she computes

$$\begin{pmatrix} 3 & 1 \\ 1 & 1 \end{pmatrix}\begin{pmatrix} 13 \\ 13 \end{pmatrix} = \begin{pmatrix} 0 \\ 0 \end{pmatrix}$$

and again finds that the corresponding ciphertext is AA. Now, if Bob receives AA as a block, he has no way of knowing whether the plaintext was AA or NN. For this reason, the K in this example is a bad key matrix to use for encryption.

In light of Example 1.4.1, we want an easy way to tell whether or not a particular key matrix will be a good one to use for encryption. Specifically, we want the matrix K to have the property that there is a matrix B so that $BK = I$. Also, we want K to have the property that if $\vec{x}_1$ and $\vec{x}_2$ are *different* vectors with entries in $\mathbb{Z}_{26}$, then $K\vec{x}_1$ and $K\vec{x}_2$ are also *different* vectors. The following theorem tells us that these two properties are equivalent and that there is an easy way to check whether or not the properties hold.

Theorem 1.4.1. For a Hill cipher with an alphabet of 26 letters, block size 2, and key matrix $K = \begin{pmatrix} a & b \\ c & d \end{pmatrix}$, the following statements are equivalent:

1. $ad - bc$ is not divisible by 2 or 13.
2. There exists a 2×2 matrix B with entries in $\mathbb{Z}_{26}$ satisfying $BK = I = \begin{pmatrix} 1 & 0 \\ 0 & 1 \end{pmatrix}$.
3. K satisfies the property that if $\vec{x}_1 \neq \vec{x}_2$ then $K\vec{x}_1 \neq K\vec{x}_2$.

In Theorem 1.4.1, all arithmetic is done in $\mathbb{Z}_{26}$.

Proof. Our strategy will be to show that the first statement implies the second, the second implies the third, and the third implies the first.

So assume that $ad - bc$ is not divisible by 2 or 13. Then by Problem 2 from Section 1.3 there exists an $h \in \mathbb{Z}_{26}$ such that $h(ad - bc) = 1$ (in $\mathbb{Z}_{26}$).

Let $B = \begin{pmatrix} hd & -hb \\ -hc & ha \end{pmatrix}$. Then,

$$BK = \begin{pmatrix} hd & -hb \\ -hc & ha \end{pmatrix} \begin{pmatrix} a & b \\ c & d \end{pmatrix} = \begin{pmatrix} h(ad - bc) & h(bd - bd) \\ h(-ac + ac) & h(-bc + ad) \end{pmatrix}$$

$$= \begin{pmatrix} 1 & 0 \\ 0 & 1 \end{pmatrix}.$$

It follows that the second property of the theorem holds.

Now, assume that the second property holds and we will show this implies that the third property holds. Suppose there is a matrix B such that $BK = I$. If $K\vec{x}_1 = K\vec{x}_2$, then $BK\vec{x}_1 = BK\vec{x}_2$, so $\vec{x}_1 = \vec{x}_2$ and it follows that the third property of the theorem holds.

For the final part of our proof, we assume that K satisfies the property that if $\vec{x}_1 \neq \vec{x}_2$ then $K\vec{x}_1 \neq K\vec{x}_2$. We assume $ad - bc$ is divisible by 2 and arrive at a contradiction. Since 2 divides $ad - bc$, it must be that $13(ad - bc) = 0$. (Remember, all arithmetic is done in $\mathbb{Z}_{26}$.) So,

$$\begin{pmatrix} a & b \\ c & d \end{pmatrix} \begin{pmatrix} 13d \\ -13c \end{pmatrix} = \begin{pmatrix} 13(ad - bc) \\ 13(cd - cd) \end{pmatrix} = \begin{pmatrix} 0 \\ 0 \end{pmatrix}$$

and

$$\begin{pmatrix} a & b \\ c & d \end{pmatrix} \begin{pmatrix} -13b \\ 13a \end{pmatrix} = \begin{pmatrix} 13(ab - ab) \\ 13(ad - bc) \end{pmatrix} = \begin{pmatrix} 0 \\ 0 \end{pmatrix}.$$

But also, we have

$$\begin{pmatrix} a & b \\ c & d \end{pmatrix} \begin{pmatrix} 0 \\ 0 \end{pmatrix} = \begin{pmatrix} 0 \\ 0 \end{pmatrix}.$$

As K satisfies the third property of the theorem, it must be that $13d = -13b = 0$ and $-13c = 13a = 0$. Now, consider

$$\begin{pmatrix} a & b \\ c & d \end{pmatrix} \begin{pmatrix} 13 \\ 13 \end{pmatrix} = \begin{pmatrix} 13(a + b) \\ 13(c + d) \end{pmatrix} = \begin{pmatrix} 0 \\ 0 \end{pmatrix}.$$

But this contradicts that K satisfies the third property. Similarly, one can find a contradiction if $ad - bc$ is divisible by 13. ❑

We note here that we can generalize this theorem. We state a generalization without proof.

Theorem 1.4.2. For a Hill cipher with an alphabet of n letters, block size m, and key matrix K where K is an $m \times m$ matrix with entries in $\mathbb{Z}_n$, the following statements are equivalent:

1. The determinant of K and n are relatively prime.
2. There exists an $m \times m$ matrix B with entries in $\mathbb{Z}_n$ satisfying $BK = I$, where I is the $m \times m$ identity matrix.
3. K satisfies the property that if $\vec{x}_1 \neq \vec{x}_2$ then $K\vec{x}_1 \neq K\vec{x}_2$.

In Theorem 1.4.2, all arithmetic is done in $\mathbb{Z}_n$.

Theorem 1.4.1 is extremely useful. Because of it, Alice and Bob can easily verify that the key matrix K they have chosen will be a good one for encrypting messages. They simply compute $ad - bc$ and make sure it is not divisible by 2 or 13. But we are still left with the problem of how, in practice, Bob finds the plaintext after receiving the ciphertext. It turns out that the answer to this problem lies in the proof of Theorem 1.4.1. We illustrate with an example.

Recall the example earlier in this section where Alice and Bob used

$$K = \begin{pmatrix} 4 & 3 \\ 1 & 2 \end{pmatrix}$$

as their key matrix and the plaintext was $SNOW$. As shown earlier, the ciphertext is $HSSG$. Assuming that Bob receives $HSSG$ and does not know the original message that Alice sent, we now show how he would go about finding the plaintext. He first creates the vectors $\vec{y}_1$ and $\vec{y}_2$ by converting the letters to numbers. So, $\vec{y}_1 = \begin{pmatrix} 7 \\ 18 \end{pmatrix}$ and $\vec{y}_2 = \begin{pmatrix} 18 \\ 6 \end{pmatrix}$. Recall that Bob is trying to find $\vec{x}_1$ and $\vec{x}_2$ and he knows that $K\vec{x}_1 = \vec{y}_1$ and $K\vec{x}_2 = \vec{y}_2$. As discussed previously, Bob wants to find a matrix B such that $BK = I$. Notice that in the proof of Theorem 1.4.1, we actually constructed such a matrix. If $K = \begin{pmatrix} a & b \\ c & d \end{pmatrix}$ then $B = \begin{pmatrix} hd & -hb \\ -hc & ha \end{pmatrix}$, where $h \in \mathbb{Z}_{26}$ satisfies $h(ad - bc) = 1$. In our case, $a = 4, b = 3, c = 1$, and $d = 2$. So $ad - bc = 5$ and we want to find h so that $5h = 1$ in $\mathbb{Z}_{26}$. Note that $5 \times 21 = 1$ in $\mathbb{Z}_{26}$, so $h = 21$. (For a systematic way of finding such an h, see Section 1.9.) Now,

$$B = \begin{pmatrix} hd & -hb \\ -hc & ha \end{pmatrix} = \begin{pmatrix} 21(2) & -21(3) \\ -21(1) & 21(4) \end{pmatrix} = \begin{pmatrix} 16 & 15 \\ 5 & 6 \end{pmatrix}.$$

So,

$$\vec{x}_1 = B\vec{y}_1 = \begin{pmatrix} 16 & 15 \\ 5 & 6 \end{pmatrix} \begin{pmatrix} 7 \\ 18 \end{pmatrix} = \begin{pmatrix} 18 \\ 13 \end{pmatrix}$$

and

$$\vec{x}_2 = B\vec{y}_2 = \begin{pmatrix} 16 & 15 \\ 5 & 6 \end{pmatrix} \begin{pmatrix} 18 \\ 6 \end{pmatrix} = \begin{pmatrix} 14 \\ 22 \end{pmatrix}.$$

Translating the numbers back into letters, Bob finds that the plaintext was $SNOW$ and has thus correctly recovered the original message that Alice sent.

EXERCISES

Problem 1
(a) Use a 26-character Hill cipher to encode the message $FOUR$ using the key matrix $K = \begin{pmatrix} 25 & 0 \\ 2 & 1 \end{pmatrix}$.

(b) Let $\alpha_1\alpha_2\alpha_3\alpha_4$ represent your answer from part (a). Now encode the message $\alpha_1\alpha_2\alpha_3\alpha_4$ using the same key matrix that you used in part (a).

(c) There should be something surprising about your answer in part (b). Is that simply a coincidence? Explain.

Problem 2. Alice and Bob agree that they will use a Hill Cipher to send messages to each other. They decide to use $K = \left(\begin{smallmatrix} 2 & 1 \\ 3 & 6 \end{smallmatrix}\right)$ for the key matrix. Bob receives the ciphertext $SMKH$ from Alice. What is the plaintext?

1.5 Attacks on the Hill Cipher

In this section, we briefly describe two methods of attack on the Hill cipher. This illustrates just how easy it is for an eavesdropper, called Eve, to crack this cipher. Note that for any Hill cipher, if Eve can find the key matrix K, then she can decipher all encrypted messages. So we focus on how she might go about finding the key matrix.

We first describe what is called a *chosen-plaintext* attack. Suppose that Eve does not know the key matrix, but she can choose any plaintext and has a way of finding out the corresponding ciphertext. In other words, she has access to the Hill cipher "machine" that encrypts the messages, but she does not know how the machine works. In this case, the cipher is extremely easy to break. Eve simply chooses to encrypt $\left(\begin{smallmatrix} 1 \\ 0 \end{smallmatrix}\right)$ and $\left(\begin{smallmatrix} 0 \\ 1 \end{smallmatrix}\right)$. This will give her the key matrix. To see this, just note that if $K = \left(\begin{smallmatrix} a & b \\ c & d \end{smallmatrix}\right)$, then $\left(\begin{smallmatrix} a & b \\ c & d \end{smallmatrix}\right)\left(\begin{smallmatrix} 1 \\ 0 \end{smallmatrix}\right) = \left(\begin{smallmatrix} a \\ c \end{smallmatrix}\right)$ and $\left(\begin{smallmatrix} a & b \\ c & d \end{smallmatrix}\right)\left(\begin{smallmatrix} 0 \\ 1 \end{smallmatrix}\right) = \left(\begin{smallmatrix} b \\ d \end{smallmatrix}\right)$. So Eve has found the key matrix K.

In practice the adversary typically cannot choose the plaintext. She still might be able to use what is called a *known-plaintext* attack. Suppose that Eve happens to know that $\vec{x}_1 = \left(\begin{smallmatrix} x_{11} \\ x_{12} \end{smallmatrix}\right)$ is encrypted as $\vec{y}_1 = \left(\begin{smallmatrix} y_{11} \\ y_{12} \end{smallmatrix}\right)$ and $\vec{x}_2 = \left(\begin{smallmatrix} x_{21} \\ x_{22} \end{smallmatrix}\right)$ is encrypted as $\vec{y}_2 = \left(\begin{smallmatrix} y_{21} \\ y_{22} \end{smallmatrix}\right)$. Then if $K = \left(\begin{smallmatrix} a & b \\ c & d \end{smallmatrix}\right)$, we have that $K\vec{x}_1 = \left(\begin{smallmatrix} a & b \\ c & d \end{smallmatrix}\right)\left(\begin{smallmatrix} x_{11} \\ x_{12} \end{smallmatrix}\right) = \left(\begin{smallmatrix} y_{11} \\ y_{12} \end{smallmatrix}\right)$ and $K\vec{x}_2 = \left(\begin{smallmatrix} a & b \\ c & d \end{smallmatrix}\right)\left(\begin{smallmatrix} x_{21} \\ x_{22} \end{smallmatrix}\right) = \left(\begin{smallmatrix} y_{21} \\ y_{22} \end{smallmatrix}\right)$. It follows that $\left(\begin{smallmatrix} a & b \\ c & d \end{smallmatrix}\right)\left(\begin{smallmatrix} x_{11} & x_{21} \\ x_{12} & x_{22} \end{smallmatrix}\right) = \left(\begin{smallmatrix} y_{11} & y_{21} \\ y_{12} & y_{22} \end{smallmatrix}\right)$. Eve now hopes that $x_{11}x_{22} - x_{21}x_{12}$ is not divisible by 2 or 13 so that, by Theorem 1.4.1, she will be able to solve for the key matrix K. Of course, it may be true that $x_{11}x_{22} - x_{21}x_{12}$ is divisible by 2 or 13, in which case Eve would have to try other techniques. We leave these to you to devise and investigate on your own.

EXERCISES

Problem 1. You discover that the key matrix for a certain Hill cipher is $K = \begin{pmatrix} 8 & 1 \\ 1 & 2 \end{pmatrix}$. You have intercepted the ciphertext *BYIC*. What is the plaintext?

Problem 2. You have intercepted the message

WGTK

and know it has been encrypted using a Hill cipher. You also happen to know that *CD* is encrypted as *RR* and *JK* is encrypted as *OV*. What is the plaintext?

Problem 3. You intercept the message

JQXMDISJZGHIVN

and know it has been encrypted using a Hill cipher. You suspect it contains the phrase *THEBEST*. Find the plaintext.

1.6 Feistel Ciphers and DES

We are now ready to discuss more modern methods of encryption. Until the 1970s cryptography was used almost exclusively for military purposes. In the two decades following the Second World War, the National Security Agency (NSA), created by Truman in 1952 as a top secret organization, was actively involved in conducting research in cryptography. In the 1950s and 1960s, the NSA was virtually the only place in the United States where this kind of research was actively pursued. However, in the early 1970s, with the development of the modern computer, businesses began to realize the value of cryptography. For example, those in the banking community realized that the concept of ATMs and electronic funds transfers could become a reality if they had the use of encryption. As a result, in 1973 the National Bureau of Standards solicited proposals for a standardized cryptosystem that could be used nationwide for commerce. In 1977, the NBS approved a cryptosystem that had been submitted by a team from IBM. That system is now known as the data encryption standard, or DES, and is currently the most widely used cryptosystem in the world.

The ideal cryptosystem should use as little computing power and computer storage space as possible, be easy to decrypt if one knows the key, and the ciphertext should look random to make it more difficult for an adversary to crack. DES has all of these desirable properties. In this section, we give an overview of the key mathematical ideas used in DES.[12] We start with several definitions and a description of a Feistel cipher – an important ingredient in DES.

DES is a binary cipher. This means that the plaintext and ciphertext are strings of zeros and ones. Since computers store and send information using binary representation for the information, it makes sense that a modern cipher would use zeros and ones for the plaintext and ciphertext.

Definition. We define $\mathbb{Z}_2^n$ to be the set $\{(a_1, a_2, \ldots, a_n) | a_i \in \mathbb{Z}_2\}$ along with componentwise addition modulo 2 and scalar multiplication modulo 2 where the set of scalars is $\mathbb{Z}_2$. The addition is denoted by $\oplus$ or *XOR*.

Example 1.6.1. Note that $(101101), (110101) \in \mathbb{Z}_2^6$ and

$$(101101) \oplus (110101) = (011000).$$

Notice that the scalar multiplication in $\mathbb{Z}_2^n$ is very easy. Since 0 and 1 are the only scalars we are allowed to use, we only need define $0\vec{v}$ and $1\vec{v}$, where $\vec{v} \in \mathbb{Z}_2^n$. We do this in the obvious way: $0\vec{v} = \vec{0}$ and $1\vec{v} = \vec{v}$, where $\vec{0}$ denotes the element of $\mathbb{Z}_2^n$ consisting of all zeros.

Definition. A function $f : \mathbb{Z}_2^n \to \mathbb{Z}_2^m$ is called *linear* if $f(\vec{x} \oplus \vec{y}) = f(\vec{x}) \oplus f(\vec{y})$ and $f(c\vec{x}) = cf(\vec{x})$ for all $\vec{x}, \vec{y} \in \mathbb{Z}_2^n$ and all $c \in \mathbb{Z}_2$.

We take a moment to consider the second condition. When $c = 1$ it is trivial and when $c = 0$, $f(c\vec{x}) = cf(\vec{x})$ is equivalent to saying that

---

[12] Those wishing for more details are encouraged to consult other sources such as Stinson (2002).

$f(\vec{0}) = \vec{0}$. But notice that if $\vec{x} = \vec{0}$ and $\vec{y} = \vec{0}$, then the first condition of the definition gives us that $f(\vec{0}) = \vec{0}$. So in practice, to check that a function $f : \mathbb{Z}_2^n \to \mathbb{Z}_2^m$ is linear, we need only check the first condition. It is reasonable then to ask why we include the second condition in the definition at all. In fact, the definition of a linear function can be generalized and in the generalization the second condition becomes meaningful.

Example 1.6.2. Define $\quad f : \mathbb{Z}_2^3 \to \mathbb{Z}_2^3 \quad$ as $\quad f((x_1, x_2, x_3)) = (x_2, x_3, x_1)$. Then, $f((x_1, x_2, x_3) \oplus (y_1, y_2, y_3)) = (x_2 \oplus y_2, x_3 \oplus y_3, x_1 \oplus y_1) = (x_1, x_2, x_3) \oplus (y_1, y_2, y_3) = f((x_1, x_2, x_3)) \oplus f((y_1, y_2, y_3))$. It follows that f is linear.

DES is a binary block cipher with block size 64. It it can therefore be thought of as a function from $\mathbb{Z}_2^{64}$ to $\mathbb{Z}_2^{64}$. Call the function *DES*. So if $\vec{x} \in \mathbb{Z}_2^{64}$ is the plaintext, then $\vec{y} = DES(\vec{x})$ is the ciphertext. Now, *DES* is not a linear function. In fact, we have introduced the notion of linearity at this point primarily to emphasize the *non*linearity of DES. Nowadays one would not want a cryptosystem to be linear (see Problem 3 at the end of this section) because linear cryptosystems possess too much structure and, as a result, are too easy to crack. (The Hill cipher that we considered in Section 1.4 is linear – though not over $\mathbb{Z}_2$ – and we saw that it is not difficult to crack.) The nonlinearity of *DES* is one of the reasons why it works well.

We start our mathematical discussion of DES by describing a particular Feistel cipher.

An *r*-Round Feistel Cipher with Block Size 64

Let $\vec{k} \in \mathbb{Z}_2^{64}$ be a key and r a positive integer. The sender and intended receiver know $\vec{k}$, but an eavesdropper must not know it or else she will easily be able to crack the code. Let $\vec{k}_i \in \mathbb{Z}_2^{48}$ for $i = 1, 2, \ldots, r$ be a subkey obtained from $\vec{k}$. The specific method of generating these subkeys is not important for this discussion, but note that the method does not need to be kept secret. In fact, it is announced publicly. Now, let $f : \mathbb{Z}_2^{80} \to \mathbb{Z}_2^{32}$ be any function from $\mathbb{Z}_2^{80}$ to $\mathbb{Z}_2^{32}$. Divide the plaintext, which will be a long string of zeros and ones, into blocks of 64. We describe here how to encrypt each block. First, divide the block of 64 into two halves – call the left half $\vec{L}_0$ and the right half $\vec{R}_0$. We will map $\vec{L}_0$ to $\vec{L}_r$ and $\vec{R}_0$ to $\vec{R}_r$ after r rounds according to the following algorithm:

$\vec{L}_1$ is defined to be $\vec{R}_0$.
$\vec{R}_1$ is defined to be $\vec{L}_0 \oplus f(\vec{R}_0, \vec{k}_1)$.

$\vec{L}_2$ is defined to be $\vec{R}_1$.
$\vec{R}_2$ is defined to be $\vec{L}_1 \oplus f(\vec{R}_1, \vec{k}_2)$.

And in general,

$\vec{L}_i$ is defined to be $\vec{R}_{i-1}$.
$\vec{R}_i$ is defined to be $\vec{L}_{i-1} \oplus f(\vec{R}_{i-1}, \vec{k}_i)$.

We stop after r rounds to obtain $\vec{L}_r$ and $\vec{R}_r$. The ciphertext will be $(\vec{R}_r, \vec{L}_r)$. Notice that we have put $\vec{R}_r$ on the left and $\vec{L}_r$ on the right. This was done on purpose so that encryption and decryption use the same algorithm.

Now we describe how to find the plaintext knowing the ciphertext and the key $\vec{k}$. Because we know the ciphertext, we know $\vec{L}_r$ and $\vec{R}_r$ and because we know $\vec{k}$, we can find $\vec{k}_i$ for all $i = 1, 2, \ldots, r$. Recall that $\vec{L}_r$ was defined to be $\vec{R}_{r-1}$ and $\vec{R}_r$ was defined to be $\vec{L}_{r-1} \oplus f(\vec{R}_{r-1}, \vec{k}_r)$. So we know $\vec{R}_{r-1} = \vec{L}_r$ and

$$\vec{L}_{r-1} = \vec{L}_{r-1} \oplus (f(\vec{R}_{r-1}, \vec{k}_r) \oplus f(\vec{R}_{r-1}, \vec{k}_r))$$
$$= (\vec{L}_{r-1} \oplus f(\vec{R}_{r-1}, \vec{k}_r)) \oplus f(\vec{R}_{r-1}, \vec{k}_r) = \vec{R}_r \oplus f(\vec{R}_{r-1}, \vec{k}_r).$$

Since we know $\vec{L}_r, \vec{R}_r, f$, and $\vec{k}_r$ we can find $\vec{R}_{r-1}$ and $\vec{L}_{r-1}$. In general, given $\vec{L}_i$ and $\vec{R}_i$ we can obtain $\vec{L}_{i-1}$ and $\vec{R}_{i-1}$ by

$\vec{R}_{i-1} = \vec{L}_i$ and
$\vec{L}_{i-1} = \vec{R}_i \oplus f(\vec{R}_{i-1}, \vec{k}_i)$.

We continue until we find $\vec{L}_0$ and $\vec{R}_0$, which gives us the plaintext as desired. Note that f can be *any* function from $\mathbb{Z}_2^{80}$ to $\mathbb{Z}_2^{32}$. The trick is to choose f in a "smart" way.

DES

The key $\vec{k}$ for DES is a 64-bit string of zeros and ones. We should note, though, that 8 of the bits are used for error correction – those 8 bits depend on the other 56 bits. In other words, from the perspective of an eavesdropper, the cipher is really based on a 56-bit key. Suppose we have our key, $\vec{k} \in \mathbb{Z}_2^{64}$. We now describe how to encrypt a message using DES. We assume the message has been converted to a string of zeros and ones. To encrypt it, break the string up into blocks of 64 and do the following to each block:

1. Permute the zeros and ones in the block using a specific permutation called $\mathbb{P}$. The actual permutation used here is not important and we leave it to the reader to look up the details if desired.[13]
2. Select sixteen 48-bit subkeys, $\vec{k}_1, \vec{k}_2, \ldots, \vec{k}_{16}$ (again, there is a specific method of doing this that the interested reader is encouraged to look up in other sources) from the key $\vec{k}$ and perform a 16-round Feistel cipher where $f(\vec{R}_{i-1}, \vec{k}_i) = P(S(E(\vec{R}_{i-1}) \oplus \vec{k}_i))$. We will describe the functions P, S, and E in a moment.
3. Do the permutation $\mathbb{P}$ backwards. In other words, perform $\mathbb{P}^{-1}$.

Of course, it remains to describe the functions P, S, and E. We will give a general idea of what these functions do. E is a function from $\mathbb{Z}_2^{32}$ to $\mathbb{Z}_2^{48}$. So it takes a string of 32 zeros and ones and outputs a string of 48 zeros and ones by simply repeating some of the bits. The purpose of the function E is to ensure that if one digit of the input is changed then more than one digit of output is affected.

The function S is really the meat of DES. In fact, there has been much controversy surrounding this function over the years. Among other things, it ensures that DES is not a linear function. (See Problem 4 at the end of this section.) The function S maps $\mathbb{Z}_2^{48}$ to $\mathbb{Z}_2^{32}$. It involves eight arrays called S-boxes. These are specific arrays and are public knowledge. For example, here is the fifth S-box:

2	12	4	1	7	10	11	6	8	5	3	15	13	0	14	9
14	11	2	12	4	7	13	1	5	0	15	10	3	9	8	6
4	2	1	11	10	13	7	8	15	9	12	5	6	3	0	14
11	8	12	7	1	14	2	13	6	15	0	9	10	4	5	3

Before giving the details of the function S, we first recall binary numbers. A binary number is of the form $a_n a_{n-1} \ldots a_1 a_0$, where $a_i \in \{0, 1\}$ for

---

[13] Stinson (2002).

every i. Now, $a_n a_{n-1} \ldots a_1 a_0$ means $a_n 2^n + a_{n-1} 2^{n-1} + \cdots + a_1 2^1 + a_0 2^0$. So, for example, to convert the binary number 110011 to base ten, we have $110011 = 1(2^5) + 1(2^4) + 0(2^3) + 0(2^2) + 1(2^1) + 1(2^0) = 32 + 16 + 2 + 1 = 51$. A table of the binary representation for the numbers 0 through 25 can be found in Section A.3 of the Appendix.

We are now ready to explain the function S. Given an element of $\mathbb{Z}_2^{48}$, first break it up into eight blocks of 6-bit strings. Each S-box will have as input a 6-bit string and will produce a 4-bit string as output. The ith 6-bit string will go through the ith S-box in the following way. Take the first and sixth bits and convert from binary to base ten. Then look in the corresponding row of the ith S-box. Take the second, third, fourth, and fifth bits and convert from binary to base ten. Look in the corresponding column of the ith S-box. The number you see converted back to binary is the output. For example, suppose your fifth 6-bit string is 101110. Since it is the fifth string, we will use the fifth S-box. Looking at the first and sixth digits, we see 10. Now, 10 is binary for the number 2. So we start counting from the zeroeth row and look in the second row. Since we started counting at zero, the second row is the one that starts with a 4. Now, the second, third, fourth, and fifth bits are 0111 and that is binary for the number 7. So we look in the seventh column, keeping in mind that we start counting from the zeroeth column. This is the column that begins with a 6. The number in the second row and the seventh column is 8. Converting this back to binary, we get 1000. Hence, 1000 is the 4-bit output for the given 6-bit string. Finally, concatenating all of the 4-bit strings will give us the output of the function S.

The function P maps $\mathbb{Z}_2^{32}$ to $\mathbb{Z}_2^{32}$ and is simply a specific permutation. The purpose of P is to ensure that the output from one round affects the input to multiple S-boxes in the next round.

We take a moment to briefly explain why the S-boxes caused such controversy. A team at IBM developed the design that DES is based on, but the NSA modified the design before they agreed to approve it as the data encryption standard. Evidently they had a list of criteria that they thought the S-boxes should satisfy. Since they refused to release those criteria, many people thought that they had designed the cipher to have a built-in "back door" that would allow the NSA to crack it easily. Another reason for criticism was that the key size of 56-bits was thought to be too small. After many years of cryptanalysis on DES without discovering an easy way to crack it, it is now believed that the NSA did not put in a "back door." However, over the years, there has been some progress in cracking DES. Computers have gotten faster, allowing an adversary to try more keys to see if they work. In addition, there have been some theoretical breakthroughs, most notably differential cryptanalysis and linear cryptanalysis, that eliminate some of those possible keys. This theoretical progress along with an increase in computing power resulted in DES being cracked by the Electronic Frontier Foundation in 1998. It was clear that a new encryption standard was needed.

EXERCISES

Problem 1

(a) Define $E : \mathbb{Z}_2^4 \longrightarrow \mathbb{Z}_2^6$ by $E((x_1, x_2, x_3, x_4)) = (x_1, x_2, x_2, x_3, x_4, x_4)$. Show that E is linear.

(b) Define $P : \mathbb{Z}_2^6 \longrightarrow \mathbb{Z}_2^6$ by $P((x_1, x_2, x_3, x_4, x_5, x_6)) = (x_3, x_4, x_1, x_5, x_2, x_6)$. Show that P is linear.

Problem 2. Let E be an invertible function from $\mathbb{Z}_2^n$ to $\mathbb{Z}_2^n$. Show that if E is linear, then E^{-1} is linear.

Problem 3. Let E be a linear invertible function from $\mathbb{Z}_2^n$ to $\mathbb{Z}_2^n$. Define a cipher of block size n in the following way. Let $\vec{x} \in \mathbb{Z}_2^n$ be the plaintext. Then the ciphertext $\vec{y} \in \mathbb{Z}_2^n$ is obtained by $\vec{y} = E(\vec{x})$. You intercept a message $\vec{z} \in \mathbb{Z}_2^n$ that has been encrypted using this cipher. Explain how can you find the plaintext using a chosen-plaintext attack. Assume you do not know the function E and hence do not know E^{-1}. But you may choose any plaintext you want and assume you can find the corresponding ciphertext.

Problem 4. Consider the fifth S-box used in DES. Think of it as a function from $\mathbb{Z}_2^6$ to $\mathbb{Z}_2^4$. Show that this function is not linear.

1.7 A Word about AES

As mentioned in the previous section, because of advances in computing power combined with progress in theoretical methods of cracking DES, the government realized that a new standard of encryption was needed. In September of 1997, the National Institute of Standards and Technology (NIST) asked for submissions of algorithms to be considered for the new encryption standard, which would be called the advanced encryption standard (AES). Twenty-one algorithms were submitted and fifteen met the criteria required by NIST. These fifteen algorithms were tested and scrutinized and, as a result, five finalists were announced in August of 1999. The five finalists were MARS, RC6, Rijndael, Serpent, and Twofish. NIST continued a more in-depth analysis of these five algorithms and even encouraged public comment on them. In October of 2000, NIST chose Rijndael as the winner. Rijndael again went through rigorous analysis and testing. Finally, the Secretary of Commerce approved Rijndael as the new official government encryption standard (AES) effective May 26, 2002. DES is expected to be phased out over the next few years and replaced by AES. It is worth noting that the mathematics involved in AES is more sophisticated than that in DES.[14] In fact, AES involves the use of a finite field much like the one you will see in Section 6.2. For more information on AES, see http://www.nist.gov/aes.

1.8 Diffie–Hellman Public Key Exchange

So far, we have discussed methods of encryption where the sender and receiver must share a secret "key." For example, in the Hill cipher, they must agree on the key matrix and if that matrix falls into an eavesdropper's hands, the cipher will be as legible to the eavesdropper as to the intended recipient. But how does one get the key safely from the sender to the receiver? In the 1960s and 1970s, as computers were becoming more powerful, it was possible to imagine millions, and possibly even billions, of computer-mediated transactions per year between businesses. And many of these transactions would require encryption. DES could be used, but for each transaction, the parties involved would somehow have to get the secret 56-bit key from one party to the other. Whitfield Diffie was one of the first people to devise a successful strategy for tackling this problem. Diffie graduated from MIT in 1965 and in the years following became

---

[14] For a mathematical description of AES, see Stinson (2002).

consumed with the dilemma we have just described. He traveled around the country learning all of the cryptography theory that he could. In the early 1970s he met Martin Hellman who was in the Electrical Engineering department at Stanford. The two started thinking about this problem together and in May of 1975, Diffie came up with the crucial idea. If two people who have never met, and therefore do not share a secret key, want to communicate in a secure way, they could *split* the key. Each would have both a public key and a private one. If Alice wants to send Bob a message, she looks up his public key and uses it to encrypt the message. Bob gets the message and uses his private key to decrypt it. An eavesdropper will know the public key but not the private one. The idea is that knowing the public key should make it easy to encrypt messages, but decrypting should not be easy unless the private key is known. A year later, in May 1976, Hellman thought of a tantalizingly simple mathematical way to implement Diffie's idea to exchange a secret key between two parties.

Diffie–Hellman Public Key Exchange

Suppose Alice wants to communicate in a secure way with Bob but they have never met and therefore do not share a secret key. The Diffie–Hellman public key exchange is a method for them to securely exchange a key so that they can use that key for encrypting messages using, for example, DES.

First choose a large prime, p. Then choose $g \in \mathbb{Z}_p$ so that the set $\{g^s | s \in \mathbb{Z}\}$ is a large set. Keep in mind that we are doing arithmetic modulo p, so g^s will be an element of $\mathbb{Z}_p$. Alice and Bob announce p and g.

Now, Alice chooses a random integer r and keeps it secret. This will be her private key. Bob also chooses a random integer t, which will be his private key. Alice computes $X = g^r \in \mathbb{Z}_p$ and Bob computes $Y = g^t \in \mathbb{Z}_p$. They exchange X and Y using a public channel, accessible to everyone. So Alice knows $p, g, r, X,$ and Y. Bob knows $p, g, t, X,$ and Y. To get the shared key, Alice computes $K = Y^r = g^{tr}$ and Bob computes $K = X^t = g^{rt}$. Thus Alice and Bob both know K and can use that as their key.

Let us briefly consider what the eavesdropper Eve knows. Alice and Bob announced $p, g, X,$ and Y. Eve also knows that $X = g^r$. If she could solve this equation for r, then she could compute $K = Y^r$ to get the secret key. She might be tempted to take the log base g of both sides to solve for r. But remember, to get X, Alice computed g^r *and reduced it modulo p.* So taking the log base g of both sides will not solve for the r that Alice used. In fact, it will rarely give Eve an integer. Solving $X = g^r$ for r is called the *discrete log problem* and turns out to be quite hard as long as Alice and Bob have arranged for the set $\{g^s | s \in \mathbb{Z}\}$ to be large. Of course, Eve could try all possible values for r. But Alice and Bob have chosen p and g so that there are so many possibilities for Eve to check that she and her computer cannot do it in a reasonable amount of time. So for practical purposes, Alice and Bob have generated a shared secret key.

EXERCISES

Problem 1. You want to exchange a secret key with a friend using the Diffie–Hellman public key exchange algorithm. You agree on $p = 13$ and $g = 2$. You choose $r = 5$. Your friend sends you $Y = 7$. What is the secret key that you share? (Of course, in reality, you would want to choose p to be much larger – we just give this exercise to illustrate the idea.)

Problem 2. Suppose you are an eavesdropper and know that a key is being exchanged using the Diffie–Hellman method. You know that $p = 17, g = 4$ and you intercept $X = 13$ and $Y = 13$. Find the key K. Why was $g = 4$ an unwise choice for this Diffie–Hellman public key exchange?

1.9 RSA

Shortly after Diffie and Hellman's groundbreaking ideas, three professors from the computer science department at MIT, Ron Rivest, Len Adleman, and Adi Shamir, started working on other mathematical approaches to public key cryptography. They were trying to make use of another function – that is, other than the modular exponentiation of Diffie–Hellman – that was easy to compute but hard to "undo." They knew that multiplying prime numbers together was easy, but given a large integer, factoring it into its prime factors ("undoing" the multiplication) was much harder. In April of 1977, they discovered how this idea could be used to implement public key cryptography. Their scheme is known as RSA, after Rivest, Shamir, and Adleman, and can be used not only for key exchange, but also for sending messages. Incidently, the RSA paper is the first occurrence of the now standard terminology of Alice, Bob, and Eve.[15]

We begin by describing the algorithm for sending messages using RSA and will spend the remainder of the section explaining why it works. As always, Alice will be the sender and Bob the receiver.

RSA

Bob

1. Choose two distinct large prime numbers, p and q and let $n = pq$.
2. Let m be the least common multiple of $p - 1$ and $q - 1$.
3. Choose a positive integer r so that r and m are relatively prime.
4. Find a positive integer s so that $rs \equiv 1 (\text{mod } m)$.
5. Announce n and r and keep all other information secret.

Alice

1. Convert the message to a string of numbers.
2. Break up the string of numbers into blocks of the same size. Call the ith block M_i.
3. Compute $R_i = M_i^r (\text{mod } n)$ for each i.
4. Send all the R_i's to Bob.

Bob

1. Compute $R_i^s (\text{mod } n)$ for all i. We claim that $R_i^s (\text{mod } n)$ will actually be M_i, so that Bob can now recover the original message sent by Alice.

Example 1.9.1. We illustrate with a simple example. Suppose Bob chooses $p = 61$ and $q = 11$. Of course, in reality, he will want to choose p and q to be very large or else an eavesdropper will easily be able to crack the cipher. Then we have $n = 61 \cdot 11 = 671$. The integer m is the least common multiple of 60 and 10, so in this case $m = 60$. Suppose Bob chooses r to be 7. Now he must find an integer s so that $rs \equiv 1 (\text{mod } m)$. We illustrate a systematic way of doing this in Example 1.9.2, but for now, note that $7 \cdot 43 = 301 \equiv 1 (\text{mod } 60)$. So $s = 43$. Now, Bob announces that $n = 671$ and $r = 7$.

---

[15] To read about the political controversy surrounding RSA, see Levy (2001).

Suppose Alice wants to send the message "be." She must convert the message to a string of numbers. Alice and Bob can agree on any way they want to do that, but we will use ASCII. The letter b in ASCII is represented by 098 and e is represented by 101. Suppose we agree to use a block size of 3. Then, $M_1 = 098$ and $M_2 = 101$. Now Alice computes $R_1 = 98^7 (\text{mod } 671)$ and $R_2 = 101^7 (\text{mod } 671)$. When she does this, she gets that $R_1 = 175$ and $R_2 = 326$. So Alice sends 175326 to Bob.

Bob receives 175326 from Alice, so he knows that $R_1 = 175$ and $R_2 = 326$. He computes $175^{43} (\text{mod } 671)$ and $326^{43} (\text{mod } 671)$. You can verify that he gets 98 and 101. He converts 098101 from ASCII back to letters to get the message "be."

Note that if an eavesdropper knows p and q, she can crack the cipher. But to find these primes, she would have to factor n. The idea is that Bob chooses the primes so large that for Eve to factor n will take an unreasonable amount of computer time.

Before explaining why this works, we first discuss a systematic method for finding the s in the above algorithm. For this we will need the Division Algorithm, which we state without proof.

Theorem 1.9.1 (The Division Algorithm). Let a and b be integers with $b > 0$. Then there exist unique integers r and q such that $a = bq + r$, where $0 \leq r < b$.

Children learning long division actually unknowingly are making use of the above theorem. When we divide an integer a by a positive integer b, we get a quotient q and a remainder r. And recall that $a/b = q + r/b$. Multiplying this equation by b, we get $a = bq + r$. So the q in the above theorem is simply the quotient when dividing a by b and the r is the remainder. We note here that the Division Algorithm is a theorem and in fact, not an algorithm. Nevertheless, since it is well known as the Division Algorithm, that is what we will call it.

Now we get back to the problem at hand. Given that m and r are relatively prime, we want to find a positive integer s so that $rs \equiv 1 (\text{mod } m)$. But this is equivalent to saying that we want m to divide $rs - 1$, which is equivalent to saying that we want there to exist an integer t so that $mt = rs - 1$. Solving this equation for 1, we get $1 = rs - mt$, or $1 = rs + m(-t)$.

In other words, we want to write 1 as a linear combination of r and m. To do this, we will use the Euclidean Algorithm, which we describe here, leaving the proof as an exercise at the end of this section.

The Euclidean Algorithm

Given $a \geq 0$ and $b > 0$, both integers, we can find the greatest common divisor of a and b in the following way. Use the Division Algorithm to find q_1 and r_1 so that $a = q_1b + r_1$ with $0 \leq r_1 < b$. If $r_1 = 0$, stop and b is the greatest common divisor of a and b. Otherwise, divide b by r_1 to obtain $b = q_2r_1 + r_2$ with $0 \leq r_2 < r_1$. If $r_2 = 0$, stop. If not, divide r_1 by r_2. Continue this process. Notice that the r_i's are all nonnegative and strictly decreasing. Hence, we will eventually get that one of the r_i's is 0 and the algorithm will stop. So we have,

$$a = q_1b + r_1 \text{ with } 0 < r_1 < b$$

$$b = q_2r_1 + r_2 \text{ with } 0 < r_2 < r_1$$

$$r_1 = q_3r_2 + r_3 \text{ with } 0 < r_3 < r_2$$

$$\vdots$$

$$r_{k-1} = q_{k+1}r_k + r_{k+1} \text{ with } 0 < r_{k+1} < r_k$$

$$r_k = q_{k+2}r_{k+1} + 0$$

Theorem 1.9.2. The integer r_{k+1} in the above algorithm is the greatest common divisor of a and b.

Proof. See Problem 3 at the end of this section.   ❏

Notice that the Euclidean Algorithm is a simple way to find the greatest common divisor of two integers. In fact, this is the algorithm that computers use to do this.

Now how does the Euclidean Algorithm help us find the integer s that we are looking for? Recall that m and r are relatively prime, so their greatest common divisor is 1. Hence, when we run through the Euclidean

Algorithm with $a = m$ and $b = r$ we will get that $r_{k+1} = 1$. We illustrate
with an example.

Example 1.9.2. Suppose $m = 696$ and $r = 13$ and we want to find s. Running through the Euclidean Algorithm, we get

$$696 = (53)13 + 7$$

$$13 = (1)7 + 6$$

$$7 = (1)6 + 1$$

$$6 = (6)1 + 0$$

The last nonzero remainder is 1, so as we already knew, the greatest common divisor of 696 and 13 is 1. Recall that we want to write 1 as a linear combination of 696 and 13. We can do this by running the Euclidean Algorithm backwards. The third equation tells us that $1 = 7 - 1(6)$. The second equation tells us that $6 = 13 - 7(1)$. Substituting this into the equation $1 = 7 - 1(6)$, we get $1 = 7 - 1(13 - 7(1))$. Grouping the 7's together, we get $1 = 2(7) - 13$. Now, the first equation tells us that $7 = 696 - 53(13)$. Substituting this into $1 = 2(7) - 13$, we get $1 = 2(696 - 53(13)) - 13$. Grouping the 13's we get $1 = 2(696) - 107(13)$. Notice that we have now written 1 as a linear combination of 696 and 13. Taking this equation modulo 696, we get that $-107(13) \equiv 1 \pmod{696}$. We would like s to be a positive integer. Noting that $-107 \equiv 589 \pmod{696}$, we infer that $589(13) \equiv 1 \pmod{696}$; so we can choose s to be 589.

Example 1.9.2 illustrates in general how to find s. We just start from the "end" of the Euclidean Algorithm and work our way backwards, solving for the remainders and then grouping the appropriate terms.

Now that we understand *how* RSA works, it remains to explain *why* it works. Recall that $R_i^s \equiv (M_i^r)^s \pmod{n}$. We want to show that $R_i^s \equiv M_i \pmod{n}$. In other words, we want to show that $(M_i^r)^s \equiv M_i \pmod{n}$. To show this, we first state and prove Fermat's Little Theorem.

Theorem 1.9.3 (Fermat's Little Theorem). Let p be a prime number and a a nonzero element in $\mathbb{Z}_p$. Then $a^{p-1} = 1$.

Proof. Recall that since we are in $\mathbb{Z}_p$, all arithmetic is done modulo p. Let $S = \mathbb{Z}_p - \{0\} = \{1, 2, 3, \ldots, p - 1\}$ and $aS = \{a, 2a, 3a, \ldots, (p - 1)a\} \subseteq \mathbb{Z}_p$. We claim that $S = aS$. Suppose $0 \in aS$. Then there is a nonzero element $x \in S$ such that $0 = ax$. By Problem 3 of Section 1.3, we have that $a = 0$ or $x = 0$. But we are given that a is nonzero and we also know that x is not 0. It follows that $0 \notin aS$ and so we have $aS \subseteq S$. We show now that aS has $p - 1$ distinct elements. Suppose it does not. Then $ax = ay$ for some $x, y \in S$ with $x \neq y$. By Problem 3 of Section 1.3, $ax = ay$ implies that $x = y$, a contradiction. It follows that $aS = S$. Therefore we can multiply all elements of S together and get the same thing as if we multiplied all elements of aS together. In other words,

$$(1)(2)(3) \cdots (p - 1) = a(2a)(3a) \cdots ((p - 1)a).$$

It follows that

$$(1)(2)(3) \cdots (p - 1) = a^{p-1}(1)(2)(3) \cdots (p - 1).$$

By cancelation, we have that $1 = a^{p-1}$ as desired. $\qquad\qquad\Box$

Note that if a is a nonzero element of $\mathbb{Z}_p$, then, by the above theorem, $1 = a^{p-1} = a(a^{p-2})$. So the multiplicative inverse of a in $\mathbb{Z}_p$ is a^{p-2}.

With the help of Fermat's Little Theorem, we are now ready to prove that RSA works.

Theorem 1.9.4. Let p and q be prime numbers with $p \neq q$. Let $n = pq$ and let m be the least common multiple of $p - 1$ and $q - 1$. Suppose r is a positive integer that is relatively prime to m. Let s be a positive integer such that $rs \equiv 1 \pmod{m}$. Then for every integer M, we have that $M^{rs} \equiv M \pmod{n}$.

Proof. Since $rs \equiv 1 \pmod{m}$, we have that $m | rs - 1$. So there exists an integer k such that $mk = rs - 1$. Rearranging this, we get that $rs = mk + 1$.

We first claim that $M^{rs} \equiv M \pmod{p}$. If $M \equiv 0 \pmod{p}$, then it is clear. On the other hand, if $M \not\equiv 0 \pmod{p}$, then $M \equiv a \pmod{p}$ for some integer a with $0 < a < p$. So by Fermat's Little Theorem, we have that $a^{p-1} \equiv 1 \pmod{p}$. It follows that $M^{p-1} \equiv a^{p-1} \equiv 1 \pmod{p}$. Now, $M^{rs} = M^{mk+1} = M^{mk} M$. Recall that m is a multiple of $p - 1$, and so $m = (p - 1)l$

for some integer l. It follows that

$$M^{mk} M = (M^{p-1})^{lk} M \equiv M(\bmod p).$$

Similarly, we can show that $M^{rs} \equiv M(\bmod q)$.

It follows that $p | M^{rs} - M$ and $q | M^{rs} - M$. As p and q are distinct primes, we have that $pq | M^{rs} - M$ and so $n | M^{rs} - M$. Hence $M^{rs} \equiv M(\bmod n)$ and the theorem holds.   ❑

EXERCISES

Problem 1. In the RSA cipher, we can never have an M_i be larger than n. Explain why.

Problem 2. Suppose you intercept the message 231. You know it has been encrypted using the RSA cipher with $n = 341, r = 7$, and block size 3. Find the original message.

Problem 3. Prove that r_{k+1} in the Euclidean Algorithm is the greatest common divisor of a and b.

Problem 4. (a) Show that if p is prime, then p divides $2^p - 2$.
(b) Show that the converse of the above statement is false. In other words, show that there is an n with $n > 1$ and n not prime such that $n | 2^n - 2$. Hint: try $n = 341$.

Problem 5. Show that if n is odd and b is an integer, then $b^n \equiv b(\bmod 3)$.

1.10 Public Key Exchanges with a Group

It turns out that given an algebraic structure called a group, we can use the group to perform a public key exchange. Recall that the goal of a public key exchange is for two parties who have never met to find a shared secret key so that they can use an encryption scheme that requires a shared secret key, such as DES or AES. In this chapter, we explain how this works. We start by defining a group.[16]

---

[16] For a comprehensive introduction to the theory of groups, see Gallian (2006).

Definition. Let G be a set together with an operation on pairs of elements of G which is usually denoted using multiplication notation. We say that G together with this operation is a *group* if the following properties are satisfied.

1. For every $a, b \in G$, we have that $ab \in G$. (G is closed under its operation)
2. For every $a, b, c \in G$, we have that $(ab)c = a(bc)$. (The operation is associative)
3. There exists an element $e \in G$ such that $ae = ea = a$ for all $a \in G$. (e is called the identity element of G).
4. For every $a \in G$, there exists a $b \in G$ satisfying $ab = ba = e$. (b is called the inverse of a and is denoted a^{-1}).

Examples:

1. If p is a prime number, $\mathbb{Z}_p - \{0\}$ is a group under the multiplication of $\mathbb{Z}_p$.
2. $\mathbb{Z}_n$ is a group under its addition.
3. The set of all nonsingular 2×2 matrices with real numbers as entries is a group under matrix multiplication.

We now take a moment to comment on notation. If G is a group and $g \in G$, then, as a convention, we say $g^0 = e$. When we write g^n, where n is a positive integer, we mean g multiplied together n times. When we write g^n, where n is a negative integer, we mean g^{-1} multiplied together $-n$ times.

We are now ready to describe a method for a public key exchange using any finite group.

Alice

1. Pick a finite group G and an element $x \in G$. This should be done in a "smart" way – we want the group G to have a large number of elements and we also want the set $\{x^n | n \in \mathbb{Z}\}$ to be large.
2. Choose a secret integer r and compute $x^r \in G$.
3. Announce G, x, and x^r.

Bob

1. Choose a secret integer t.
2. Compute $x^t \in G$.
3. Send x^t to Alice.

Now, Alice computes $K = (x^t)^r = x^{rt} \in G$ and Bob computes $K = (x^r)^t = x^{rt} \in G$. Then they both share K and can use it as their secret key.

We take a moment to consider what the eavesdropper, Eve, will know. She knows G, x, x^r, and x^t. So Alice should choose a group G so that if one knows $y = x^r$, then it is difficult to find r. We will discuss such a group in the next section.

You should also note that when $G = \mathbb{Z}_p - \{0\}$, then this is exactly the Diffie–Hellman public key exchange. So this method is actually a generalization of the Diffie–Hellman method.

Sometimes it is more convenient to use additive notation for a group instead of multiplicative notation. For example, $\mathbb{Z}$ is a group under addition and so it would be confusing to use multiplicative notation in this case. When we use additive notation, the four properties used in the definition of a group can be rephrased as follows.

1. For every $a, b \in G$, we have that $a + b \in G$. (Closure)
2. For every $a, b, c \in G$, we have that $(a + b) + c = a + (b + c)$. (Associative)
3. There exists an element $0 \in G$ such that $a + 0 = 0 + a = a$ for all $a \in G$. (0 is called the identity element of G)
4. For every $a \in G$, there exists a $b \in G$ satisfying $a + b = b + a = 0$. (b is called the inverse of a and is denoted $-a$)

When we use additive notation for a group, if g is an element of the group and n is a positive integer, then we will use ng to mean g added to itself n times. If n is a negative integer, then ng means $-g$ added to itself $-n$ times. As a convention, $0g = 0$.

We now describe the public key exchange described earlier in this section with multiplicative notation replaced with additive notation.

Alice

1. Pick a finite group G and an element $P \in G$. This should be done in a "smart" way – we want the group G to have a large number of elements and we also want the set $\{nP \mid n \in \mathbb{Z}\}$ to be large.
2. Choose a secret integer r and compute $rP \in G$.
3. Announce G, P, and rP.

Bob

1. Choose a secret integer t.
2. Compute $tP \in G$.
3. Send tP to Alice.

Now, Alice computes $K = trP = rtP \in G$ and Bob computes $K = rtP = trP \in G$. Then they both share K and can use it as their secret key.

EXERCISES

Problem 1. Prove that the identity element in a group is unique.

Problem 2. Prove that if G is a group and $a \in G$, then a^{-1} is unique.

Problem 3. Let $U(n) \subseteq \mathbb{Z}_n$ be the set of elements of $\mathbb{Z}_n$ that are relatively prime to n. Show that $U(n)$ is a group under multiplication modulo n.

1.11 Public Key Exchange Using Elliptic Curves

In this section, we define a group using points on an elliptic curve. Not only is this group elegant and useful in its own right, but it also has properties beneficial for applications in cryptography. We use the group we describe here for public key exchange as explained in Section 1.10.[17]

Consider the equation

$$y^2 = x^3 + ax + b, \tag{1.4}$$

where a and b are rational numbers satisfying $4a^3 + 27b^2 \neq 0$. (This will ensure that the elliptic curve is smooth.) Equation (1.4) is a specific

---

[17] We will give a brief introduction to the subject and a reader interested in more details should consult other sources such as Koblitz (1994).

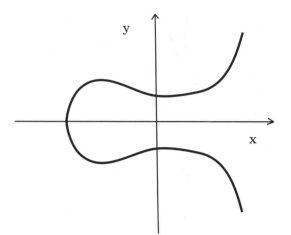

Figure 1.3: The points satisfying $y^2 = x^3 - 3x + 4$.

example of an elliptic curve and the only type that we will consider here. Now let H be the set of points (c, d) such that (c, d) satisfies Eq. (1.4) (i.e., $d^2 = c^3 + ac + b$) and c and d are both rational numbers. We define the elements of our group G to be $H \cup \mathcal{O}$ where we will call $\mathcal{O}$ "the point at infinity." For example, suppose $a = -3$ and $b = 4$. Then we can graph the set of points that satisfy

$$y^2 = x^3 - 3x + 4$$

as in Fig. 1.3. So the elements of G are $\mathcal{O}$ along with the points on the curve for which both coordinates are rational.

Recall that for G to be a group, we must define an operation, denoted in this case by $+$, on pairs of elements of G that satisfies the appropriate properties. We break up our definition into five different cases as follows.

Case 1: For any point P in G, we define $P + \mathcal{O} = \mathcal{O} + P = P$.

We now define $+$ for the other cases. In other words, suppose that $P \neq \mathcal{O}$ and $Q \neq \mathcal{O}$. Then we can write $P = (x_1, y_1)$ and $Q = (x_2, y_2)$, where x_1, x_2, y_1, and y_2 are all rational numbers.

Case 2: If $x_1 \neq x_2$, draw the line through the points P and Q. As we will prove after we finish defining $+$, that line will intersect the elliptic curve at exactly one more point $R = (x_3, y_3)$. For this case, we define

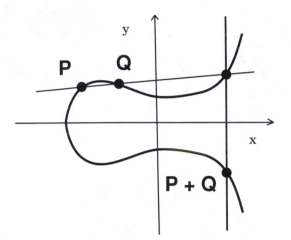

Figure 1.4: $P + Q$ in Case 2.

$P + Q = (x_3, -y_3)$. So $P + Q$ is the reflection of the point R about the x-axis. See Fig. 1.4 for an illustration of this case. Here we use the convention that if the line is tangent to the elliptic curve, we say that it intersects the elliptic curve twice. So, if the line through P and Q is tangent to the elliptic curve at the point P, then $R = P$.

Case 3: If $x_1 = x_2$ and $y_1 \neq y_2$ then we define $P + Q = \mathcal{O}$.

Case 4: If $P = Q$, then draw the line tangent to the elliptic curve at the point P. If the tangent line is not vertical, it will intersect the elliptic curve at exactly one more point $R = (x_3, y_3)$ (we will prove this later). In this case, we define $P + Q = P + P = (x_3, -y_3)$. See Fig. 1.5 for an illustration of this case.

Case 5: On the other hand, if in the above case the tangent line is vertical, then we define $P + Q = P + P = \mathcal{O}$.

One natural question to ask now is: Unless $P + Q = \mathcal{O}$, how do we algebraically find the coordinates of the point $P + Q$? Since the answer for Case 1 is clear, we need only work out the answer for Case 2 and Case 4. We start with Case 2.

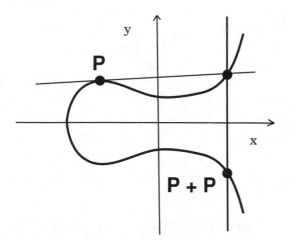

y

P

P + P

x

Figure 1.5: $P + Q$ in Case 4.

Let $P = (x_1, y_1)$ and $Q = (x_2, y_2)$ with $x_1 \neq x_2$ and P and Q both on the elliptic curve given by Eq. (1.4). Then $m = \frac{y_2 - y_1}{x_2 - x_1}$ is the slope of the line through P and Q. So the equation of the line through P and Q is

$$y = mx + h, \tag{1.5}$$

where h is the y-intercept of the line. We know that (x_1, y_1) is on the line, so plugging this into Eq. (1.5) and solving for h, we get

$$h = y_1 - mx_1 = y_1 - \left(\frac{y_2 - y_1}{x_2 - x_1} \right) x_1.$$

Now, we want to find the points of intersection of the line described in Eq. (1.5) and the elliptic curve given by Eq. (1.4). Plugging Eq. (1.5) into Eq. (1.4), we get

$$(mx + h)^2 = x^3 + ax + b.$$

Squaring out the left-hand side and rearranging terms, we get

$$x^3 - m^2 x^2 + (a - 2mh)x + (b - h^2) = 0.$$

Since (x_1, y_1) and (x_2, y_2) are on both the line and the elliptic curve, we know that x_1 and x_2 are solutions to the above equation. Now recall that if $f(x)$ is a nonzero polynomial with real coefficients and r is a real number, then r satisfies $f(r) = 0$ if and only if $x - r$ is a factor of the polynomial

$f(x)$. It follows that

$$f(x) = x^3 - m^2 x^2 + (a - 2mh)x + (b - h^2)$$

can be factored as $(x - x_1)(x - x_2)g(x)$, where $g(x)$ is a polynomial of degree 1. Since the coefficient of the x^3 term of $f(x)$ is 1, we know that $g(x)$ must be of the form $(x - k)$, where k is a real number. Now, $f(x)$ has degree 3, so $f(x) = 0$ has at most three solutions. It follows that x_1, x_2, and k are the only solutions. We are given x_1 and x_2 and so we want to find the third solution, k, in terms of quantities that we know. Now, we have

$$x^3 - m^2 x^2 + (a - 2mh)x + (b - h^2) = (x - x_1)(x - x_2)(x - k).$$

Multiplying everything out, we get

$$\begin{aligned} & x^3 - m^2 x^2 + (a - 2mh)x + (b - h^2) \\ & = x^3 + (-x_1 - x_2 - k)x^2 + (x_1 x_2 + kx_1 + kx_2)x - kx_1 x_2. \end{aligned}$$

Equating the coefficients of the x^2 term on both sides and solving for k, we get

$$k = m^2 - x_1 - x_2.$$

From our above discussion, we know that the line given by Eq. 1.5 intersects the elliptic curve in exactly three points, namely (x_1, y_1), (x_2, y_2), and $(k, mk + h)$. So the point R described in Case 2 of the definition of $P + Q$ is

$$R = (x_3, y_3) = (k, mk + h).$$

Therefore, we must have that

$$x_3 = k = m^2 - x_1 - x_2 = \left(\frac{y_2 - y_1}{x_2 - x_1} \right)^2 - x_1 - x_2$$

and

$$\begin{aligned} y_3 = mk + h = mx_3 + h &= \left(\frac{y_2 - y_1}{x_2 - x_1} \right) x_3 + y_1 - \left(\frac{y_2 - y_1}{x_2 - x_1} \right) x_1 \\ &= y_1 + \left(\frac{y_2 - y_1}{x_2 - x_1} \right) (x_3 - x_1). \end{aligned}$$

It follows that

$$P + Q = \left(\left(\frac{y_2 - y_1}{x_2 - x_1} \right)^2 - x_1 - x_2, \, -y_1 + \left(\frac{y_2 - y_1}{x_2 - x_1} \right)(x_1 - x_3) \right). \quad (1.6)$$

Recall that $P + Q$ is defined to be $(x_3, -y_3)$. So given the coordinates of P and Q, we can use Eq. (1.6) to find the coordinates of $P + Q$.

We now describe how to find the coordinates of $P + Q$ for Case 4. Suppose $P = (x_1, y_1)$ is on the elliptic curve given by Eq. (1.4) and the tangent line at P is not vertical. Using implicit differentiation on Eq. (1.4), we get that $2yy' = 3x^2 + a$. Solving for y', we know that for $y \neq 0$, $y' = \frac{3x^2 + a}{2y}$. So the slope of the tangent line to the elliptic curve at the point $P = (x_1, y_1)$ is

$$m = \frac{3x_1^2 + a}{2y_1}.$$

Notice that $y_1 \neq 0$ since the tangent line is not vertical. Running through the same argument as in Case 2 with our new value for m and with $P = Q$ so that $x_1 = x_2$ and $y_1 = y_2$, we arrive at

$$R = (x_3, y_3) = (k, mk + h).$$

Therefore, we must have that

$$x_3 = k = m^2 - x_1 - x_2 = \left(\frac{3x_1^2 + a}{2y_1} \right)^2 - 2x_1$$

and

$$y_3 = mk + h = mx_3 + h = \left(\frac{3x_1^2 + a}{2y_1} \right) x_3 + y_1 - \left(\frac{3x_1^2 + a}{2y_1} \right) x_1$$

$$= y_1 + \left(\frac{3x_1^2 + a}{2y_1} \right)(x_3 - x_1).$$

It follows that

$$P + P = \left(\left(\frac{3x_1^2 + a}{2y_1} \right)^2 - 2x_1, \, -y_1 + \left(\frac{3x_1^2 + a}{2y_1} \right)(x_1 - x_3) \right). \quad (1.7)$$

Recall that $P + P$ is defined to be $(x_3, -y_3)$. So given the coordinates of P, we can use Eq. (1.7) to find the coordinates of $P + P$.

We have completed the definition of our group G and the operation $+$. Now we must argue that G is in fact a group under $+$. To see that G is closed, let P and Q be elements of G. By the definition in Cases 1, 3, and 5 and by Eq. (1.6) in Case 2 and Eq. (1.7) in Case 4, it follows that $P + Q$ is an element of G. (Notice that by Eq. (1.6) and (1.7), the coordinates of $P + Q$ in those cases are in fact rational numbers.) It turns out that to prove $(P + Q) + S = P + (Q + S)$ for all points P, Q, and S in G is quite difficult and so will be omitted from our discussion. But rest assured that $+$ does satisfy the associative property. It is not difficult to see that $\mathcal{O}$ serves as the identity for G. The inverse of $\mathcal{O}$ is clearly $\mathcal{O}$ and the inverse of $P = (x_1, y_1)$, where $P \neq \mathcal{O}$ is $(x_1, -y_1)$, the reflection of P about the x-axis. It follows that G is a group under the operation $+$.

After all the work we just did to define the group G, we now admit that it is not the one we will use for public key exchange. But it will be clear in a moment that G serves as a geometric motivation for the group that we *will* use. This latter group $\mathcal{G}$ (notationally distinguished by the calligraphic symbol) is defined as follows. First let p be a prime number satisfying $p > 3$ and let a and b be elements of $\mathbb{Z}_p$ satisfying $4a^3 + 27b^2 \neq 0 \pmod{p}$. Let $\mathcal{H}$ be the set of ordered pairs (x_1, y_1) such that x_1 and y_1 are elements of $\mathbb{Z}_p$ and x_1 and y_1 satisfy Eq. (1.4), in $\mathbb{Z}_p$ where a and b are now elements of $\mathbb{Z}_p$. In other words, we must have that

$$y_1^2 = x_1^3 + ax_1 + b \pmod{p}.$$

Then we define the elements of the group $\mathcal{G}$ to be $\mathcal{H} \cup \mathcal{O}$ where, as before, we call $\mathcal{O}$ the "point at infinity." We now work to define the operation $+$ that we will use on $\mathcal{G}$. First recall that if $a \in \mathbb{Z}_p$ with $a \neq 0$, then there is an element $b \in \mathbb{Z}_p$ such that $ab = 1$. When we write $\frac{1}{a}$ in the following discussion, we mean b. We are now ready to define $+$.

Case 1: For any point P in $\mathcal{G}$, we define $P + \mathcal{O} = \mathcal{O} + P = P$.

We now define $+$ for the other cases. In other words, suppose that $P \neq \mathcal{O}$ and $Q \neq \mathcal{O}$. Then we can write $P = (x_1, y_1)$ and $Q = (x_2, y_2)$ where x_1, x_2, y_1, and y_2 are now elements of $\mathbb{Z}_p$.

Case 2: If $x_1 \neq x_2$ then we define $P + Q$ to be the point $\left(\left(\frac{y_2 - y_1}{x_2 - x_1}\right)^2 - x_1 - x_2, -y_1 + \left(\frac{y_2 - y_1}{x_2 - x_1}\right)(x_1 - x_3)\right)$, where $x_3 = \left(\frac{y_2 - y_1}{x_2 - x_1}\right)^2 - x_1 - x_2$ and all arithmetic is done in $\mathbb{Z}_p$.

Case 3: If $x_1 = x_2$ and $y_1 \neq y_2$ then we define $P + Q = \mathcal{O}$.

Case 4: If $P = Q$ and $y_1 \neq 0$ then we define $P + Q = P + P = \left(\left(\frac{3x_1^2 + a}{2y_1}\right)^2 - 2x_1, -y_1 + \left(\frac{3x_1^2 + a}{2y_1}\right)(x_1 - x_3)\right)$, where $x_3 = \left(\frac{3x_1^2 + a}{2y_1}\right)^2 - 2x_1$ and all arithmetic is done in $\mathbb{Z}_p$.

Case 5: On the other hand, if, in the above case, $y_1 = 0$ then we define $P + Q = P + P = \mathcal{O}$.

With the above definition it can be shown that $\mathcal{G}$ is a group under the operation $+$. As with the group G described earlier, the element $\mathcal{O}$ is the identity element of the group $\mathcal{G}$, the inverse of $\mathcal{O}$ is itself, and the inverse of any other element (x_1, y_1) in $\mathcal{G}$ is $(x_1, -y_1)$. This is the group we will use for public key exchange as described in Section 1.10.

We end with an example.

Example 1.11.1. Let $p = 7$, $a = -3$, and $b = 4$ as before. Since $-3 \equiv 4 \pmod 7$, we want to find the pairs of elements in $\mathbb{Z}_7$ that satisfy the equation $y^2 = x^3 + 4x + 4$. It is not hard to do this by hand to get the group $\mathcal{G}$.

$$\mathcal{G} = \{\mathcal{O}, (0, 2), (0, 5), (1, 4), (1, 3), (3, 1), (3, 6), (4, 0), (5, 4), (5, 3)\}$$

Suppose Alice and Bob agree to do a public key exchange with the above $\mathcal{G}$ using the method described in Section 1.10. If Alice chooses $P = (0, 2)$ and $r = 3$, then she must compute $rP = 3(0, 2) = (0, 2) + (0, 2) + (0, 2)$. Now,

$$(0, 2) + (0, 2) = \left(\left(\frac{3(0)^2 + 4}{4}\right)^2 - 0, -2 + \left(\frac{3(0)^2 + 4}{4}\right)(0 - x_3)\right)$$
$$= (1, 5 + (0 - 1))$$
$$= (1, 4).$$

Note that for the above calculation we used Case 4 of the definition. Now $3(0, 2) = (0, 2) + (1, 4)$, so we have

$$(0, 2) + (1, 4) = \left(\left(\frac{4 - 2}{1 - 0}\right)^2 - 0 - 1, -2 + \left(\frac{4 - 2}{1 - 0}\right)(0 - x_3)\right)$$
$$= (3, -2 + (2)(0 - 3))$$
$$= (3, 6).$$

So Alice announces that $P = (0, 2)$ and $rP = (3, 6)$.

Now suppose that Bob chooses $t = 4$. Then $tP = 4(0, 2) = 2(0, 2) + 2(0, 2) = (1, 4) + (1, 4)$. So

$$(1, 4) + (1, 4) = \left(\left(\frac{3(1)^2 + 4}{2(4)} \right)^2 - 2(1), -4 + \left(\frac{3(1)^2 + 4}{(2)4} \right)(1 - x_3) \right)$$
$$= (0 - 2, -4 + (0)(1 - x_3))$$
$$= (5, 3).$$

Bob sends $tP = (5, 3)$ to Alice. Alice now computes $K = trP = r(tP) = 3(5, 3)$ as follows.

$$(5, 3) + (5, 3) = \left(\left(\frac{3(5)^2 + 4}{2(3)} \right)^2 - 2(5), -3 + \left(\frac{3(5)^2 + 4}{(2)3} \right)(5 - x_3) \right)$$
$$= (1, -3 + (-2)(5 - 1))$$
$$= (1, 3)$$

and

$$(1, 3) + (5, 3) = \left(\left(\frac{3 - 3}{5 - 1} \right)^2 - 1 - 5, -3 + \left(\frac{3 - 3}{5 - 1} \right)(1 - x_3) \right)$$
$$= (1, 4).$$

Alice now knows that $K = (1, 4)$.
Bob computes $K = trP = 4(3, 6)$.

$$(3, 6) + (3, 6) = \left(\left(\frac{3(3)^2 + 4}{2(6)} \right)^2 - 2(3), -6 + \left(\frac{3(3)^2 + 4}{(2)6} \right)(3 - x_3) \right)$$
$$= (5, 4)$$

and

$$(5, 4) + (5, 4) = \left(\left(\frac{3(5)^2 + 4}{2(4)} \right)^2 - 2(5), -4 + \left(\frac{3(5)^2 + 4}{(2)4} \right)(5 - x_3) \right)$$
$$= (1, 4).$$

Now Bob and Alice share the secret key $K = (1, 4)$.

Of course, the above example is a very simple one that could be broken easily. In practice, Alice and Bob choose p to be much larger. Because the operation on the group $\mathcal{G}$ is so complicated, it is difficult to "undo" the operation and that makes it more challenging for an eavesdropper to find the shared key K.

This concept can be modified so that we can use the group $\mathcal{G}$ not only for public key exchange but also for sending encrypted messages.[18]

EXERCISES

Problem 1. In the group described in Example 1.11.1, compute $(3, 6) + (5, 4)$.

Problem 2. Let $p = 7$ and $a = b = 1$. Find the elements of the group $\mathcal{G}$.

Problem 3. Alice and Bob decide to do a public key exchange using the group from Problem 2. Suppose Alice chooses $P = (2, 2)$ and $r = 4$. Find rP. Suppose Bob chooses $t = 3$. Find tP. Go through the steps that Alice will to find K. Do the same for Bob to verify that they will find the same K.

---

[18] See Koblitz (1994).

2   Quantum Mechanics

The early twentieth century was a revolutionary time in the history of physics. People often think of Einstein's special theory of relativity of 1905, which changed our conceptions of time and space. But among physicists, quantum mechanics is usually regarded as an even more radical change in our thinking about the physical world. Quantum mechanics, which was developed between 1900 and 1926, began as a theory of atoms and light but has now become the framework in terms of which all basic physical theories are expected to be cast. We need quantum ideas not only to understand atoms, molecules, and elementary particles, but also to understand the electronic properties of solids and even certain astronomical phenomena such as the stability of white dwarf stars. The theory was radical in part because it introduced probabilistic behavior as a fundamental aspect of the world, but even more because it seems to allow mutually exclusive situations to exist simultaneously in a "quantum superposition." We will see later that the possibility of quantum superposition is largely responsible for a quantum computer's distinctive advantage over an ordinary computer. The present chapter is devoted to introducing the basic principles of quantum mechanics.[1]

---

[1] In this book, because of the applications we consider, we focus on the quantum mechanics of systems having only a finite number of perfectly distinguishable states. A thorough introduction with a similar focus can be found in the book by Peres (1995). See also the article by Mermin (2003), which covers some of the same material starting with ideas from classical computer science. Most quantum mechanics textbooks, reasonably enough, deal primarily with the quantum mechanics of continuous variables such as position and momentum, and with applications to atomic and molecular physics. Two widely used books along these lines are Griffiths (1995) and Park (1992). For a more conceptual approach, but still assuming the mathematical background of an undergraduate student in physics

There are essentially four components of the mathematical structure of quantum mechanics. We need to know how to represent (i) states, (ii) measurements, (iii) reversible transformations, and (iv) composite systems. We will develop the first three in stages, starting with a very simple case – linear polarization of photons – and working toward the most general case. The treatment of composite systems will be saved for the last few sections of the chapter.

2.1 Photon Polarization

Any object you can think of – an atom, a baseball, a tree – can in principle be described by quantum mechanics, though in practice we would never want to give an exhaustive quantum description of anything as complex as a baseball. In this book we will mainly be thinking about extremely simple objects, and even then we will restrict our attention to very simple properties.

A photon, or particle of light, is a particularly simple object. It has essentially only two properties, or *quantum variables*: momentum and polarization. We use the word *state* to refer to the most complete characterization that one can give of a quantum variable at a particular moment in time. The state of a quantum variable can change from one moment to the next, but at any given moment, you cannot know more about a quantum variable than its state.[2] Of the two quantum variables that describe a photon, the simpler by far is its polarization. So let us consider just that variable.

For some purposes it is useful to divide the set of possible polarization states of a photon into three classes: linear, circular, and elliptical. The linear polarizations are the easiest ones to visualize and we will start by focusing just on these states. Our discussion of linear polarization is somewhat informal and is intended to introduce ideas that will be used throughout our work on quantum mechanics. The terms introduced in that

---

or engineering, see Greenstein and Zajonc (1997). A less technical introduction to the fundamental ideas is Styer (2000).

[2] We use the word "state" to refer to what is more precisely known as a *pure* state. If one has less than maximal knowledge about a quantum variable, one describes it by a state that is not pure but *mixed*. We will not explicitly consider mixed states in this book.

discussion will be defined more precisely when we generalize to circular and elliptical polarizations.

2.1.1 Linear polarization

In classical physics (that is, nonquantum physics), the polarization of a linearly polarized light wave is represented by an axis in a plane perpendicular to the direction of propagation of the wave; this axis is understood to be the axis along which the electric field vector is oscillating. In quantum physics we cannot properly speak of an electric field oscillating along an axis, but we can still speak of a photon's polarization, and linear polarization can still be represented as an axis in a plane. Moreover, it is still helpful to think of this plane as perpendicular to the direction of motion of the photon, because visualizing the polarization in this way aids the intuition as we think about how the polarization will change in various situations.

Suppose that a photon is traveling directly into this page – its direction of propagation is perpendicular to the page – so that the plane of possible polarization vectors can be identified with the plane of the page; the plane has a horizontal axis (which we will call the s_1-axis) and a vertical axis (the s_2-axis). Any other axis in the plane can be represented by a vector lying along that axis, so that we can represent states of linear polarization by two-dimensional real vectors. In fact we will always use normalized vectors, that is, vectors of unit length, and we will usually write them as column vectors. Thus a general linear polarization state can be represented by the vector $|s\rangle = \begin{pmatrix} s_1 \\ s_2 \end{pmatrix} = \begin{pmatrix} \cos\theta \\ \sin\theta \end{pmatrix}$, where θ is the angle measured counterclockwise from the positive s_1-axis, as in Fig. 2.1. Here we use the physicists' notation $|\cdots\rangle$ to denote a vector that represents a quantum state. (One might have expected $\vec{s}$ but this notation is not normally used for quantum states.) We will also use the special symbols $|\leftrightarrow\rangle$ and $|\updownarrow\rangle$ to indicate the horizontal and vertical polarizations as represented by the vectors $\begin{pmatrix} 1 \\ 0 \end{pmatrix}$ and $\begin{pmatrix} 0 \\ 1 \end{pmatrix}$ respectively. Thus we can write our general linear polarization state $|s\rangle$ as $|s\rangle = s_1 |\leftrightarrow\rangle + s_2 |\updownarrow\rangle$. Note that the two vectors $|s\rangle = \begin{pmatrix} s_1 \\ s_2 \end{pmatrix}$ and $-|s\rangle = \begin{pmatrix} -s_1 \\ -s_2 \end{pmatrix}$, which are diametrically opposite each other, lie on the same axis and therefore represent the same polarization state. So there is not a one-to-one correspondence between normalized vectors and polarization states. This feature is quite general in quantum mechanics: we

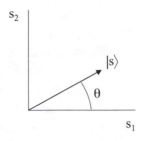

Figure 2.1: A vector representing a state of linear polarization.

will see that two vectors that are proportional to each other (as in this case where one is the negative of the other) always represent the same quantum state. (As we will see, in the general case the proportionality constant can be a *complex* number.)

We now introduce the concepts of *measurements* and *reversible transformations* as they apply to linear polarizations.

We can imagine a measuring device for a quantum variable as a sort of box that can accept as input the quantum object (which for now will be a photon) and produce as output one of several possible outcomes. The outcomes are physical events but they can be labeled by mathematical symbols. We will say more below about the labeling scheme we will use. If you have not seen any quantum mechanics before, you might expect that a measuring device for photon polarization would simply ascertain the polarization state of the input photon. That is, if you were to insert into the device a photon in the polarization state $\left(\begin{smallmatrix}\cos\theta\\\sin\theta\end{smallmatrix}\right)$, the observed outcome would tell us the value of θ. It turns out, though, that no such device exists. Moreover, according to quantum mechanics, no such device could ever be built. In other words, it is impossible for a measuring device to ask of a photon, "What is your polarization state?" Instead, it can ask only *binary* questions, giving the photon a choice between two *orthogonal* (i.e., perpendicular) states. For example, there exists a measuring device that asks, in effect, "Which of the following two polarizations do you have: vertical or horizontal?" Of course the photon may well not have either of these polarizations – it may be polarized along some intermediate axis – but the measuring device *forces* the photon to choose between the two options given. As we will discuss further below, the photon's polarization state typically must change in response to the question posed by the measuring device. Mathematically, a device that measures linear polarization is represented by an ordered pair of normalized, mutually perpendicular state vectors $M = (|m^{(1)}\rangle, |m^{(2)}\rangle)$. A set of vectors that are normalized and mutually perpendicular is called an *orthonormal* set. The pair M also constitutes a *basis* for the space of states (i.e., any vector in the space can be written as a linear combination of $|m^{(1)}\rangle$ and $|m^{(2)}\rangle$); so the measurement is represented by an *orthonormal basis*. The two vectors $|m^{(1)}\rangle$ and $|m^{(2)}\rangle$ correspond to the two possible outcomes of the measurement.

At this point you may well be wondering how the photon makes its decision. For example, if the photon's initial polarization makes an angle of 30° with the horizontal axis, and it is forced to choose between horizontal and vertical, how does it decide which outcome to give? According to quantum mechanics the decision is made *probabilistically*: if the state of the photon before measurement is $|s\rangle$, then the probability p_i of the outcome $|m^{(i)}\rangle$ (where $i = 1$ or 2) is the squared cosine of the angle between $|s\rangle$ and $|m^{(i)}\rangle$. Notice that because the two vectors $|m^{(1)}\rangle$ and $|m^{(2)}\rangle$ are orthogonal, the two probabilities add up to one, as they must. Notice also that if the polarization vector $|s\rangle$ is only a few degrees away from one of the allowed outcome vectors $|m^{(i)}\rangle$, then it is much more likely to yield that outcome than the other one. This rule for computing probabilities is consistent with the experimental evidence, and indeed one can easily produce more such evidence in a simple demonstration that we will describe shortly.

We can reexpress the above probability rule in a more succinct form by introducing the *inner product* between two polarization vectors. If $|s\rangle = \binom{s_1}{s_2}$ and $|m\rangle = \binom{m_1}{m_2}$ are two real vectors representing linear polarization states, then the inner product between $|s\rangle$ and $|m\rangle$ is denoted $\langle s|m\rangle$ and is defined to be $\langle s|m\rangle = s_1 m_1 + s_2 m_2$. The probability rule can now be restated as follows: if a photon with linear polarization $|s\rangle$ is subjected to the linear polarization measurement $M = (|m^{(1)}\rangle, |m^{(2)}\rangle)$, then the probability of the outcome $|m^{(i)}\rangle$ is $|\langle s|m^{(i)}\rangle|^2$. (The absolute value sign is not necessary here, but we include it because it will be necessary for more general polarizations, for which $\langle s|m^{(i)}\rangle$ can be a complex number.)

Example 2.1.1. In a certain polarization measurement M, one of the possible outcomes is represented by the vector $|m^{(1)}\rangle = \binom{1/2}{\sqrt{3}/2}$. (i) How can

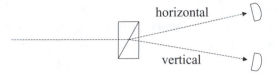

Figure 2.2: Distinguishing horizontal and vertical polarizations by means of a Wollaston prism and two photon detectors.

we represent the other outcome vector? (ii) If M is applied to a photon with horizontal polarization, what are the probabilities of the two outcomes?

Answers: (i) The vector $|m^{(2)}\rangle$ must be orthogonal to $|m^{(1)}\rangle$. This requirement forces $|m^{(2)}\rangle$ to be proportional to $\left(\begin{smallmatrix}\sqrt{3}/2\\-1/2\end{smallmatrix}\right)$. Since we insist on normalization, the only real vectors we can use for $|m^{(2)}\rangle$ are $\left(\begin{smallmatrix}\sqrt{3}/2\\-1/2\end{smallmatrix}\right)$ and $\left(\begin{smallmatrix}-\sqrt{3}/2\\1/2\end{smallmatrix}\right)$. (ii) If the incoming photon has horizontal polarization, represented by $|s\rangle = \left(\begin{smallmatrix}1\\0\end{smallmatrix}\right)$, then the probability of the first outcome is $p_1 = |\langle s|m^{(1)}\rangle|^2 = (1/2)^2 = 1/4$, and the probability of the second outcome is $p_2 = |\langle s|m^{(2)}\rangle|^2 = (\sqrt{3}/2)^2 = 3/4$.

In practice the measuring device represented by an orthonormal basis $M = (|m^{(1)}\rangle, |m^{(2)}\rangle)$ can be realized in a number of ways. One such realization consists of what is called a Wollaston prism, together with a pair of photon detectors. A Wollaston prism will direct into one path all photons that are polarized along a certain axis, and will direct into a different path all photons that are polarized along the orthogonal axis. A photon detector is placed in each of these two paths to record each photon's choice, as illustrated in Fig. 2.2. If a photon's polarization is neither of the two special states picked out by the Wollaston prism, then the photon chooses one of the two detectors probabilistically in accordance with the above rule. By counting how many photons land in each detector, one can estimate the probabilities, and one indeed finds that the observations agree with the theory. Detecting and counting individual photons requires rather fancy equipment and cannot be done in practice unless the beam of light is extremely weak. On the other hand, it is quite easy to measure the *intensity* of a normal beam of light, and the intensity is proportional to the number of photons arriving per unit time.

Another very common way to make a measurement of linear polarization is with a polarizing filter. Like a Wollaston prism, a polarizing filter distinguishes two orthogonal polarization axes, but instead of sending them along different paths, it simply absorbs photons having one polarization and transmits photons having the orthogonal polarization. For example, the polarizing filters used in polarizing sunglasses are oriented so as to transmit vertically polarized light and to absorb horizontally polarized light. This is because glare tends to be horizontally polarized, for reasons having to do with the behavior of light upon reflection.

So far we have treated measurements primarily as indicators of one outcome or the other. But if the photon survives the measurement, we can also ask how the measurement affects the photon's state. In classical physics, an ideal measurement would be one that does not affect the object being measured. But in quantum physics this ideal must be abandoned. Consider, for example, the following experiment. A photon is prepared in the state $\left(\begin{smallmatrix} 1/\sqrt{2} \\ 1/\sqrt{2} \end{smallmatrix}\right)$, that is, with its polarization 45° from the horizontal. It now encounters a polarizing filter whose preferred axis (that is, the axis of polarization that is transmitted) is vertical. If the photon gets through this filter, it encounters a second polarizing filter, which likewise favors vertical polarization. Let us try to predict the probability that the photon will pass through both filters.

First, the photon has a 50% chance of passing through the first filter, since $\sin^2(45°) = 1/2$. If the first filter does not affect the photon's polarization, then the same calculation applies to the second filter, so that the probability of passing both filters is $(1/2)(1/2) = 25\%$. When one actually does the experiment, though, one finds that *half* of the light gets through both filters. We explain this by saying that in the first measurement, in which the photon is forced to choose between outcomes corresponding to vertical and horizontal polarizations, if it chooses "vertical," then it *becomes* vertical. It does not remember that it was originally polarized at 45°. Having become vertically polarized, it now has a 100% chance of passing through the second filter. So the probability of passing through both filters is not 25% but 50%.

This behavior is quite typical of quantum measurements. Therefore standard quantum mechanics includes another rule about measurements: When a quantum particle is measured and gives the outcome associated with $|m^{(i)}\rangle$, its state *becomes* $|m^{(i)}\rangle$, regardless of what it was before. Note that this effect gives us a way of *preparing* a quantum state.

For example, to prepare a beam of photons having vertical polarization, we can send an unpolarized beam of light through a vertically polarizing filter; the photons that make it through the filter are vertically
polarized.

Example 2.1.2. Consider a sequence of three polarizing filters, oriented
at angles $0°$, $45°$, and $90°$ from the horizontal. If a photon passes through
the first filter, with what probability will it pass through both of the other
filters? *Answer:* The probability of passing through the second filter is
$1/2$, and if the photon does pass through that filter, it becomes polarized
at $45°$. It then has probability $1/2$ of passing through the final filter. So
the probability of passing through both is $(1/2)(1/2) = 1/4$. (Notice that
if the middle filter had not been there, the photon would certainly have
been absorbed by the final filter. This example thus nicely illustrates the
fact that a quantum measurement can make a difference.)

We have just seen that a photon's polarization state can change upon
measurement. It can also change in situations not involving measurement.
For example, if a photon with linear polarization passes through a solution
of ordinary table sugar, the polarization will rotate counterclockwise (as
viewed from directly behind the photon) by an angle proportional to both
the concentration of sugar and the distance the photon travels through
the solution. So it is possible to rotate polarizations. In fact, one finds after
much experimentation that the only physically possible transformations
that are reversible (unlike measurements) and that take linear polarizations into linear polarizations are (i) rotations and (ii) reflections around
an axis. (One device that effects a reflection is called a half-wave plate.)
There is no device, for example, that effects the following transformation
for all angles θ:

$$\begin{pmatrix} \cos\theta \\ \sin\theta \end{pmatrix} \longrightarrow \frac{1}{\sqrt{(2\cos\theta)^2 + (\sin\theta)^2}} \begin{pmatrix} 2\cos\theta \\ \sin\theta \end{pmatrix}.$$

Such a transformation, which stretches the polarization vector in the
horizontal direction and then shrinks it back to unit length, would always produce an allowed *state*, but the *transformation* itself is not allowed by the laws of physics. The allowed transformations – rotations and

reflections – can be represented by matrices. If $|s\rangle$ is the initial polarization state and $|s'\rangle$ is the final state, we can write

$$|s'\rangle = R|s\rangle, \tag{2.1}$$

where R is a 2×2 real matrix satisfying $R^T R = I$. Here T denotes the transpose and I is the 2×2 identity matrix. Any real matrix satisfying this condition is called an *orthogonal* matrix, and one can show that every orthogonal matrix represents a rotation or a reflection.

At this point we should confess that there do exist other measurements and transformations that one can perform on a photon's polarization, even if one restricts one's attention to linear polarization. For example, there are "generalized measurements" of polarization that can have more than two possible outcomes (though for such measurements it will *not* be the case that each outcome has a corresponding state that will produce that outcome with certainty). And there are nonreversible transformations that are not measurements. However, these alternative operations can always be constructed from measurements and transformations of the types we have introduced above, in combination with familiar operations such as "throwing information away." So we restrict our attention to these basic types, which we will distinguish by the terms "standard measurement" and "reversible transformation."

Let us summarize, then, the quantum mechanics of linear polarization.

1. A state is represented by a normalized vector in two real dimensions, and the negative of a vector represents the same state as the vector itself.

2. A standard measurement is represented by an orthonormal basis $(|m^{(1)}\rangle, |m^{(2)}\rangle)$ for the two-dimensional vector space, and the probability of the outcome $|m^{(i)}\rangle$ when the initial state is $|s\rangle$ is $|\langle s|m^{(i)}\rangle|^2$. After the measurement, the photon's state is the chosen outcome vector $|m^{(i)}\rangle$.

3. The allowed reversible physical transformations are represented by orthogonal matrices acting on the two-dimensional vector space, and every such matrix represents an allowed transformation.

Before we end this section, it is worth saying a few more words about the concept of a quantum state. In this informal introduction we have been speaking as if the polarization state of a photon resides in the photon itself, that is, as if it were a literal description of the photon. This is surely the easiest way to think of a quantum state, but it is problematic, as we will see later when we discuss composite systems. Some physicists argue that it is best to think of a quantum state as a *state of knowledge*, not a literal property of the object itself. Probably the safest approach is to regard the quantum state as characterizing the *preparation* of the object in question. Thus, the change in state when an object is measured can be taken as indicating that the measuring device has effected a new preparation of the object.

You might also be bothered by our focus on *measurements*. One would normally think that the aim of physics is simply to describe how the world works, not how *we* interact with the world or how *we* find things out about the world. So why not just state the rules governing the workings of the world, and leave us and our measurements out of the picture? If you are bothered about this, you are not alone. Many physicists and philosophers have addressed this issue, and there are various strategies for expressing the content of quantum mechanics without invoking the concept of a measurement. But these alternative strategies likewise challenge one's ordinary views about physics and are no easier to swallow on a first encounter. (We did mention at the beginning of this chapter that quantum mechanics was revolutionary!) We have chosen the language of measurements partly because it is the most commonly used formulation but also because it is the one that is most useful for describing quantum cryptography and quantum computation.

There remain many interesting questions about the interpretation of quantum mechanics. Fortunately, the observable predictions of the theory are not in dispute, and these are all that we need for our purposes.

EXERCISES

Problem 1. Consider the following state vector $|s\rangle$ and measurement vectors $|m_1\rangle$ and $|m_2\rangle$ for photon polarization:

$$|s\rangle = \begin{pmatrix} 4/5 \\ 3/5 \end{pmatrix}$$

$$M = (|m_1\rangle, |m_2\rangle) = \left(\begin{pmatrix} 3/5 \\ 4/5 \end{pmatrix}, \begin{pmatrix} -4/5 \\ 3/5 \end{pmatrix} \right)$$

(a) Show that $|s\rangle$ is indeed a legitimate state vector and that M is indeed a legitimate pair of measurement vectors.

(b) When the measurement M is performed on a photon in the state $|s\rangle$, what are the probabilities of the two outcomes?

Problem 2. Consider the matrix $R = \left(\begin{smallmatrix} \cos\phi & -\sin\phi \\ \sin\phi & \cos\phi \end{smallmatrix}\right)$. (a) Show that R is an orthogonal matrix. (b) Apply R to the linear polarization state $|s\rangle = \left(\begin{smallmatrix} \cos\theta \\ \sin\theta \end{smallmatrix}\right)$. Describe in everyday language the effect of this transformation on a state of linear polarization.

Problem 3. We have asserted that orthogonal matrices represent allowed *reversible* transformations. If we had simply said that they represent allowed transformations, how would you know that the transformations they represent are indeed reversible?

Problem 4. Let $R = \left(\begin{smallmatrix} \cos(\pi/(2n)) & -\sin(\pi/(2n)) \\ \sin(\pi/(2n)) & \cos(\pi/(2n)) \end{smallmatrix}\right)$.

(a) Compute R^n. (That is, compute the product of n factors of R, where the multiplication is matrix multiplication. You may find the following trigonometric identities helpful: $\cos\alpha\cos\beta - \sin\alpha\sin\beta = \cos(\alpha+\beta)$; $\cos\alpha\sin\beta + \sin\alpha\cos\beta = \sin(\alpha+\beta)$.)

(b) A horizontally polarized photon passes successively through n small containers of sugar water, each of which effects the transformation R. The photon then encounters a polarizing filter whose preferred axis is horizontal. What is the probability of the photon passing the filter?

(c) Another horizontally polarized photon passes through the same n containers of sugar water. But now, just after each container there is a polarizing filter whose preferred axis is horizontal. What is the probability that the photon will pass through all n filters?

(d) Find the limit of your answer to part (c) as n approaches infinity.

Problem 5. A half-wave plate is a transparent sheet of material that has the effect of reflecting any linear polarization around a certain axis. Suppose that this special axis makes an angle ϕ with the horizontal axis (measured counterclockwise from the horizontal axis). (a) Write down a 2×2 orthogonal matrix that represents the effect of the half-wave plate. (b) Is the answer to part (a) unique? If not, find *all* orthogonal matrices that could be used to express this effect.

2.1.2 Review of complex numbers

In the preceding subsection, all our vectors and matrices had only real-valued components. But when we extend the discussion to more general quantum states, the components of our vectors and matrices will be *complex* numbers. We now review the basic definitions pertaining to complex numbers and highlight the properties that will be most useful for our purpose.

Definition. The *field of complex numbers* $\mathbb{C}$, consists of all numbers of the form $a + ib$, where a and b are real numbers and i is the imaginary unit defined by $i^2 = -1$. Addition and multiplication are defined as follows:

$$(a + ib) + (c + id) = (a + c) + i(b + d)$$
$$(a + ib)(c + id) = (ac - bd) + i(ad + bc)$$

One can show that both addition and multiplication are commutative and associative, and that together they have the distributive property. Moreover, both operations have inverses. For example, the reciprocal of $a + ib$ can be written as

$$\frac{1}{a + ib} = \frac{1}{a + ib} \cdot \frac{a - ib}{a - ib} = \frac{a - ib}{a^2 + b^2} = \frac{a}{a^2 + b^2} + i\left(\frac{-b}{a^2 + b^2}\right), \quad (2.2)$$

which exists as long as $a + ib \neq 0$ (that is, as long as a and b are not both zero). Thus the complex numbers indeed constitute a *field*. The complex numbers are usually visualized as points in a Cartesian plane, with a being the horizontal coordinate and b the vertical coordinate. The horizontal axis is usually called the *real axis*, the vertical axis is the *imaginary axis*, and the plane itself is called the *complex plane*. Note that the addition of complex numbers can be visualized as ordinary vector addition in this plane. It is also possible to visualize multiplication, but this will be easier after we have developed a few more conceptual tools.

Definition. The *complex conjugate* (sometimes called simply the conjugate) of the complex number $z = a + ib$ is the complex number $a - ib$ and is denoted $\bar{z}$.

In the complex plane, one obtains the complex conjugate of a number z by reflecting z around the real axis.

Definition. Let $z = a + ib$ be a complex number. The *real part* of z is the real number a and is denoted Re z. The *imaginary part* of z is the real number b and is denoted Im z. A complex number is called *imaginary* if its real part is zero and its imaginary part is nonzero.

Sometimes it is useful to compute the real and imaginary parts as follows:

$$\frac{z + \bar{z}}{2} = \frac{(a + ib) + (a - ib)}{2} = a = \text{Re } z.$$

$$\frac{z - \bar{z}}{2i} = \frac{(a + ib) - (a - ib)}{2i} = b = \text{Im } z.$$

Definition. The *magnitude* of the complex number $z = a + ib$ (also called the modulus, norm, or absolute value) is denoted $|a|$ and is equal to the nonnegative real number $\sqrt{a^2 + b^2}$.

In the complex plane, the magnitude of z is the distance between the origin and the point representing z. Sometimes it is convenient to compute the magnitude of z via the complex conjugate:

$$\sqrt{z\bar{z}} = \sqrt{(a + ib)(a - ib)} = \sqrt{a^2 + b^2} = |z|.$$

We now introduce a notion that will be extremely useful, namely, the concept of an imaginary exponent. Recall that the exponential function e^x, for real x, can be expressed as an infinite Taylor series:

$$e^x = 1 + x + \frac{x^2}{2!} + \frac{x^3}{3!} + \cdots. \tag{2.3}$$

We now formally replace x everywhere in this expression by $i\theta$, where θ is real. This gives us

$$e^{i\theta} = 1 + i\theta + \frac{(i\theta)^2}{2!} + \frac{(i\theta)^3}{3!} + \cdots = 1 + i\theta - \frac{\theta^2}{2!} - i\frac{\theta^3}{3!} + \cdots. \tag{2.4}$$

Rearranging so as to separate the real terms from the imaginary terms, we get

$$e^{i\theta} = \left(1 - \frac{\theta^2}{2!} + \frac{\theta^4}{4!} - \cdots\right) + i\left(\theta - \frac{\theta^3}{3!} + \frac{\theta^5}{5!} - \cdots\right), \tag{2.5}$$

which we can resum to arrive at

$$e^{i\theta} = \cos\theta + i\sin\theta. \tag{2.6}$$

These formal manipulations lead us to the following definition.

Definition. Let θ be a real number. We define $e^{i\theta}$ to be the complex number $\cos\theta + i\sin\theta$.

In fact the above manipulations are more than formal. One can rigorously define convergence of a complex infinite series and show that the series expressed in Eq. (2.4) converges to $\cos\theta + i\sin\theta$ for all θ. Indeed the definition can be extended to make sense of e^z for all complex numbers z (not just purely imaginary numbers), but we will not need this more general concept.

The ordinary exponential function e^x has the property that $e^x e^y = e^{x+y}$. Let us check that our newly defined function $e^{i\theta}$ has this property also. We have

$$\begin{aligned}
e^{i\theta}e^{i\phi} &= (\cos\theta + i\sin\theta)(\cos\phi + i\sin\phi) \\
&= (\cos\theta\,\cos\phi - \sin\theta\sin\phi) + i(\cos\theta\sin\phi + \sin\theta\cos\phi) \\
&= \cos(\theta + \phi) + i\sin(\theta + \phi) = e^{i(\theta+\phi)}.
\end{aligned}$$

In fact this property actually follows from the Taylor expansion (2.3), so it is not surprising that it holds for $e^{i\theta}$.

The relation $e^{i\theta} = \cos\theta + i\sin\theta$ gives us another way of writing complex numbers. Consider an arbitrary nonzero complex number $z = a + ib$, and write both a and b in terms of polar coordinates: $a = r\cos\theta$ and $b = r\sin\theta$, where r is a nonnegative real number. These relations define r uniquely – r is the magnitude $|z|$ – and they define θ (in radians) uniquely up to the addition of a multiple of 2π. One possible value of θ is the smallest angle by which the positive real axis has to be rotated *counterclockwise* in order to reach z. The angle θ is usually called the *phase* of the complex number z. In terms of r and θ, we can write z as

$$z = a + ib = r\cos\theta + ir\sin\theta = r(\cos\theta + i\sin\theta) = re^{i\theta}. \tag{2.7}$$

The expression $re^{i\theta}$, illustrated in Fig. 2.3, is usually called the *polar form* of z. This alternative way of writing complex numbers is often much more convenient than the Cartesian form $z = a + ib$. Consider, for example, the

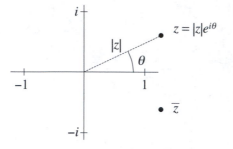

Figure 2.3: The polar representation of a complex number. The figure also indicates the location of the complex conjugate $\bar{z}$.

multiplication of two complex numbers z_1 and z_2. If we write them both in polar form, we have

$$z_1 z_2 = \left(r_1 e^{i\theta_1}\right)\left(r_2 e^{i\theta_2}\right) = r_1 r_2 e^{i(\theta_1 + \theta_2)}.$$

Thus when we multiply two complex numbers, the magnitudes multiply as real numbers, and the angles, as measured counterclockwise from the positive real axis, simply add.

EXERCISES

Problem 1. Let z_1 and z_2 be complex numbers.
    (a) Show that the complex conjugate of $z_1 z_2$ is $\bar{z}_1 \bar{z}_2$.
    (b) Show that if $z_2 \neq 0$, the complex conjugate of z_1/z_2 is $\bar{z}_1/\bar{z}_2$.
    (c) Show that $|z_1 z_2| = |z_1||z_2|$.
    (d) Show that if $z_2 \neq 0$, $|z_1/z_2| = |z_1|/|z_2|$.

Problem 2. Starting with $e^{3i\theta} = \left(e^{i\theta}\right)^3$, derive a formula for $\cos(3\theta)$ in terms of $\cos\theta$ and $\sin\theta$.

Problem 3. Evaluate each of the following quantities.
    (a) $e^{i\pi}$
    (b) $|1 + i|$
    (c) $\frac{2+3i}{3+2i}$
    (d) $(1 + i)^{16}$. (Hint: There is more than one way to approach this problem.)

2.1.3 Circular and elliptical polarization

It is easy to do an experiment showing that linear polarization is not the last word on the polarization of photons. One can, for example, reversibly convert a linearly polarized photon into a new polarization state with the following property: it has a 50% chance of passing through any linearly polarizing filter, *regardless* of the orientation of that filter. In other words, the photon's new polarization has no preferred axis. Its polarization state is called "circular." (We will discuss this experiment further in Examples 2.1.6 and 2.1.7.) As we have said in the preceding section, in order to express this polarization and other polarizations mathematically, we need to generalize our earlier formalism. Specifically, we need to let our state vectors have complex components. In this section we develop the mathematical rules for expressing these new states, and we explore some of the physical consequences of these rules. Of course the rules themselves were formulated only after much experimentation. You can regard them as very succinct summaries of a lot of data.

As we will see, the laws of quantum mechanics with complex numbers are very similar to the ones we have used to describe linear polarization. But there are some subtleties in the generalization; in particular, we need to define the inner product carefully.

Definition. Let $|s\rangle = \left(\begin{smallmatrix} s_1 \\ s_2 \end{smallmatrix}\right)$ and $|m\rangle = \left(\begin{smallmatrix} m_1 \\ m_2 \end{smallmatrix}\right)$ be a pair of two-dimensional complex vectors. The *inner product* between $|s\rangle$ and $|m\rangle$ is denoted $\langle s|m\rangle$ and is defined to be the complex number $\bar{s}_1 m_1 + \bar{s}_2 m_2$, where the bar indicates complex conjugation.

This definition of the inner product also determines what we mean by "orthogonality" and "length" for complex vectors.

Definition. Let $|s\rangle$ and $|m\rangle$ be a pair of two-dimensional complex vectors. The two vectors are *orthogonal* if and only if $\langle s|m\rangle = 0$.

Definition. Let $|s\rangle$ be a two-dimensional complex vector. The *length* of $|s\rangle$ is $\langle s|s\rangle^{1/2}$, and a vector is said to be *normalized* if its length is 1. (Note that $\langle s|s\rangle$ is always real and nonnegative. The square root is understood to be the nonnegative square root.)

The presence of complex conjugation in the definition of the inner product makes sense. The magnitude of the inner product between two normalized vectors is supposed to indicate how similar the two quantum states are that are represented by those vectors. Orthogonal vectors are supposed to represent states that are as different from each other as possible. If we removed the bars in the above definition of inner product, so that $\langle s|m \rangle$ were simply $s_1 m_1 + s_2 m_2$, then a nonzero vector could be orthogonal to itself, and this would violate the intended interpretation of orthogonality.

The notation $\langle s|m \rangle$ for the inner product can be understood in the following way. We will consistently regard state vectors written with a rightward pointing bracket, such as $|m \rangle$, as column vectors. A symbol with a leftward pointing bracket, such as $\langle s|$, can be understood on its own as a row vector, so that the $\langle s||m \rangle$, regarded as a product of two matrices, automatically comes out to be a single number. We abbreviate the notation $\langle s||m \rangle$ to $\langle s|m \rangle$ to express the inner product. But in order to understand the above definition of the inner product in this way, we cannot take $\langle s|$ to be the transpose of $|s \rangle$. Rather, it is the *complex conjugate* of the transpose. This notation will frequently prove useful in what follows.

Example 2.1.3. Consider the two vectors $|s \rangle = \left(\begin{smallmatrix} 1/\sqrt{2} \\ i/\sqrt{2} \end{smallmatrix} \right)$ and $|t \rangle = \left(\begin{smallmatrix} 1/\sqrt{2} \\ -i/\sqrt{2} \end{smallmatrix} \right)$. Find the length of each vector and the inner product $\langle s|t \rangle$.
Answers: The squared length of $|s \rangle$ is $\langle s|s \rangle = \left(1/\sqrt{2} \; -i/\sqrt{2} \right) \left(\begin{smallmatrix} 1/\sqrt{2} \\ i/\sqrt{2} \end{smallmatrix} \right) = 1/2 + 1/2 = 1$. So the length itself is also 1. (Here we have used the row-vector interpretation of $\langle s|$ and ordinary matrix multiplication to express the sum required in our definition of the inner product.) One finds similarly that the length of $|t \rangle$ is 1. The inner product $\langle s|t \rangle$ is $\left(1/\sqrt{2} \; -i/\sqrt{2} \right) \left(\begin{smallmatrix} 1/\sqrt{2} \\ -i/\sqrt{2} \end{smallmatrix} \right) = 1/2 - 1/2 = 0$. Thus these two vectors are orthogonal.

There is one more concept that has to be generalized, namely, the notion of an orthogonal matrix. Recall that any reversible transformation that takes linear polarizations to linear polarizations can be represented by an orthogonal matrix. In the world of complex numbers, the natural generalization is the notion of a *unitary* matrix, or unitary operator. It often aids one's intuition to think of a unitary operator as a rotation, albeit a more abstract sort of rotation. Though for the time being we need to define unitary transformations only on two-component vectors, we give the definition for the more general case of N-component vectors because we will need it later.

Definition. An *operator* (or linear operator) acting on N-component complex vectors is an $N \times N$ matrix, also having complex components.

Definition. Let M be an operator. The *adjoint* of M, denoted $M^\dagger$, is the complex conjugate of the transpose of M. (That is, one takes the complex conjugate of each component of the transpose.)

Definition. Let U be an operator. We say that U is *unitary* if and only if $U^\dagger U = I$, where I is the identity matrix.

Example 2.1.4. Any real orthogonal matrix is also unitary. For a real matrix R, $R^\dagger = R^T$; so the unitarity condition becomes $R^T R = I$, which is the defining property of an orthogonal matrix.

Example 2.1.5. Consider the matrix $V = (1/\sqrt{2})\left(\begin{smallmatrix} 1 & i \\ i & 1 \end{smallmatrix}\right)$. V is unitary, since $V^\dagger V = (1/2)\left(\begin{smallmatrix} 1 & -i \\ -i & 1 \end{smallmatrix}\right)\left(\begin{smallmatrix} 1 & i \\ i & 1 \end{smallmatrix}\right) = \left(\begin{smallmatrix} 1 & 0 \\ 0 & 1 \end{smallmatrix}\right)$.

We can now state the basic quantum mechanical rules for arbitrary polarizations of a photon.

1. A polarization state is represented by a normalized complex vector in two dimensions. Moreover, two vectors $|s\rangle$ and $|t\rangle$ represent the same polarization state if and only if they differ by no more than an overall factor, that is, if $|s\rangle = \gamma |t\rangle$ for some complex number γ. Since $|s\rangle$ and $|t\rangle$ are both normalized, γ must have unit magnitude; that is, $\gamma = e^{i\phi}$ for some real ϕ.
2. A standard polarization measurement is represented by an orthonormal basis $(|m^{(1)}\rangle, |m^{(2)}\rangle)$ for the two-dimensional complex vector space, and every such basis represents a possible measurement. The probability of the outcome $|m^{(i)}\rangle$ when the initial state is $|s\rangle$ is $|\langle s|m^{(i)}\rangle|^2$.
3. Every allowed reversible physical transformation on the polarization of a photon is represented by a 2×2 unitary matrix U, and every such U represents an allowed transformation.

Thus, in generalizing from linear polarizations to general polarizations, real vectors and matrices become complex vectors and matrices, and in inner products and the condition for reversible transformations, one of the factors has to be complex-conjugated.

We have not yet said what counts as elliptical polarization and what counts as circular polarization. It is easy enough to make this distinction mathematically: a vector $|s\rangle = \begin{pmatrix} s_1 \\ s_2 \end{pmatrix}$ represents "right-hand circular polarization" if and only if $s_2 = is_1$; it represents "left-hand circular polarization" if and only if $s_2 = -is_1$. If s_2/s_1 is any complex number other than i and $-i$, but still having a nonzero imaginary part, then $|s\rangle$ represents a state of elliptical polarization. If s_2/s_1 is real or if $s_1 = 0$, then the polarization is linear, because $|s\rangle$ is proportional to a real vector. Note that the expression "right-hand circular polarization" describes a single quantum state, as does "left-hand circular polarization" – all vectors satisfying $s_2 = is_1$, for example, are related to each other by an overall factor and therefore describe the same state – whereas "elliptical polarization" and "linear polarization" describe whole sets of quantum states, each containing an infinite number of elements.

To begin to give these distinctions physical meaning, in the following example we imagine performing a linear polarization measurement on a photon with circular polarization.

Example 2.1.6. We can represent a general linear polarization measurement as follows:

$$M_\theta = \left(|m_\theta^{(1)}\rangle, |m_\theta^{(2)}\rangle \right) = \left(\begin{pmatrix} \cos\theta \\ \sin\theta \end{pmatrix}, \begin{pmatrix} -\sin\theta \\ \cos\theta \end{pmatrix} \right). \tag{2.8}$$

The orthonormal basis M_θ is obtained from the horizontal–vertical basis by rotating it counterclockwise through an angle θ. Any such measurement could be implemented with a Wollaston prism suitably oriented. Now consider a photon in the state $|s\rangle = \begin{pmatrix} 1/\sqrt{2} \\ i/\sqrt{2} \end{pmatrix}$, which represents right-hand circular polarization. Let us calculate the probability that this photon will give each of the two possible outcomes of the measurement M. The probability of the outcome $|m^{(1)}\rangle$ is

$$p_1 = |\langle s | m^{(1)} \rangle|^2 = \left| \frac{1}{\sqrt{2}} \cos\theta - \frac{i}{\sqrt{2}} \sin\theta \right|^2 = \frac{1}{2}. \tag{2.9}$$

One finds similarly that the probability p_2 of the outcome $|m^{(2)}\rangle$ is also equal to 1/2. (This is the example mentioned at the beginning of this section.)

What is notable about the result of Example 2.1.6 is that the probabilities do not depend on the angle θ. Regardless of the orientation of the Wollaston prism, the photon has an equal chance of taking either of the two allowed paths. This behavior is one of the reasons why the photon's state is called "circular polarization": the polarization does not favor any particular axis. Another reason is that in the corresponding state of a classical light wave, the electric field vector at a given point in space rotates in a circular motion as the wave passes through that point. (A state of elliptical polarization does favor one axis over all the others, but not as strongly as linear polarization does. You can see an example of this in Problem 4 of the exercises at the end of this section.)

You might wonder how one creates a photon in a state of circular polarization. We have seen how a Wollaston prism or a polarizing filter can be used to generate linearly polarized photons. (Indeed there are other ways to create such photons. Reflecting a light beam off a window pane or a puddle of water at the proper angle can also create linearly polarized photons.) One way to generate circularly polarized photons is to start with a linearly polarized beam and to let the light pass through a device known as a *quarter-wave plate*, as we discuss in the following example.

Example 2.1.7. A quarter-wave plate executes a reversible transformation and can therefore be represented by a unitary transformation. In fact the following simple unitary transformation represents such a device:

$$U = \begin{pmatrix} 1 & 0 \\ 0 & i \end{pmatrix}. \tag{2.10}$$

This transformation leaves horizontal polarization horizontal and leaves vertical polarization vertical, but it significantly changes the 45°-polarized state $|s\rangle = \binom{1/\sqrt{2}}{1/\sqrt{2}}$:

$$|s'\rangle = U|s\rangle = \begin{pmatrix} 1 & 0 \\ 0 & i \end{pmatrix} \begin{pmatrix} 1/\sqrt{2} \\ 1/\sqrt{2} \end{pmatrix} = \begin{pmatrix} 1/\sqrt{2} \\ i/\sqrt{2} \end{pmatrix}, \tag{2.11}$$

which we identified earlier as right-hand circular polarization. It is interesting to note, by the way, that if we allow a photon generated in this way to pass through a second quarter-wave plate represented by the same transformation U, the circular polarization will return to linear polarization, but now flipped around the vertical axis. (The term "quarter-wave plate" is related to the fact that the two diagonal components of U are separated by a $90°$ rotation of the complex plane, that is, by one-quarter of a complete cycle.)

So far, the only polarization measurements we have considered explicitly are measurements that distinguish between two orthogonal *linear* polarizations. But according to our general rules many other measurements must be possible. Right- and left-hand circular polarizations, for example, are orthogonal to each other; so it should be possible to perform a measurement that distinguishes between these two states. In fact one can do this quite simply, by allowing the photon to pass through a quarter-wave plate before it hits a Wollaston prism.

EXERCISES

Problem 1. For each of the following state vectors, find a normalized vector that is orthogonal to the given vector.

$$\begin{pmatrix} \frac{\sqrt{3}}{2} \\ \frac{1}{2} \end{pmatrix} \qquad \begin{pmatrix} \frac{1}{\sqrt{2}} \\ \frac{i}{\sqrt{2}} \end{pmatrix} \qquad \begin{pmatrix} \frac{1-i}{2} \\ \frac{1+i}{2} \end{pmatrix}$$

Problem 2. Prove the assertion made in the last paragraph of this section, that a combination of a quarter-wave plate (see Example 2.1.7) and a Wollaston prism can be used to distinguish between the two circularly polarized states $\begin{pmatrix} 1/\sqrt{2} \\ i/\sqrt{2} \end{pmatrix}$ and $\begin{pmatrix} 1/\sqrt{2} \\ -i/\sqrt{2} \end{pmatrix}$.

Problem 3. The rotation operation R_ϕ, defined by

$$R_\phi = \begin{pmatrix} \cos\phi & -\sin\phi \\ \sin\phi & \cos\phi, \end{pmatrix}$$

rotates any linear polarization state by an angle ϕ. What does this transformation do to the right-hand circular polarization state? Is the resulting state a state of linear polarization, circular polarization, or elliptical polarization? Does the answer to this question depend on the value of ϕ?

Problem 4. Consider the elliptical polarization represented by $|s\rangle = \left(\begin{smallmatrix} 1/\sqrt{2} \\ (1+i)/2 \end{smallmatrix}\right)$. Suppose the measurement M_θ of Example 2.1.6 is applied to a photon in the state $|s\rangle$. (a) Find the probabilities of the two outcomes as functions of θ. (b) For what value of θ do the two probabilities differ the most from each other? The basis defined by M_θ for this value of θ can be thought of as giving the "principal axes" of the elliptical polarization.

Problem 5. Consider the polarization state $|s\rangle = \left(\begin{smallmatrix} 1/2 \\ i\sqrt{3}/2 \end{smallmatrix}\right)$. (a) Is $|s\rangle$ a state of linear, circular, or elliptical polarization? (b) Find a unitary transformation U that turns $|s\rangle$ into the (linear) vertically polarized state. (c) Let U_0 be a particular answer to part (b). Is *every* possible answer to part (b) of the form $e^{i\phi}U_0$ for some real number ϕ?

Problem 6. In this problem we are looking for three photon-polarization measurements that are related to each other in a special way. Call the measurements $A = (|a_1\rangle, |a_2\rangle)$, $B = (|b_1\rangle, |b_2\rangle)$, and $C = (|c_1\rangle, |c_2\rangle)$. The special relationship is this: If a photon has just been subjected to one of the measurements (and has survived intact) and is about to be subjected to a different one, then the two outcomes of the second measurement are always equally likely. (Assume, as we have been doing so far, that if the first measurement was, say, B, the photon will emerge from that measurement either in the state $|b_1\rangle$ or in the state $|b_2\rangle$.) Does such a set of measurements exist? If so, find one, writing down explicitly the components of all six measurement vectors.

2.2 General Quantum Variables

Suppose someone "hands" you a photon and tells you that it is either in the state $|s\rangle$ or in the state $|t\rangle$. Your mission is to determine which of these two states is actually the case. You are guaranteed to be able to accomplish this task only if $|s\rangle$ and $|t\rangle$ are *orthogonal*, because only then does there exist a measurement whose outcomes correspond to the two given states. In any other case, there exists no measurement that will always tell you unambiguously which of the two states you actually hold. Moreover, if someone hands you a photon and tells you that its polarization is in one of the three states $|s\rangle$, $|t\rangle$, and $|u\rangle$, then regardless of the relationship among the three states, there does not exist a measurement that can reliably distinguish the three states from each other. Thus, for photon polarizations, the maximum number of perfectly distinguishable states is two. As we think about generalizing the rules of quantum mechanics from photon polarization to arbitrary quantum variables, this quantity – the maximum number of perfectly distinguishable states – is crucially important. We will usually call this number N, and for reasons that will become clear, we will refer to it as the *dimension* of the quantum variable. The dimension can be either a positive integer or infinity. Now, it is a remarkable physical fact that once the value of the dimension is specified for a quantum variable, the mathematical description of that variable – how one expresses its states, measurements, and transformations – is completely determined. In other words, if two quantum variables have the same maximum number of perfectly distinguishable states, then their quantum descriptions are essentially the same.

Examples of quantum variables are the following: for photons – polarization and momentum; for electrons – spin and momentum; for quarks – spin, color, and momentum. The following table gives the value of the dimension N for each of these variables.

Variable	N
Photon polarization	2
Photon momentum	∞
Electron spin	2
Electron momentum	∞
Quark spin	2
Quark color	3
Quark momentum	∞

Note that the value of N for electron or quark spin is the same as for photon polarization. This is a very helpful fact, because it means that if you understand the quantum mechanics of a photon's polarization, you also understand the quantum mechanics of an electron's or quark's spin. This equivalence, and the special importance of quantum variables with $N = 2$, has led researchers in quantum cryptography and quantum computation to adopt the generic word "qubit" to refer to any such variable. Thus electron spin and photon polarization are two examples of qubits. In Chapter 3, on quantum cryptography, we will mostly be concerned with qubits. In Chapter 7, on quantum computation, we will need to consider systems with much larger dimension, namely, quantum computers consisting of many qubits. However, in this book we will never need to consider the value $N = \infty$. So we restrict our attention to finite values of N. In this section we present the basic quantum rules pertaining to any quantum variable with finite dimension. After our study of photon polarization, the rules will probably not be surprising. We begin with some definitions, which will also not be surprising.

Definition. Let $|s\rangle = \begin{pmatrix} s_1 \\ \vdots \\ s_N \end{pmatrix}$ and $|m\rangle = \begin{pmatrix} m_1 \\ \vdots \\ m_N \end{pmatrix}$ be a pair of complex N-dimensional vectors. The *inner product* $\langle s|m\rangle$ between $|s\rangle$ and $|m\rangle$ is the complex number $\bar{s}_1 m_1 + \cdots + \bar{s}_N m_N$. The vectors $|s\rangle$ and $|m\rangle$ are *orthogonal* if and only if $\langle s|m\rangle = 0$. An N-dimensional space of complex vectors, with the inner product defined above, is called a *state space*.

Definition. The *length* of a complex vector $|s\rangle$ is $\langle s|s\rangle^{1/2}$, and $|s\rangle$ is said to be *normalized* if its length is 1. A normalized complex vector is called a *state vector*.

With these definitions in hand, we can now state the rules of quantum mechanics for a variable with N perfectly distinguishable states.

1. A state is represented by an N-dimensional state vector, and two vectors $|s\rangle$ and $|t\rangle$ represent that same state if and only if they are complex scalar multiples of each other. Note that, because $|s\rangle$ and $|t\rangle$ are both normalized, a complex scalar factor relating them must be of unit magnitude; that is, it must be of the form $e^{i\phi}$ for some real ϕ.

2. A standard measurement is represented by an orthonormal basis $(|m^{(1)}\rangle, \ldots, |m^{(N)}\rangle)$ for the state space, and every such basis in principle represents a possible measurement. Each possible outcome of the

measurement is associated with one of the vectors $|m^{(i)}\rangle$, and the probability of the outcome $|m^{(i)}\rangle$ when the initial state is $|s\rangle$ is $|\langle s|m^{(i)}\rangle|^2$.

3. Every allowed reversible physical transformation on the state is represented by an $N \times N$ unitary matrix U, and every such U represents an allowed transformation.

Two aspects of rule 2 need further comment. First, note that the N possible outcomes of a standard measurement are exhaustive and mutually exclusive events – in any given trial, one and only one of the outcomes will actually happen. Therefore, the probabilities should add up to 1. Is the mathematics of rule 2 consistent with this requirement? The following theorem, whose proof can be found in linear algebra texts, guarantees that it is.

Theorem 2.2.1. Let $|s\rangle$ be an N-dimensional, normalized complex vector, and let $M = \{|m^{(1)}\rangle, \ldots, |m^{(N)}\rangle\}$ be an orthonormal basis for the space. Let $p_i = |\langle s|m^{(i)}\rangle|^2$, $i = 1, \ldots, N$. Then $p_1 + \cdots + p_N = 1$.

Second, though we will typically not need to worry about generalizations of our notion of a "standard" measurement, there is one generalization that we will need, and it applies only to cases where the dimension N is greater than 2. This is the notion of an *incomplete* measurement. Sometimes we do not want our measurement to distinguish all N of the elements of an orthogonal basis. For example, if the variable in question has dimension 4, we may want only to distinguish dimensions 1 and 2 from dimensions 3 and 4. In other words, we might be trying to distinguish one subspace from another, without separating vectors that lie in the same subspace. Such measurements are possible, and they can be less disruptive than our standard measurements, which are called *complete*. We will treat incomplete measurements in Sections 2.4 and 2.5. For now, we just wanted to point out that such measurements are allowed.

To make our three rules of quantum mechanics somewhat more concrete, it is helpful to consider a few examples.

Example 2.2.1. As we have said, the spin of an electron is characterized by the value $N = 2$; so it is possible to find two spin states of an electron that are perfectly distinguishable from each other by measurement. One such set of states is usually labeled $|\uparrow\rangle$ and $|\downarrow\rangle$; we will represent these states as

$$|\uparrow\rangle = \begin{pmatrix} 1 \\ 0 \end{pmatrix} \quad \text{and} \quad |\downarrow\rangle = \begin{pmatrix} 0 \\ 1 \end{pmatrix}. \tag{2.12}$$

These vectors are orthogonal and constitute a basis for the state space. The two states can be distinguished by sending the electron (not by itself but as part of a neutral atom) through a suitably designed magnetic field. One can arrange that an electron in the state $|\uparrow\rangle$ is pushed upward by the field, while an electron in the state $|\downarrow\rangle$ is pushed downward. Because $|\uparrow\rangle$ and $|\downarrow\rangle$ constitute a basis, any spin state can be represented as $|s\rangle = s_1 |\uparrow\rangle + s_2 |\downarrow\rangle = \begin{pmatrix} s_1 \\ s_2 \end{pmatrix}$. If we perform the up-vs-down measurement on this state, the probability of the outcome $|\uparrow\rangle$ is $p_\uparrow = |\langle s |\uparrow\rangle|^2 = |(\bar{s}_1)(1) + (\bar{s}_2)(0)|^2 = |s_1|^2$, and the probability of the outcome $|\downarrow\rangle$ is $p_\downarrow = |\langle s |\downarrow\rangle|^2 = |(\bar{s}_1)(0) + (\bar{s}_2)(1)|^2 = |s_2|^2$.

In the above example we have labeled the two basis states of the electron's spin as $|\uparrow\rangle$ and $|\downarrow\rangle$, because the states $|\uparrow\rangle$ and $|\downarrow\rangle$ are associated with two diametrically opposite directions in space as we have said. This contrasts with the photon polarization states $|\leftrightarrow\rangle$ and $|\updownarrow\rangle$, which are associated with perpendicular directions in space. Thus even though the mathematics of electron spin is essentially the same as the mathematics of photon polarization, the *physical interpretations* of the two cases are quite different. This difference, though utterly crucial for researchers studying possible implementations of, say, quantum computation, does not affect the more formal considerations that we focus on in this book. Later in the book, when we want to consider a general *qubit*, which might be realized physically as a photon's polarization or an electron's spin or in some other way, we will represent the basis vectors not as $\{|\leftrightarrow\rangle, |\updownarrow\rangle\}$ or as $\{|\uparrow\rangle, |\downarrow\rangle\}$ but with the more generic notation $\{|0\rangle, |1\rangle\}$.

Example 2.2.2. The matrix $U = \frac{1}{\sqrt{2}}\begin{pmatrix} 1 & 1 \\ 1 & -1 \end{pmatrix}$ is unitary and therefore represents an allowed transformation of the spin state of an electron. (It can be realized by placing the electron in a magnetic field for a short time.) (i) If this transformation is applied to an electron in the "up" state, what is the spin state after the transformation? (ii) If we then perform the up-vs-down measurement on the electron, what is the probability of the outcome "up"?

Answers: (i) The state after the transformation is $|s'\rangle = U|s\rangle = \frac{1}{\sqrt{2}}\begin{pmatrix} 1 & 1 \\ 1 & -1 \end{pmatrix}\begin{pmatrix} 1 \\ 0 \end{pmatrix} = \begin{pmatrix} 1/\sqrt{2} \\ 1/\sqrt{2} \end{pmatrix}$. (ii) The probability of "up" is $p_\uparrow = |\langle\uparrow|s'\rangle|^2 = 1/2$.

Example 2.2.3. A ρ meson is an unstable particle whose spin variable has three orthogonal states. If the state of a certain ρ meson is represented by the vector $|s\rangle = \begin{pmatrix} 1 \\ 0 \\ 0 \end{pmatrix}$, find a measurement M such that when it is performed on this particle, the three outcomes are all equally likely.

Answer: We need to find three orthonormal vectors $\{|m^{(1)}\rangle, |m^{(2)}\rangle, |m^{(3)}\rangle\}$, each of which has as its first component a complex number of magnitude $1/\sqrt{3}$. Here is one such set:

$$M = \left\{ \frac{1}{\sqrt{3}}\begin{pmatrix} 1 \\ 1 \\ 1 \end{pmatrix}, \frac{1}{\sqrt{3}}\begin{pmatrix} 1 \\ \omega \\ \bar{\omega} \end{pmatrix}, \frac{1}{\sqrt{3}}\begin{pmatrix} 1 \\ \bar{\omega} \\ \omega \end{pmatrix} \right\}, \tag{2.13}$$

where $\omega = e^{2\pi i/3}$.

We have now covered most of the essential structure of quantum mechanics, but the one remaining piece is crucially important. It is the description of composite systems, which is the subject of the following section.

EXERCISES

Problem 1 (a) Show that for any complex vectors $|s\rangle$ and $|t\rangle$ in the same vector space, $\langle t|s\rangle$ is the complex conjugate of $\langle s|t\rangle$. (b) Show that the inner product is linear in its second argument. That is, if $|c\rangle = x|a\rangle + y|b\rangle$, then $\langle s|c\rangle = x\langle s|a\rangle + y\langle s|b\rangle$. (c) Show that the inner product is *conjugate linear* (or antilinear) in its first argument. That is, if $|c\rangle = x|a\rangle + y|b\rangle$, then $\langle c|s\rangle = \bar{x}\langle a|s\rangle + \bar{y}\langle b|s\rangle$.

Problem 2. Consider the measurement M given in Example 2.2.3. (a) Show that the vectors in M are normalized and orthogonal, so that the ordered triple does indeed represent a standard measurement. (b) For each of the following state vectors $|a\rangle$, $|b\rangle$, and $|c\rangle$, find the probabilities of the three outcomes of the measurement M if the ρ meson is in the given state.

$$|a\rangle = \begin{pmatrix} 1 \\ 0 \\ 0 \end{pmatrix} \quad |b\rangle = \frac{1}{\sqrt{2}} \begin{pmatrix} 0 \\ 1 \\ 1 \end{pmatrix} \quad |c\rangle = \frac{1}{3\sqrt{2}} \begin{pmatrix} 4 \\ 1 \\ 1 \end{pmatrix}$$

(c) If we had a thousand ρ mesons all guaranteed to be in the same state, and if we knew that that state was either $|a\rangle$, $|b\rangle$, or $|c\rangle$, would we be able to tell which of these three states the particles were actually in by performing the measurement M on each of them? Explain.

Problem 3. We are given an electron in the state $|\uparrow\rangle$ and want to change its spin to the quantum state represented by $|\downarrow\rangle$ (or by any scalar multiple of $|\downarrow\rangle$). There are many unitary transformations that will effect this change. Find the *complete set* of such transformations, and prove that there are no others.

2.3 Composite Systems

We now know everything we need to know about the quantum mechanics of, say, a single qubit. But later we will want to think about a quantum computer, which might consist of thousands of qubits. We therefore need to know the quantum mechanics of composite systems. In classical physics, the transition from a single object to a system of many objects is entirely trivial. For example, in order to describe the state of nine planets at any given moment, it is sufficient to describe the state of each of the planets separately. The whole is the collection of the parts. But in quantum mechanics the situation is quite different. We can illustrate it by considering a pair of photons. These two photons could be close to each other or in different galaxies; the principle is the same in either case.

As we have seen, the most general polarization state of a single photon can be represented as $|s\rangle = s_1 |\leftrightarrow\rangle + s_2 |\updownarrow\rangle$. One might therefore think that the most general polarization state of a *pair* of photons should be represented by a pair of vectors, one for each photon:

$$|s\rangle = s_1 |\leftrightarrow\rangle + s_2 |\updownarrow\rangle; \quad |t\rangle = t_1 |\leftrightarrow\rangle + t_2 |\updownarrow\rangle. \tag{2.14}$$

Such a state is *possible*, but there are other states that cannot be expressed in this form. To write down the most general possible state, we first focus on the basis states. For a single photon, we have been using the basis states $|\leftrightarrow\rangle$ and $|\updownarrow\rangle$. For a pair of photons, we may regard the following as our basis states: $|\leftrightarrow\leftrightarrow\rangle$, $|\leftrightarrow\updownarrow\rangle$, $|\updownarrow\leftrightarrow\rangle$, $|\updownarrow\updownarrow\rangle$. Within each bracket, the first symbol refers to the first photon and the second to the second. (We assume that the physical situation gives us some way to distinguish the two photons; for example, they could be distinguished by their locations.) The most general polarization state of a pair of photons is a normalized linear combination of these four basis states, that is, a vector of the form

$$|s\rangle = s_1\,|\leftrightarrow\leftrightarrow\rangle + s_2\,|\leftrightarrow\updownarrow\rangle + s_3\,|\updownarrow\leftrightarrow\rangle + s_4\,|\updownarrow\updownarrow\rangle, \qquad (2.15)$$

where the complex numbers s_i satisfy $\sum_i |s_i|^2 = 1$.

We will have to do some thinking about the physical interpretation of this expression. For now we simply note that this prescription is quite different from that given in Eq. (2.14). For one thing, once we take into account the normalization of the vectors and the fact that states differing only by an overall factor are equivalent, we find that the total number of real parameters needed to specify the two states in Eq. (2.14) is *four* (that is, two parameters for each photon). But the number of real parameters needed to specify a state of the form given in Eq. (2.15) is *six*.[3] So it cannot be the case that every state of the latter form can be expressed as a pair of states as in Eq. (2.14).

The generalization of this idea to arbitrary combinations of quantum variables can be made via the notion of a *tensor product*, which we now define in enough generality to serve our needs for the rest of the book. The tensor product will also help us make the connection between the description in Eq. (2.14) – which again applies only in certain cases – and the more general description in Eq. (2.15).

---

[3] In Eq. (2.14), we can count parameters as follows. Frist, using our freedom to multiply $|s\rangle$ by an overall constant, we lose no generality by forcing s_1 to be real and nonnegative. Once s_1 is fixed, the magnitude of s_2 is determined by the fact that $|s\rangle$ is normalized, leaving only the phase of s_2 to be specified. Thus it requires two real parameters to specify $|s\rangle$, namely, the magnitude of s_1 and the phase of s_2. The same is true for $|t\rangle$; so Eq. (2.14) entails four real parameters. In Eq. (2.15), we can again take s_1 to be real and nonnegative. Then the parameters needed to specify the state are (i) the magnitude of s_1, (ii) the magnitudes and phases of s_2 and s_3, and (iii) the phase of s_4 (the magnitude of s_4 is fixed by normalization once the other magnitudes have been determined). This is a total of six real parameters.

Definition. *The tensor product of two vector spaces.*
Let $\{|b^{(1)}\rangle, \ldots, |b^{(N)}\rangle\}$ and $\{|c^{(1)}\rangle, \ldots, |c^{(M)}\rangle\}$ be orthonormal bases for two complex vector spaces $\mathcal{H}_N$ and $\mathcal{H}_M$, respectively. The *tensor product* of $\mathcal{H}_N$ with $\mathcal{H}_M$ is denoted $\mathcal{H}_N \otimes \mathcal{H}_M$ and is constructed as follows. First, we formally write down a new set of basis vectors $\{|b^{(i)}c^{(j)}\rangle\}$, $i = 1, \ldots, N$, $j = 1, \ldots, M$, which are *defined* to be orthonormal. The tensor product $\mathcal{H}_N \otimes \mathcal{H}_M$ is the vector space consisting of all complex linear combinations $\sum_{ij} s_{ij} |b^{(i)}c^{(j)}\rangle$, together with an inner product given by the following rule: if $|s\rangle = \sum_{ij} s_{ij} |b^{(i)}c^{(j)}\rangle$ and $|t\rangle = \sum_{ij} t_{ij} |b^{(i)}c^{(j)}\rangle$, then $\langle s|t\rangle = \sum_{ij} \bar{s}_{ij} t_{ij}$. (Note that because the space $\mathcal{H}_N \otimes \mathcal{H}_M$ is spanned by NM orthogonal vectors, its dimension is NM.)

Definition. *The tensor product of two vectors.*
Let $|v\rangle = \sum_i v_i |b^{(i)}\rangle$ be an element of $\mathcal{H}_N$ and let $|w\rangle = \sum_j w_j |c^{(j)}\rangle$ be an element of $\mathcal{H}_M$. The *tensor product* of $|v\rangle$ with $|w\rangle$ is denoted $|v\rangle \otimes |w\rangle$ (or sometimes simply $|vw\rangle$ for brevity) and is defined to be the vector $\sum_{ij} v_i w_j |b^{(i)}c^{(j)}\rangle$ in $\mathcal{H}_N \otimes \mathcal{H}_M$. What this says, in essence, is that the tensor product obeys the distributive rule.

Example 2.3.1. Let $|s\rangle = \binom{s_1}{s_2} = s_1 |\leftrightarrow\rangle + s_2 |\updownarrow\rangle$ be the state of polarization of photon a, and let $|t\rangle = \binom{t_1}{t_2} = t_1 |\leftrightarrow\rangle + t_2 |\updownarrow\rangle$ be the state of polarization of photon b. Then the polarization state of the pair ab is

$$|s\rangle \otimes |t\rangle = (s_1 |\leftrightarrow\rangle + s_2 |\updownarrow\rangle) \otimes (t_1 |\leftrightarrow\rangle + t_2 |\updownarrow\rangle)$$

$$= s_1 t_1 |\leftrightarrow\leftrightarrow\rangle + s_1 t_2 |\leftrightarrow\updownarrow\rangle + s_2 t_1 |\updownarrow\leftrightarrow\rangle + s_2 t_2 |\updownarrow\updownarrow\rangle = \begin{pmatrix} s_1 t_1 \\ s_1 t_2 \\ s_2 t_1 \\ s_2 t_2 \end{pmatrix}.$$

In writing the column vector in the last step, we have used the following convention (as we always will):

$$|\leftrightarrow\leftrightarrow\rangle = \begin{pmatrix} 1 \\ 0 \\ 0 \\ 0 \end{pmatrix} \quad |\leftrightarrow\updownarrow\rangle = \begin{pmatrix} 0 \\ 1 \\ 0 \\ 0 \end{pmatrix} \quad |\updownarrow\leftrightarrow\rangle = \begin{pmatrix} 0 \\ 0 \\ 1 \\ 0 \end{pmatrix} \quad |\updownarrow\updownarrow\rangle = \begin{pmatrix} 0 \\ 0 \\ 0 \\ 1 \end{pmatrix}.$$

We thus get the following rule, which is often the easiest way to get the tensor product in practice.

$$\begin{pmatrix} s_1 \\ s_2 \end{pmatrix} \otimes \begin{pmatrix} t_1 \\ t_2 \end{pmatrix} = \begin{pmatrix} s_1 t_1 \\ s_1 t_2 \\ s_2 t_1 \\ s_2 t_2 \end{pmatrix}.$$

Note that each element of the first vector multiplies the entire second vector.

In the following section we will also need the concept of the tensor product of two operators, which we present here.

Definition. *The tensor product of two operators.*
Let T be an operator on $\mathcal{H}_N$ and let V be an operator on $\mathcal{H}_M$. The *tensor product* $T \otimes V$ is an operator on $\mathcal{H}_N \otimes \mathcal{H}_M$. Its action on each basis vector $|b^{(i)}c^{(j)}\rangle$ is given by $(T \otimes V)|b^{(i)}c^{(j)}\rangle = (T|b^{(i)}\rangle) \otimes (V|c^{(j)}\rangle)$. Its action on all other vectors is determined by linearity; e.g., $(T \otimes V)(s_1|b^{(1)}c^{(1)}\rangle + s_2|b^{(2)}c^{(2)}\rangle)) = s_1(T \otimes V)|b^{(1)}c^{(1)}\rangle + s_2(T \otimes V)|b^{(2)}c^{(2)}\rangle$.

Example 2.3.2. It is actually quite easy to compute the tensor product, given the two matrices T and V. For example, let T and V be operators on a pair of two-dimensional vector spaces. Thus

$$T = \begin{pmatrix} a & b \\ c & d \end{pmatrix} \quad \text{and} \quad V = \begin{pmatrix} w & x \\ y & z \end{pmatrix}.$$

Then

$$T \otimes V = \begin{pmatrix} aw & ax & bw & bx \\ ay & az & by & bz \\ cw & cx & dw & dx \\ cy & cz & dy & dz \end{pmatrix}$$

That is, each element of the first matrix multiplies the entire second matrix in order to produce the tensor product.

In terms of the tensor product, we can now state the general rule by which quantum variables are combined into composite systems:

The composite system rule

Let $\mathcal{H}_N$ and $\mathcal{H}_M$, of dimensions N and M respectively, be the state spaces of two quantum variables A and B. (For example, A could be the polarization of one photon and B could be the polarization of another.) Then the allowed states of the combined system consisting of both A and B – let us call the combined system AB – are represented by the normalized vectors in $\mathcal{H}_N \otimes \mathcal{H}_M$. Moreover, the combined system AB follows all the rules of quantum mechanics, as given in the preceding section, for a variable with NM dimensions.

Note that if $|s\rangle$ is a state of the variable A and $|t\rangle$ is a state of the variable B, then $|s\rangle \otimes |t\rangle$, being a normalized vector in $\mathcal{H}_N \otimes \mathcal{H}_M$, is a possible state of AB. A state of this form is called a *product state* and is exactly the kind of state for which one can use a description such as that given in Eq. (2.14). That is, one can specify a product state by giving the two factors separately. As we have noted above, not all states of a two-part system are product states. If the state of a two-part system does not factor, then neither of the parts of the system has a state of its own. We will say more about such nonfactorable states shortly, but first let us look at some examples of states of composite systems.

Example 2.3.3. Consider again a system consisting of two photons. The first photon is polarized at an angle $\theta = 45°$, and the second is horizontally polarized. Let us write down the polarization state of the pair, as an element of the tensor product space. Each photon has a state of its own, so the joint state is a product state, namely,

$$|t\rangle = \left[\frac{1}{\sqrt{2}} (|\leftrightarrow\rangle + |\updownarrow\rangle) \right] \otimes |\leftrightarrow\rangle = \frac{1}{\sqrt{2}} (|\leftrightarrow\leftrightarrow\rangle + |\updownarrow\leftrightarrow\rangle). \tag{2.16}$$

We can also write the state as a column vector, in which the four components are the coefficients of the basis vectors $(|\leftrightarrow\leftrightarrow\rangle, |\leftrightarrow\updownarrow\rangle, |\updownarrow\leftrightarrow\rangle, |\updownarrow\updownarrow\rangle)$:

$$|t\rangle = \begin{pmatrix} 1/\sqrt{2} \\ 1/\sqrt{2} \end{pmatrix} \otimes \begin{pmatrix} 1 \\ 0 \end{pmatrix} = \begin{pmatrix} 1/\sqrt{2} \\ 0 \\ 1/\sqrt{2} \\ 0 \end{pmatrix}. \tag{2.17}$$

Example 2.3.4. Here is a possible polarization state of a pair of photons:

$$|s\rangle = \frac{1}{\sqrt{2}}(|\leftrightarrow\leftrightarrow\rangle + |\updownarrow\updownarrow\rangle). \tag{2.18}$$

Is this state a product state? We can see by the following argument that it is not. By definition, a product state is of the form

$$|t\rangle = (a\,|\leftrightarrow\rangle + b\,|\updownarrow\rangle) \otimes (c\,|\leftrightarrow\rangle + d\,|\updownarrow\rangle)$$
$$= ac\,|\leftrightarrow\leftrightarrow\rangle + ad\,|\leftrightarrow\updownarrow\rangle + bc\,|\updownarrow\leftrightarrow\rangle + bd\,|\updownarrow\updownarrow\rangle. \tag{2.19}$$

In the state $|s\rangle$, the coefficient of $|\leftrightarrow\updownarrow\rangle$ is zero; so if $|s\rangle$ is of the form given in Eq. (2.19), either a or d must be zero. But then either the coefficient of $|\leftrightarrow\leftrightarrow\rangle$ or the coefficient of $|\updownarrow\updownarrow\rangle$ would also have to be zero, which is not the case. So $|s\rangle$ is not a product state.

By an extension of the argument used in this example, one can show that a general polarization state of a pair of photons, $|s\rangle = s_1\,|\leftrightarrow\leftrightarrow\rangle + s_2|\leftrightarrow\updownarrow\rangle + s_3\,|\updownarrow\leftrightarrow\rangle + s_4\,|\updownarrow\updownarrow\rangle$, is a product state if and only if $s_1 s_4 = s_2 s_3$. (We leave the proof for the exercises.)

By applying the composite system rule repeatedly, we can construct the state space of a collection of any number of quantum variables. Thus, if a quantum computer consists of n qubits – recall that a qubit is any quantum variable with two orthogonal states – then the state space of the quantum computer has 2^n dimensions. A state $|s\rangle$ of *any* composite system, with any number n of components, is called a product state if it can be written as $|s\rangle = |s_1\rangle \otimes \cdots \otimes |s_n\rangle$. There is no need to use parentheses in the multiple tensor product, because the tensor product operation is associative. (See Problem 1.)

Any state of any composite system that is not a product state is called an *entangled* state. (So "entangled" means the same thing as "not completely factorable." For a two-part sytem, "entangled" and "nonfactorable" mean the same thing.) As we have said earlier for the case of a bipartite system, if a multicomponent system is in an entangled state, then some of its components do not have states of their own. In this sense the whole is literally more than the collection of the parts. Erwin Schrödinger, one of the pioneers of quantum mechanics, gave this meaning to the word "entangled" in 1935 and identified entanglement as *the* feature of quantum mechanics that forces its departure from the concepts of classical physics. Indeed there is nothing quite like entanglement in any area of classical physics. We will see later that entanglement plays an important role in quantum computation: every promising quantum algorithm involves operations capable of entangling the computer's qubits. Entanglement also enters into quantum cryptography: one strategy that an eavesdropper might use is to entangle each transmitted photon with a quantum variable controlled by the eavesdropper. The following example shows how this sort of entangling might be described mathematically.

Example 2.3.5. The polarization state of a pair of photons is represented by a vector in a four-dimensional complex space. Therefore the allowed reversible transformations on such a state are represented by 4×4 unitary matrices. Here is one such matrix[4]:

$$U = \begin{pmatrix} 1 & 0 & 0 & 0 \\ 0 & 1 & 0 & 0 \\ 0 & 0 & 0 & 1 \\ 0 & 0 & 1 & 0 \end{pmatrix}. \qquad (2.20)$$

This matrix acts on states in the form of four-dimensional column vectors such as the one shown in Example 2.3.3. By applying U to the four basis states, one finds that it has the following effect: if the first photon is in the state $|\leftrightarrow\rangle$, it leaves the whole state unchanged; if the first photon is in the state $|\updownarrow\rangle$, it interchanges the states $|\leftrightarrow\rangle$ and $|\updownarrow\rangle$ of the second photon. Let us apply U to the state $|t\rangle$ we considered in Example 2.3.3:

$$U|t\rangle = \begin{pmatrix} 1 & 0 & 0 & 0 \\ 0 & 1 & 0 & 0 \\ 0 & 0 & 0 & 1 \\ 0 & 0 & 1 & 0 \end{pmatrix} \begin{pmatrix} 1/\sqrt{2} \\ 0 \\ 1/\sqrt{2} \\ 0 \end{pmatrix} = \begin{pmatrix} 1/\sqrt{2} \\ 0 \\ 0 \\ 1/\sqrt{2} \end{pmatrix}. \qquad (2.21)$$

Note that the resulting state is precisely the state $|s\rangle$ of Example 2.3.4, which we have seen to be entangled. Thus, the operation U is capable of entangling a pair of photons.

In Problem 6 we describe a practical method of producing an entangled pair of photons. It is important to note that, though entanglement

---

[4] This is the controlled-not operation CNOT that we will frequently encounter in Chapter 7.

beween two particles is usually created when the particles are close together, the entanglement can persist even after the particles have become
widely separated.

Let us now consider what happens when one makes a *measurement*
on a composite system in an entangled state. For a pair of photons,
a standard polarization measurement is represented by an orthonor-
mal basis for the four-dimensional state space. So one possible
measurement is defined by our standard basis, $M = (|\leftrightarrow\leftrightarrow\rangle, |\leftrightarrow\updownarrow\rangle,$
$|\updownarrow\leftrightarrow\rangle, |\updownarrow\updownarrow\rangle)$. If we perform this measurement on the entangled state $|s\rangle$ of
Example 2.3.4 – recall that $|s\rangle = \frac{1}{\sqrt{2}}(|\leftrightarrow\leftrightarrow\rangle + |\updownarrow\updownarrow\rangle)$ – we get the following
probabilities of the outcomes: $p_1 = 1/2$, $p_2 = 0$, $p_3 = 0$, $p_4 = 1/2$. That
is, the only possible outcomes are $|\leftrightarrow\leftrightarrow\rangle$ and $|\updownarrow\updownarrow\rangle$, so that the observed
polarizations of the two photons are correlated. In the following example,
we show than the potential for correlation that exists in the state $|s\rangle$ is a
little more subtle than one might at first think.

Example 2.3.6. Again let us consider the state $|s\rangle$ of Example 2.3.4, but
instead of performing a measurement in the standard basis, let us per-
form the following measurement: $Q = (|rr\rangle, |rl\rangle, |lr\rangle, |ll\rangle)$, where $|r\rangle =$
$(1/\sqrt{2})(|\leftrightarrow\rangle + i\ |\updownarrow\rangle)$, $|l\rangle = (1/\sqrt{2})(|\leftrightarrow\rangle - i\ |\updownarrow\rangle)$, and we are using the ab-
breviated notation for the tensor product, for example, $|rr\rangle = |r\rangle \otimes |r\rangle$.
The measurement Q checks each photon to see whether it is right- or
left-circularly polarized. ($|r\rangle$ is right-circular and $|l\rangle$ is left-circular.) It is a
straightforward calculation to compute the probabilities of the four out-
comes; one finds that $p_1 = 0$, $p_2 = 1/2$, $p_3 = 1/2$, $p_4 = 0$. Thus the only
possible outcomes are $|rl\rangle$ and $|lr\rangle$. That is, when one performs this mea-
surement, the observed polarizations are *anticorrelated*. This fact is by no
means obvious just by looking at the form of the state $|s\rangle$.

One might be tempted to think that if a pair of photons is in the state
we have just been considering – $|s\rangle = (1/\sqrt{2})(|\leftrightarrow\leftrightarrow\rangle + |\updownarrow\updownarrow\rangle)$ – then what
is really going on is that the photons are *actually* either in the state $|\leftrightarrow\leftrightarrow\rangle$
or in the state $|\updownarrow\updownarrow\rangle$, but we simply do not happen to know which one is
correct. Example 2.3.6 makes it clear that this interpretation is *wrong*. If
the photons really were in the state $|\leftrightarrow\leftrightarrow\rangle$, then all four outcomes of the
measurement Q defined in that example would be equally likely, and the
same would be true if the photons were really in the state $|\updownarrow\updownarrow\rangle$. There is

no way that our *ignorance* could cause two of the probabilities to be zero if they would not be zero otherwise. So it is not a question of ignorance on our part. Rather, the pair of photons is in a *quantum superposition* of the states $|\leftrightarrow\leftrightarrow\rangle$ and $|\updownarrow\updownarrow\rangle$. There is no good way to interpret the concept of a quantum superposition in the familiar terms of classical physics. Our best handle on the concept comes from the predictions we get by following our mathematical rules. If one is forced to describe a quantum superposition in ordinary language, perhaps the best one can do is to say that the physical system (e.g., the pair of photons) is in two states *at the same time*. But the meaning of such a statement has to come from the mathematics.

EXERCISES

Problem 1. Prove that the tensor product operation on vectors is associative.

Problem 2. Let $|s\rangle$ and $|t\rangle$ be any two states of polarization of photon A. Let $|v\rangle$ be any state of polarization of photon B. Using the definition of tensor product, show that the inner product between $|s\rangle \otimes |v\rangle$ and $|t\rangle \otimes |v\rangle$ is the same as the inner product between $|s\rangle$ and $|t\rangle$. The physical interpretation of this fact is utterly trivial: the degree of distinguishability of two states of photon A is not changed merely because we decide to regard photon B as part of our system.

Problem 3. Each of the following vectors represents a state of a pair of photons. The ordering of the basis vectors is the same as in the examples of this section. For each vector, determine whether or not it represents a product state. If it does represent a product, write the vector explicitly as the tensor product of two two-component vectors.

$$\begin{pmatrix} 1 \\ 0 \\ 0 \\ 0 \end{pmatrix} \begin{pmatrix} 1/2 \\ 1/2 \\ 1/2 \\ -1/2 \end{pmatrix} \begin{pmatrix} 1/2 \\ i/2 \\ i/2 \\ -1/2 \end{pmatrix}$$

Problem 4. Prove that if the state $|s\rangle = s_1 |\leftrightarrow\leftrightarrow\rangle + s_2 |\leftrightarrow\updownarrow\rangle + s_3 |\updownarrow\leftrightarrow\rangle + s_4 |\updownarrow\updownarrow\rangle$ is a product state, then $s_1 s_4 = s_2 s_3$.

Problem 5. Prove the converse of the statement in Problem 4: If $s_1 s_4 = s_2 s_3$, then $|s\rangle$ is a product state.

Problem 6. The following is an interesting example of an entangled state of a pair of photons:

$$|v\rangle = \frac{1}{\sqrt{2}}(|\leftrightarrow\updownarrow\rangle - |\updownarrow\leftrightarrow\rangle) = \frac{1}{\sqrt{2}} \begin{pmatrix} 0 \\ 1 \\ -1 \\ 0 \end{pmatrix}.$$

Such a state can be produced by passing an ultraviolet pulse through a special kind of transparent crystal. Most of the photons in the pulse pass straight through, but sometimes a photon will split into two lower-energy photons going off in two specifically selected directions not parallel to the direction of the original pulse. These two lower-energy photons are in the state $|v\rangle$ defined above. In this problem, we ask what happens when a polarization measurement is made on each of the two entangled photons. In particular, we imagine making the measurement

$$\mathcal{M}_\theta = (|m_1\rangle, |m_2\rangle) = \left(\begin{pmatrix} \cos\theta \\ \sin\theta \end{pmatrix}, \begin{pmatrix} -\sin\theta \\ \cos\theta \end{pmatrix} \right)$$

on each photon. (We've seen this measurement before: it distinguishes between two orthogonal states of linear polarization.) The two measurements, one performed on each photon, can be thought of as a single measurement $\mathcal{M}_\theta$ performed on the *pair* of photons. The measurement $\mathcal{M}_\theta$ has four possible outcomes and can be written as follows:

$$\mathcal{M}_\theta = (|m_1\rangle \otimes |m_1\rangle, |m_1\rangle \otimes |m_2\rangle, |m_2\rangle \otimes |m_1\rangle, |m_2\rangle \otimes |m_2\rangle).$$

Find the probabilities of the four possible outcomes of $\mathcal{M}_\theta$ when it is performed on the pair state $|v\rangle$ defined above. In particular, show that no matter what the value of θ is, the two photons *must* give opposite outcomes: if one of them chooses to be polarized in the θ direction, the other will choose the orthogonal direction.

2.4 Measuring a Subsystem

In Section 2.1, we mentioned that we would sometimes want to consider *incomplete* measurements on a quantum system. The case of a composite system is a case in which we often want to make such a measurement. Suppose, for example, that we have a pair of photons in some joint state of polarization. We might choose to measure only the first photon and leave the second one unmeasured. We have not yet explained (i) how to compute the probabilities of the outcomes of such a measurement, or (ii) how to figure out the state of the measured particle and the unmeasured particle after the measurement. Fortunately, the rules that answer these questions are fairly straightforward. In this section we offer a practical approach to the issue, which will be sufficient for almost all of the applications in this book. The final section of this chapter gives a more thorough mathematical treatment that applies to other incomplete measurements; it will be needed in Section 7.9.

Consider the most general polarization state of a pair of photons:

$$|s\rangle = a\,|\leftrightarrow\leftrightarrow\rangle + b\,|\leftrightarrow\updownarrow\rangle + c\,|\updownarrow\leftrightarrow\rangle + d\,|\updownarrow\updownarrow\rangle,$$

which may or may not be entangled. Suppose that we perform the measurement $M = (|\leftrightarrow\rangle, |\updownarrow\rangle)$ on the first photon and leave the second photon unmeasured. To figure out the effect of this measurement, it is helpful to rewrite the state as

$$|s\rangle = |\leftrightarrow\rangle \otimes (a\,|\leftrightarrow\rangle + b\,|\updownarrow\rangle) + |\updownarrow\rangle \otimes (c\,|\leftrightarrow\rangle + d\,|\updownarrow\rangle),$$

which is of the form

$$|s\rangle = |\leftrightarrow\rangle \otimes |v\rangle + |\updownarrow\rangle \otimes |w\rangle, \tag{2.22}$$

where $|v\rangle$ and $|w\rangle$ are *unnormalized* vectors associated with the second photon. When we make the measurement M on the first photon, what are the probabilities of the outcomes $|\leftrightarrow\rangle$ and $|\updownarrow\rangle$? If there were no second particle, and if the first particle were in a state of the form $v\,|\leftrightarrow\rangle + w\,|\updownarrow\rangle$ with v and w being complex numbers, the two probabilities would be $|v|^2$ and $|w|^2$ respectively. When the state is of the form given in Eq. (2.22), quantum mechanics predicts – according to a general rule to be stated shortly – that the probabilities will be $\langle v|v\rangle$ and $\langle w|w\rangle$ respectively. That is, instead of using the squared magnitudes of complex coefficients, we use the squared *lengths* of the *vectors* that serve as coefficients.

Figuring out the final states of the photons is easier. If the first photon gives the outcome $|\leftrightarrow\rangle$, its final state is $|\leftrightarrow\rangle$ – that is, the photon takes on the state that defines its outcome, as always – and the final state of the second photon is proportional to $|v\rangle$; that is, the second photon takes on the state that is paired with $|\leftrightarrow\rangle$ in $|s\rangle$. (We say "proportional" because a state vector has to be normalized, but $|v\rangle$ is not normalized.)

We express these ideas more generally in the following rule.

Rule for measurements on subsystems

Consider a system AB consisting of two parts A and B, and suppose that AB as a whole is in the state $|s\rangle$. Part A is now subjected to a measurement $(|m_1\rangle, \ldots, |m_N\rangle)$, where N is the dimension of part A. One can show that the state $|s\rangle$ can always be written in the form

$$|s\rangle = |m_1\rangle \otimes |v_1\rangle + \cdots + |m_N\rangle \otimes |v_N\rangle,$$

where $|v_1\rangle, \ldots, |v_N\rangle$ are unnormalized vectors associated with part B (it is possible for one or more of the $|v_i\rangle$'s to be the zero vector).

i. The probability of the outcome $|m_i\rangle$ is $p_i = \langle v_i | v_i \rangle$.
ii. If the ith outcome occurs, the final state of part A is $|m_i\rangle$ and the final state of part B is $|v_i\rangle/\sqrt{\langle v_i|v_i\rangle}$.

Example 2.4.1. A pair of photons is in the state

$$|s\rangle = \frac{1}{\sqrt{2}}\left(|\leftrightarrow\leftrightarrow\rangle + |\updownarrow\updownarrow\rangle\right). \tag{2.23}$$

We now perform on the first photon the measurement

$$M = (|m_1\rangle, |m_2\rangle) = \left(\frac{1}{\sqrt{2}}(|\leftrightarrow\rangle + |\updownarrow\rangle), \frac{1}{\sqrt{2}}(|\leftrightarrow\rangle - |\updownarrow\rangle)\right).$$

(i) What is the probability of the outcome $|m_1\rangle$? (ii) If the outcome is $|m_1\rangle$, what is the final state of the second photon?
Answers: To answer these questions, we want to reexpress the state $|s\rangle$ in the form

$$|s\rangle = |m_1\rangle \otimes |v_1\rangle + |m_2\rangle \otimes |v_2\rangle.$$

That is, we want

$$|s\rangle = \frac{1}{\sqrt{2}}\left[(|\leftrightarrow\rangle + |\updownarrow\rangle) \otimes |v_1\rangle + (|\leftrightarrow\rangle - |\updownarrow\rangle) \otimes |v_2\rangle\right].$$

Each $|v_i\rangle$ can be written as $|v_i\rangle = a_i |\leftrightarrow\rangle + b_i |\updownarrow\rangle$, so that we get

$$\begin{aligned}
|s\rangle &= \frac{1}{\sqrt{2}}[(|\leftrightarrow\rangle + |\updownarrow\rangle) \otimes (a_1 |\leftrightarrow\rangle + b_1 |\updownarrow\rangle) \\
&\quad + (|\leftrightarrow\rangle - |\updownarrow\rangle) \otimes (a_2 |\leftrightarrow\rangle + b_2 |\updownarrow\rangle)] \\
&= \frac{1}{\sqrt{2}}[(a_1 + a_2) |\leftrightarrow\leftrightarrow\rangle + (b_1 + b_2) |\leftrightarrow\updownarrow\rangle \\
&\quad + (a_1 - a_2) |\updownarrow\leftrightarrow\rangle + (b_1 - b_2) |\updownarrow\updownarrow\rangle].
\end{aligned}$$

Comparing this last expression with Eq. (2.23), we see that we must have $a_1 + a_2 = 1$, $b_1 + b_2 = 0$, $a_1 - a_2 = 0$, and $b_1 - b_2 = 1$. The only solution is $a_1 = a_2 = b_1 = 1/2$ and $b_2 = -1/2$. Thus

$$|v_1\rangle = \frac{1}{2}(|\leftrightarrow\rangle + |\updownarrow\rangle) \quad \text{and} \quad |v_2\rangle = \frac{1}{2}(|\leftrightarrow\rangle - |\updownarrow\rangle).$$

We can now answer the questions. (i) The probability of the outcome $|m_1\rangle$ is $\langle v_1|v_1\rangle = (1/2)^2 + (1/2)^2 = 1/2$. (ii) If the outcome $|m_1\rangle$ occurs, the final state of the second photon is $|v_1\rangle/\sqrt{\langle v_1|v_1\rangle} = (1/\sqrt{2})(|\leftrightarrow\rangle + |\updownarrow\rangle)$.

The results of this last example may strike you as suspicious. First of all, it seems that by making a measurement on the first photon, we have had an effect on the state of the second photon. Now, the two photons do not have to be close to each other; they may be lightyears apart. How, then, can a measurement on the first photon have any effect on the second photon? This is the sort of issue that causes one to question the interpretation of a quantum state as a *literal* description of the quantum object. Does the second photon change its state at the *exact moment* that the first photon is measured? But according to the special theory of relativity, the notion of simultaneity depends on the observer's state of motion; so what could be meant by "at the exact moment"? On the other hand, if we regard the quantum state as a state of *knowledge*, then the effect on the second photon is not surprising: making a measurement can certainly change one's *knowledge* about something that is far away. But if the quantum state is only a state of knowledge, does this mean that there is some underlying *actual* state that we do not yet know how to express, or have we abandoned the notion of an underlying reality? Fortunately it is not our mission to resolve these matters here. The observable prediction is perfectly clear, regardless of how one chooses to interpret it.

There is a related question, however, that we cannot avoid. In the above example, it is not just that making a measurement on one photon affects the state of the second photon. In addition, the final state of the second photon depends on our *choice* of what measurement to perform on the first photon. If Alice is standing near the first photon and Bob is standing near the second one, could Alice send an instantaneous signal to Bob by her *choice* of what to measure? There is no argument about the answer to this question. Alice can choose what measurement to make, but she cannot control the outcome of her measurement. One can show that this lack of control prevents her from using the photons' entanglement to send a signal to Bob. (See Problem 1 below.)

EXERCISES

Problem 1. (a) Suppose that Alice and Bob share the entangled state $|s\rangle$ of Example 2.4.1: Alice holds the first photon while Bob holds the second. Bob has decided to perform the measurement $(|\leftrightarrow\rangle, |\updownarrow\rangle)$ on his photon. If, before Bob makes his measurement, Alice measures her photon, using some arbitrary measurement $M = (|m^{(1)}\rangle, |m^{(2)}\rangle)$, show that the probabilities of the outcomes of Bob's measurement are *independent* of M. Thus Alice cannot use her choice of measurement to send a signal to Bob. (b) Show that the same conclusion holds no matter what measurement Bob chooses to make on his photon.

2.5   Other Incomplete Measurements

In the preceding section we presented the quantum mechanical rule describing the effects of a measurement on *part* of a system. This is one example of an incomplete measurement, but it is not the most general case. We now give a more general account of incomplete measurements in quantum mechanics.

We begin with the familiar example just mentioned – measuring only the first of two photons – but we now treat the problem in a way that can be extended to other cases. The standard basis, $(|\leftrightarrow\leftrightarrow\rangle, |\leftrightarrow\updownarrow\rangle, |\updownarrow\leftrightarrow\rangle, |\updownarrow\updownarrow\rangle)$, represents a certain complete measurement on the pair of photons. But suppose we simply want to make the measurement $(|\leftrightarrow\rangle, |\updownarrow\rangle)$ on the first photon. In terms of our four-element standard basis, this amounts to distinguishing the first two basis elements from the last two. To express this measurement mathematically, it is helpful to introduce the notion of a *projection operator*. Expressed in our standard basis, multiplication by the matrix

$$P_1 = \begin{pmatrix} 1 & 0 & 0 & 0 \\ 0 & 1 & 0 & 0 \\ 0 & 0 & 0 & 0 \\ 0 & 0 & 0 & 0 \end{pmatrix} \tag{2.24}$$

has the effect of projecting any two-photon state vector onto the subspace spanned by the first two basis vectors, that is, the subspace in which the first photon is in the state $|\leftrightarrow\rangle$. Similarly, the matrix

$$P_2 = \begin{pmatrix} 0 & 0 & 0 & 0 \\ 0 & 0 & 0 & 0 \\ 0 & 0 & 1 & 0 \\ 0 & 0 & 0 & 1 \end{pmatrix} \tag{2.25}$$

projects onto the last two basis vectors, in which the first photon is in the state $|\updownarrow\rangle$. The measurement we have in mind does not discriminate among all four basis vectors; rather, it discriminates between the two subspaces specified by the above projection operators. This is typical of incomplete measurements, and in general an incomplete measurement in quantum mechanics can be specified in terms of projection operators. We therefore spend the next few paragraphs getting more familiar with this class of operators.

In general, a projection operator is defined as follows.

Definition. A *projection operator* P acting on a vector space of N dimensions is an $N \times N$ matrix with the following properties: (i) $P^\dagger = P$, (ii) $P^2 = P$.

One might well wonder why these two properties characterize an operator that projects an arbitrary vector onto a specific subspace. We can make sense of the definition as follows. First, an operator Q such that

$Q^\dagger = Q$, called a self-adjoint operator, has the (nonobvious) property that its eigenvalues are all real and that eigenvectors corresponding to distinct eigenvalues are orthogonal. We can therefore think of such an operator in the following way: there exists an orthogonal basis for the space such that the operator Q squeezes or stretches the space along each basis vector (or reflects, in the case of negative eigenvalues). The additional requirement $P^2 = P$ implies that the eigenvalues λ, that is, the squeezing or stretching factors, themselves satisfy $\lambda^2 = \lambda$; that is, the only eigenvalues are 0 and 1. Thus there is a preferred subspace (corresponding to the eigenvalue 1) that is left unchanged by P, and there is the orthogonal subspace (with eigenvalue 0) that is "squeezed flat" by P. Thus when it operates on any given vector, P in effect preserves the component in the favored subspace, and removes the orthogonal component. We now give a couple of examples of projection operators.

Example 2.5.1. Let $|s\rangle$ be any state vector in an N-dimensional state space. The matrix $P = |s\rangle\langle s|$ is a projection operator that projects onto the one-dimensional subspace spanned by $|s\rangle$. (Here we are using the interpretation of $\langle s|$ as a row vector.) To see this, consider an arbitrary state $|\psi\rangle$, and express it in an orthonormal basis that includes $|s\rangle$: $|\psi\rangle = c_1|b^{(1)}\rangle + \cdots + c_N|b^{(N)}\rangle$, where $|b^{(1)}\rangle = |s\rangle$. When we apply P to $|\psi\rangle$, all but one of the terms vanish because of the orthogonality of the basis elements, and we are left with the equation $P|\psi\rangle = c_1|s\rangle$. That is, the resulting vector is proportional to $|s\rangle$, and the proportionality constant is the component of $|\psi\rangle$ along $|s\rangle$.

Example 2.5.2. Let $|s^{(1)}\rangle$ and $|s^{(2)}\rangle$ be two orthogonal states in an N-dimensional state space. Together they span a two-dimensional subspace. The operator that projects onto this subspace can be written as $P = |s^{(1)}\rangle\langle s^{(1)}| + |s^{(2)}\rangle\langle s^{(2)}|$.

In terms of projection operators, we can now write down the general quantum mechanical rules for incomplete measurements, for a system with a state space of arbitrary dimension:

1. A general measurement can be represented by an ordered set of projection operators $M = (P_1, \ldots, P_n)$ such that $\sum_i P_i = I$, the identity operator.

2. If the initial state of the system is $|s\rangle$ and the measurement M is performed, the probability of the ith outcome is

$$p_i = \langle s|P_i|s\rangle. \tag{2.26}$$

3. If the initial state is $|s\rangle$ and the ith outcome occurs, the final state of the system is

$$|s_i\rangle = \frac{P_i|s\rangle}{\sqrt{\langle s|P_i|s\rangle}}. \tag{2.27}$$

Example 2.5.3. A pair of photons is initially in the state $|s\rangle = (1/\sqrt{2})(|\leftrightarrow\leftrightarrow\rangle + |\updownarrow\updownarrow\rangle)$. We now perform on the first photon the measurement $(|\leftrightarrow\rangle, |\updownarrow\rangle)$. What are the probabilities of the two outcomes, and for each outcome, what is the final state of the pair of photons?

Answer: First we have to interpret the measurement in terms of projection operators on the full four-dimensional state space. We have already done this in the above discussion: the measurement is $M = (P_1, P_2)$, where P_1 and P_2 are given by Eqs. (2.24) and (2.25) respectively. Using Eq. (2.26), we find that the probability of the first outcome is

$$p_1 = \begin{pmatrix} \frac{1}{\sqrt{2}} & 0 & 0 & \frac{1}{\sqrt{2}} \end{pmatrix} \begin{pmatrix} 1 & 0 & 0 & 0 \\ 0 & 1 & 0 & 0 \\ 0 & 0 & 0 & 0 \\ 0 & 0 & 0 & 0 \end{pmatrix} \begin{pmatrix} 1/\sqrt{2} \\ 0 \\ 0 \\ 1/\sqrt{2} \end{pmatrix} = \frac{1}{2}.$$

One similarly finds that the probability of the second outcome is also $1/2$. If the first outcome occurs, then according to Eq. (2.27) the resulting state of the pair is

$$|s_1\rangle = \frac{1}{\sqrt{1/2}} \begin{pmatrix} 1 & 0 & 0 & 0 \\ 0 & 1 & 0 & 0 \\ 0 & 0 & 0 & 0 \\ 0 & 0 & 0 & 0 \end{pmatrix} \begin{pmatrix} 1/\sqrt{2} \\ 0 \\ 0 \\ 1/\sqrt{2} \end{pmatrix} = \begin{pmatrix} 1 \\ 0 \\ 0 \\ 0 \end{pmatrix} = |\leftrightarrow\leftrightarrow\rangle.$$

Thus the measurement not only leaves the measured photon in the state $|\leftrightarrow\rangle$, it also leaves the unmeasured photon in the same state. Note that this result is consistent with our earlier results concerning the state $|s\rangle$ in Sections 2.3 and 2.4; for example, when we make a complete measurement on the pair, it is impossible to get the outcome $|\leftrightarrow\updownarrow\rangle$.

Example 2.5.4. Assume the same initial state $|s\rangle$ as in the preceding example, but now let us perform on the first photon the measurement $(|r\rangle, |l\rangle)$, with $|r\rangle$ and $|l\rangle$ defined as in Example 2.3.6. That is, we are asking the first photon to choose between right- and left-hand circular polarization. For each of the two outcomes, what is the final state of the pair?

Answer: First we need to find the relevant projection operators. Consider, for example, the first outcome, corresponding to the first photon being found in the right-hand circular polarization state $|r\rangle$. The subspace in question is spanned by the two orthogonal vectors $|r\rangle \otimes |\leftrightarrow\rangle$ and $|r\rangle \otimes |\updownarrow\rangle$. Using the method of Example 2.5.2, we find that the operator that projects onto this subspace is

$$
P = \frac{1}{\sqrt{2}} \begin{pmatrix} 1 & 0 & -i & 0 \\ 0 & 1 & 0 & -i \\ i & 0 & 1 & 0 \\ 0 & i & 0 & 1 \end{pmatrix}.
$$

Alternatively, we can obtain this matrix P as the tensor product $(|r\rangle\langle r|) \otimes I$, where I is the identity operator on the second photon. Using Eq. (2.27), we find that if the first outcome occurs, the final state of the pair is $|rl\rangle$. Similarly, if the second outcome occurs, the final state of the pair is $|lr\rangle$. That is, the second photon ends up in the state *opposite* to that of the first photon. This again is consistent with the result of Example 2.3.6 in which we considered a complete measurement.

Example 2.5.5. Let us now consider the following incomplete measurement on a pair of photons:

$$
P_1 = |\leftrightarrow\leftrightarrow\rangle\langle\leftrightarrow\leftrightarrow| + |\updownarrow\updownarrow\rangle\langle\updownarrow\updownarrow|
$$

$$
P_2 = |\leftrightarrow\updownarrow\rangle\langle\leftrightarrow\updownarrow| + |\updownarrow\leftrightarrow\rangle\langle\updownarrow\leftrightarrow|.
$$

Roughly speaking, this measurement asks whether the two photons have the *same* polarization or *opposite* polarizations, in the horizontal–vertical basis, without asking each individual photon to reveal its own polarization. Note that unlike the measurements of the last two examples, this one cannot be realized as a measurement on just one photon. This is a joint measurement on the pair, which one might perform by bringing the two photons together and letting them interact in some way. It is a difficult measurement to perform on photons, because it is difficult to make photons interact with each other in the right way. But the analogous measurement on other quantum variables, such as electron spin, can be easier.

If we perform this measurement on the state $|s\rangle$ of the preceding examples, we find that the probabilities of the outcomes are

$$p_1 = \langle s|P_1|s\rangle = \frac{1}{2}((\langle\leftrightarrow\leftrightarrow| + \langle\updownarrow\updownarrow|)(|\leftrightarrow\leftrightarrow\rangle\langle\leftrightarrow\leftrightarrow| + |\updownarrow\updownarrow\rangle\langle\updownarrow\updownarrow|)$$
$$\times(|\leftrightarrow\leftrightarrow\rangle + |\updownarrow\updownarrow\rangle)) = 1$$

$$p_2 = \langle s|P_2|s\rangle = \frac{1}{2}((\langle\leftrightarrow\leftrightarrow| + \langle\updownarrow\updownarrow|)(|\leftrightarrow\updownarrow\rangle\langle\leftrightarrow\updownarrow| + |\updownarrow\leftrightarrow\rangle\langle\updownarrow\leftrightarrow|)$$
$$\times(|\leftrightarrow\leftrightarrow\rangle + |\updownarrow\updownarrow\rangle)) = 0$$

(We see that we do not need to use matrix notation to compute such probabilities. The bracket notation can sometimes be more convenient.) Thus the first outcome will definitely occur. When it does, the pair of photons is, according to our rule, left in the state

$$|s_1\rangle = \frac{P_1|s\rangle}{\sqrt{\langle s|P_1|s\rangle}} = |s\rangle.$$

That is, the measurement has not disturbed the state. Notice that it certainly *would have* disturbed the state if we had measured the polarization of each individual photon. By making this sort of incomplete measurement, we can often learn something about the state without destroying the subtle quantum superposition between its components.

EXERCISES

Problem 1. This problem explores further the incomplete measurement (P_1, P_2) described in Example 2.5.5.

(a) In this example, we considered the initial state $|s\rangle = \frac{1}{\sqrt{2}}(|\leftrightarrow\leftrightarrow\rangle + |\updownarrow\updownarrow\rangle)$, and found (i) the probabilities of the two outcomes and (ii) the final state of the pair of photons when the first outcome occurs. Go through the same calculations, doing the algebra by means of matrices rather than by relying on the bracket notation.

(b) Consider the same incomplete measurement, but now suppose that the initial state is $|t\rangle = \frac{1}{2}(|\leftrightarrow\leftrightarrow\rangle + |\leftrightarrow\updownarrow\rangle + |\updownarrow\leftrightarrow\rangle + |\updownarrow\updownarrow\rangle)$. Find (i) the probability of the first outcome and (ii) the final state of the pair of photons if the first outcome occurs.

(c) Starting with a product state, is it possible to create an entangled state merely by performing an incomplete measurement? (Hint: Is the state $|t\rangle$ in part (b) a product state?)

3   Quantum Cryptography

As we have said, quantum mechanics has become the standard framework for most of what is done in physics and indeed has played this role for three-quarters of a century. For just as long, physicists and philosophers have, as we have already suggested, raised and discussed questions about the *interpretation* of quantum mechanics: Why do we single out *measurement* as a special kind of interaction that evokes a probabilistic, irreversible response from nature, when other kinds of interaction cause deterministic, reversible changes? How should we talk about quantum superpositions? What does entanglement tell us about the nature of reality? These are interesting questions and researchers still argue about the answers. However, in the last couple of decades researchers have also been thinking along the following line: Let us accept that quantum objects act in weird ways, and see if we can *use* this weirdness technologically. The two best examples of potential uses of quantum weirdness are quantum computation and quantum cryptography.

One of the first quantum cryptographic schemes to appear in the literature, and the only one we consider in detail in this book, was introduced by Charles Bennett and Gilles Brassard in 1984.[1] Their idea is *not* to use quantum signals directly to convey secret information. Rather, they suggest using quantum signals to generate a secret cryptographic *key* shared between two parties. Thus the Bennett–Brassard scheme is an example

---

[1] Bennett and Brassard (1984). A good nonmathematical review of the basic ideas and early investigations into quantum key distribution is Bennett, Brassard, and Ekert (1992). The Bennett–Brassard scheme was inspired by ideas in a paper by Wiesner (1983), which had been written more than a decade before it was published. An alternative approach to quantum key distribution, based on entanglement, was devised by Ekert (1991).

of "quantum key distribution." Laboratory implementations of quantum key distribution always use photons to carry the quantum signals. Usually these photons are transmitted via optical fiber, but in some cases they are sent directly through the air.[2] (It is no mean feat to detect a single photon sent to you through the air, and to distinguish it from all the other photons that happen to be in the vicinity!) In principle, a secret key distributed by quantum cryptography could be used in one of two ways: (i) it could be used as a one-time pad; (ii) it could be used as the shared key in a standard secret-key protocol such as DES or AES. Let us consider these two cases briefly.

(i) We have discussed one-time pads earlier but we recall the scheme here. The shared key might be a sequence of zeros and ones, for example, 011101001000010. The sender, Alice, somehow translates her message into binary digits; let us say that her translated message is 101010101010101. She adds each bit of the key to the corresponding bit of the message, mod 2, to generate the ciphertext:

        101010101010101
        011101001000010
        110111100010111

She then sends this last string of bits to Bob, who performs the same operation to recover the original message:

        110111100010111
        011101001000010
        101010101010101

In this one-time pad scheme, if the key is random and is truly known only to Alice and Bob, then the cryptography is unbreakable. But as we have noted in Chapter 1, it is awkward to have to convey new bits of the secret key as fast as message bits are being sent. Quantum key distribution offers a potential solution to this problem, and indeed some experiments have

---

[2] For a review of both theory and experiment, see Gisin et al. (2002), Dusek et al. (2006), Lo, Popescu, and Spiller (2001), or Bouwmeester, Ekert, and Zeilinger (2000). For a recent high-key-rate result, see Tang et al. (2006).

already produced net key rates sufficient to transmit a video signal with one-time-pad encryption.

(ii) If Alice and Bob do not need a one-time pad but only a secret key for use with a secret-key cryptosystem, they could, of course, generate such a key via Diffie–Hellman or RSA. However, as we will discuss in Chapter 7, these public-key cryptosystems ultimately risk being cracked by a quantum computer. *Quantum* key distribution systems are not vulnerable to attack by a quantum computer; so they offer a distinct advantage here. Moreover, this way of using quantum key distribution can tolerate a slower secret key rate than would be needed for a one-time pad. As we will discuss later, though, the main challenge for quantum cryptography at the present time is not transmission rate but *distance*. There exist prototype systems that connect sites within several miles of each other, but, as we will see, qualitatively new challenges arise when one tries to extend the system to several hundreds of miles.

In the following section we present the basic ideas of the Bennett–Brassard protocol. We will, however, have to delay until Chapter 5 a more detailed discussion of the final steps of the protocol, in which the parties correct errors and enhance the security of their shared key. To discuss these issues, we will need the ideas on error correction that will be developed in Chapter 4.

3.1 The Bennett–Brassard Protocol

As we have seen, a quantum measurement is not a passive acquisition of information. Rather, it is an invasive procedure that typically changes the state of the variable being measured. Bennett and Brassard's scheme uses this fact about quantum measurements to foil a potential eavesdropper.

More specifically, we imagine the following scenario. Alice and Bob want to generate a shared, random, secret key. The eavesdropper, Eve, wants to gain some information about this key without being detected. If she can accomplish this, she will later be able to read at least part of an actual secret message encrypted with that key. Now, because the

Alice's Bit String and Bases:

0	0	1	0	0	1	1	1	1	0	0	0	0	1	0	1	0	0	1	0	1	1	0	0	1	0	0	1	0	1
+	x	+	+	x	x	+	+	+	x	+	x	+	+	+	+	+	+	+	+	x	x	+	x	x	x	+	+	+	+

Bob's Bases:

x	x	x	x	x	+	x	+	x	x	+	x	x	x	+	+	x	x	x	x	x	x	x	+	+	+	x	+	+	x

Figure 3.1: Illustration of the first four steps of the Bennett–Brassard protocol if there is no eavesdropper and no other source of noise. The shaded entries represent the cases in which Alice and Bob chose different bases; the corresponding bits are discarded. In this example, the bit strings A' and B' are both equal to 001000011110.

Bennett–Brassard key distribution protocol has Alice sending *quantum* signals to Bob, Eve will typically not be able to measure these signals without causing some disturbance. In this way Alice and Bob hope to detect Eve's presence and thereby foil her plan.

But if Eve cannot measure the signals without causing a disturbance, then Bob likewise cannot measure the signals without changing them. So the protocol has to be designed in such a way as to let Bob get the *correct* key, in spite of the disturbance caused by his measurements. The Bennett–Brassard protocol solves this problem by making it possible for Alice and Bob to know *when* Bob has made a disruptive measurement, so that they can discard the resulting data and keep only the data that Bob has not disturbed.

Here, then, are the steps of the Bennett–Brassard protocol. The first four steps are illustrated in Fig. 3.1.

1. Alice generates two random binary strings $A = (a_1, \ldots, a_n)$ and $S = (s_1, \ldots, s_n)$. The entries a_i are zeros and ones; a subset of these entries will eventually be used to create a shared secret key. The entries s_i are chosen from the binary set $\{+, \times\}$, where the characters "+" and "×" will represent two different *bases* for the state space of a photon's polarization.

2. Alice now sends a sequence of n photons to Bob, the polarization of the ith photon being determined as follows. If $s_i = +$, the polarization will be chosen from the orthogonal basis $M_+ = (|\updownarrow\rangle, |\leftrightarrow\rangle)$;

if $s_i = \times$, the polarization will be chosen from the alternative basis $M_\times = ((|\updownarrow\rangle + |\leftrightarrow\rangle)/\sqrt{2}, (|\updownarrow\rangle - |\leftrightarrow\rangle)/\sqrt{2})$, whose elements make a $45°$ angle with the elements of M_+. In either case, Alice uses the first element of the basis if $a_i = 0$ and the second if $a_i = 1$. We think of a_i as the bit Alice is trying to send to Bob, and s_i as determining the means by which she will encode this bit.

3. Before he receives any photons, Bob generates a random string $R = (r_1, \ldots, r_n)$ in which each entry is chosen from the set $\{+, \times\}$. When he receives the ith photon, he measures its polarization in the basis labeled by r_i and records the result. Regardless of which basis he uses, if he obtains the first of the two possible outcomes, he records a 0, and if he obtains the second of the possible outcomes he records a 1. Thus at the end of this process he has a sequence $B = (b_1, \ldots, b_n)$ of zeros and ones, the results of his measurements. Note that for any given photon i, there is no reason to assume that Alice and Bob used the same basis; that is, s_i need not equal r_i. However, if they *have* used the same basis, then provided that the photon was not disturbed on route from Alice to Bob, we should have $a_i = b_i$. For example, if Alice used the basis $(|\updownarrow\rangle, |\leftrightarrow\rangle)$ and sent the bit 0, that is, if she sent Bob a photon in the state $|\updownarrow\rangle$, and if Bob measured this photon in the same basis, then he should have gotten the outcome $|\updownarrow\rangle$ and recorded the bit 0. On the other hand, if Alice and Bob used different bases, then there should be no correlation between Alice's bit a_i and Bob's bit b_i.

4. After all the photons have been sent, Alice and Bob use a public channel to tell each other their sequences of bases S and R. Each of them compares these two sequences and makes a note of the values of the index i for which the two sequences disagree. (Note that they do *not* at this point transmit or compare any values from their bit strings A and B; they are only comparing the bases.) Then Alice removes from her bit string A the bits corresponding to these values of i, and Bob does the same with his bit string B. Let the remaining, shorter strings be called A' and B'. Again, assuming that there has been no interference, the strings A' and B' should be identical. Note that the expected length of each of these strings is $n/2$, since for each photon transmitted, there is a 50% chance that Alice and Bob used the same basis.

5. In reality there will always be errors in transmission even if there is no eavesdropper. So Alice and Bob now want to estimate the number of errors, that is, the number of bits in B' that are not equal to their counterparts in A'. To do this, Alice sends to Bob, over a public channel, a small random sample of her actual bits from A', which Bob then compares to the corresponding bits in B'. After the comparison, Alice and Bob discard these bits since Eve could know them. Assuming that the remaining bits have about the same proportion of errors as the ones they checked, they now want to correct these remaining errors. Remarkably, they can do this without necessarily giving everything away. We will see in Chapter 5 how this can be done.[3] At the end of this step Alice and Bob should possess strings A'' and B'', which are shorter than A' and B' but are almost certain to be identical.

6. From the number of errors that Alice and Bob have discovered in step 5, they estimate the maximum amount of information an eavesdropper is likely to have obtained about the remaining bits. They use this information to replace their strings A'' and B'' with even shorter strings A''' and B''' about which the eavesdropper has essentially no knowledge whatsoever.

Though the details of steps 5 and 6 will have to wait until Chapter 5, we can and should explain here why there is any connection between the number of errors that Alice and Bob find in step 5, and the amount of information an eavesdropper might have gained. As we have suggested before, in the long run an eavesdropper cannot gain information without causing errors.

To understand this point better, we need to think about how an eavesdropper (Eve) would try to intercept Alice's bits. For a given photon i, if Eve knew the basis s_i, she would be able to find out what bit Alice was sending, without disturbing the signal: she could simply measure the photon in the correct basis and then generate and send on to Bob a new photon having the same polarization. Eve would thus learn Alice's bit a_i but her action would be invisible to Alice and Bob. However, because

---

[3] It is not actually necessary for Alice and Bob to estimate the number of errors before taking steps to correct them. The estimation can be done as part of the process of error correction. But it is probably simpler conceptually to keep these two tasks separate.

of the sending protocol used in step 2, Eve cannot know which basis Alice uses to encode any given bit. Let us suppose, then, that she simply guesses which basis Alice is using and makes a measurement according to her guess. If she is correct, she will get the bit as before. But suppose she guesses incorrectly. For definiteness let us suppose that Alice is using the basis $M_+ = (|\updownarrow\rangle, |\leftrightarrow\rangle)$ and in fact is sending the bit 0, that is, the state $|\updownarrow\rangle$. Eve now measures the photon in the wrong basis, the diagonal basis $M_\times$. The two possible outcomes of her measurement are equally likely, and in either case, her measurement does not tell her what state Alice actually sent. So she has failed to learn anything about Alice's bit a_i. In fact, she still does not know that she used the wrong basis, so she prepares and sends to Bob a new photon having the diagonal polarization that corresponds to her measurement outcome.

What happens, now, at Bob's end? If Bob is using the diagonal basis $M_\times$, then it does not matter what happens, because according to step 4, the bits associated with this photon will eventually be discarded. So we may as well restrict our attention to the case in which Bob uses the same basis that Alice used, which in our example is the vertical–horizontal basis M_+. Thus Bob is measuring a diagonally polarized photon in the vertical–horizontal basis, and the two outcomes are equally likely. If Bob happens to get the vertical outcome, Eve is lucky, because he then records the bit $b_i = 0$, which happens to match Alice's bit a_i. Thus this photon has not given Alice and Bob any evidence of Eve's interference. (At this point, "lucky" for Eve refers simply to damage control. We have already established that she has learned nothing about Alice's bit. But she can hope that her attempt will not be detected.) On the other hand, if Bob gets the horizontal outcome, he will record the bit $b_i = 1$, so that $b_i \neq a_i$. This discrepancy will be present in the strings A' and B' and might be detected in step 5. If so, Eve's efforts to possess information about a key shared between Alice and Bob will have provided Alice and Bob some information about Eve's activity. We illustrate in Fig. 3.2 Eve's effect on Bob's bit string.

Let us work out the relevant probabilities. Suppose that for each photon, Eve decides probabilistically whether to measure it or not; the probability that she will measure it is p. Now consider a photon whose bit will be included in the strings A' and B'. What is the probability that Eve will cause an error in such a bit? The answer is $p/4$: there is a probability

Alice's Bit String and Bases:

```
1 1 0 0 0 1 1 1 1 1 0 1 0 1 0 0 0 0 1 0 0 0 1 1 0 1 0 0 1 0 0 0 1 0 1 0
+ x x x x + x x x x + x + + x + + + x + + + x + + + x + x + x + x x x x +
```

Eve's Bases and Measurements:

```
x               + x             x         x +             x x x + +     +
0               1 1             0         1 1             1 0 1 1 1     0
```

Bob's Bases and Measurements:

```
+ + + + + x + x + + x + x + x + + x + x x + + x x x + + + + x x x x + x
1 0 1 0 0 1 0 1 1 1 1 1 0 1 0 0 0 0 1 1 0 1 0 1 0 1 0 0 1 0 0 1 0 0 0 1
```

Figure 3.2: Illustration of the effect of an eavesdropper. Eve has measured certain randomly chosen photons, and in some cases her measurements have caused errors that Alice and Bob might detect in step 5. In this example the strings A' and B' are, respectively, 11100010000010 and 11100000000000.

p that she will measure the photon, then a probability $1/2$ that she will choose the wrong basis, and if she chooses the wrong basis, a probability $1/2$ that she will cause an error. We can also figure out the probability that she will learn the value of the bit: this probability is $p/2$, since she learns the value whenever she chooses the correct basis. Thus in the long run, for every two bits whose values she learns, she causes one error.

Of course there are other strategies that Eve might use, and we consider some of them in the exercises and in the following section. For any such strategy, though, it is useful to have a way of quantifying its success. For now let us restrict our attention to strategies in which Eve acts on each successive photon independently, without regard to what she has done with the earlier photons or what she has learned from them. A strategy is good for Eve if she gains a lot of information from a photon while minimizing her probability of causing a detectable error. We know how to compute the probability of an error, but how do we compute the amount of information she gains? In the above example it was relatively easy, because for each bit, Eve either learned its value with certainty or she learned nothing. But for other strategies, the information she gains may be probabilistic: she might end up thinking that the value 0 is more *likely* than the value 1, without being certain. It turns out that a useful mathematical tool for measuring Eve's information in such a situation is the *Rényi entropy*, which we now define.

Before Eve has made any measurement on a given photon, the two possible bit values, 0 and 1, are for Eve equally likely. That is, their probabilities are $p_0 = 1/2$ and $p_1 = 1/2$. After she has made her measurement (and after she had heard the public communication between Alice and Bob), her probabilities are, she hopes, more lopsided, for example, $p_0 = 3/4$ and $p_1 = 1/4$. Whether before or after her measurement, the *Rényi entropy of order 2* of her probability distribution, which we call "Rényi entropy" for short, is defined by[4]

$$H_R = -\log_2\left(p_0^2 + p_1^2\right), \tag{3.1}$$

and is a measure of the amount of information she *lacks* about the bit. (It can be helpful to read the word "entropy" as a synonym for "uncertainty.") Rényi entropy is a pure number and does not need units, but one usually speaks of it as being measured in "bits."[5] So if Eve's probabilities were $p_0 = 1$ and $p_1 = 0$, her Rényi entropy would be $H_R = -\log_2(1^2 + 0^2) = 0$ bits, indicating that she lacks no information. On the other hand, if the two probabilities are equal, as they are for Eve before she makes her measurement, her Rényi entropy is $H_R = -\log_2((1/2)^2 + (1/2)^2) = 1$ bit, which is its largest possible value: if you know nothing about the value of a bit, you lack one bit of information. If after her measurement the probabilities are $p_0 = 3/4$ and $p_1 = 1/4$, her Rényi entropy is now

$$H_R = -\log_2((3/4)^2 + (1/4)^2) = 0.678 \text{ bits}, \tag{3.2}$$

which is less than the maximum value. For convenience we will also speak of Eve's "Rényi *information*," defined as the amount by which her Rényi entropy falls short of its maximum possible value.[6] Thus,

$$\text{Rényi information} = 1 - (\text{Rényi entropy}) = 1 - H_R. \tag{3.3}$$

---

[4] Rényi (1965). For a binary probability distribution, the Rényi entropy of order α is defined by $(1/(1-\alpha))\log_2(p_0^\alpha + p_1^\alpha)$.

[5] This *is* a helpful way of speaking, in part because it distinguishes the definition given in Eq. (3.2) from an alternative definition using the natural logarithm in place of $\log_2$. In the latter case, the entropy would be measured in "nats."

[6] For valid technical reasons, the term "Rényi information" is not standard in the literature: specifically, it is impossible to talk about the amount of Rényi information that each of two random variables provides about the other. However, our more limited definition of Rényi information is not problematic, and we use it because it simplifies certain statements and makes them more intuitive.

In the above example, Eve ends up with $1 - 0.678 = 0.322$ bits of Rényi information.

What makes Rényi entropy useful is its role in a theorem, which we will discuss in Chapter 5, that relates the Rényi entropy to the ultimate security of Alice's and Bob's shared strings. Because of this theorem, it is reasonable to use Rényi entropy in comparing different eavesdropping strategies. For example, we might measure the effectiveness of an eavesdropping strategy by the ratio

$$\frac{\text{Eve's Rényi information}}{\text{Probability of causing an error}}.$$

Eve is trying to make this ratio as large as possible, while Alice and Bob are hoping that it can be kept low.

Example 3.1.1. Alice sends a photon to Bob, which Eve intercepts and measures in the basis

$$(|m_1\rangle, |m_2\rangle) = \left(\begin{pmatrix} 1/2 \\ \sqrt{3}/2 \end{pmatrix}, \begin{pmatrix} \sqrt{3}/2 \\ -1/2 \end{pmatrix} \right),$$

obtaining the first of these two outcomes. Later, Eve learns that Alice originally prepared the photon in one of the two polarization states $|\leftrightarrow\rangle$ and $|\updownarrow\rangle$. How much Rényi information has her measurement given her about the original state of the photon? (Assume that in the absence of any evidence from her measurement, the states $|\leftrightarrow\rangle$ and $|\updownarrow\rangle$ would be equally likely for Eve.)

Answer: To figure out Eve's Rényi information after she has taken her measurement into account, we need to find $p(\leftrightarrow |m_1)$ and $p(\updownarrow |m_1)$, where the vertical line is read "given." For example, $p(\leftrightarrow |m_1)$ is the probability that Alice sent $|\leftrightarrow\rangle$, *given* that Eve has obtained the outcome $|m_1\rangle$. This is not the sort of probability we have been computing using quantum rules. Rather, we have been computing probabilities such as $p(m_1| \leftrightarrow)$, the probability of the outcome $|m_1\rangle$ given that Alice sent the state $|\leftrightarrow\rangle$. In order to obtain the probabilities we want, we need to use Bayes' rule:

$$p(B|A) = \frac{p(A|B)p(B)}{p(A)}. \tag{3.4}$$

Here A and B are two propositions, and $p(A)$ and $p(B)$ are the overall probabilities of A and B, not conditioned on each other. Applying this rule to our problem, we have

$$p(\leftrightarrow \,|m_1) = \frac{p(m_1|\,\leftrightarrow)p(\leftrightarrow)}{p(m_1)}.$$

Let us compute each factor on the right in turn. Quantum rules tell us that $p(m_1|\,\leftrightarrow) = |\langle m_1|\,\leftrightarrow\rangle|^2 = 1/4$. We are given that $p(\leftrightarrow) = 1/2$. Finally, we compute $p(m_1)$ as follows: $p(m_1) = p(\leftrightarrow)p(m_1|\,\leftrightarrow) + p(\updownarrow)p(m_1|\,\updownarrow) = (1/2)(1/4) + (1/2)(3/4) = 1/2$. Putting the numbers together, we get

$$p(\leftrightarrow \,|m_1) = \frac{(1/4)(1/2)}{(1/2)} = \frac{1}{4}.$$

In a similar way, we find that $p(\updownarrow \,|m_1) = 3/4$ (as must be the case, since the probabilities must add up to 1). So Eve's final Rényi entropy is 0.678 bits, as computed in Eq. (3.2), and her final Rényi information is $1 - 0.678 = 0.322$ bits.

In the following section we explore a particular eavesdropping strategy that might have already occurred to you. What if Eve does not measure the photons at all? Rather, she makes a *copy* of each photon as it passes and she holds on to the copy until she learns, from the public discussion, which basis Alice used for that photon. Then she can measure each copy in its proper basis and get every bit that Alice sent. We show below why this strategy fails.

EXERCISES

Problem 1. In the Bennett–Brassard scheme, suppose that Eve performs on each photon the measurement

$$M(\theta) = \left(\begin{pmatrix} \cos\theta \\ \sin\theta \end{pmatrix}, \begin{pmatrix} -\sin\theta \\ \cos\theta \end{pmatrix} \right).$$

(Recall our convention that the horizontal polarization $|\leftrightarrow\rangle$ is represented by the vector $\binom{1}{0}$.) Let us suppose that she uses the "intercept-resend" strategy: if she gets the first outcome, she sends the state $\binom{\cos\theta}{\sin\theta}$ to Bob, and if she gets the second outcome, she sends the state $\binom{-\sin\theta}{\cos\theta}$.

(a) Assume that Bob measures his received photon in the same basis that Alice used in her preparation. (As we have said, ultimately this is the only case that matters.) For each of the four possible states that Alice might send, find the probability that the bit Bob receives will *not* agree with the bit that Alice sent (because of Eve's interference). That is, find the probability of error, as a function of θ, for each of Alice's four states.

(b) Find the *average* probability of error as a function of θ. (The average is over Alice's four states, which are equally likely.)

(c) For what value of θ does Eve's measurement cause the least disturbance, in the sense of minimizing the average probability of error? Or does it not matter which value of θ she chooses?

Problem 2. Assume the same eavesdropping strategy as in Problem 1.

(a) For each of Eve's two possible outcomes, and for each of the two possible bases that Alice might have used, compute Eve's final Rényi information about the bit that Alice sent.

(b) Find Eve's *average* Rényi information about the bit that Alice sent. (The average is over Eve's two possible outcomes and Alice's two possible bases.)

(c) For what value of θ does Eve's measurement tell her the most about Alice's bit, in the sense of maximizing the average Rényi information? Or does it not matter which value of θ she chooses?

Problem 3. There are many other possible measurements Eve could perform besides the ones considered in Problem 1. The most general complete orthogonal measurement she can perform on a photon can be written either as

$$M = \left(\begin{pmatrix} m_1 \\ m_2 \end{pmatrix}, \begin{pmatrix} -\bar{m}_2 \\ \bar{m}_1 \end{pmatrix} \right),$$

where m_1 and m_2 are arbitrary complex numbers satisfying $|m_1|^2 + |m_2|^2 = 1$, or in terms of a specific parameterization, as

$$M = \left(\begin{pmatrix} \cos\theta \\ \sin\theta e^{i\phi} \end{pmatrix}, \begin{pmatrix} -\sin\theta e^{-i\phi} \\ \cos\theta \end{pmatrix} \right).$$

Show that none of these measurements creates less disturbance, that is, yields a smaller average probability of error, than the measurements considered in Problem 1. (You may use either of the above representations of the measurement; they are equivalent.) In other words, show that if Eve is trying not to be detected, it does not help to use a measurement with complex components.

Problem 4. Show that when there are just two possibilities – so far we have defined Rényi entropy only for this case – the maximum value of the Rényi entropy is indeed 1 as we have claimed.

3.2 The No-Cloning Theorem

For ordinary information – called "classical information" within the framework of quantum information theory – there is no theoretical limit on one's ability to copy it. We can download files from the Internet and copy them onto our own computer's disk, as long as there is enough space to hold the copy. However, for quantum information such copying is impossible except when the information is essentially classical. We now prove this assertion.[7]

Consider a quantum object that could be in any of a number of states $|s_1\rangle, |s_2\rangle, \ldots, |s_m\rangle$. Suppose that we want to copy the state of this object. We are not interested in copying an *arbitrary* state; we are interested only in the specific states $|s_i\rangle$. For example, in the Bennett–Brassard scheme Eve would like to copy each photon, but she cares only about the four states $|\updownarrow\rangle, |\leftrightarrow\rangle, (|\updownarrow\rangle + |\leftrightarrow\rangle)/\sqrt{2}$, and $(|\updownarrow\rangle - |\leftrightarrow\rangle)/\sqrt{2}$. She does not care if other states are not copied faithfully. Assume that we are also given a similar quantum object in a known state $|0\rangle$. This is the object onto which we wish to copy the state of the first object, and the state $|0\rangle$ is the "blank" state, like the state of a piece of paper stored in a photocopier. To copy the state of the first object onto the second object, we would look for a unitary transformation U with the following effect:

$$U(|s_i\rangle \otimes |0\rangle) = |s_i\rangle \otimes |s_i\rangle, \tag{3.5}$$

for each of the possible states $|s_i\rangle$. The question is, does there exist such a U? Let us suppose that there is, and see what consequences follow.

It is a fact from linear algebra that unitary transformations preserve inner products. That is, if $|v\rangle$ and $|w\rangle$ are two vectors, and $|y\rangle$ and $|z\rangle$ are

---

[7] The impossibility of copying a general quantum state was pointed out in Dieks (1982) and Wootters and Zurek (1982). The stronger proof that we give here can be found in Nielsen and Chuang (2000, p. 532).

their respective images under U, then

$$\langle y|z \rangle = \langle v|w \rangle. \tag{3.6}$$

Indeed it is not hard to show this. We use the fact that since $|y\rangle = U|v\rangle$, the conjugate transpose of $|y\rangle$ is $\langle y| = \langle v|U^\dagger$. (You can convince yourself that this is true by writing out $|v\rangle$, U, and $|y\rangle$ as vectors and matrices and seeing what operations are entailed by the matrix multiplication.) So we have

$$\langle y|z \rangle = \langle v|U^\dagger U|w \rangle = \langle v|w \rangle, \tag{3.7}$$

in which we have used the definition of unitarity: $U^\dagger = U^{-1}$.

Applying this fact to Eq. (3.5) for two different states $|s_i\rangle$ and $|s_j\rangle$, we get

$$((\langle s_i| \otimes \langle 0|)(|s_j\rangle \otimes |0\rangle)) = ((\langle s_i| \otimes \langle s_i|)(|s_j\rangle \otimes |s_j\rangle)). \tag{3.8}$$

Here each side of the equation is the inner product of two four-dimensional vectors, each of which is a tensor product. Now, how does one take the inner product of two tensor product states? One of the problems at the end of this section asks you to show that the inner product is simply the ordinary product of the two separate inner products. That is, in general,

$$((\langle a| \otimes \langle b|)(|c\rangle \otimes |d\rangle)) = \langle a|c \rangle \langle b|d \rangle. \tag{3.9}$$

In the case of Eq. (3.8), this gives us

$$\langle s_i|s_j \rangle \langle 0|0 \rangle = \langle s_i|s_j \rangle \langle s_i|s_j \rangle. \tag{3.10}$$

The inner product $\langle 0|0 \rangle$ is equal to 1; so Eq. (3.10) tells us simply that the inner product $\langle s_i|s_j \rangle$ must be equal to its own square. That is, it must be 0 or 1. An inner product of 1 means that the two states are identical; an inner product of 0 means that they are orthogonal. Thus a quantum state chosen from a given set of possible states can be cloned perfectly only if the states in the set that are distinct are mutually orthogonal. But if a set of states is orthogonal, the states are related to each other in the same way that classical alternatives are related to each other. There is none of the ambiguity that typically characterizes the relation among quantum states. This is what we meant when we said that cloning is possible only if the information being cloned is essentially classical.

In the Bennett–Brassard scheme, the four states in question are not all orthogonal. This was necessary in order to keep Eve from knowing how to measure each photon, and we have just shown that it also foils any attempt she might make to copy a photon's state faithfully. Much work has been done on quantifying the *extent* to which one can copy quantum states. It turns out that one can achieve a kind of partial copying, and indeed, there is a partial copying strategy that works better for Eve than the measurement strategy that we discussed in the preceding section. This partial copying strategy is explored in the exercises.

Returning for a moment to the copying of classical information, we note that an ordinary fax machine makes a copy but achieves an additional feat: it produces the copy at some distance from the original. In the processing of quantum information it can likewise be advantageous to produce a replica at a distance. But because of the no-cloning theorem this can be done only if the original is destroyed in the process. It is as if the fax machine were required to eat the original document in order to produce a replica somewhere else. Such "faxing with destruction" is indeed possible in the quantum world, and it is the subject of the following section.

EXERCISES

Problem 1. Let $|a\rangle$ and $|c\rangle$ be two possible quantum states of object A, and let $|b\rangle$ and $|d\rangle$ be two possible states of object B. Starting from the definition of the tensor product, show that $((\langle a| \otimes \langle b|)(|c\rangle \otimes |d\rangle)) = \langle a|c\rangle \langle b|d\rangle$.

Problem 2. One of the best eavesdropping strategies against the Bennett–Brassard quantum key distribution scheme is the "partial cloning" strategy that we now describe.[8] As Alice's photon is on its way to Bob, Eve allows it to interact with her own photon, which she has prepared in the right-hand circular polarization state. The interaction, designed by Eve, is

---

[8] This strategy was described by Fuchs *et al.* (1997). (Those authors use a different but equivalent set of polarization states.)

given by the following unitary transformation U:

$$U = \frac{1}{4} \begin{pmatrix} 2+\sqrt{2} & -i\sqrt{2} & i\sqrt{2} & -2+\sqrt{2} \\ -i\sqrt{2} & 2+\sqrt{2} & 2-\sqrt{2} & -i\sqrt{2} \\ i\sqrt{2} & 2-\sqrt{2} & 2+\sqrt{2} & i\sqrt{2} \\ -2+\sqrt{2} & -i\sqrt{2} & i\sqrt{2} & 2+\sqrt{2} \end{pmatrix}$$

Here we are using our usual convention, in which

$$|\leftrightarrow\leftrightarrow\rangle = \begin{pmatrix} 1 \\ 0 \\ 0 \\ 0 \end{pmatrix}, \quad |\leftrightarrow\updownarrow\rangle = \begin{pmatrix} 0 \\ 1 \\ 0 \\ 0 \end{pmatrix}, \quad \text{etc.,}$$

and the first and second photons are Alice's photon and Eve's photon respectively. After the interaction, Eve allows Alice's photon to go on to Bob with no further disturbance (e.g., no measurement), and she holds on to her probe photon until she learns in which basis Alice encoded her bit. At that point, she measures her photon *in the correct basis*. The advantage of this scheme is that she does not have to guess the basis. However, her cloning is less than ideal for Eve in two ways: (i) her probe does not emerge as an exact copy of Alice's photon, and (ii) the partial cloning process has disturbed Alice's photon and this disturbance could later be detected when Alice and Bob check for errors. Still, this strategy turns out to be better than the "measure-resend" strategy that we considered in an earlier section.

(a) Suppose that Alice uses the vertical–horizontal basis, and specifically that she sends the state $|\updownarrow\rangle$. Compute the polarization state of Alice's photon and Eve's photon after Eve has applied her transformation. (Since Alice's photon travels on to Bob, we will henceforth refer to it as Bob's photon.)

(b) Assume that Bob and Eve both measure their respective photons in the correct basis, that is, the vertical–horizontal basis. (We assume this for Bob because otherwise the bit will be discarded. We assume it for Eve because she does not measure her photon until she has learned what basis Alice used.) What are the probabilities of the four possible outcomes?

(c) What is the probability that Bob gets the outcome $|\leftrightarrow\rangle$, that is, the probability of an error?

(d) How much Rényi information does Eve gain about Alice's bit? Compute the ratio, (Rényi information)/(probability of causing an error). Show that this is better than the optimal value that Eve can obtain using the intercept-resend strategy. (See Problems 1 and 2 of Section 3.1.)

(e) Show that for the partial-cloning strategy, the value of this ratio is the same for *each* of the four states that Alice might send.

3.3 Quantum Teleportation

Though the no-cloning theorem is crucial for preventing Eve from accessing the bits sent by Alice, it also causes problems for Alice and Bob. In real life each photon sent by Alice has to pass through some channel, typically an optical fiber, in which the photon has some probability of being degraded or destroyed. If photons could be cloned, one could place cloning devices at regular intervals along the fiber to make sure that for each photon Alice sends, there is a reasonable probability that Bob will receive a photon in the same state. But cloning is not possible, so this strategy is out of the question. Of course, even with a very long fiber, one might still hope to create a secret key out of the extremely small percentage of Alice's photons that actually make it to Bob. However, any photon detector that Bob might use in practice will occasionally produce false detections ("dark counts"); so at some point it becomes impossible for Bob to distinguish Alice's photons from the background noise. With the best optical fibers and photon detectors currently available, quantum key distribution by direct transmission of photons is limited to a few hundred kilometers in principle, and actual demonstrations of quantum key distribution have in fact rarely exceeded 100 kilometers.

One way around this problem is quantum teleportation.[9] Consider two locations A and B along the fiber. If it can be arranged that two particles, one at location A and the other at B, are *perfectly entangled* with each other, then, as we will see shortly, the state of a photon arriving at A

---

[9] Bennett et al. (1993). The theory and some early experimental implementations of quantum teleporation are reviewed in Bouwmeester, Ekert, and Zeilinger (2000). Two recent experiments realizing precisely the protocol that we describe here are reported in Riebe et al. (2004) and Barrett et al. (2004).

can be *teleported* directly to B, without having to traverse the intervening fiber. (The fiber will probably still be necessary to get the entangled pair to A and B in the first place.) By repeating this process over many successive lengths of fiber, it is possible in principle to convey each of Alice's key-distribution states over an arbitrary distance. Arranging for the sharing of a well-separated entangled pair is quite tricky and we discuss this issue toward the end of this section. For now we assume the existence of such a pair and show how teleportation can in principle be done. For this discussion we will not insist that the state to be teleported is one of the four Bennett–Brassard states; rather it is some generic state $|s\rangle$. In fact, to emphasize that teleportation is not just for photons, we will use the more generic labels $|0\rangle$ and $|1\rangle$ to represent an orthonormal basis for each particle, instead of the polarization labels $|\leftrightarrow\rangle$ and $|\updownarrow\rangle$. (For the sake of simplicity we do restrict our discussion to qubits, though the whole argument can be generalized to arbitrary quantum variables.)

To explain teleportation it is helpful to define the following four two-qubit states, each of which is maximally entangled:

$$
\begin{aligned}
|\Phi^+\rangle &= (1/\sqrt{2})(|00\rangle + |11\rangle) \\
|\Phi^-\rangle &= (1/\sqrt{2})(|00\rangle - |11\rangle) \\
|\Psi^+\rangle &= (1/\sqrt{2})(|01\rangle + |10\rangle) \\
|\Psi^-\rangle &= (1/\sqrt{2})(|01\rangle - |10\rangle)
\end{aligned}
\tag{3.11}
$$

Notice that these four states are mutually orthogonal, so that in principle one can make a measurement on the two qubits, whose outcomes correspond to these states. This particular measurement has a name: it is called the Bell measurement, after John S. Bell who considerably advanced our understanding of entanglement. We will make use of this measurement shortly.

Let us assume the existence of two particles, one at A and the other at B, in the entangled state $|\Phi^+\rangle$. In fact, let us call these particles "particle a" and "particle b," and let us imagine people at these locations called Anna and Boris who will carry out the teleportation procedure.[10] (These people are usually called Alice and Bob, but in this chapter Alice and Bob have already been assigned other roles.) At some moment another

---

[10] We have taken these names from Elliott et al. (2005).

particle, labeled c, arrives at location A; particle c is the one whose state is to be teleported to B. Particle c has been prepared (possibly by Alice) in some state $|s\rangle = \alpha|0\rangle + \beta|1\rangle$, which is unknown to both Anna and Boris.

Before outlining the teleportation process, let us note that the combined state of particles c, a, and b can be written as follows:

$$|s\rangle \otimes |\Phi^+\rangle = \frac{1}{\sqrt{2}}(\alpha|000\rangle + \alpha|011\rangle + \beta|100\rangle + \beta|111\rangle), \qquad (3.12)$$

where the order of the particles in each term is cab. As we will see shortly, in the first step of the teleportation protocol, Anna performs the Bell measurement on particles c and a, which are both at the same location. She necessarily leaves particle b unmeasured since she does not have access to particle b. This is an example of a measurement on a subsystem, as described in Section 2.4. Recall that to analyze such a measurement, it is helpful to reexpress the state of the whole system in terms of the outcome vectors of the measurement. A little algebra shows that when we do this for the state $|s\rangle \otimes |\Phi^+\rangle$, we get

$$\begin{aligned}
|s\rangle \otimes |\Phi^+\rangle = \frac{1}{2}[&|\Phi^+\rangle \otimes (\alpha|0\rangle + \beta|1\rangle) \\
+ &|\Phi^-\rangle \otimes (\alpha|0\rangle - \beta|1\rangle) \\
+ &|\Psi^+\rangle \otimes (\beta|0\rangle + \alpha|1\rangle) \\
+ &|\Psi^-\rangle \otimes (-\beta|0\rangle + \alpha|1\rangle)].
\end{aligned} \qquad (3.13)$$

Here we have expanded $|s\rangle \otimes |\Phi^+\rangle$ in terms of the Bell states of particles c and a, and we see that each of these states is correlated with a specific state of particle b. Notice that this is merely a mathematical reexpression of the original state; there is no physical change. In particular, even though each of the Bell states is entangled, particle c is still not entangled with particles a and b.

The teleportation procedure can now be explained quite simply:

1. Anna makes the Bell measurement on particles c and a. Once the outcome of this measurement is determined, the state of particle b is also determined in accordance with Eq. (3.13). For example, if Anna gets the outcome $|\Phi^+\rangle$, the state of particle b is $\alpha|0\rangle + \beta|1\rangle$. Here we are following the rule for measurements of subsystems as presented in Section 2.4.

2. Anna conveys to Boris, by a classical signal, the outcome of her measurement.

3. Boris performs a unitary transformation on particle b, the transformation depending on the result of Anna's measurement according to the following table. Here $I = \begin{pmatrix} 1 & 0 \\ 0 & 1 \end{pmatrix}$ is the identity operator, and Z and X are defined as $Z = \begin{pmatrix} 1 & 0 \\ 0 & -1 \end{pmatrix}$ and $X = \begin{pmatrix} 0 & 1 \\ 1 & 0 \end{pmatrix}$.

Outcome	Transformation
$\lvert \Phi^+ \rangle$	I
$\lvert \Phi^- \rangle$	Z
$\lvert \Psi^+ \rangle$	X
$\lvert \Psi^- \rangle$	XZ

Once Boris has performed the appropriate transformation, his particle is guaranteed to be in the state $\lvert s \rangle$, regardless of the outcome of Anna's measurement (as you will show in one of the exercises).

As an example of how this works, suppose that Anna gets the outcome $\lvert \Psi^+ \rangle$. Then, in accordance with Eq. (3.13), we can take Boris's particle to be in the state $\beta \lvert 0 \rangle + \alpha \lvert 1 \rangle$. This is not the desired state $\lvert s \rangle$, but when Boris applies the transformation X, it *becomes* $\lvert s \rangle$:

$$\begin{pmatrix} 0 & 1 \\ 1 & 0 \end{pmatrix} \begin{pmatrix} \beta \\ \alpha \end{pmatrix} = \begin{pmatrix} \alpha \\ \beta \end{pmatrix} = \lvert s \rangle.$$

Note that Boris does not need to know anything about α or β to carry out this transformation. The same transformation works for any values of these parameters.

There are a few things to notice about the teleportation process. First, the state $\lvert s \rangle$ has not been cloned. When Anna makes the joint measurement on her two particles, she "collapses" their state into one of the four states defined by the Bell measurement. Whereas originally particle c was in the state $\lvert s \rangle$, it is now one member of an entangled pair. The state $\lvert s \rangle$ no longer exists at Anna's end but has been teleported to Boris. This is the sense in which teleportation is a kind of "destructive faxing."

Second, the classical communication from Anna to Boris, in which she tells him the outcome of her measurement, in itself contains *no information* about the state $\lvert s \rangle$. Regardless of the values of α and β, the probabilities of the four outcomes of Anna's measurement are all equal to 1/4, as you will show in the exercises. Thus neither an eavesdropper nor

Boris himself learns anything about $|s\rangle$. Nevertheless, Boris ends up with a particle in the state $|s\rangle$ because he began with a half of an entangled pair shared with Anna. He knows that his particle b is in the correct state, but he does not know the state itself.

Finally, teleportation is not instantaneous. Until Boris receives the signal from Anna telling him the outcome of her measurement, he has nothing useful. As you showed in an exercise from Section 2.4, no measurement performed by Anna on her half of an entangled pair can have any effect that Boris can observe. Thus teleportation is no faster than any other form of communication. What is special about teleportation is that it conveys a quantum state directly from one place to another, avoiding any sources of noise in the intervening space.

Of course this is all assuming that Anna and Boris started with two perfectly entangled particles, one at location A and one at B, which might be miles away. For the purpose of quantum key distribution, one might reasonably ask how a pair of photons with this property might be generated if A and B are connected only by an imperfect optical fiber. If an entangled pair is created at A and one member of the pair is sent to B over the fiber, the pair will not be perfectly entangled by the time this photon arrives. Researchers have studied this problem theoretically and have found that it is in fact possible in principle to create well-separated entangled pairs over a noisy fiber. The key idea, called "entanglement purification," is based on the following scenario. Anna generates many entangled pairs of photons at her end and sends one member of each pair to Boris via the imperfect channel. (Alternatively, a source halfway between Anna and Boris could generate the pairs and send the two photons in each pair to the two parties.) The result is that Anna and Boris share many imperfectly entangled pairs. Now, by a series of measurements made locally by Anna and Boris, coupled with classical communication between them, Anna and Boris can sacrifice some fraction of their imperfect pairs and leave the remaining pairs more entangled than they were.[11] We will not go into the details here but the idea is explored in the exercises. In principle, as long as the channel is not too noisy, Anna and Boris can achieve arbitrarily perfect entanglement while sacrificing a fixed fraction of their pairs, a fraction that depends on the noisiness of the channel.

---

[11] Bennett et al. (1996a, 1996b), Deutsch et al. (1996).

An optical fiber running from New York to Los Angeles would disturb the photons so much that it would be impossible to purify any entanglement after sending one photon from each of many entangled pairs over the entire length of the fiber. However, one can imagine dividing the fiber into sections of, say, 10 kilometers each, and generating many entangled pairs shared between the two ends of each section. (There could be computers playing the roles of Anna and Boris at the ends of each section.) Once these pairs have been prepared, the Bennett–Brassard key distribution scheme can be carried out over an arbitrarily long distance. For each photon generated by Alice in New York, its state can be teleported over each section in turn, until it finally reaches Bob in Los Angeles.[12]

Alternatively, once there is a pure entangled pair spanning each section, these pairs can in principle be combined, by teleportation, to create an entangled pair shared between Alice and Bob.[13] This pair can then be used *directly* to create a shared secret bit: Alice and Bob simply measure the pair in the same basis – they can use public communication to decide on this basis – and use the result of the measurement as their shared bit. If their photons really were perfectly entangled, then the bit is secret because no other party could have been entangled with their two photons. This entanglement-based method of generating a shared secret key, which has also served as a basis for some proofs of security, goes back to a 1991 paper by Artur Ekert.[14]

Although teleportation itself has been successfully demonstrated in a number of experiments, at present we do not have the technology to do entanglement purification on a large scale, and quantum key distribution is therefore limited to modest distances. Purifying entanglement requires holding on to quantum states for some time and protecting them from degradation. This is a scientific and technological challenge on which progress is constantly being made. Presumably it is only a matter of time before quantum key distribution is possible over arbitrary distances.

---

[12] Alternatively, rather than doing entanglement purification over each 10-km section separately, one can achieve greater efficiency with a nested scheme as described in Briegel et al. (1998).

[13] The fact that entanglement can be created between particles that have never directly interacted was pointed out by Yurke and Stoler (1993).

[14] Ekert (1991).

EXERCISES

Problem 1. Verify that the teleportation scheme as described in this section does indeed leave Boris with the desired state $|s\rangle$ regardless of the outcome of Anna's measurement.

Problem 2. Verify that when Anna performs the Bell measurement on particles c and a, each of the four possible outcomes has probability $1/4$. (Here you will have to use the rule for measurements of subsystems from Section 2.4.)

Problem 3. Suppose that instead of starting with particles b and c in the state $|\Phi^+\rangle$, Anna and Boris start with a and b in the state $|\Psi^-\rangle$. How should the table be changed that gives Boris's unitary transformation for each outcome of Anna's measurement? (Anna still performs the standard Bell measurement on particles c and a.)

Problem 4. This problem extends the teleportation scheme to states belonging to a three-dimensional state space. Let $\{|0\rangle, |1\rangle, |2\rangle\}$ be an orthonormal basis for this space, and let $|s\rangle = \alpha|0\rangle + \beta|1\rangle + \gamma|2\rangle$ be the state that is to be teleported.

(a) Consider the following states $|\Phi^{jk}\rangle$, $j, k = 0, 1, 2$, of a *pair* of particles each having a three-dimensional state space:

$$|\Phi^{jk}\rangle = \frac{1}{\sqrt{3}} \sum_{l=0}^{2} e^{2\pi i l k/3} |l, l + j \,(\mathrm{mod}\ 3)\rangle.$$

Show that these nine states form an orthonormal basis for the state space of such a pair. The measurement whose outcome vectors are $|\Phi^{jk}\rangle$ can be called a generalized Bell measurement.

(b) We assume three particles, a, b, and c, with the same roles as before, but now each particle has a three-dimensional state space. Suppose that particles a and b start out in the entangled state $|\Phi^{00}\rangle$ and particle c starts in the state $|s\rangle$. Anna performs the above generalized Bell measurement on particles c and a. For each of the nine possible outcomes of Anna's measurement, find the unitary transformation $U^{(ij)}$ that Boris should perform in order to bring particle b to the desired state $|s\rangle$.

Problem 5. This problem should give you an indication of how it is possible to purify entanglement that has been corrupted by noise. Suppose that at one end of an optical fiber, Anna creates two perfectly entangled qubits in the state $|\Phi^+\rangle = (1/\sqrt{2})(|00\rangle + |11\rangle)$. She sends the second member of each pair through the fiber to Boris. With probability p, the fiber leaves the state of any particle unchanged, but with probability $q = 1 - p$ it performs on the particle the transformation $X = \left(\begin{smallmatrix} 0 & 1 \\ 1 & 0 \end{smallmatrix}\right)$. That is, with probability q the fiber interchanges $|0\rangle$ and $|1\rangle$. (This is simpler than what an actual fiber would do, but it will serve to illustrate the essential idea.) Thus at the end of this process Anna and Boris share two pairs in one of the following four states:

$$
\begin{array}{ll}
|\Phi^+\rangle_{A_1 B_1} \otimes |\,\Phi^+\rangle_{A_2 B_2}, & \text{probability } p^2 \\
|\Phi^+\rangle_{A_1 B_1} \otimes |\,\Psi^+\rangle_{A_2 B_2}, & \text{probability } pq \qquad (3.14) \\
|\Psi^+\rangle_{A_1 B_1} \otimes |\,\Phi^+\rangle_{A_2 B_2}, & \text{probability } pq \\
|\Psi^+\rangle_{A_1 B_1} \otimes |\,\Psi^+\rangle_{A_2 B_2}, & \text{probability } q^2
\end{array}
$$

Here the subscripts indicate the particles involved in each state.

(a) Write out each of these four states explicitly in terms of vectors such as $|0_{A_1} 0_{A_2} 0_{B_1} 0_{B_2}\rangle$, in which the states of Anna's two particles appear first. (This ordering will be very convenient for the next steps.)

(b) Both Anna and Boris perform the following unitary transformation on their two particles:

$$
U = \begin{pmatrix} 1 & 0 & 0 & 0 \\ 0 & 1 & 0 & 0 \\ 0 & 0 & 0 & 1 \\ 0 & 0 & 1 & 0 \end{pmatrix},
$$

where the ordering of the basis vectors is $(|00\rangle, |01\rangle, |10\rangle, |11\rangle)$. Write out the four possible states (with their probabilities) as modified by this transformation.

(c) Anna and Boris now both measure their second qubits in the standard basis $\{|0\rangle, |1\rangle\}$; that is, Anna measures particle A_2 and Boris measures B_2. They discard the measured qubits but compare the results of their measurements. If their results are the same, they keep their first pair (which has not been measured). If their results differ, they discard their first pair. Find the probability that, *if* they keep their first pair, it is in the original state $|\Phi^+\rangle$.

(d) Show that as long as p is greater than 1/2, the probability that you found in part (c) is greater than p. That is, the pair is now more likely to be in the uncorrupted state $|\Phi^+\rangle$. By repeating this procedure many times – and using up many pairs of qubits – one can distill a much smaller number of qubits for which the probability of the state $|\Phi^+\rangle$ is arbitrarily close to one. Moreover, one can design an extension of this procedure that will work under a more general class of errors. (But designing such an extension is not part of this problem!)

4 An Introduction to Error-Correcting Codes

In the preceding chapter we mentioned the inevitable errors that occur when one tries to send quantum signals over, say, an optical fiber, even when there is no eavesdropper. But errors in transmission are not a problem just for quantum cryptography. For this entire chapter we forget about sending *quantum* information and instead focus on simply transmitting ordinary data faithfully over some kind of channel. Moreover, we assume that the data either is not sensitive or has already been encrypted. Unfortunately, many methods for transmitting data are susceptible to outside influences that can cause errors. How do we protect information from these errors? Error-correcting codes provide a mathematical method of not only detecting these errors, but also correcting them. Nowadays error-correcting codes are ubiquitous; they are used, for example, in cell-phone transmissions and satellite links, in the representation of music on a compact disk, and even in the bar codes in grocery stores.

The story of modern error-correcting codes began with Claude Shannon's famous paper "A Mathematical Theory of Communication,[1]" which was published in 1948. Shannon worked for Bell Labs where he specialized in finding solutions to problems that arose in telephone communication. Quite naturally, he started considering ways to correct errors that occurred when information was transmitted over phone lines. Richard Hamming, who also worked at Bell Labs on this problem, published a groundbreaking paper in 1950 on the subject.[2] Hamming continued his

---

[1] Shannon (1948).
[2] Hamming (1950).

work and today is known as one of the greatest contributers to coding theory. In fact, there is a famous class of error-correcting codes called Hamming codes that we introduce in Section 4.8. This chapter is intended to be a basic introduction to techniques used for error correction.[3] We encourage those readers interested in recent breakthroughs in the theory of error correction to consult sources on such codes as turbo codes[4] and low-density parity check codes.[5] Researchers have shown that using these, one can construct highly efficient codes.[6] These results, however, are beyond the scope of this book. We now begin with an elementary discussion on the theory of error correction.

4.1 A Few Binary Examples

To make things simple, suppose we start with a message expressed in an alphabet consisting of only eight letters: a, b, c, d, e, f, g, h. In deciding how to protect our transmission from noise, it is helpful to assume that the transmission itself will be binary; that is, it will consist of a string of zeros and ones. The error correction in digital communication is indeed usually based on protocols whose output is binary. So we will think about reasonable ways to encode our eight letters using strings of zeros and ones. Though it is quite possible, and sometimes very useful, to use strings of different lengths to encode different letters, for simplicity we assume here that every letter is encoded in a string of the same length. As always, our sender will be Alice and the receiver will be Bob.

Since we have eight letters that we want to code with blocks of zeros and ones, the shortest block size we can use is 3. There are exactly eight strings of zeros and ones of length 3, namely:

$$000 \quad 001 \quad 010 \quad 011 \quad 100 \quad 101 \quad 110 \quad 111$$

---

[3] For a more in-depth introduction see Pless (1998).
[4] Berrou, Glaneux, and Thitimijashima (1993).
[5] Gallager (1963) and Mackay and Neal (1996).
[6] Specifically, they come very close to reaching Shannon's limit, an efficiency theorem proved in Shannan (1948).

So we first try making the following assignments assuming that both Alice and Bob agree on this way to code the eight letters of the alphabet:

Example 4.1.1

$$a \longrightarrow 000$$
$$b \longrightarrow 001$$
$$c \longrightarrow 010$$
$$d \longrightarrow 011$$
$$e \longrightarrow 100$$
$$f \longrightarrow 101$$
$$g \longrightarrow 110$$
$$h \longrightarrow 111$$

If no errors occur, this is a perfectly good way to code the eight letters. For example, if Alice wants to send the message *bad* to Bob, she sends the string 001000011. If no errors occur, then Bob receives the string 001000011. He then breaks it up into blocks of three: 001, 000, and 011. He knows 001 represents the letter b, 000 represents a, and 011 represents d and so he decodes the message correctly as *bad*.

But what happens if an error occurs? We note here that the only type of errors we will consider is when one or more of the numbers in the string Bob receives is different than the corresponding entry in the string Alice sent. We will not consider, for example, when one of the numbers is simply dropped. Suppose Alice sends the same string as before – 001000011 – but Bob receives 101000011. Notice that there is only one error – the first zero has been erroneously received as a one – and everything else in the string has been received correctly. When Bob decodes the string, he gets $101 \longrightarrow f, 000 \longrightarrow a, 011 \longrightarrow d$. So he thinks the message that Alice sent him was *fad* – a perfectly good English word. Not only does he get the wrong message, but he is not even aware that an error has occurred. In other words, he has not even *detected* the error.

What kind of scheme can Bob and Alice use to be able to at least *detect* an error? We first try adjusting the previous example by repeating each length-three string. In other words, we consider the following assignments.

Example 4.1.2

$$a \longrightarrow 000000$$
$$b \longrightarrow 001001$$
$$c \longrightarrow 010010$$
$$d \longrightarrow 011011$$
$$e \longrightarrow 100100$$
$$f \longrightarrow 101101$$
$$g \longrightarrow 110110$$
$$h \longrightarrow 111111$$

If the string Bob receives is different than the string Alice sent in exactly one position, then Bob will be able to tell that an error occurred in transmission. For example, if Alice sends the word *bad*, she transmits the string 001001000000011011. Suppose that the first number in the string is received incorrectly, so that Bob receives 101001000000011011. He breaks up the message into blocks of six: 101001, 000000, and 011011. Now, he knows that 000000 represents *a* and 011011 represents *d*. But the string 101001 was not assigned to any letter, so an error must have occurred. Of course, Bob cannot tell if the intended message was *bad* or *fad*, but at least he knows there was an error and he can ask Alice to resend the message.

You might notice that our new assignments are not very efficient. In fact, compared to Example 4.1.1 we have doubled the number of digits it takes to send a message. Is there a better way? Can we come up with a way to detect a single error, but use strings of length less than 6? It turns out that, in fact, we can. Again, suppose we have an alphabet of eight letters. Consider the following assignment of strings of length 4 to each letter.

Example 4.1.3

$$a \longrightarrow 0000$$
$$b \longrightarrow 0011$$
$$c \longrightarrow 0101$$
$$d \longrightarrow 0110$$
$$e \longrightarrow 1001$$
$$f \longrightarrow 1010$$
$$g \longrightarrow 1100$$
$$h \longrightarrow 1111$$

Note that the first three digits of each string are exactly the same as we used in Example 4.1.1. To find the last digit, we simply make sure that there are an even number of ones in each string of four digits. Now when Alice sends Bob a message, there are an even number of ones in each block of four. If exactly one error occurs, then one of the blocks of four that Bob receives will have an odd number of ones, so he can tell that there has been a transmission error. Thus this method will detect one error and is more efficient than Example 4.1.2. Note, though, that in the above example, if exactly two errors occur, Bob will not be able to detect that errors have occurred during transmission. For example, if Alice sends the letter *c* to Bob, she transmits the string 0101. Suppose the first two digits are exchanged, so that two errors have occurred. Then Bob receives 1001 and believes that Alice has sent him the letter *e*. He has no way of detecting that there has been an error. Example 4.1.3 is called the binary parity check code of length 4 and can be generalized. We will discuss it in more detail in the next section.

Now we get back to the question at hand. We know how to detect an error, but how do we correct an error? We could take Example 4.1.1 and repeat the message three times instead of two. So the assignments to the letters would be:

Example 4.1.4

$$a \longrightarrow 000000000$$
$$b \longrightarrow 001001001$$
$$c \longrightarrow 010010010$$
$$d \longrightarrow 011011011$$
$$e \longrightarrow 100100100$$
$$f \longrightarrow 101101101$$
$$g \longrightarrow 110110110$$
$$h \longrightarrow 111111111$$

Admittedly, a string of nine digits to represent each letter is excessive, but let us see if we can use this scheme to correct a single error. Suppose Alice sends the message *bad* to Bob. In that case she transmits the string

$$001001001000000000011011011.$$

What happens if the string Bob receives has an error in the first position? He then receives

$$101001001000000000011011011.$$

He breaks up this string into blocks of nine, namely, 101001001, 000000000, 011011011, and knows that 000000000 represents *a* and 011011011 represents *d*. But 101001001 does not represent any letter. He can use the "best two out of three" approach to correct the error. All the letters are represented by a string of three that is repeated three times. So Bob takes the string 101001001, breaks it into the three strings 101, 001, and 001. Since two out of the three of these agree, he declares that the error occurred in the first string of three and that the first string should have been 001. In this way, he can accurately correct any single error. Note that if two errors occur, this scheme may fail. For example, if Bob receives

$$101101001000000000011011011$$

so that errors have occurred in the first and fourth positions, then when he looks at the first string of nine, 101101001, and breaks it up into three strings of three 101, 101, 001, he believes that the 001 should have been 101 and decodes the message incorrectly as *fad*.

So Example 4.1.4 will correct one error, but we used blocks of length 9 to represent each letter. Our goal is to find a more efficient way. In general, our goal is to find a way to transmit information in a reasonably efficient way so that we can also correct a reasonable number of errors.

EXERCISES

Problem 1. Use Example 4.1.2 to encode the message *beef*.

Problem 2. Suppose Alice and Bob agree to use Example 4.1.2 to send messages. Bob receives the message

$$010110111111100100101101$$

from Alice. What is his best guess as to the message that Alice sent?

Problem 3. Suppose Alice and Bob agree to use Example 4.1.3 to send messages. Bob receives the message

$$1111000100000110000101011111001$$

from Alice. What is his best guess as to the message that Alice sent?

Problem 4. Find a way to encode the letters a, b, c, d, e, f, g, h using blocks of zeros and ones of length 6 so that if two or fewer errors occur in a block, Bob will be able to detect that errors have occurred but not necessarily be able to correct them.

Problem 5. Find a way to encode the letters a, b, c, d, e, f, g, h using blocks of zeros and ones of length 6 so that if one error occurs in a block, Bob will be able to correct the error. To test your answer, first go to the Construct-A-Code applet on the website www.williams.edu/crypto/. Then, in the boxes below the blocks of length 3, enter the blocks of length 6 you used for your eight letters. Now, set the Noise Control to Specify Error Rate Per Block and set it at one or fewer flips per 6 bits. Type in a message in the Transmitted Text Box and hit the Simulate Message Transmission several times. Does your message transmit correctly every time? If so, there is a good chance your answer is a correct one. Play around with other examples on the applet to try and decide what criterion must hold so that the errors in the transmitted messages are corrected accurately.

Problem 6. Prove that there is no way to encode the letters $a, b, c, d,$ e, f, g, h using blocks of zeros and ones of length 5 so that Bob will be able to correct a single error.

4.2   Preliminaries and More Examples

We first define several mathematical tools we will need for error correction.

Definition. Let A be any set and $n \geq 1$ an integer. We define

$$A^n = \{(a_1, a_2, \ldots, a_n) | a_i \in A\}.$$

Definition. Let A be a finite set and $n \geq 1$ an integer. A code C of length n is any subset of A^n. In this setting, we call A^n the *codespace* and the elements of A^n are called *words*. We call the elements of the code C *codewords*.

Suppose Alice wants to send Bob a message. It will be a string of codewords as defined above with each codeword representing a piece of information that is not necessarily an actual English word. For example, a codeword as defined above may represent a letter in the English language, or it may represent an element of A^m where m is less than n. In this setting, n is the length of each codeword and A is the set of characters Alice has to choose from for each position of the codeword. The codespace A^n is all the words Bob could possibly receive, taking into account that errors might occur. The elements of our code C are the codewords themselves; that is, C is the set of words that Alice could send. Consider Example 4.1.1 from Section 4.1. First, note that each word represents a letter of our alphabet. For this example, $A = \{0, 1\}$ because for each position, Alice must choose either a 0 or a 1 to send. And $n = 3$ because that is the length of each word we used to represent a letter. So we have that

$$A^n = \{000, 001, 010, 011, 100, 101, 110, 111\}$$

and

$$C = \{000, 001, 010, 011, 100, 101, 110, 111\}.$$

Note that in this case, $C = A^n$ and this is why Bob cannot detect errors using this scheme. All the possible words received are codewords, that is, words that Alice might have actually sent, and so he cannot tell if an error occurred.

On the other hand, in Example 4.1.3 from Section 4.1, we have $A = \{0, 1\}$, $n = 4$,

$$A^n = \{0000, 0001, 0010, 0011, 0100, 0101, 0110, 1000,$$
$$1000, 1001, 1010, 1011, 1100, 1101, 1110, 1111\}$$

and

$$C = \{0000, 0011, 0101, 0110, 1001, 1010, 1100, 1111\}.$$

In this example, C is not equal to A^n. In other words, the set of words that Bob could possibly receive is larger than the set of words Alice could send. So Bob could receive a word that Alice could not possibly have sent. For example, Bob could receive the word 0001, but since that is not an element of C, he knows it is not the word that Alice intended to send him and so an error must have occurred.

Notice that in all our examples so far we have had $A = \{0, 1\}$. Since this is the simplest possible alphabet and since many practical cases can be expressed in such terms, we will use this A for most of our examples. However, sometimes it is useful to use a different set for A. So we will include several examples of those codes as well.

Definition. If $A = \{0, 1\}$ and C is a code of length n, we say C is a binary code of length n.

Example: The Binary Repetition Code of Length n

Let n be any integer greater than or equal to 1. A^n is the set of all possible strings of zeros and ones of length n. Note that A^n contains 2^n elements. We define the binary repetition code of length n – call it C – to be the set containing only two elements: the word consisting of all zeros and the word consisting of all ones. For example, if $n = 5$, then

$$A^n = \{00000, 00001, 00010, 00011, 00100, 00101, 00110, 00111,$$
$$01000, 01001, 01010, 01011, 01100, 01101, 01110, 01111,$$
$$10000, 10001, 10010, 10011, 10100, 10101, 10110, 10111,$$
$$11000, 11001, 11010, 11011, 11100, 11101, 11110, 11111\}$$

and

$$C = \{00000, 11111\}.$$

The advantage to this code is that it can correct two errors accurately. Bob just takes the best three out of five. For example, suppose Alice sends 11111 to Bob and he receives the word 01011. Then he knows an error has occurred because the only two words Alice can send are 00000 and 11111. Bob notes that since 01011 has three ones and two zeros, Alice probably meant to send 11111. This method of error correction will work as long as no more than two errors occur. The disadvantage to this method is that it severely limits the amount of information that Alice can send. Since there are two codewords, she can only code two alternative pieces of information. Bob and Alice might use this code when they do not need to send much information, but when correcting errors is important. For example, suppose Alice wanted to send a message to Bob telling him to buy or sell a certain stock. They might use 00000 to represent "buy" and 11111 for "sell." Correcting errors is important (Bob stands to lose a lot of money if he "buys" when he should "sell"), and there are only two possible messages that Alice needs to be able to send to Bob. So they might choose to use a binary repetition code.

Example: The Binary Parity Check Code of Length n

For this code, we again let n be any integer greater than or equal to 1. A^n is the set of all possible strings of zeros and ones of length n. We define the binary parity check code of length n to be the set of elements of A^n with an even number of ones. For example, if $n = 5$, then

$$
\begin{aligned}
A^n = \{ &00000, 00001, 00010, 00011, 00100, 00101, 00110, 00111, \\
&01000, 01001, 01010, 01011, 01100, 01101, 01110, 01111, \\
&10000, 10001, 10010, 10011, 10100, 10101, 10110, 10111, \\
&11000, 11001, 11010, 11011, 11100, 11101, 11110, 11111\}
\end{aligned}
$$

and

$$
\begin{aligned}
C = \{ &00000, 00011, 00101, 00110, 01001, 01010, 01100, 01111, \\
&10001, 10010, 10100, 10111, 11000, 11011, 11101, 11110\}
\end{aligned}
$$

The binary parity check code will detect an error but not correct it. Example 4.1.3 in the previous section is the binary parity check code of length 4. The advantage of the binary parity check code is that Alice can code a lot of information. The disadvantage is that errors cannot be corrected.

Example: A Binary [7,4] Hamming Code

For this code, we let $n = 7$ and $A = \{0, 1\}$. Then $A^n = A^7$ is the set of all possible strings of length 7 consisting of zeros and ones. There are

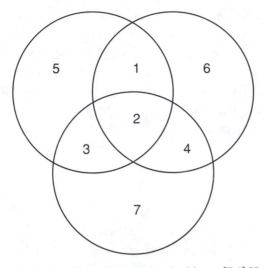

Figure 4.1: Venn diagram for the binary [7,4] Hamming code.

$2^7 = 128$ of them. We define a binary [7,4] Hamming code by

$$C = \{0000000, 0001011, 0010101, 0011110, 0100111, 0101100,$$
$$0110010, 0111001, 1000110, 1001101, 1010011, 1011000,$$
$$1100001, 1101010, 1110100, 1111111\}.$$

At first glance, it is not apparent how these codewords were chosen. But notice that if we look at the first four positions of all the codewords, all 16 possible combinations of zeros and ones occur. So to get the 16 codewords, we first just list those strings of length 4. Then, to get the last three positions, we use the following three rules:

The sum of the numbers in the first, second, third, and fifth positions must be even.

The sum of the numbers in the first, second, fourth, and sixth positions must be even.

The sum of the numbers in the second, third, fourth, and seventh positions must be even.

Alternatively, we could view this code using the Venn diagram of Fig. 4.1. We put the first four digits of the codeword in the areas of the diagram labeled 1, 2, 3, and 4 respectively. Then we must put either a zero or a one in the area labeled 5. We choose this bit by making sure that the sum of the digits in the upper left circle is even. Similarly, we put either a zero or a one in the area labeled 6 and 7, making sure that their respective circles have an even sum. It turns out that this code will correct one error. We will prove this in the next section.

We end this section with an example where $A = \{0, 1, 2\}$. Alice and Bob might choose this A if Alice has three choices of input for each position instead of two.

Example: A Ternary Code

Let $n = 3$ and $A = \{0, 1, 2\}$. Then,

$$
\begin{aligned}
A^n = \{&(000), (001), (002), (010), (011), (012), (020), (021), (022), \\
        &(100), (101), (102), (110), (111), (112), (120), (121), (122), \\
        &(200), (201), (202), (210), (211), (212), (220), (221), (222)\}.
\end{aligned}
$$

We define

$$C = \{(000), (110), (001), (111), (220), (002), (222), (221), (112)\}.$$

Note that C can be described as the set

$$\{\alpha_1(110) + \alpha_2(001) | \alpha_1, \alpha_2 \in \mathbb{Z}_3\}$$

where all arithmetic is done component-wise and modulo 3. For example, if $\alpha_1 = 1$ and $\alpha_2 = 2$, then $\alpha_1(110) + \alpha_2(001) = 1(110) + 2(001) = (110) + (002) = (112) \in C$.

EXERCISES

Problem 1. Let n and r be positive integers. If $A = \mathbb{Z}_r$, how many elements does A^n have? Explain your answer.

Problem 2. How many errors will the binary repetition code of length 7 correct? Explain.

Problem 3. Explain why the binary parity check code of length n will not detect two errors.

Problem 4. Let $A = \mathbb{Z}_5$ and $n = 3$. Let

$$C = \{\alpha_1(100) + \alpha_2(011) | \alpha_1, \alpha_2 \in \mathbb{Z}_5\}$$

where all arithmetic is done component-wise and modulo 5. Write down the elements of C.

Problem 5. Let n and r be positive integers. Let $A = \mathbb{Z}_r$ and $\vec{x}_i \in \mathbb{Z}_r^n$ be the element with a one in the ith position and zeros in all other positions. Let Ω be a nonempty subset of $\{1, 2, \ldots, n\}$. Describe the set

$$C = \left\{ \sum_{j \in \Omega} \alpha_j \vec{x}_j \,|\, \alpha_j \in \mathbb{Z}_r \right\}$$

where all arithmetic is done component-wise and modulo r. How many elements does C contain?

Problem 6. Let n and r be positive integers. Let $A = \mathbb{Z}_r$ and $\vec{x}_i \in \mathbb{Z}_r^n$ for $i = 1, 2, \ldots, k$ be a set of k linearly independent vectors. For a definition of linearly independent, see Section 4.5. Let

$$C = \left\{ \sum_{i=1}^{k} \alpha_i \vec{x}_i \,|\, \alpha_i \in \mathbb{Z}_r \right\}$$

where all arithmetic is done component-wise and modulo r. How many elements does C contain? How does your answer change if $\vec{x}_1, \vec{x}_2, \ldots, \vec{x}_k$ are not linearly independent? Explain.

4.3 Hamming Distance

When Bob receives a word from Alice and wants to know if an error has occurred, he simply looks at the list of codewords and determines whether or not the word he received is on that list. If so, he assumes no error has occurred. If not, then an error has occurred. So the method for detecting errors is clear. Stated in mathematical terms, suppose Alice and Bob have agreed on a code to use as described in Section 4.2. When Bob receives the word $\vec{r}$, he checks to see if $\vec{r}$ is an element of C. If so, he assumes no error has occurred. If not, then he assumes at least one error occurred in the transmission of the word Alice sent.

On the other hand, when Bob receives a word from Alice and wants to correct the possible errors, he picks the codeword that is "closest" to his received word. In other words, he wants to find the codeword whose entries agree with his received word in as many places as possible. In this section, we use mathematical terms to explain this more precisely. We also prove useful theorems that tell us how many errors a code will detect and how many it will correct.

Definition. Let $\vec{x}, \vec{y} \in A^n$. We define the Hamming distance between $\vec{x}$ and $\vec{y}$, denoted $d_H(\vec{x}, \vec{y})$, to be the number of places where $\vec{x}$ and $\vec{y}$ are different.

Examples:
1. Let $n = 6$, $A = \{0, 1\}$, $\vec{x} = (110100)$, and $\vec{y} = (101010)$. Then $d_H(\vec{x}, \vec{y}) = 4$ since these two words are different in four positions, namely, the second, third, fourth, and fifth ones.
2. Let $n = 5$, $A = \{0, 1, 2, 3, 4\}$, $\vec{x} = (34201)$, and $\vec{y} = (30210)$. Then $d_H(\vec{x}, \vec{y}) = 3$ since these two words are different in three positions, namely, the second, fourth, and fifth ones.

The Hamming distance satisfies the following desirable properties for all $\vec{x}, \vec{y}$, and $\vec{z}$ in A^n. The proof of this will be left as an exercise.

(*i*) $d_H(\vec{x}, \vec{y}) \geq 0$
(*ii*) $d_H(\vec{x}, \vec{y}) = 0$ if and only if $\vec{x} = \vec{y}$
(*iii*) $d_H(\vec{x}, \vec{y}) = d_H(\vec{y}, \vec{x})$
(*iv*) $d_H(\vec{x}, \vec{y}) \leq d_H(\vec{x}, \vec{z}) + d_H(\vec{z}, \vec{y})$

This list may look familiar. These are exactly the properties used to define a metric. So in fact, d_H is a metric on A^n. Property (*iv*) is known as the triangle inequality.

Using the concept of Hamming distance, we can mathematically describe the method we will use for error correction. When a word $\vec{r}$ is received, we decode it by finding a codeword $\vec{x}$ such that $d_H(\vec{r}, \vec{x})$ is the smallest possible. This method is called *minimum distance decoding*. Notice that given a received word $\vec{r}$, there may be more than one valid codeword whose Hamming distance to $\vec{r}$ is the smallest possible. In that case we cannot correct the word with confidence, but we could guess by choosing one of the closest codewords.

Of course Alice and Bob want to find "good" codes. But what do they mean by "good"? They would like to have a reasonably large set of codewords, so that they can code a lot of information, and they would like to detect and correct as many errors as possible. Given a code C, how can we determine how many errors it will detect and how many errors will it correct? Imagine a code C where all the codewords are a distance of at least 3 from each other using the Hamming distance. Suppose Alice sends Bob a word and we know that no more than one error can occur. Then, the Hamming distance between the received word $\vec{r}$ and the intended message $\vec{x}$ is 1 or 0. Is it possible that there could be another codeword that is a distance 1 or less from $\vec{r}$? Suppose so. Then there is a $\vec{y} \in C$ with $\vec{y} \neq \vec{x}$ satisfying $d_H(\vec{r}, \vec{y}) \leq 1$. By the triangle inequality, we have $d_H(\vec{x}, \vec{y}) \leq d_H(\vec{x}, \vec{r}) + d_H(\vec{r}, \vec{y}) \leq 2$. So there are two codewords that are a distance less than 3 from each other. But this contradicts our assumption that all codewords are a distance at least 3 from each other. It follows that $\vec{x}$ is the *only* closest codeword to $\vec{r}$, so that Bob can confidently decode $\vec{r}$ as $\vec{x}$. As long as no more than one error occurs, Bob will correct all errors accurately. Notice that our assumption that all codewords were a distance of at least 3 apart was quite important in our argument. Putting this concept into mathematical terms, we get the following definition.

Definition. Let $C \subseteq A^n$ be a code. We define the *minimum distance* of the code to be

$$\min_{\vec{x}, \vec{y} \in C, \vec{x} \neq \vec{y}} d_H(\vec{x}, \vec{y}).$$

We denote the minimum distance of a code by $d_{\min}(C)$ or $d(C)$, or sometimes just d.

To find the minimum distance of a code, we simply compute the Hamming distance between all possible pairs of distinct codewords. The smallest number we get is the minimum distance of the code.

Examples:
1. Let C be the binary repetition code of length 4. Then we have that $C = \{(0000), (1111)\}$. So the minimum distance of C is 4. In fact, the minimum distance of the binary repetition code of length n is n.
2. Let C be the binary parity check code of length 5. We listed the elements of C in Section 4.2. You can verify that the minimum distance

of C is 2. In fact, the minimum distance of the binary parity check code of length n is 2.

3. Let C be the binary [7,4] Hamming code that we defined in Section 4.2. The minimum distance of C in that case is 3.

4. Let C be the ternary code we defined in Section 4.2. The minimum distance of C in that case is 1.

We are now in a position to prove how many errors a code C will detect and how many errors it will correct. As you might guess from our above discussion, the answer to these questions involves the minimum distance of the code.

We first discuss precisely what we mean by a code detecting a certain number of errors. Recall our method for detecting errors. When Bob receives a word $\vec{r}$ from Alice, he checks to see if $\vec{r}$ is an element of C. If so, he assumes no error has occurred. If not, then he assumes an error occurred in the transmission of the word Alice sent. We say that a code C detects e errors if whenever e or fewer errors occur during transmission, no matter what codeword Alice sent or where the errors occur, Bob is guaranteed to accurately tell whether or not an error has occurred.

Now, recall our method for correcting errors. When a word $\vec{r}$ is received, Bob decodes it by finding a codeword $\vec{x}$ such that $d_H(\vec{r}, \vec{x})$ is the smallest possible. We say that a code C corrects e errors if whenever e or fewer errors occur during transmission, no matter what codeword Alice sent or where the errors occur Bob is guaranteed to accurately correct the errors. Remember that when Bob receives $\vec{r}$, for him to accurately correct errors it must be that the codeword Alice sent is the *unique* closest codeword to $\vec{r}$.

We now prove that if we know the minimum distance of a code, then we know how many errors it will detect and how many errors it will correct.

Theorem 4.3.1. Let $C \subseteq A^n$ be a code with minimum distance d. Then C detects $d - 1$ errors.

Proof. Suppose $\vec{c} \in C$ is the codeword that Alice sends to Bob. We assume that no more than $d - 1$ errors occur and we will show that Bob is guaranteed to accurately tell whether or not an error occurred. Let $\vec{r} \in A^n$ be the word that Bob receives. Now, suppose that no errors occurred. Then,

$\vec{r} = \vec{c} \in C$ and so Bob correctly assumes that no error has occurred. On the other hand, suppose that there were some errors in the transmission, but remember, no more than $d - 1$. Then, $1 \leq d_{\mathrm{H}}(\vec{c}, \vec{r}) \leq d - 1$. Now, as the minimum distance of C is d, it must be that $\vec{r} \notin C$. So Bob correctly assumes that an error occurred. It follows that C detects $d - 1$ errors. ❑

We note here that if l is a real number we will use $\lfloor l \rfloor$ to denote the largest integer that is less than or equal to l.

Theorem 4.3.2. Let $C \subseteq A^n$ be a code with minimum distance d. Then, C corrects e errors where $e = \lfloor \frac{d-1}{2} \rfloor$.

Proof. Suppose $\vec{c} \in C$ is the word that Alice sends to Bob and let $\vec{r}$ be the word that Bob receives. We assume no more than $e = \lfloor \frac{d-1}{2} \rfloor$ errors occur and we show that Bob can accurately correct the errors. Note that $d_{\mathrm{H}}(\vec{c}, \vec{r}) \leq e$. We want to show that $\vec{c}$ is the closest element of C to $\vec{r}$. Suppose on the contrary that there is another codeword $\vec{y} \in C$ with $\vec{y} \neq \vec{c}$ that is within a distance e of $\vec{r}$. Then, $d_{\mathrm{H}}(\vec{y}, \vec{r}) \leq e$. So by the triangle inequality, we get

$$d_{\mathrm{H}}(\vec{y}, \vec{c}) \leq d_{\mathrm{H}}(\vec{y}, \vec{r}) + d_{\mathrm{H}}(\vec{r}, \vec{c}) \leq e + e = 2e = 2 \left\lfloor \frac{d-1}{2} \right\rfloor \leq d - 1.$$

Then there are two different elements of C that are a distance less than d apart. This contradicts that the minimum distance of C is d. It follows that C corrects e errors. ❑

Examples:
1. Recall that the binary repetition code of length n has minimum distance n. So it will detect $n - 1$ errors and correct $\lfloor \frac{n-1}{2} \rfloor$ errors. This code is very good for error correction, but remember that we can code only two pieces of information with it.
2. The binary parity check code of length n has minimum distance 2. So it will detect a single error and will not correct any errors. But remember the advantage of this code is that we can code a lot of information.
3. The binary [7,4] Hamming Code that we discussed in Section 4.2 has minimum distance 3. So it will detect two errors and it will correct a single error.

4. Recall the ternary code we defined in Section 4.2 has minimum distance 1. It will neither detect nor correct any errors.

There you have it. If we know what the minimum distance of a code is, we also know how many errors it can detect and how many it can correct. Of course, our above two theorems imply that the larger the minimum distance of a code is, the more errors it will detect and will correct. So codes with large minimum distance are desirable for error correction.

EXERCISES

Problem 1. Prove that for all $\vec{x}$, $\vec{y}$, and $\vec{z}$ in A^n the following properties hold.

(i) $d_H(\vec{x}, \vec{y}) \geq 0$
(ii) $d_H(\vec{x}, \vec{y}) = 0$ if and only if $\vec{x} = \vec{y}$
(iii) $d_H(\vec{x}, \vec{y}) = d_H(\vec{y}, \vec{x})$
(iv) $d_H(\vec{x}, \vec{y}) \leq d_H(\vec{x}, \vec{z}) + d_H(\vec{z}, \vec{y})$

Problem 2. How many errors will the code described in Problem 4 of Section 4.2 detect? How many errors will it correct?

Problem 3. Let $A = \mathbb{Z}_3$, $n = 4$ and define C to be

$$C = \{\alpha_1(2101) + \alpha_2(0112) | \alpha_1, \alpha_2 \in \mathbb{Z}_3\}$$

where all arithmetic is done component-wise modulo 3. How many errors will C detect? How many errors will C correct?

Problem 4. Find a binary code of length 6 containing eight elements that will correct one error.

Problem 5. Let C be a binary code of length 8 that corrects two errors. What is the largest number of elements that C can possibly contain?

4.4 Linear Codes

Let $A = F$ where F is any field. For the definition of and examples of fields, refer to Section A.1. In most of our examples, F will be $\mathbb{Z}_p$ where p

is a prime number, so this is the example you should keep in mind when we are discussing fields. We define an addition and scalar multiplication on $A^n = F^n$ component-wise. In other words,

$$(a_1, a_2, \ldots, a_n) + (b_1, b_2, \ldots, b_n) = (a_1 + b_1, a_2 + b_2, \ldots a_n + b_n) \text{ and}$$
$$\text{If } \alpha \in F, \text{ then } \alpha(a_1, a_2, \ldots, a_n) = (\alpha a_1, \alpha a_2, \ldots, \alpha a_n)$$

where all the addition and multiplication is done in the field F. Note that $A^n = F^n$ is a vector space with the set of scalars being F. For example, if $F = \mathbb{Z}_7$ and $n = 4$, then $(3, 5, 4, 1) + (6, 4, 1, 0) = (2, 2, 5, 1)$ and $4(4, 5, 2, 0) = (2, 6, 1, 0)$.

We now define a set of "good" codes.

Definition. Let $A = F$ where F is any finite field. Let $C \subseteq A^n$ be a code. We say that C is a *linear code* if

(*i*) C is not empty,
(*ii*) For every $\vec{x}, \vec{y} \in C$ we have that $\vec{x} + \vec{y} \in C$, and
(*iii*) For every $\alpha \in F$ and every $\vec{x} \in C$, we have that $\alpha \vec{x} \in C$.

In other words, a code C is linear if it is nonempty and closed under addition and scalar multiplication. Saying that a code is linear is the same thing as saying that C is a subspace of the vector space $A^n = F^n$.

The binary repetition code, the binary parity check code, and the binary [7,4] Hamming code are all linear codes where $F = \mathbb{Z}_2$. You can verify on your own that they are closed under addition and scalar multiplication. The ternary code that we defined in Section 4.2 is linear with $F = \mathbb{Z}_3$.

Let $A = \mathbb{Z}_2, n = 4$, and $C = \{(1100), (1110)\}$. Then C is not linear because it is not closed under addition. In particular, $(1100) + (1110) = (0010) \notin C$.

Note that if C is a linear code, then the word consisting of all zeros must be in C. To see this, first let $\vec{0}$ denote the word with zeros in every position. Then, note that $0 \in F$. Since C is linear, it is not empty, so there is an $\vec{x} \in C$. We also know that C is closed under scalar multiplication. So $0\vec{x} \in C$. But $0\vec{x} = \vec{0}$ and it follows that the word consisting of all zeros must be in C.

We will spend the rest of this chapter studying linear codes. It turns out that in many ways linear codes are easier to describe and analyze than codes that are not linear. Remember that to find the minimum distance of a code, we have to check the Hamming distance of all pairs of codewords. For linear codes, it is much easier to determine the minimum distance. Our goal in this section is to prove this. We begin with a definition.

Definition. Let $\vec{x} \in A^n$. We define the *Hamming weight*, or simply the weight, of $\vec{x}$ to be the number of nonzero entries in $\vec{x}$. We will denote the Hamming weight of $\vec{x}$ by $w(\vec{x})$.

For example, if $\vec{x} = (1001110) \in \mathbb{Z}_2^7$, then $w(\vec{x}) = 4$. If $\vec{x} = (41060) \in \mathbb{Z}_7^5$, then $w(\vec{x}) = 3$. Note that for any $\vec{x} \in A^n$, we have $w(\vec{x}) = d_H(\vec{x}, \vec{0})$.

Definition. Let $C \subseteq A^n$ be a code. We define the *minimum weight of C*, denoted $w_{\min}(C)$, as

$$w_{\min}(C) = \min_{\vec{x} \in C, \vec{x} \neq \vec{0}} \{w(\vec{x})\}.$$

So to find the minimum weight of a code C, just compute the weights of all the nonzero codewords of C. The smallest value we get is the minimum weight of C. For example, the minimum weight of the binary repetition code of length n is n, the minimum weight of the binary check code of length n is 2, and the minimum weight of the binary [7,4] Hamming code is 3. The minimum weight of the ternary code we defined in Section 4.2 is 1. Looking at these four examples as evidence, we might guess that the minimum weight of a code is equal to the minimum distance of the code. It turns out that this guess is correct for linear codes.

Theorem 4.4.1. Let $C \subseteq F^n$ be a linear code. Then, $w_{\min}(C) = d_{\min}(C)$.

Proof. Let $\vec{x} \neq \vec{y}$ be two elements of C satisfying $d_H(\vec{x}, \vec{y}) = d_{\min}(C)$. We know that two such vectors exist by the definition of minimum distance. Now, let $-\vec{x}$ denote the word that satisfies $\vec{x} + -\vec{x} = \vec{0}$. Note that $-\vec{x} \in C$. The proof of this will be left as an exercise at the end of the section. So we have

$$d_{\min}(C) = d_H(\vec{x}, \vec{y}) = d_H(\vec{x} + -\vec{x}, \vec{y} + -\vec{x})$$
$$= d_H(\vec{0}, \vec{y} + -\vec{x}) = w(\vec{y} + -\vec{x}).$$

Now, since $\vec{y} \in C$ and $-\vec{x} \in C$, and C is linear, we know that $\vec{y} + -\vec{x} \in C$. Note also that $\vec{y} + -\vec{x} \neq \vec{0}$. It follows that $d_{\min}(C) \geq w_{\min}(C)$. Suppose $d_{\min}(C) > w_{\min}(C)$. Then, there is a nonzero codeword $\vec{f} \in C$ such that $w(\vec{f}) < d_{\min}(C)$. But then

$$d_H(\vec{f}, \vec{0}) = w(\vec{f}) < d_{\min}(C),$$

contradicting the definition of minimum distance. It follows that $d_{\min}(C) = w_{\min}(C)$ as desired. ❏

Notice that computing the minimum weight for a code is easier than computing the minimum distance for the code. So this theorem has made finding the minimum distance for linear codes easier. This is useful since by knowing the minimum distance of a code, we can determine how many errors it will detect and how many it will correct.

EXERCISES

Problem 1. Let C be a linear code. If $\vec{x} \in F^n$, we let $-\vec{x}$ denote the word in F^n satisfying $\vec{x} + -\vec{x} = \vec{0}$. Show that if $\vec{x} \in C$, then $-\vec{x} \in C$.

Problem 2. Let $F = \mathbb{Z}_3, n = 3$, and

$$C = \{(000), (110), (111), (221), (001), (002)\}.$$

Determine whether or not C is linear. Explain.

Problem 3. Give an example of a binary code C where $d_{\min}(C) \neq w_{\min}(C)$.

Problem 4. Let $F = \mathbb{Z}_2$ and $C \subseteq F^4 = \mathbb{Z}_2^4$ be a linear code. Show that the number of elements in C must be $1, 2, 4, 8,$ or 16.

Problem 5. Let F be a field containing r elements. Let $C \subseteq F^n$ be a linear code. What can you say about the number of elements in C?

4.5   Generator Matrices

Recall from the last section that an advantage of a linear code is that we can compute the minimum distance by computing the minimum weight.

It turns out that another advantage of using a linear code is that there is a neat, concise way to represent it using a matrix called a generator matrix. Before we define generator matrices, we need some terminology.

Definition. Let G be a $k \times n$ matrix with entries from a field F. Let $\vec{x}_i$ be the ith row of G. We define the *rowspace* of G, denoted $RS(G)$, to be

$$RS(G) = \{\alpha_1 \vec{x}_1 + \alpha_2 \vec{x}_2 + \cdots + \alpha_k \vec{x}_k | \alpha_i \in F\} \subseteq F^n.$$

So $RS(G)$ is simply the span of the rows of G.

Examples:
1. If $F = \mathbb{Z}_2$ and $G = \begin{pmatrix} 1 & 0 & 0 & 1 \\ 0 & 1 & 0 & 1 \\ 0 & 0 & 1 & 1 \end{pmatrix}$, then

   $$RS(G) = \{(0000), (1001), (0101), (0011), (1100), (1010),$$
   $$(0110), (1111)\}.$$

   Note that this is the binary parity check code of length 4.
2. If $F = \mathbb{Z}_2$ and $G = (1 \quad 1 \quad 1 \quad 1 \quad 1)$, then

   $$RS(G) = \{(00000), (11111)\}.$$

   This is the binary repetition code of length 5.
3. If $F = \mathbb{Z}_3$ and $G = \begin{pmatrix} 1 & 1 & 0 \\ 0 & 0 & 1 \end{pmatrix}$ then

   $$RS(G) = \{(000), (110), (001), (111), (220), (002), (222), (221), (112)\}.$$

   This is the ternary code we described in Section 4.2.

We now recall the definition of linearly independent elements in F^n.

Definition. Let $\vec{x}_1, \vec{x}_2, \ldots, \vec{x}_k \in F^n$ where F is a field. Suppose that the only $\alpha_i \in F$ that satisfy the equation

$$\alpha_1 \vec{x}_1 + \alpha_2 \vec{x}_2 + \cdots + \alpha_k \vec{x}_k = \vec{0}$$

are $\alpha_i = 0$ for $i = 1, 2, \ldots, k$. Then we say that $\vec{x}_1, \vec{x}_2, \ldots, \vec{x}_k$ are *linearly independent*. If $\vec{x}_1, \vec{x}_2, \ldots, \vec{x}_k$ are not linearly independent, we say $\vec{x}_1, \vec{x}_2, \ldots, \vec{x}_k$ are *linearly dependent*.

Note that if $\vec{x}_1, \vec{x}_2, \ldots, \vec{x}_k \in F^n$ then $\alpha_1 = 0, \alpha_2 = 0, \ldots, \alpha_k = 0$ will *always* satisfy the equation $\alpha_1 \vec{x}_1 + \alpha_2 \vec{x}_2 + \cdots + \alpha_k \vec{x}_k = \vec{0}$ no matter whether $\vec{x}_1, \vec{x}_2, \ldots, \vec{x}_k$ are linearly independent or not. For $\vec{x}_1, \vec{x}_2, \ldots, \vec{x}_k$ to be linearly independent, then, means that $\alpha_1 = 0, \alpha_2 = 0, \ldots, \alpha_k = 0$ is the *only* way to choose the α_i's so that the equation $\alpha_1 \vec{x}_1 + \alpha_2 \vec{x}_2 + \cdots + \alpha_k \vec{x}_k = \vec{0}$ is satisfied.

Examples:

1. Let $F = \mathbb{Z}_2$. Are $(0101), (1110), (0001)$ linearly independent? To find out, we must find all the solutions in $\mathbb{Z}_2$ to the equation

$$\alpha_1(0101) + \alpha_2(1110) + \alpha_3(0001) = (0000).$$

   For this equation to hold, we must have

   $\alpha_2 = 0$ from the first component
   $\alpha_1 + \alpha_2 = 0$ from the second component
   $\alpha_2 = 0$ from the third component, and
   $\alpha_1 + \alpha_3 = 0$ from the fourth component.

   The only solution to these equations is when $\alpha_1 = \alpha_2 = \alpha_3 = 0$. So $(0101), (1110), (0001)$ are linearly independent.

2. Let $F = \mathbb{Z}_2$. $(1101), (0011), (1110)$ are linearly dependent since $(1101) + (0011) + (1110) = (0000)$.

3. Let $F = \mathbb{Z}_5$. Then (241) and (032) are linearly independent since for the equation

$$\alpha_1(241) + \alpha_2(032) = (000)$$

   to hold, we must have $2\alpha_1 = 0$ from the first component. But the only α_1 in $\mathbb{Z}_5$ that satisfies this equation is $\alpha_1 = 0$. So our equation becomes

$$\alpha_2(032) = (000).$$

   From the third component, we get that $2\alpha_2 = 0$ and so $\alpha_2 = 0$. It follows that (241) and (032) are linearly independent.

4. Let $F = \mathbb{Z}_3$. Then $(011), (211)$, and (200) are linearly dependent since $2(011) + (211) = (200)$.

If $C \subseteq F^n$ is a linear code containing more than one element, then there exists a $k \times n$ matrix G with entries in F such that the rows of G are linearly independent and such that $C = RS(G)$. To find such a G, just find a basis for C and use the basis elements as the rows of the matrix G.

Definition. Let $C \subseteq F^n$ be a linear code. Let G be a $k \times n$ matrix with entries in F such that the rows of G are linearly independent and such that $C = RS(G)$. Then, G is called a *generator matrix* for C and C is called an $[n, k]$ linear code. The number k is called the *dimension of C*. If $C = \{\vec{0}\}$ then we say that C is a linear code with dimension 0.

Note that if we know a generator matrix for a linear code C, then we can find all elements of C by computing the row space of the matrix. In other words, the generator matrix provides a concise way of describing a linear code.

Example:
Let C be the binary [7,4] Hamming code that we defined in Section 4.2. You can show that it contains all elements $(x_1, x_2, x_3, x_4, x_5, x_6, x_7)$ where x_1, x_2, x_3, x_4 can be any elements of $\mathbb{Z}_2$ and $x_5 = x_1 + x_2 + x_3 (\mathrm{mod}\, 2)$, $x_6 = x_1 + x_2 + x_4 (\mathrm{mod}\, 2)$, and $x_7 = x_2 + x_3 + x_4 (\mathrm{mod}\, 2)$. So we can describe C as any element of $\mathbb{Z}_2^7$ that can be written as

$$(x_1, x_2, x_3, x_4, x_1 + x_2 + x_3, x_1 + x_2 + x_4, x_2 + x_3 + x_4)$$

where the arithmetic is done modulo 2. Now, we claim that

$$G = \begin{pmatrix} 1 & 0 & 0 & 0 & 1 & 1 & 0 \\ 0 & 1 & 0 & 0 & 1 & 1 & 1 \\ 0 & 0 & 1 & 0 & 1 & 0 & 1 \\ 0 & 0 & 0 & 1 & 0 & 1 & 1 \end{pmatrix}$$

is a generator matrix for C. To see this, you can verify that the rows of G are linearly independent. We will show here that $C = RS(G)$. Now,

$RS(G)$
$\quad = \{\alpha_1(1000110) + \alpha_2(0100111) + \alpha_3(0010101) + \alpha_4(0001011) | \alpha_i \in \mathbb{Z}_2\}.$

Multiplying this out and adding, we get

$RS(G)$
$$= \{(\alpha_1, \alpha_2, \alpha_3, \alpha_4, \alpha_1 + \alpha_2 + \alpha_3, \alpha_1 + \alpha_2 + \alpha_4, \alpha_2 + \alpha_3 + \alpha_4) | \alpha_i \in \mathbb{Z}_2\}.$$

But this is exactly the way we described C above (with the x_i's replaced with α_i's). So $RS(G) = C$.

Generator matrices for linear codes are *not* unique! There are many generator matrices for each linear code. For example, if we take any generator matrix and exchange two rows then the result will still be a generator matrix for the code. Recall from linear algebra that most vector spaces have many different bases. Since we use the elements of a basis as the rows of G, it follows that there are many different possible generator matrices for a given linear code. The generator matrix we found above for the binary [7,4] Hamming code, however, has an especially nice property. Remember, we can pick our first four digits to be anything. Once we pick those, though, the last three are determined. So sometimes we think of the first four digits as the "information" digits and the last three as "check" digits. Let us see what happens if we take the 1×4 matrix with the information digits as its entries and multiply that by the generator matrix:

$$(x_1, x_2, x_3, x_4) \begin{pmatrix} 1 & 0 & 0 & 0 & 1 & 1 & 0 \\ 0 & 1 & 0 & 0 & 1 & 1 & 1 \\ 0 & 0 & 1 & 0 & 1 & 0 & 1 \\ 0 & 0 & 0 & 1 & 0 & 1 & 1 \end{pmatrix}$$
$$= (x_1, x_2, x_3, x_4, x_1 + x_2 + x_3, x_1 + x_2 + x_4, x_2 + x_3 + x_4).$$

The result is the codeword that Alice sends! Now, why did this happen? Notice that the G we found has the identity matrix on the left-hand side. Think of the first k digits of the word as the "information." You can verify for yourself that when you multiply the "information" vector times a generator matrix that has the $k \times k$ identity matrix on the left, you will get an element of C that has the "information" vector as its leftmost entries. So generator matrices for linear codes that have the identity matrix on the left are desirable. However, not all linear codes have such generator matrices. Finding an example of a linear code that does not have a generator matrix with the identity matrix on the left will be left as an exercise. What is true, though, is that for any linear code we can find a generator matrix that has all k columns of the $k \times k$ identity matrix. But these columns do not necessarily occur at the left. We make these ideas more precise using the following definitions.

Definition. Let $C \subseteq F^n$ be an $[n, k]$ linear code. A generator matrix for C that contains all k columns of the $k \times k$ identity matrix is called *systematic*.

All linear codes of positive dimension have systematic generator matrices. To convince yourself this is true, first show that performing elementary row operations on a generator matrix yields another generator matrix. Then perform elementary row operations on any generator matrix until it is in reduced row echelon form. Because the rows of the matrix are linearly independent, we know all k columns of the $k \times k$ identity matrix will appear in this new generator matrix.

Definition. Let $C \subseteq F^n$ be an $[n, k]$ linear code. A generator matrix for C where the $k \times k$ identity matrix appears at the left is called a *standard generator matrix*.

As noted above, not all linear codes have standard generator matrices.

Definition. Let C_1 and C_2 be codes. If by permuting the coordinates of C_1, we get C_2, then C_1 and C_2 are said to be *equivalent*.

Example:
Let $F = \mathbb{Z}_2$,

$$C_1 = \{(0000), (1100), (0011), (1111)\}$$

and

$$C_2 = \{(0000), (0110), (1001), (1111)\}.$$

Then, C_1 is equivalent to C_2 because by switching the first and third coordinates of the elements of C_1, we get the elements of C_2.

It is not hard to show that every linear code of positive dimension is equivalent to a linear code that has a standard generator matrix. The proof of this fact will be left as an exercise.

EXERCISES

Problem 1. Find a linear code C of positive dimension such that C does not have a standard generator matrix.

Problem 2. Prove that every linear code of positive dimension is equivalent to a linear code that has a standard generator matrix.

Problem 3. Are the following linearly independent? Explain.

(a) $(101111), (000001), (110111) \in \mathbb{Z}_2^6$.
(b) $(000), (101) \in \mathbb{Z}_2^3$.
(c) $(10000), (01001), (00111) \in \mathbb{Z}_2^5$.
(d) $(0212), (0010), (2212) \in \mathbb{Z}_3^4$.
(e) $(32410), (01215), (60051) \in \mathbb{Z}_7^5$.

Problem 4. Let

$$C = \{(000000), (101110), (001010), (110111),$$
$$(100100), (011001), (111101), (010011)\} \subseteq \mathbb{Z}_2^6$$

Note that C is linear.

(a) What is the minimum distance of C?
(b) How many errors will C detect?
(c) How many errors will C correct?
(d) Find a generator matrix for C.
(e) What is the dimension of C?

Problem 5. Let $F = \mathbb{Z}_5$ and C be the code with generator matrix

$$G = \begin{pmatrix} 1 & 2 & 4 \\ 0 & 1 & 1 \end{pmatrix}.$$

(a) List the elements of C.
(b) What is the minimum distance of C?
(c) How many errors will C detect?
(d) How many errors will C correct?
(e) Find a generator matrix for C that is in reduced row echelon form.

Problem 6. Let F be a field with $r < \infty$ elements in it. Let C be an $[n, k]$ linear code over F. How many elements does C contain? Prove your answer.

Problem 7. Prove that if C is a binary $[n, k]$ linear code then the sum of the weights of all the elements in C is less than or equal to $n2^{k-1}$.

Problem 8. Find the smallest n such that there exists a binary $[n, 3]$ linear code that corrects two errors.

4.6 Dual Codes

Recall Bob's method for correcting errors. He receives a word from Alice and then computes the Hamming distance of that word with every codeword, a possibly time-consuming task. It turns out that there are more efficient ways for Bob to correct errors. We describe one of these ways in the next two sections. To get started, we define the dual code.

Definition. Let $C \subseteq F^n$ be a code. The *dual code* of C, denoted $C^\perp$ is the code

$$C^\perp = \{\vec{x} \in F^n | \vec{x} \cdot \vec{c} = 0 \text{ for every } \vec{c} \in C\} \subseteq F^n$$

where $\vec{x} \cdot \vec{c}$ is the dot product computed in the field F.

Examples:
1. Let C be the binary parity check code of length 4. So,

   $$C = \{(0000), (0011), (0101), (1001), (0110), (1010), (1100), (1111)\}.$$

   To find the elements of $C^\perp$, we test all elements of $\mathbb{Z}_2^4$ to see which ones have a dot product of zero with all the elements of C. Remember, all arithmetic is done in $\mathbb{Z}_2$. So, for example, when we test whether or not (0111) is in $C^\perp$ we notice that $(0111) \cdot (1111) = 0 + 1 + 1 + 1 = 1$ in $\mathbb{Z}_2$. Since there is a codeword (1111) whose dot product with (0111) is not zero, (0111) is not in $C^\perp$. Going through all 16 elements of $\mathbb{Z}_2^4$ in this way, you can verify that

   $$C^\perp = \{(0000), (1111)\}.$$

   This is the binary repetition code of length 4. Of course, we could compute the dual code of the binary repetition code of length 4. When we do, we get the binary parity check code of length 4. In other words in this case, $(C^\perp)^\perp = C$.

2. Let C be the ternary code we defined in Section 4.2. You can verify that $C^\perp = \{(000), (120), (210)\}$ and that $(C^\perp)^\perp = C$.

In light of the above examples, you may conjecture that $(C^\perp)^\perp = C$ for all codes. This, however, is not the case. Let $F = \mathbb{Z}_2$ and $C = \{(001), (010), (110)\}$. Then, $C^\perp = \{(000)\}$ and

$$(C^\perp)^\perp = \{(000), (001), (010), (011), (100), (101), (110), (111)\} \neq C.$$

But not all is lost. If C is linear, then in fact we do have $(C^\perp)^\perp = C$. We will prove this soon.

On another note, you may have noticed that for some examples, although C may not be linear, $C^\perp$ is linear. In fact, for all C, linear or not, it can be shown that $C^\perp$ is linear. The proof of this will be left as an exercise.

Note that determining whether or not an element of F^n is in the dual of a code using the definition of the dual code requires us to compute the dot product of that element and all elements of the code. We now prove a theorem that shows us an easier method for linear codes. In fact, we use a generator matrix to test whether or not an element is in the dual of the code. We note here that if $\vec{x} \in F^n$, then we use $\vec{x}^T$ to denote the transpose of $\vec{x}$.

Theorem 4.6.1. Let $C \subseteq F^n$ be a linear code and G a generator matrix for C. An element $\vec{x} \in F^n$ is in $C^\perp$ if and only if $G\vec{x}^T = \vec{0}$.

Proof. Let $\vec{c}_1, \vec{c}_2, \ldots, \vec{c}_k \in F^n$ be the rows of G. Now, suppose $\vec{x} \in C^\perp$. Then, $\vec{x} \cdot \vec{c} = 0$ for all $\vec{c} \in C$. In particular, $\vec{x} \cdot \vec{c}_i = 0$ for all $i = 1, 2, \ldots, k$. It follows that $G\vec{x}^T = \vec{0}$.

On the other hand, suppose $G\vec{x}^T = \vec{0}$ for some $\vec{x} \in F^n$. Then, $\vec{x} \cdot \vec{c}_i = 0$ for all $i = 1, 2, \ldots, k$. Let $\vec{c} \in C$. So,

$$\vec{c} = \alpha_1 \vec{c}_1 + \alpha_2 \vec{c}_2 + \cdots + \alpha_k \vec{c}_k$$

for some $\alpha_i \in F$. It follows that

$$\vec{c} \cdot \vec{x} = \alpha_1 (\vec{c}_1 \cdot \vec{x}) + \alpha_2 (\vec{c}_2 \cdot \vec{x}) + \cdots + \alpha_k (\vec{c}_k \cdot \vec{x}) = 0.$$

Hence we have that $\vec{x} \in C^\perp$ as desired.   ❏

Example:

Recall that $G = \left(\begin{smallmatrix} 1 & 1 & 0 \\ 0 & 0 & 1 \end{smallmatrix}\right)$ is a generator matrix for the ternary code we defined in Section 4.2. If we want to find out whether or not (120) is in $C^\perp$, we simply compute $G(120)^T = \left(\begin{smallmatrix} 1 & 1 & 0 \\ 0 & 0 & 1 \end{smallmatrix}\right)\left(\begin{smallmatrix} 1 \\ 2 \\ 0 \end{smallmatrix}\right) = \left(\begin{smallmatrix} 0 \\ 0 \end{smallmatrix}\right)$. By the theorem above, we know that $(120) \in C^\perp$.

Theorem 4.6.2. If $C \subseteq F^n$ is an $[n, k]$ linear code, then $C^\perp$ is an $[n, n - k]$ linear code. Moreover, we have $(C^\perp)^\perp = C$.

Proof. The fact that $C^\perp$ is linear will be an exercise. Let G be a generator matrix for C. Then, G is a $k \times n$ matrix of rank k. By Theorem 4.6.1, we know that the dimension of the dual of C is equal to the dimension of the nullspace of G. But Theorem A.2.6 tells us that the rank of a matrix plus the dimension of the nullspace is n. So the dimension of the nullspace of G is $n - k$. It follows that $C^\perp$ is an $[n, n - k]$ linear code. Using the same argument, we can show that the dimension of $(C^\perp)^\perp$ is k. Now, it is easy to show that for any code C, we have $C \subseteq (C^\perp)^\perp$. This will be an exercise at the end of this section. So in our case, we have a subspace of dimension k contained in another subspace of dimension k. It follows by Theorem A.2.3 that the two subspaces are equal. In other words, we have $(C^\perp)^\perp = C$. ❑

The above theorem turns out to be rather useful. Consider a linear code C. Since we know that $C^\perp$ is a linear code, it must have a generator matrix. Call this matrix H. By Theorem 4.6.1, then, we know that $\vec{x} \in (C^\perp)^\perp$ if and only if $H\vec{x}^T = \vec{0}$. But since we know $(C^\perp)^\perp = C$, this is the same as saying $\vec{x} \in C$ if and only if $H\vec{x}^T = \vec{0}$. In other words, the matrix H allows us to check whether or not elements of F^n are in our code. In mathematical language, we have

$$C = \{\vec{x} \in F^n \,|\, H\vec{x}^T = \vec{0}\}.$$

In view of this discussion, we have the following definition.

Definition. Let $C \subseteq F^n$ be a linear code. A generator matrix H for $C^\perp$ is called a *check matrix* for C.

Example:

We will find a check matrix for the binary [7,4] Hamming code. Recall that a generator matrix for this code is

$$G = \begin{pmatrix} 1 & 0 & 0 & 0 & 1 & 1 & 0 \\ 0 & 1 & 0 & 0 & 1 & 1 & 1 \\ 0 & 0 & 1 & 0 & 1 & 0 & 1 \\ 0 & 0 & 0 & 1 & 0 & 1 & 1 \end{pmatrix}.$$

Now, let $\vec{x} = (x_1, x_2, x_3, x_4, x_5, x_6, x_7)$ be an element of $\mathbb{Z}_2^7$. Then, by Theorem 4.6.1, we know $\vec{x}$ is in the dual of C if and only if its dot product with every row of G is zero. In other words, $\vec{x} \in C^\perp$ if and only if

$(1000110) \cdot (x_1, x_2, x_3, x_4, x_5, x_6, x_7) = 0,$
$(0100111) \cdot (x_1, x_2, x_3, x_4, x_5, x_6, x_7) = 0,$
$(0010101) \cdot (x_1, x_2, x_3, x_4, x_5, x_6, x_7) = 0,$ and
$(0001011) \cdot (x_1, x_2, x_3, x_4, x_5, x_6, x_7) = 0,$

where remember that all arithmetic is done modulo 2. But the above equations hold if and only if

$x_1 = x_5 + x_6$ and
$x_2 = x_5 + x_6 + x_7$ and
$x_3 = x_5 + x_7$ and
$x_4 = x_6 + x_7.$

So $\vec{x} \in C^\perp$ if and only if it is of the form

$$(x_5 + x_6, x_5 + x_6 + x_7, x_5 + x_7, x_6 + x_7, x_5, x_6, x_7).$$

But we can write this as

$$x_5(1110100) + x_6(1101010) + x_7(0111001).$$

So if we let

$$H = \begin{pmatrix} 1 & 1 & 1 & 0 & 1 & 0 & 0 \\ 1 & 1 & 0 & 1 & 0 & 1 & 0 \\ 0 & 1 & 1 & 1 & 0 & 0 & 1 \end{pmatrix}$$

then we know that $C^\perp = RS(H)$. It is easy to verify that the rows of H are linearly independent. So H is a generator matrix for $C^\perp$ and hence by definition a check matrix for C. We can use this check matrix to tell whether a word is an element of C or not. Given a word $\vec{x}$, we simply compute $H\vec{x}^T$. If we get $\vec{0}$, then $\vec{x} \in C$. If we do not get $\vec{0}$, then $\vec{x} \notin C$. For example, let $\vec{x} = (0101110)$. Now,

$$H\vec{x}^T = \begin{pmatrix} 1 & 1 & 1 & 0 & 1 & 0 & 0 \\ 1 & 1 & 0 & 1 & 0 & 1 & 0 \\ 0 & 1 & 1 & 1 & 0 & 0 & 1 \end{pmatrix} \begin{pmatrix} 0 \\ 1 \\ 0 \\ 1 \\ 1 \\ 1 \\ 0 \end{pmatrix} = \begin{pmatrix} 0 \\ 1 \\ 0 \end{pmatrix}$$

and since $\begin{pmatrix} 0 \\ 1 \\ 0 \end{pmatrix} \neq \begin{pmatrix} 0 \\ 0 \\ 0 \end{pmatrix}$, we know $(0101110) \notin C$.

EXERCISES

Problem 1. Let $C \subseteq F^n$ be a code.
(a) Show that $C^\perp$ is a linear code.
(b) Show that $C \subseteq (C^\perp)^\perp$.

Problem 2. Let $C \subseteq \mathbb{Z}_2^4$ be defined as

$$C = \{(0000), (1110), (0001)\}$$

(a) Find $C^\perp$.
(b) Find a generator matrix for $C^\perp$.
(c) Find $(C^\perp)^\perp$.
(d) Find a generator matrix for $(C^\perp)^\perp$.

Problem 3. Let $C \subseteq \mathbb{Z}_2^5$ be defined as

$$C = \{(11010), (01101), (11000)\}$$

(a) Find $C^\perp$.
(b) Find a generator matrix for $C^\perp$.
(c) Find $(C^\perp)^\perp$.
(d) Find a generator matrix for $(C^\perp)^\perp$.

Problem 4. Let $C \subseteq \mathbb{Z}_2^6$ be the linear code with generator matrix

$$G = \begin{pmatrix} 1 & 0 & 1 & 0 & 1 & 1 \\ 1 & 1 & 0 & 1 & 0 & 0 \\ 0 & 0 & 0 & 0 & 1 & 1 \end{pmatrix}.$$

Note that the rows of G are linearly independent.
  (a) Find a check matrix H for C.
  (b) Use H to determine which of the following are in C.
      (i) (011111)
      (ii) (110110)
      (iii) (011100)

Problem 5. Let $C \subseteq \mathbb{Z}_3^4$ be the linear code with generator matrix

$$G = \begin{pmatrix} 1 & 2 & 1 & 0 \\ 0 & 0 & 2 & 1 \end{pmatrix}.$$

Note that the rows of G are linearly independent.
  (a) Find a check matrix H for C.
  (b) Use H to determine which of the following are in C.
      (i) (2110)
      (ii) (1201)
      (iii) (0220)

Problem 6. Let C be a linear code with check matrix H. Prove that if one column of H is a multiple of another column of H then C will not correct any errors.

Problem 7. Let C be a linear code with check matrix H. Prove that if no column of H is a multiple of another column then C will correct at least one error.

4.7 Syndrome Decoding

In this section, we will discuss a way for Bob to correct errors that does not require him to compute the Hamming distance from the received word to all of the codewords. Suppose Alice sends the codeword $\vec{c}$ to Bob and let $\vec{r}$ be the word that Bob receives. Then, we can write $\vec{r} = \vec{c} + \vec{e}$ where $\vec{e} \in F^n$. Notice that $\vec{e}$ tells us what kind of errors occurred in transmission. For that reason, we call $\vec{e}$ the error vector. Bob knows $\vec{r}$ and he wants to find $\vec{c}$. But since $\vec{c} = \vec{r} - \vec{e}$, if he can find $\vec{e}$, then he will be able to compute $\vec{c}$. So our goal for this section will be to find $\vec{e}$. We will assume that messages are transmitted over some reasonable channel where not very many errors occur, and hence $w(\vec{e})$ is small. So Bob can use the following strategy. He knows that $\vec{e} = \vec{r} - \vec{c}$. He computes $\vec{r} - \vec{c}$ for all codewords $\vec{c}$ and the answer he gets that has the smallest weight he assumes is $\vec{e}$. Note that this is a perfectly good strategy, but it does not seem to save Bob much time. In fact, we have really just restated our old way of correcting errors. But thinking about correcting errors in this way will soon prove useful. We start by defining mathematically the set of words $\vec{r} - \vec{c}$ for all codewords $\vec{c}$. The concept of coset we introduce in the definition below is the same as the cosets seen in Abstract Algebra books.

Definition. Let $C \subseteq F^n$ be a linear code and $\vec{x} \in F^n$. We define the coset $\vec{x} + C$ to be

$$\vec{x} + C = \{\vec{x} + \vec{c} \mid \vec{c} \in C\}.$$

It will be left as an exercise that in the above definition, replacing the "+" sign with a "−" sign will result in the same set. So in terms of our new definition, Bob computes the weight of all elements of the set $\vec{r} + C$, and the element with the smallest weight, if a unique one exists, will be $\vec{e}$.

Example:
Let $C \subseteq \mathbb{Z}_2^4$ be defined as

$$C = \{(0000), (1100), (0011), (1111)\}.$$

Then, if $\vec{x} = (1010)$, we have

$$\vec{x} + C = \{(1010), (0110), (1001), (0101)\}.$$

We now define the syndrome of a word. Syndromes will help us characterize cosets for linear codes.

Definition. Let $C \subseteq F^n$ be an $[n, k]$ linear code and H a check matrix for C. Let $\vec{r} \in F^n$. Then $\vec{s} = H\vec{r}^T \in F^{n-k}$ is called the *syndrome* of $\vec{r}$.

Example:
Recall that $H = \begin{pmatrix} 1 & 1 & 1 & 0 & 1 & 0 & 0 \\ 1 & 1 & 0 & 1 & 0 & 1 & 0 \\ 0 & 1 & 1 & 1 & 0 & 0 & 1 \end{pmatrix}$ is a check matrix for the binary [7,4] Hamming code. So if we want to compute the syndrome of (1110000), we

get

$$\begin{pmatrix} 1 & 1 & 1 & 0 & 1 & 0 & 0 \\ 1 & 1 & 0 & 1 & 0 & 1 & 0 \\ 0 & 1 & 1 & 1 & 0 & 0 & 1 \end{pmatrix} \begin{pmatrix} 1 \\ 1 \\ 1 \\ 0 \\ 0 \\ 0 \\ 0 \end{pmatrix} = \begin{pmatrix} 1 \\ 0 \\ 0 \end{pmatrix}.$$

So the syndrome of (1110000) is $\begin{pmatrix} 1 \\ 0 \\ 0 \end{pmatrix}$.

Now, this should look familar. By our arguments in the last section, we know that $\vec{r} \in C$ if and only if $H\vec{r}^T = \vec{0}$. Using our new terminology, we can restate that $\vec{r} \in C$ if and only if its syndrome is $\vec{0}$. So Bob now has a better way to detect errors. Instead of comparing the received word $\vec{r}$ with all the codewords, he can simply compute its syndrome. The syndrome is $\vec{0}$ if and only if no errors have occurred. Next we will use the concept of syndrome to correct errors.

Recall that we can write the word Bob receives as $\vec{r} = \vec{c} + \vec{e}$ where $\vec{c}$ is the word that Alice sent. Now, $\vec{r}$ and $\vec{e}$ have the same syndrome if and only if $H\vec{r}^T = H\vec{e}^T$, which is true if and only if $H(\vec{r} - \vec{e})^T = \vec{0}$, which is true if and only if $\vec{r} - \vec{e} \in C$. But Bob knows $\vec{r} - \vec{e} = \vec{c} \in C$. It follows that $\vec{r}$ and $\vec{e}$ must have the same syndrome. So Bob wants to find a word $\vec{e}$ with small weight such that $\vec{e}$ has the same syndrome as $\vec{r}$. We now state a theorem that tells us that two words have the same syndrome if and only if they are in the same coset.

Theorem 4.7.1. Let $C \subseteq F^n$ be a linear code. Then $\vec{x}, \vec{y} \in F^n$ have the same syndrome if and only if $\vec{x} \in \vec{y} + C$.

The proof will be left as an exercise.

Theorem 4.7.2. Let $C \subseteq F^n$ be a linear code.

(*i*) If $\vec{x} \in \vec{y} + C$, then $\vec{x} + C = \vec{y} + C$.
(*ii*) For every $\vec{x}, \vec{y} \in F^n$, either $\vec{x} + C = \vec{y} + C$ or $\vec{x} + C \cap \vec{y} + C = \emptyset$.

The proof will be left as an exercise.

So the cosets break up F^n into disjoint subsets on the basis of their syndromes.

Now, we can restate Bob's goal. He knows that the word $\vec{r}$ he receives and the error word $\vec{e}$ have the same syndrome. He also knows that all words with the same syndrome as $\vec{r}$ are in the coset $\vec{r} + C$. So he looks at the elements of $\vec{r} + C$ and chooses $\vec{e}$ to be the one whose weight is smallest.

Definition. A word of minimal weight in a coset is called a *coset leader*. (Note that there could be more than one coset leader for a given coset.)

We can summarize Bob's algorithm as follows:

1. Bob receives a word $\vec{r}$.
2. He calculates the syndrome $\vec{s} = H\vec{r}^T$ of $\vec{r}$.
3. If $\vec{s} = \vec{0}$ then no errors have occurred.
4. If $\vec{s} \neq \vec{0}$, Bob looks at the coset whose elements all have syndromes equal to $\vec{s}$. He finds the coset leader and assumes it is $\vec{e}$. Now, $\vec{r} = \vec{c} + \vec{e}$, so he computes $\vec{c} = \vec{r} - \vec{e}$ to correct errors.

One advantage to this method is that Bob's computer can compute and store a chart of syndromes and coset leaders before Alice starts sending messages to him. Then, when he receives messages, correcting errors is very fast.

Example:
Recall that

$$H = \begin{pmatrix} 1 & 1 & 1 & 0 & 1 & 0 & 0 \\ 1 & 1 & 0 & 1 & 0 & 1 & 0 \\ 0 & 1 & 1 & 1 & 0 & 0 & 1 \end{pmatrix}$$

is a check matrix for the binary [7,4] Hamming code. If Bob and Alice agree to use this code, then Bob computes the following chart before Alice starts sending messages.

Syndrome	Coset leader		Syndrome	Coset leader
$\begin{pmatrix}0\\0\\0\end{pmatrix}$	$(0\ 0\ 0\ 0\ 0\ 0\ 0)$		$\begin{pmatrix}0\\1\\1\end{pmatrix}$	$(0\ 0\ 0\ 1\ 0\ 0\ 0)$
$\begin{pmatrix}0\\0\\1\end{pmatrix}$	$(0\ 0\ 0\ 0\ 0\ 0\ 1)$		$\begin{pmatrix}1\\0\\1\end{pmatrix}$	$(0\ 0\ 1\ 0\ 0\ 0\ 0)$
$\begin{pmatrix}0\\1\\0\end{pmatrix}$	$(0\ 0\ 0\ 0\ 0\ 1\ 0)$		$\begin{pmatrix}1\\1\\0\end{pmatrix}$	$(1\ 0\ 0\ 0\ 0\ 0\ 0)$
$\begin{pmatrix}1\\0\\0\end{pmatrix}$	$(0\ 0\ 0\ 0\ 1\ 0\ 0)$		$\begin{pmatrix}1\\1\\1\end{pmatrix}$	$(0\ 1\ 0\ 0\ 0\ 0\ 0)$

Suppose Bob receives $\vec{r} = (1011100)$. Then, computing the syndrome of $\vec{r}$, he gets $\vec{s} = H\vec{r}^T = \begin{pmatrix}1\\0\\0\end{pmatrix}$.

He then refers to the chart to find the coset leader/error vector for $\begin{pmatrix}1\\0\\0\end{pmatrix}$. Since he gets the word (0000100) he knows that $(1011100) - (0000100) = (1011000)$ is a valid codeword. So Bob corrects (1011100) as (1011000).

In the above example, every coset has a unique coset leader. This is not always the case. Suppose Alice and Bob are using a linear code that corrects e errors. If Bob receives a word, computes the syndrome, and the corresponding coset has more than one coset leader then he knows that more than e errors have occurred. In this case, of course, it cannot be guaranteed that Bob can accurately correct the errors.

EXERCISES

Problem 1. Let $C \subseteq F^n$ be a linear code and $\vec{x} \in F^n$. Define

$$\vec{x} - C = \{\vec{x} - \vec{c} \mid \vec{c} \in C\}.$$

Prove that $\vec{x} + C = \vec{x} - C$.

Problem 2. Let $C \subseteq F^n$ be a linear code. Prove that $\vec{x}, \vec{y} \in F^n$ have the same syndrome if and only if $\vec{x} \in \vec{y} + C$.

Problem 3. Let $C \subseteq F^n$ be a linear code.

(a) Prove that if $\vec{x} \in \vec{y} + C$, then $\vec{x} + C = \vec{y} + C$.

(b) Prove that for every $\vec{x}, \vec{y} \in F^n$, either $\vec{x} + C = \vec{y} + C$ or $\vec{x} + C \cap \vec{y} + C = \emptyset$.

Problem 4. Let $C \subseteq \mathbb{Z}_2^4$ be the linear code with generator matrix

$$G = \begin{pmatrix} 1 & 1 & 0 & 0 \\ 0 & 1 & 1 & 1 \end{pmatrix}.$$

List all the cosets of C.

Problem 5. Let $C \subseteq \mathbb{Z}_2^6$ be the $[6, 3]$ linear code with generator matrix

$$G = \begin{pmatrix} 1 & 0 & 0 & 1 & 1 & 0 \\ 0 & 1 & 0 & 0 & 1 & 1 \\ 0 & 0 & 1 & 1 & 1 & 1 \end{pmatrix}.$$

(a) List the elements of C.

(b) Find the minimum distance of C.

(c) How many errors will C correct?

(d) Find a check matrix for C.

(e) Make a syndrome chart for C.

(f) Use the syndrome chart to correct the errors in the following:

    (i) (110101)

    (ii) (010111)

    (iii) (110111)

Problem 6. Let $C \subseteq \mathbb{Z}_3^4$ be the $[4, 2]$ linear code with generator matrix
$G = \begin{pmatrix} 1 & 2 & 1 & 0 \\ 0 & 1 & 1 & 2 \end{pmatrix}$.

(a) List the elements of C.

(b) Find the minimum distance of C.

(c) How many errors will C correct?

(d) Find a check matrix for C.

(e) Make a syndrome chart for C.

(f) Use the syndrome chart to decode the following:

    (i) (2222)

    (ii) (0121)

    (iii) (1022)

4.8   The Hat Problem

The uses of linear codes are surprisingly diverse. As an example, we now show how the theory of linear codes can be used to come up with a good strategy for a game called The Hat Problem, a problem that does not at first look like it has anything to do with coding. Suppose there are three people, call them Alice, Bob, and Carol, who will be the team playing the game. They are allowed to have an initial strategy meeting but after the game starts, they are not allowed to communicate in any way. The game starts as they all walk into a room. As the players enter, a hat is placed on each of their heads. All hats are either blue or red, where the probability of each color is 0.5. When they are in the room, each player can see the other players' hats, but not her own. Each player is then asked to guess the color of the hat on his own head by writing down "red," "blue," or "pass" on a piece of paper. The players may not communicate with each other in any way; they cannot even reveal to each other what they have written down. The team wins if at least one player has correctly guessed the color of the hat on his head and no player has guessed incorrectly. For example, suppose Bob guesses correctly and Alice and Carol pass. Then the team wins. If all three players pass or if one or more of them guesses wrong, they lose. The question is, then, what strategy should Alice, Bob, and Carol use? Certainly it is not hard to devise a strategy in which the probability of the team winning is 0.5. They could, for example, have Alice and Bob always pass and Carol randomly choose red or blue. But surprisingly there is a better way. In fact, in this chapter we prove (see Theorem 4.8.4) an amazing theorem which we now state as a claim.

Claim. Suppose n people are on a team playing The Hat Game where $n = 2^r - 1$ for some positive integer r. Then there exists a strategy such that the probability of the team winning is $1 - \frac{1}{2^r}$.

In our above example $n = 2^2 - 1$, so according to our claim, there is a strategy that Alice, Bob, and Carol can use where they will win with probability $1 - \frac{1}{2^2} = \frac{3}{4}$. Indeed, suppose that they use the following strategy. Each player looks at the other two players' hats. If the colors of the hats they see are the same, they guess the opposite color. If the colors are different, they pass. For example, suppose that we know Alice has on a red hat and Bob and Carol both blue. Alice sees two red hats and so she guesses blue. Bob sees a red hat and a blue hat so passes. Carol does the same and they win the game. Using this strategy the team will win with probability .75. To see this, we first write down the possibilities of the hat arrangements on the players in the following table.

Alice	Bob	Carol
Red	Red	Red
Red	Red	Blue
Red	Blue	Red
Red	Blue	Blue
Blue	Red	Red
Blue	Red	Blue
Blue	Blue	Red
Blue	Blue	Blue

Notice that there are a total of eight possibilities, each one occurring with probability $\frac{1}{8}$. With the strategy described above, the team will lose when all players have red hats and when all players have blue hats. Otherwise, the team wins. In other words, the team wins six out of the eight times and so they win with probability $\frac{6}{8} = .75$ as we claimed above.

So we have a good strategy to use when there are three players. What happens if there are more? In this section we assume that there are n players where $n = 2^r - 1$ for some positive integer r. There are, of course, ways to analyze the case when n is not of this form but we will not consider those cases here. The claim stated above tells us that as the number of players increases, the probability of winning increases – that is, if the players use a good strategy. To illustrate, suppose that $n = 7$. Then $r = 3$ and so the team should be able to win with probability $\frac{7}{8}$. If $n = 63$ then $r = 6$ and so the players should be able to win with probability $\frac{63}{64}$ – pretty good odds. And we can see that the larger the n is, the better the odds that the team wins. But what is this "good" strategy? We have successfully described one for the case $n = 3$, but things get more complicated as n increases. We now work to describe a strategy that will yield the probability of winning that the above claim promises. Surprisingly, the theory of binary linear codes will be the language we use to do so.

Suppose $n = 2^r - 1$ for some positive integer r. We first construct an $r \times n$ matrix H with entries in $\mathbb{Z}_2$ such that no column consists of all zeros and such that no column is repeated. For example, if $n = 7$ then $r = 3$ and we could choose H to be the following matrix.

$$H = \begin{pmatrix} 1 & 1 & 1 & 1 & 0 & 0 & 0 \\ 1 & 1 & 0 & 0 & 1 & 1 & 0 \\ 1 & 0 & 1 & 0 & 1 & 0 & 1 \end{pmatrix}.$$

Note that there are many different possibilities for the matrix H – we can choose any of them. You should convince yourself that the number of possible nonzero columns for an $r \times n$ matrix whose entries are elements of $\mathbb{Z}_2$ is $2^r - 1 = n$ and so all possible nonzero columns must appear in H, as illustrated in our example.

We now let $C \subseteq \mathbb{Z}_2^n$ be the code defined as follows: $\vec{x} \in \mathbb{Z}_2^n$ is an element of C if and only if $H\vec{x}^T = \vec{0}$, where all arithmetic is done modulo 2. It is not difficult to show that C is an $[n, k]$ linear code where $k = n - r$ and that H is a check matrix for C (See Problem 1 at the end of this section). This leads us to the following definition.

Definition. Let $n = 2^r - 1$ for some positive integer r. Suppose H is an $r \times n$ matrix with entries in $\mathbb{Z}_2$ such that all possible nonzero columns occur exactly once. Let $C \subseteq \mathbb{Z}_2^n$ be the code consisting of all $\vec{x} \in \mathbb{Z}_2^n$ such that $H\vec{x}^T = \vec{0}$. Then C is called a binary $[n, n - r]$ Hamming code. (Note that C is an $[n, n - r]$ linear code and H is a check matrix for C.)

We now describe the strategy that our team of n players will use in order to achieve the promised probability of winning.

The Strategy

During the strategy session before the game begins, the players agree on a binary $[n, n - r]$ Hamming code C and a check matrix H for C. The players also number themselves 1 through n. They agree to let the number 0 represent blue and 1 represent red. They use the convention that the vector $\vec{v} \in \mathbb{Z}_2^n$ will represent the correct description of the way the hats are distributed. For example, suppose that $n = 7$ and the hats are as follows.

Person 1	Person 2	Person 3	Person 4	Person 5	Person 6	Person 7
Red	Red	Red	Blue	Red	Blue	Blue

Mile End Library

Queen Mary, University of London
Reading Week 8th-12th November

Extended Reading Week Loans
One Week Loans borrowed
from Thursday 4th Nov
will be due back on Monday 15th Nov

Don't forget to renew your loans
if you are going away for Reading Week

Borrowed Items 10/11/2010 22:47

XXXXX5091

Item Title	Due Date
Java 2D graphics	08/12/2010
Killer game programming in	17/11/2010
Red corner [DVD]	11/11/2010
* Protecting information : fro	17/11/2010
* Cryptography and network	17/11/2010

---

* Indicates items borrowed today

PLEASE NOTE
If you still have overdue books on loan
you may have more fines to pay

Then $\vec{v} = (1110100)$. Notice that no one on the team will know the vector $\vec{v}$ when they walk into the room, but nonetheless, it does exist. Now, after the game begins, the ith person will know all the entries of $\vec{v}$ except for the ith entry. Person i then forms the two possible vectors for $\vec{v}$. Let $\vec{v}_0$ denote the description of the way the hats are distributed if Person i has on a blue hat and $\vec{v}_1$ denote the description if Person i has on a Red hat. Notice that it must be the case that either $\vec{v} = \vec{v}_0$ or $\vec{v} = \vec{v}_1$. Now the ith person does the following:

If $H\vec{v}_0^T \neq \vec{0}$ and $H\vec{v}_1^T \neq \vec{0}$ then he passes.
If $H\vec{v}_0^T = \vec{0}$ and $H\vec{v}_1^T \neq \vec{0}$ then he guesses Red.
If $H\vec{v}_0^T \neq \vec{0}$ and $H\vec{v}_1^T = \vec{0}$ then he guesses Blue.

The case where $H\vec{v}_0^T = \vec{0}$ and $H\vec{v}_1^T = \vec{0}$ will never occur. (See Problem 2 at the end of this section.)

As an example, suppose $n = 7$, H is the matrix we decribed above, and the correct arrangements of the hats is the arrangement described above so that $\vec{v} = (1110100)$. We will go through the strategy for Person 3. He computes $\vec{v}_0 = (1100100)$ and $\vec{v}_1 = (1110100)$ Now, $H\vec{v}_0^T = (010)^T \neq \vec{0}$ and $H\vec{v}_1^T = (111)^T \neq \vec{0}$, so Person 3 passes. If we go through the actions of all the players, we will find that all of them pass except for Person 1. Person 1 will compute $\vec{v}_0 = (0110100)$ and $\vec{v}_1 = (1110100)$ and $H\vec{v}_0^T = (000)^T$ and $H\vec{v}_1^T = (111)^T \neq \vec{0}$. So he will guess (correctly) that his hat is red.

This completes the description of the strategy. We will now prove that using it, our team wins with probability $1 - \frac{1}{2^r}$. The idea of the proof is to show that if $H\vec{v}^T \neq \vec{0}$ then our strategy guarantees we win, but if $H\vec{v}^T = \vec{0}$, we are guaranteed to lose. We then argue that the probability that $H\vec{v}^T \neq \vec{0}$ is exactly $1 - \frac{1}{2^r}$.

Lemma 4.8.1. Let $n = 2^r - 1$ for some positive integer r and suppose C is a binary $[n, n - r]$ Hamming code. If $\vec{v} \in \mathbb{Z}_2^n$ such that $\vec{v} \notin C$ then there is a unique codeword $\vec{c} \in C$ satisfying $d_H(\vec{v}, \vec{c}) = 1$.

Proof. As a convention, let $\vec{e}_i \in \mathbb{Z}_2^n$ denote the vector with a 1 in the ith position and a 0 in every other position. Let H be a check matrix for C so that all possible nonzero columns occur in H. We first show that $\vec{c}$ exists and then we show it is unique.

Let $\vec{s}$ be the syndrome of $\vec{v}$. In other words, $\vec{s} = H\vec{v}^T$. Since $\vec{v} \notin C$ we know that $\vec{s} \neq \vec{0}$, and so $\vec{s}$ is a column of the matrix H. Suppose it is the ith column and note that $H\vec{e}_i^T = \vec{s}$. Now, $H(\vec{v} + \vec{e}_i)^T = H\vec{v}^T + H\vec{e}_i^T = \vec{s} + \vec{s} = \vec{0}$. So we have $\vec{v} + \vec{e}_i \in C$. Now let $\vec{c} = \vec{v} + \vec{e}_i$ and note that $d_H(\vec{v}, \vec{c}) = 1$.

We now show the uniqueness of $\vec{c}$. Suppose $\vec{c}_1, \vec{c}_2 \in C$ with $d_H(\vec{v}, \vec{c}_1) = 1$ and $d_H(\vec{v}, \vec{c}_2) = 1$. We will show $\vec{c}_1 = \vec{c}_2$. Since $d_H(\vec{v}, \vec{c}_1) = 1$ we know that $\vec{v} + \vec{c}_1 = \vec{e}_i$ for some i satisfying $1 \leq i \leq n$. Likewise, $\vec{v} + \vec{c}_2 = \vec{e}_j$ for some j satisfying $1 \leq j \leq n$. Note that $\vec{e}_i + \vec{e}_j = \vec{v} + \vec{c}_1 + \vec{v} + \vec{c}_2 = \vec{c}_1 + \vec{c}_2 \in C$. It follows that $H(\vec{e}_i + \vec{e}_j)^T = \vec{0}$ and so $H\vec{e}_i^T = H\vec{e}_j^T$. Let $H\vec{e}_i^T = \vec{s}_i$ and $H\vec{e}_j^T = \vec{s}_j$ and note that $\vec{s}_i = \vec{s}_j$. Now, $\vec{s}_i$ is the ith column of H and $\vec{s}_j$ is the jth column of H. Since these two columns have the same entries, it follows that $i = j$. This follows since the matrix H cannot have any repeated columns. Hence we have $\vec{c}_1 = \vec{v} + \vec{e}_i = \vec{v} + \vec{e}_j = \vec{c}_2$ as desired.   ❑

We now show that in the case $H\vec{v}^T \neq \vec{0}$ the strategy works.

Theorem 4.8.2. Let H and $\vec{v}$ be as described in The Strategy. If $H\vec{v}^T \neq \vec{0}$, then when a team uses The Strategy, they will win the Hat Game. On the other hand, if $H\vec{v}^T = \vec{0}$ then the team loses.

Proof. First assume that $H\vec{v}^T \neq \vec{0}$. We will show that using the strategy, exactly one player will guess correctly and all others will pass. It follows that the team wins. As in the previous proof, we define $\vec{e}_i \subseteq \mathbb{Z}_2^n$ to be the vector with a 1 in the ith position and a 0 in all other positions. Note that since $H\vec{v}^T \neq \vec{0}$ we have that $\vec{v} \notin C$ and so we can use Lemma 4.8.1. Consider the set of vectors

$$X = \{\vec{v} + \vec{e}_i \mid 1 \leq i \leq n\}.$$

X is simply the set of vectors that are a distance 1 from $\vec{v}$. By Lemma 4.8.1 there is exactly one vector $\vec{c} \in X$ such that $\vec{c} \in C$. Let $\vec{c} = \vec{v} + \vec{e}_t$ be that vector where $1 \leq t \leq n$. So if $i \neq t$ then $\vec{v} + \vec{e}_i \notin C$. For the tth player in the Hat Game, we have $\{\vec{v}_0, \vec{v}_1\} = \{\vec{v}, \vec{v} + \vec{e}_t\}$, so

$$\left\{ H\vec{v}_0^T, H\vec{v}_1^T \right\} = \{H\vec{v}^T, H(\vec{v} + \vec{e}_t)^T\} = \{H\vec{v}^T \neq \vec{0}, \vec{0}\}.$$

It follows that player t will make a guess. If $H\vec{v}_0^T = \vec{0}$, then $\vec{v}$ cannot be $\vec{v}_0$ since $H\vec{v}^T \neq \vec{0}$. So it must be that $\vec{v} = \vec{v}_1$. According to our strategy, player t correctly guesses the color corresponding to $\vec{v}_1$, that is, Red. Likewise, if $H\vec{v}_1^T = \vec{0}$, then $\vec{v} = \vec{v}_0$ and player t also guesses correctly in this case.

We now show that all other players will pass. First recall from above that if $i \neq t$ then $\vec{v} + \vec{e}_i \notin C$. For the ith player where $i \neq t$, we have $\{\vec{v}_0, \vec{v}_1\} = \{\vec{v}, \vec{v} + \vec{e}_i\}$, so

$$\left\{ H\vec{v}_0^T, H\vec{v}_1^T \right\} = \{H\vec{v}^T \neq \vec{0}, H(\vec{v} + \vec{e}_i)^T \neq \vec{0}\}.$$

This set contains two nonzero vectors and so person i passes.

It follows that if $H\vec{v}^T \neq \vec{0}$ the team wins the Hat Game.

Now suppose $H\vec{v}^T = \vec{0}$. Then every player will compute $H\vec{v}_0^T$ and $H\vec{v}_1^T$, one of which will be the zero vector and the other a nonzero vector. Each player will guess the color corresponding to the nonzero vector and thus will guess incorrectly. ❏

So we have shown that the team wins if and only if $H\vec{v}^T \neq \vec{0}$. We now show that $H\vec{v}^T \neq \vec{0}$ occurs the vast majority of the time.

Lemma 4.8.3. Suppose C is a binary $[n, k]$ linear code. Then the number of elements in C is equal to 2^k.

Proof. We leave this as an exercise for the reader (see Problem 3 at the end of this section). ❏

We are now ready to prove the main result of this section.

Theorem 4.8.4. Suppose n people are on a team playing The Hat Game where $n = 2^r - 1$ for some positive integer r. Then there exists a strategy such that the probability of the team winning is $1 - \frac{1}{2^r} = \frac{n}{n+1}$.

Proof. Let C, H, and $\vec{v}$ be as described in The Strategy and recall that the dimension of C is $k = n - r$. Now $\mathbb{Z}_2^n$ has 2^n elements in it. So by Lemma 4.8.3, we know the probability that $\vec{v} \in C$ is $\frac{2^k}{2^n} = \frac{1}{2^{n-k}} = \frac{1}{2^r}$. It follows that the probability that $H\vec{v}^T = \vec{0}$ is $\frac{1}{2^r}$ and so the probability that $H\vec{v}^T \neq \vec{0}$ is $1 - \frac{1}{2^r}$. By Theorem 4.8.2 the team using our strategy wins if and only if $H\vec{v}^T \neq \vec{0}$. It follows that the probability of the team winning is $1 - \frac{1}{2^r}$. Note that $1 - \frac{1}{2^r} = \frac{2^r - 1}{2^r} = \frac{n}{n+1}$. ◻

The Hat Problem that we have discussed in this section can be generalized. For example, we could consider the case where n is not of the form $2^r - 1$ or when there are more than two hat colors. These cases are quite interesting but beyond the scope of this book. You might want to play around with such problems on your own.

EXERCISES

Problem 1. Let $n = 2^r - 1$ for some positive integer r and let H be an $r \times n$ matrix with entries in $\mathbb{Z}_2$ such that the zero column does not appear and such that each column is different. Let $C \subseteq \mathbb{Z}_2^n$ be the code defined by the property that if $\vec{x} \in \mathbb{Z}_2^n$ then $\vec{x}$ is an element of C if and only if $H\vec{x}^T = \vec{0}$. Show that C is an $[n, k]$ linear code where $k = n - r$ and H is a check matrix for C.

Problem 2. Show that in the strategy described in this section, the case where $H\vec{v}_0^T = \vec{0}$ and $H\vec{v}_1^T = \vec{0}$ will never occur.

Problem 3. Show that if C is a binary $[n, k]$ linear code then C contains 2^k elements.

5 Quantum Cryptography Revisited

Recall that in the Bennett–Brassard key distribution scheme, after Alice and Bob have obtained bit strings that ideally are *supposed* to be identical, they have to do some further processing to make sure they end up with strings that really are identical. Our first goal in this chapter is to show how they can do this.

As you might expect, we will use error-correcting codes of the sort we have been discussing in the preceding chapter. However, the way we use error-correcting codes in quantum key distribution is not quite the same as in classical communication. Normally, one corrects errors by encoding one's message into special codewords that are sufficiently different from each other that they will still be distinguishable after passing through a noisy channel. But in quantum key distribution the "noise" of the channel might actually be the effect of an eavesdropper who is free to manipulate the signals sent by Alice. Ordinary error correction is not designed for such a setting. So instead of using codewords to encode the original transmission, we wait until all the bits have been sent and then use an error-correcting code *after the fact*.[1] In this respect error correction in quantum key distribution is similar to the use of an error-correcting code in the "hat problem" discussed at the end of Chapter 4. There also, the error-correcting code is applied only after all the data – in that case the vector of hat colors – has been generated and conveyed to the participants.

The following section shows how Alice and Bob can repair discrepancies between their strings. They do this by communicating with each other

---

[1] This strategy was proposed for quantum key distribution by Bennett, Brassard, and Robert (1988).

publicly, thus inevitably giving the eavesdropper additional information. So the eavesdropper has two sources of relevant information: (i) her own surreptitious monitoring of the original quantum transmission, and (ii) Alice's and Bob's public communication.

Once Alice and Bob are confident that they have corrected all the errors and therefore share identical strings, they need to estimate how much information Eve has gained from all sources and modify their strings so as to render useless whatever information Eve may have acquired. From the observed frequency of errors, they can estimate how much relevant information an eavesdropper might have obtained through her measurements of photons. They are also aware of the information they have given to Eve during the process of correcting errors. They now use further public communication to produce, from their shared string, a shorter string that is almost certainly private. This process, called *privacy amplification*, is outlined in Section 6.2. The subject of privacy amplification can be quite technical and in this book we only scratch the surface. We will consider first a limited kind of privacy amplification, in which Eve is assumed simply to know the values of a certain number of the elements of the shared bit string. We then consider more general kinds of knowledge that Eve might have, and we end the chapter by quoting an important theorem that applies to all such cases.

We note that in real life there will *always* be errors, even if there is no eavesdropping, because, for example, optical fibers are not perfect. Thus error correction is an indispensable part of the Bennett–Brassard protocol. Moreover, even though many of the errors are likely to have perfectly innocent explanations, Alice and Bob must assume that *all* the errors have been caused by eavesdropping. For all they know, Eve has replaced their imperfect optical fiber with a *perfect* one, and has allowed herself to do as much eavesdropping as she can without causing more errors than an ordinary fiber would cause. Thus privacy amplification is also an indispensable part of the protocol.

5.1   Error Correction for Quantum Key Distribution

We join Alice and Bob at the point in the protocol where they have already discarded all the data resulting from photons for which they used different bases. So if the channel were perfect and there were no eavesdropping, Alice's string A' and Bob's string B' would be identical. Alice and Bob now estimate the number of errors in Bob's string, that is, the number of places where the two strings differ, by publicly comparing a small random sample of the two bit strings. They throw out the bits that they have checked, since Eve now has access to them. Alice and Bob use their comparisons to estimate the frequency with which errors have occurred. For example, if Alice randomly chooses 2000 bits of A' and finds that 100 of them do not agree with the corresponding bits of B', she will assume that approximately one out of every twenty of Bob's remaining bits is also likely to be wrong. Alice and Bob certainly do not want to check *all* of their bits to find out which ones are wrong. This would give Eve *all* of their information and they would have no secret bits left. So they will try to correct the errors in the remaining bits without knowing anything about where these errors occur. It may seem remarkable that they can do this without telling Eve everything. Indeed, it is impossible to do it with *absolute* certainty. But it is quite possible to do it with sufficient confidence for all practical purposes.

To see how it is possible in principle to correct the errors, let us consider first an unrealistically simple example. Suppose that Alice and Bob each has a bit string consisting of exactly 7 bits, and suppose they are confident that their strings differ in at most one place. Here is Alice's string $\vec{a}$:

$$\vec{a} = (a_1, a_2, a_3, a_4, a_5, a_6, a_7),$$

where each a_i is in $\mathbb{Z}_2$. Bob's string is

$$\vec{b} = (b_1, b_2, b_3, b_4, b_5, b_6, b_7).$$

Alice and Bob are sure that at most one of the b_i's is different from the corresponding a_i, but each of the b_i's is equally suspect. How can they correct such an error?

Here is a strategy that works.

1. Alice and Bob agree (publicly) on a check matrix H for the binary [7,4] Hamming code:

$$H = \begin{pmatrix} 1 & 1 & 1 & 0 & 1 & 0 & 0 \\ 1 & 1 & 0 & 1 & 0 & 1 & 0 \\ 0 & 1 & 1 & 1 & 0 & 0 & 1 \end{pmatrix} \tag{5.1}$$

2. Alice applies H to $\vec{a}^T$ to get $\vec{s}^A = H\vec{a}^T$ – recall that $\vec{s}^A$ is the syndrome of $\vec{a}$ – and she sends $\vec{s}^A$ to Bob over a public channel.
3. Bob applies H to $\vec{b}^T$ to get $\vec{s}^B = H\vec{b}^T$.
4. Bob computes $\vec{s} = \vec{s}^B - \vec{s}^A = H\vec{b}^T - H\vec{a}^T = H(\vec{b} - \vec{a})^T$. Let $\vec{e} = \vec{b} - \vec{a}$. Then $\vec{s} = H\vec{e}^T$.
5. If indeed there is no more than one error in the string of seven bits, then $w(\vec{e}) \leq 1$. We know that for this code there is a unique minimum-weight vector $\vec{v}$ that satisfies $H\vec{v}^T = \vec{s}$. So that vector must be $\vec{e}$. Bob now replaces his string $\vec{b}$ with the corrected version $\vec{b} - \vec{e}$.

Example 5.1.1. Suppose $\vec{a} = (1000111)$ and $\vec{b} = (1100111)$. Then

$$H\vec{a}^T = \begin{pmatrix} 0 \\ 0 \\ 1 \end{pmatrix}, \quad H\vec{b}^T = \begin{pmatrix} 1 \\ 1 \\ 0 \end{pmatrix}, \quad \vec{s} = \begin{pmatrix} 1 \\ 1 \\ 0 \end{pmatrix} - \begin{pmatrix} 0 \\ 0 \\ 1 \end{pmatrix} = \begin{pmatrix} 1 \\ 1 \\ 1 \end{pmatrix};$$

so $\vec{e} = (0100000)$, and Bob replaces $\vec{b}$ with $\vec{b} - \vec{e} = (1100111) - (0100000) = (1000111)$, which is the correct string $\vec{a}$.

Thus Bob has been able to correct his error without having to check each of his bits against the corresponding bit in Alice's string. (He has been able to do this only because Alice and Bob had obtained evidence that limited the number of likely errors in the string.) Of course the public communication has given the eavesdropper new information about Alice's string, and our participants will have to take further steps to compensate for this leak. This problem belongs to the subject of privacy amplification and will be considered in the following section.

One can imagine applying the above strategy on a much larger scale. Suppose that Alice and Bob each has a string of n bits, and they are very confident that there are no more than e discrepancies between Alice's string and Bob's. Then for as large a value of k as possible, they choose an $[n, k]$ code that corrects e errors, and they use a check matrix for that code just as we had them do in the preceding example. That is, Alice computes and transmits the syndrome of her bit string – the syndrome will be a string of $n - k$ bits – and Bob computes his syndrome, and the *difference* between the syndromes will tell him how to bring his string into agreement with Alice's. Of course this also gives Eve $n - k$ bits that she probably did not have before, but the main point is that Alice and Bob did not have to give away *all* their bits in order to correct the errors.

Notice that the error-correction strategy we have been considering so far involves only one-way communication from Alice to Bob. Bob corrects the errors in his string, and Alice never needs to hear back from him about where those errors occurred. Schemes of this kind have been found useful in mathematical proofs of the security of quantum key distribution.[2] However, it can be more computationally efficient, and in some respects simpler, to use an interactive error-correction protocol in which Alice sends Bob very limited information at first, and then waits to hear back from him before sending the next piece of information.

Here is a fairly simple interactive protocol, based on a sequence of parity checks, that will do the job as long as the error rate, that is, the number of errors divided by the length of the string, is not too high.[3]

1. Alice and Bob agree publicly on a random permutation of their bit strings, and they both apply this permutation. This step has the effect of distributing the errors randomly over the length of the string.
2. Alice and Bob break their respective strings into blocks of a certain length, the length being chosen so that it is unlikely that a given block contains more than one error.
3. For each block, Alice and Bob compute and publicly compare the *parity* of the block, that is, the sum mod 2 of the bits in the block. Blocks for which the parities agree are tentatively accepted as correct (though they may contain an even number of errors).
4. For each block showing a disagreement in step 3, the block is broken into two subblocks of roughly equal size, and the parities of Alice's first subblock and Bob's first subblock are publicly compared. This tells them in which half the parity discrepancy lies. The offending subblock is then itself divided in half, and the process continues until an error is located in a specific bit. At that point Bob flips the value of the bit that has been found to be in error.
5. Since the protocol as presented so far will miss errors whenever a block or subblock has an even number of errors, Alice and Bob now repeat

---

[2] See, for example, Mayers (2001), Section 4.
[3] Bennett, et al. (1992).

the whole process several times, each time starting with a different random permutation. But in each repetition, the starting block size will typically be larger than it was before, since Alice and Bob will typically estimate that there are fewer errors remaining.[4]

6. Once the block size becomes comparable to the length of their bit strings, that is, once there are just a few errors remaining, Alice and Bob shift to a somewhat different strategy: instead of using blocks, they choose a random subset (about half as large as the whole string) and compare parities for this subset. Each time they find a discrepancy, they break the subset in half as before, repeating the process until they find and correct the error. They then repeat this random-subset protocol until several successive repetitions have uncovered no more errors, at which point it is extremely unlikely that any further errors remain.

Example 5.1.2. Let us try out steps 3 and 4 on a block of length 8. Suppose Alice's and Bob's strings are $\vec{a} = (11011001)$ and $\vec{b} = (11011011)$. Alice sends to Bob the parity of her string, which is 1. Bob tells her that this is not his parity; so they know that there is an error. Therefore they compare the parities of the first four bits: these parities agree, so they leave these bits unchanged and they know that there is a discrepancy in the last four bits. This leads them to check the parity of $a_5 a_6$ against $b_5 b_6$: the parities agree; so they know the discrepancy is in the last two bits. They check a_7 against b_7 and find the error. Bob now changes b_7 from 1 to 0. At this point Alice and Bob cannot be sure that they have corrected all the errors in the block. For example, there could still be two errors in the first four bits. Further checking for such errors would come in later rounds. Finally, note that in the above process Alice has given away only four parity bits; so as in our earlier technique, she has not had to tell Eve everything.

---

[4] One can refine this protocol, and make it more efficient in the sense of revealing fewer bits to Eve, by keeping careful track of the parity checks that one has made in earlier rounds. For example, if Alice and Bob previously found no parity discrepancy in the bit string $b_5 b_8 b_9 b_{16}$, but now, in a subsequent round, they find and correct an error in bit b_8, they know that the new version of block $b_5 b_8 b_9 b_{16}$ has an odd number of errors. So they return to this bit string and correct an error by dividing the string into substrings as usual. This approach leads to the "cascade" protocol devised by Brassard and Salvail (1993).

In general, as long as the error rate is limited and the starting strings are very long, Alice and Bob will in principle be able to correct the errors by public communication as in the above examples, without giving all their information to Eve. If Alice and Bob estimate that the error rate is large, they should still be able to correct the errors, but only by sharing with Eve almost as many bits as they share with each other. Even this would be all right, if it were not for the fact that Eve may have already gained some information from her initial eavesdropping. When the two sources of Eve's information are combined, it could happen that Eve knows everything about Alice's and Bob's string. Thus even with error correction, quantum key distribution will not work if the error rate is too high. (See the references cited on p. 190.)

EXERCISES

Problem 1. Alice and Bob have determined that it is very unlikely that a string of seven bits will contain more than one error; so they have decided to use the binary [7,4] Hamming code to correct their errors, with the check matrix of Eq. (5.1).

(a) Suppose Bob's string is 1110110. Alice sends him the syndrome 111. What does Bob's string become after error correction?

(b) In another case, Bob's initial string is 0000111. Alice sends him the syndrome 111. What does Bob's string become after error correction?

Problem 2. Consider again steps 3 and 4 of the protocol described just before Example 5.1.2 and used in that example. Consider a block of 32 bits and suppose that there is indeed a discrepancy in only one of the bits. If Alice and Bob use this error correcting technique, how many parity bits will they have to give away to Eve in order to correct the error? Does the answer to this question depend on the location of the error in Bob's bit string?

5.2 Introduction to Privacy Amplification

We assume now that Alice and Bob have made all the corrections necessary to assure themselves that their strings are identical. Let us call the shared string $\vec{a}$. Moreover, they have combined their knowledge of the error rate with their knowledge of the information that they themselves have leaked to Eve, to estimate how much information Eve has obtained altogether. Their goal is to produce a shorter shared string $\vec{\alpha}$ about which Eve knows nothing. We proceed by considering different kinds of knowledge that Eve might have, starting with the simplest case, in which Eve's knowledge is limited to a fixed number of elements of Alice and Bob's shared string. We confess that this is not a very realistic case in the context of quantum key distribution, but it is useful for showing how privacy amplification is possible.

5.2.1 Eve knows a fixed number of elements of the bit string

We begin with a simple 3-bit example.

Example 5.2.1. Let $\vec{a} = (a_1, a_2, a_3)$. Suppose that Eve knows at most one of the bits a_1, a_2, a_3 and nothing else. Let $\vec{\alpha} = (a_1 + a_3, a_2 + a_3)$. We claim that Eve knows nothing about $\vec{\alpha}$. To verify this claim, consider the following table showing the relation between $\vec{a}$ and $\vec{\alpha}$:

$\vec{a}$	$\vec{\alpha}$
000	00
001	11
010	01
011	10
100	10
101	01
110	11
111	00

Suppose that Eve knows that $a_1 = 0$. This knowledge restricts $\vec{a}$ to the first four entries in the table. But these entries include all four possible values of $\vec{\alpha}$; so Eve knows nothing about α. One can check that the same argument works regardless of which bit a_i Eve knows and what value it has. So if Alice and Bob start with the shared string $\vec{a}$, they can agree, publicly, on the above method of creating the shorter string $\vec{\alpha}$. Eve will eavesdrop on their discussion and will therefore know exactly what Alice and Bob are doing, but there is nothing she can do about it: she will end up with no information whatsoever about $\vec{\alpha}$.

Note for future reference that in this example we can express the relation between $\vec{a}$ and $\vec{\alpha}$ in matrix form as follows:

$$\vec{\alpha}^T = \begin{pmatrix} \alpha_1 \\ \alpha_2 \end{pmatrix} = \begin{pmatrix} 1 & 0 & 1 \\ 0 & 1 & 1 \end{pmatrix} \begin{pmatrix} a_1 \\ a_2 \\ a_3 \end{pmatrix},$$

or

$$\vec{\alpha}^T = G\vec{a}^T, \quad \text{where } G = \begin{pmatrix} 1 & 0 & 1 \\ 0 & 1 & 1 \end{pmatrix}.$$

Again, we assume that Eve knows the matrix G and how it is being used. That is, the matrix itself is not a secret, even though it is used to help generate a secret key.

Now we give a very similar example that does not work so well.

Example 5.2.2. Let $\vec{a} = (a_1, a_2, a_3, a_4)$. Suppose that Eve knows exactly two of the four bits and that she knows nothing about the other two. Let us try the following privacy amplification scheme: $\alpha_1 = a_1 + a_2 + a_3$ and $\alpha_2 = a_2 + a_3 + a_4$. In matrix form,

$$\vec{\alpha}^T = G\vec{a}^T, \quad \text{where } G = \begin{pmatrix} 1 & 1 & 1 & 0 \\ 0 & 1 & 1 & 1 \end{pmatrix}.$$

The string $\vec{\alpha}$ is two bits shorter than $\vec{a}$. Since Eve knows exactly two bits, one might hope that $\vec{\alpha}$ is completely secret. But this is not necessarily the case. Note that $\alpha_1 + \alpha_2 = a_1 + a_4$. So if Eve happens to know a_1 and a_4, then she knows $\alpha_1 + \alpha_2$. Thus the string $\vec{\alpha}$ is not entirely secret.

Why did the first example work for Alice and Bob while the second example did not? If we think of G as the generator matrix of a linear code, we can see that the problem with the G of the second example is that one of its codewords, namely (1001), has too small a weight. Its weight is equal to the number of bits that Eve knows. So if she happens to know the correct bits, a_1 and a_4, then she also knows a certain linear combination of α_1 and α_2 (namely, their sum). This example leads us to make the following conjecture.

Conjecture 5.2.1. The string $\vec{\alpha}^T = G\vec{a}^T$ is guaranteed to be secret if and only if the minimum weight of the code generated by G is strictly greater than the number of bits that Eve knows.

In the case where $\vec{a}$ contains four bits of which Eve knows two, one can verify that this condition can be met only if G has just one row. For example, we can use

$$\vec{\alpha}^T = \begin{pmatrix} 1 & 1 & 1 & 0 \end{pmatrix} \begin{pmatrix} a_1 \\ a_2 \\ a_3 \\ a_4 \end{pmatrix},$$

so that the code generated by G has minimum weight 3. So in this case Alice and Bob have to make their string three bits shorter in order to guarantee secrecy.

In fact, the above conjecture is correct. We state it now more carefully as a theorem.[5]

Theorem 5.2.1. Let $\vec{a} \in \mathbb{Z}_2^n$. Suppose that Eve knows the values of exactly t bits of $\vec{a}$ and nothing else. (That is, for Eve, t of the bits of $\vec{a}$ have fixed values and the remaining collection of $n - t$ bits take all 2^{n-t} possible values with equal probability.) Let G generate a linear $[n, k]$ code $C \subset \mathbb{Z}_2^n$ with minimum weight w. Let $\vec{\alpha}^T = G\vec{a}^T$. Then if $w > t$, Eve knows nothing about $\vec{\alpha}$. (That is, all 2^k values of $\vec{\alpha}$ are equally likely.) If $w \leq t$, then Eve could know something about $\vec{\alpha}$. (That is, there exists a set of indices $\{i_1, i_2, \ldots, i_t\}$ such that if the bits $a_{i_1}, \ldots, a_{i_t}$ are the ones whose values are fixed, then not all values of $\vec{\alpha}$ are equally likely.)

Proof. The second part, "If $w \leq t \ldots$," will be covered in the problems at the end of this section. The rest of the proof is left as an exercise for the adventurous student.   ❑

The above discussion shows that privacy amplification is possible, at least in a certain context. But the approach we have taken so far demands too much in a certain sense, and too little in another. It demands too much in that in real life we cannot insist on perfect security. For example,

---

[5] Bennett, Brassard, and Robert (1988); Chor et al. (1985).

Alice and Bob could never put a strict and nontrivial upper bound on the amount of information that Eve has learned about a given block of bits; so there will always be some probability that part of Eve's initial information will survive the privacy amplification. The best we can do is to make it extremely unlikely that Eve knows much of anything. On the other hand, the above approach demands too little in that the nature of Eve's information could in fact be much more subtle than what we have considered. Indeed, already in our examples of the preceding section, Eve did not end up simply knowing the values of certain bits in the string $\vec{a}$. Rather, she learned the values of certain *sums* of bits. The above theorem does not cover this case.

5.2.2 Eve knows the parities of certain subsets of the bit string

Another case that is mathematically interesting, though still not quite what we need for quantum key distribution, is the case in which Eve knows the parities of certain subsets of Alice's bit string. This is the kind of information Alice leaked to Eve in the error-correction protocols we considered in Section 5.1. In this subsection we assume that such parities are the *only* information that Eve has obtained; she has not done any actual eavesdropping on the original quantum signals. It is this assumption that makes the considerations of the present subsection not quite applicable to quantum key distribution.

Recall that in Example 5.1.1, Alice starts with a 7-bit string $\vec{a}$, and in effect tells Eve the values of the three syndrome bits given in the following equation.

$$\vec{s} = H\vec{a}^T = \begin{pmatrix} 1 & 1 & 1 & 0 & 1 & 0 & 0 \\ 1 & 1 & 0 & 1 & 0 & 1 & 0 \\ 0 & 1 & 1 & 1 & 0 & 0 & 1 \end{pmatrix} \begin{pmatrix} a_1 \\ a_2 \\ a_3 \\ a_4 \\ a_5 \\ a_6 \\ a_7 \end{pmatrix}$$

$$= \begin{pmatrix} a_1 + a_2 + a_3 + a_5 \\ a_1 + a_2 + a_4 + a_6 \\ a_2 + a_3 + a_4 + a_7 \end{pmatrix} = \begin{pmatrix} s_1^A \\ s_2^A \\ s_3^A \end{pmatrix}. \tag{5.2}$$

Eve does not know the value of any of the bits a_i, but she knows the values of the three sums that appear in $\vec{s}$. What can Alice and Bob do about this? As before, we expect that they will have to throw away some of their bits. But how many bits should they throw away, and does it matter which ones they choose? To get a feel for this problem, let us try a few different strategies.

1. Throw away a_4, a_6, and a_7. In this case the remaining bits are a_1, a_2, a_3, and a_5. But according to Eq. (5.2), Eve knows the sum of these four bits: this sum is the syndrome bit s_1^A. This is bad for Alice and Bob.
2. Throw away a_1, a_2, and a_7. Now the remaining bits are a_3, a_4, a_5, and a_6. But the sum of these bits is the sum of s_1^A and s_2^A, which Eve knows. So again this is bad.
3. Throw away a_5, a_6, and a_7. In this case the remaining bits are a_1, a_2, a_3, and a_4. Does Eve know anything about these bits? We claim that she does not. Eve has been given only the syndrome $\vec{s}$ and the check matrix H. One can see that given any values for a_1, a_2, a_3, and a_4, there exist unique values for a_5, a_6, and a_7 such that the syndrome of $\vec{a}$ is the given $\vec{s}$. It follows that Eve cannot rule out any of the possibilities for $a_1, a_2,$ $a_3,$ and a_4, and that all of these possibilities are equally likely. That is, she has no information about the bits that Alice and Bob have kept.

Notice that in this last strategy, Alice and Bob threw away the check bits of the code and kept the information bits. By an extension of the argument just given, this strategy – throwing away the check bits – will always leave Eve with no information about the remaining bits, assuming that she had no information to start with.

Similarly, in the interactive error-correcting protocol that we considered in Section 5.1, each time Alice conveys to Bob the parity of a string of bits, Alice and Bob could discard, say, the last bit in the string in order to keep Eve ignorant of the remaining bits. This would indeed keep Eve from learning anything useful if it is true that she did not already know anything. In fact, one can show that this strategy also works well for Alice and Bob even if Eve does have some initial information, as long as this information is of a certain form, such as knowing the values of particular bits.

However, the strategy of throwing away the check bits does not work for more general kinds of knowledge that Eve might have (and it was therefore not recommended by the authors of the interactive protocol). To see this, consider the following example.

Example 5.2.3. Let (a_1, a_2) be a 2-bit string held by Alice. As part of an error-correction protocol, she conveys to Bob over a public channel the parity $a_1 \oplus a_2$, which happens to be 0. (Here $\oplus$ means addition mod 2.) She then discards the bit a_2, and Bob discards the corresponding bit in his string, hoping to make the revealed parity bit useless to Eve. However, it happened that Eve had already done some fancy eavesdropping that ruled out the specific string 00. That is, for Eve, the only possibilities were 01, 10, and 11. When she hears that the parity $a_1 \oplus a_2$ has the value 0, she knows immediately that the string is 11. In particular, she knows that the bit a_1, which Alice is keeping, has the value 1, a fact that she did not know previously. So the strategy of discarding the last bit after a parity check does not always prevent Eve from learning something.

The following subsection considers the problem of privacy amplification in a more realistic setting.

5.2.3 The general case

To get a sense of how subtle Eve's information could be, consider the following eavesdropping strategy. Rather than making a complete measurement on certain photons sent by Alice, Eve could build a probe that interacts weakly with each of the photons. Then, once she has learned what basis Alice used for each photon, Eve could measure her probe, choosing her measurement so as to provide as much information as possible about the *whole* string of bits. In one of the problems in Chapter 3 we considered something along these lines, which we called "the partial cloning strategy." But that strategy treated each photon separately, so that the information Eve obtained was always about individual bits of Alice's string. Now we are imagining that her probe interacts with *all* the photons before she makes her measurement, so that the information she gains could take the form of *correlations* among the bits and could be entirely probabilistic. For example, she may end up knowing that the sum (mod 2) of a_1, a_6, and a_{17} has a 75% chance of being zero. Even though she may not be certain about the value of *any* particular bit, or any sum of bits, this sort of probabilistic information is quite valuable. It would give her a way to start decrypting any secret message that Alice might send to Bob using their shared key. Thus it is crucially important that Alice and Bob find a way, in such circumstances, to produce a new string about which Eve knows essentially nothing.

Below we list various ways in which one might characterize Eve's information about the n-bit string $\vec{a}$ shared by Alice and Bob. Each item in the list includes the items that precede it as special cases. Since Eve may be capable of making a joint measurement on many photons, as in the above example in which she uses a probe, ultimately the only kind of bound that Alice and Bob can safely place on Eve's knowledge will be a statement about probabilities. The last item in the following list is a bound of this sort.

1. Eve knows t of the bits in the string $\vec{a}$ (as in Subsection 5.2.1).
2. Eve knows the parities of t substrings of $\vec{a}$ (as in Subsection 5.2.2).
3. Eve knows the value of $f(\vec{a})$, where f is a function from $\mathbb{Z}_2^n$ to $\mathbb{Z}_2^t$. (This is still deterministic information, whereas Eve is much more likely to have obtained probabilistic information.)
4. Eve's knowledge of $\vec{a}$ is characterized by a probability distribution $p(\vec{a})$ whose *Rényi information* is no greater than t.

We encountered Rényi information in Chapter 3. But there we defined it only for a probability distribution (p_0, p_1) over the two possible values of a single bit. Now we are thinking of a string of bits $\vec{a}$, which has 2^n possible values if $\vec{a}$ consists of n bits. So we need to define Rényi information more generally. We begin, as before, with the more standard notion of *Rényi entropy*.[6]

Definition. Let $\{\vec{a}\}$ be a string of bits, and let p be a probability distribution over all possible values of this string. That is, p is a function taking nonnegative values such that $\sum_{\vec{a}} p(\vec{a}) = 1$. The Rényi entropy H_R of the probability distribution is defined by

$$H_R = -\log_2 \left(\sum_{\vec{a}} [p(\vec{a})]^2 \right). \tag{5.3}$$

[6] More generally, the Rényi entropy of order α is defined as $(1/(1-\alpha))\log_2(\sum[p(\vec{a})]^\alpha)$. As in Chapter 3, we are using the Rényi entropy of order 2.

As we noted in Chapter 3, the Rényi entropy is usually expressed in units of bits.

As before, the Rényi entropy can be interpreted as the amount of information that one *lacks* about the string $\vec{a}$. To get a feeling for this quantity, let us consider a few examples.

Example 5.2.4. Suppose that all possible bit strings $\vec{a}$ of length n have the same probability $1/2^n$. Then the Rényi entropy is $H_R = -\log_2[\sum_{\vec{a}}(1/2^{2n})] = n$. This expresses the fact that if all strings are equally likely for Eve, she lacks n bits of information. One can thus see better why "bit" is used as a unit of entropy: if you know nothing about a string of n bits, you lack n bits of information.

Example 5.2.5. At the other extreme, suppose that one of the strings has probability 1 and the rest have probability 0. In this case the Rényi entropy is $H_R = -\log_2 1 = 0$, and we say that Eve lacks zero bits of information about the string.

Example 5.2.6. Suppose that Eve knows the values of exactly t bits of $\vec{a}$ and nothing else. Then the number of strings that are possible for Eve is 2^{n-t}, and each of these has probability $1/2^{n-t}$. So Eve's Rényi entropy is

$$H_R = -\log_2\left[2^{n-t}\left(\frac{1}{2^{n-t}}\right)^2\right] = n - t.$$

Thus when Eve knows the values of a specific set of bits, her Rényi entropy is simply equal to the number of remaining bits, about which she knows nothing.

Whereas the Rényi entropy H_R measures the amount of information that Eve *lacks*, the Rényi information measures the amount that she *has*, by comparing her value of H_R to its maximum possible value. For a string of n bits, this maximum possible value is n. So we define the Rényi information as follows.

Definition. Let $\vec{a}$ be a string of bits of length n, and let p be a probability distribution over all possible values of this string. The *Rényi information*

I_R of the probability distribution is defined by

$$I_R = n - H_R = n + \log_2 \left(\sum_{\vec{a}} [p(\vec{a})]^2 \right). \tag{5.4}$$

Rényi entropy is by no means the most common way of quantifying one's lack of information. The most common such quantification was given by Shannon and is the focus of the most central theorems of information theory. The Shannon entropy of a probability distribution $p(\vec{a})$ is defined as[7]

$$H = - \sum_{\vec{a}} p(\vec{a}) \log_2 p(\vec{a}), \tag{5.5}$$

a quantity that, like the Rényi entropy H_R, ranges from 0 to n for an n-bit string $\vec{a}$. In fact H is an upper bound for H_R:

$$H \geq H_R \tag{5.6}$$

If the focus of this book had been on the theoretical limits on error-correcting codes, for example, we would have devoted several chapters to Shannon entropy and its applications. Indeed, even in quantum key distribution, Alice and Bob ultimately want to limit the amount of Shannon information that Eve possesses about their final shared key, the Shannon information being defined as $I = n - H$, which is analogous to Eq. (5.4). But for assessing whether they can *achieve* this goal, and for figuring out *how* to achieve this goal, it is not sufficient to estimate Eve's Shannon information about the string that they share *before* privacy amplification. Instead, they should estimate her Rényi information. The justification for this statement comes from an important theorem to be stated shortly.

The examples of the preceding subsections suggest that in order to achieve security, Alice and Bob will have to discard at least as many bits as Eve knows. It turns out that this intuition remains valid even when Eve does not know t specific bits but has t bits of Rényi information manifested in some other way. Alice and Bob will have to discard at least t bits, and the more bits they discard in excess of t bits, the more secret their final shared string will be.

---

[7] It is interesting that the Shannon entropy is the limit of the Rényi entropy of order α (see the preceding footnote) as α approaches one. It is a fun exercise to take this limit!

Clearly, though, it is not sufficient for Alice and Bob simply to discard a specified set of bits. For example, if Eve has t bits of Rényi information about the string as a whole, it will almost certainly not be sufficient for Alice and Bob to lop off the last t bits of their strings: at least part of Eve's information was probably about some of the other bits. Rather, they should do what we had them doing earlier in this section: they select a matrix G which they apply to $\vec{a}$ to create the shorter string $\vec{\alpha}$. (As always, we assume that Eve will know exactly what matrix G Alice and Bob are using.) But what matrix should they use? The following theorem, in addition to expressing precisely how the security is enhanced by shortening the string, also tells us that one can do very well by choosing G *at random*. In fact, the matrix does not even have to be a generator matrix; that is, Alice and Bob do not have to check to see whether the rows are linearly independent. We state the theorem without proof.[8]

Theorem 5.2.2. Suppose that Eve has Rényi information $I_R \leq t$ about the n-bit string $\vec{a}$, where t is a nonnegative integer less than n. Let s be any positive integer less than $n - t$, and let $k = n - t - s$. Finally, let $\vec{\alpha}^T = G\vec{a}^T$, where G is a randomly chosen $k \times n$ binary matrix. Then Eve's average Rényi information about the k-bit string $\vec{\alpha}$ – that is, averaged over all possible matrices G – is no larger than $2^{-s}/\ln 2$. (Note that Eve's Rényi information about $\vec{\alpha}$ is defined to be $I_R = k - H_R$, since k is the number of bits in $\vec{\alpha}$.)

It follows that Eve's final Shannon information about $\vec{\alpha}$, which is what Alice and Bob ultimately care about, is *also* bounded by $2^{-s}/\ln 2$. This is because of the inequality (5.6):

$$I = k - H \leq k - H_R = I_R.$$

Note that Eve's information shrinks *exponentially* with increasing s: each additional bit that Alice and Bob are willing to sacrifice reduces the upper bound on Eve's information by another factor of 2. If the original string $\vec{a}$ is very long, the additional s bits that provide the cushion of

---

[8] Bennett et al. (1995). Their theorem is actually more general in that it allows other ways of producing the shorter string. We also note that the authors state their theorem in terms of Rényi entropy rather than the less standard notion of Rényi information.

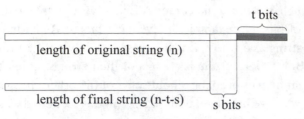

Figure 5.1: Illustration of the effect of privacy amplification. Eve initially has t bits of Rényi information about Alice and Bob's string. (These bits do not literally lie at the end of the string.) After privacy amplification, her information is bounded by $2^{-s}/\ln 2$. The s bits of further shortening represent a security cushion for Alice and Bob.

security can represent quite a small fraction of the bits that Alice and Bob finally keep. The effect of privacy amplification is illustrated schematically in Fig. 5.1.

We see, then, that the complete protocol for quantum key distribution includes several steps: (i) The original quantum transmission and comparison of bases. (After this step Alice and Bob have strings which are not necessarily identical and not necessarily secret.) (ii) Checking some bits for errors and discarding these bits. (iii) Correcting the errors in the remaining bits. (After this step the strings are almost certainly identical but not private.) (iv) Privacy amplification.

Quantum key distribution has been an area of active research, both mathematical and experimental, for some decades now and progress continues to be made on both fronts. One of the greatest mathematical challenges was to prove that the Bennett–Brassard scheme is indeed secure against all conceivable eavesdropping strategies allowed by the rules of quantum mechanics. The strategy we mentioned earlier, in which Eve lets her probe interact with all the photons and then delays her measurement until she knows the whole sequence of bases, is particularly subtle. But it has now been proven in a few different ways that the scheme is indeed secure against such attacks.[9]

Ironically, while quantum cryptography in principle provides new ways to transmit information securely, another quantum technology, quantum computation, threatens to subvert the ingenious and widely used

[9] Mayers (1996); Lo and Chau (1999); Shor and Preskill (2000); Biham et al. (2000). For recent results on tolerable error rates, see Kraus, Gisin, and Renner (2005) and Chau (2002).

public key cryptosystems that we studied in Chapter 1. We will study this quantum technology in Chapter 7.

EXERCISES

Problem 1. Prove the second statement of Theorem 5.2.1. That is, if the weight of the code is less than or equal to the number of bits that Eve knows about the string $\vec{a}$, then if she knows the right bits of $\vec{a}$ she will also have some information about the string $\vec{\alpha}$.

Problem 2. Alice and Bob share a string $\vec{a}$ of n bits. They know that Eve might know the values of up to t of their bits. So, as in subsection 5.2.1, they create a k-bit string $\vec{\alpha}$ defined as

$$\vec{\alpha}^T = G\vec{a}^T,$$

where G is a generator matrix for an $[n, k]$ linear code. Let $m(n, t)$ be the largest value of k for which one can find a G such that the resulting string $\vec{\alpha}$ is guaranteed to be entirely secret. That is, $m(n, t)$ be the greatest number of genuinely secret bits Alice and Bob can share after privacy amplification by this method. Use Theorem 5.2.1 to find the value of $m(n, t)$ for $n = 2, 3, 4, 5$ and for $t = 1, \ldots, n - 1$. (You will have to optimize over various G's.)

Problem 3. As in problem 2, Alice and Bob share a string of n bits. But now Eve knows the values of exactly two of the bits. With $m(n, t)$ being defined as in Problem 2, we are now interested specifically in $m(n, 2)$. Show that for any fixed positive integer q, one can find an integer n such that $m(n, 2) < n - q$. (That is, there is no limit on the number of bits Alice and Bob might have to sacrifice for *perfect* secrecy, even though Eve knows only two bits.)

Problem 4. Alice and Bob share a 3-bit string $\vec{a} = (a_1, a_2, a_3)$. Eve has made a measurement on this string suggesting that $(0, 0, 0)$ is the most likely value of $\vec{a}$. Specifically, she assigns probability 1/2 to $(0, 0, 0)$ and splits the remaining probability evenly among the other possibilities.

   (a) What is Eve's Rényi entropy about the string $\vec{a}$?
   (b) What is Eve's Shannon entropy about the string $\vec{a}$?

(c) Now suppose that Alice and Bob share an n-bit string. Eve assigns probability 1/2 to the string $(0, 0, 0, \ldots, 0)$ and regards all the other possibilities as equally likely. Compute Eve's Rényi and Shannon entropies. Show that as n approaches infinity, the Shannon entropy also approaches infinity while the Rényi entropy remains bounded. This example shows that even if Eve lacks a lot of information in the Shannon sense, she may not lack much information in the Rényi sense, and therefore Alice and Bob may still have to do a lot of privacy amplification.

6 Generalized Reed-Solomon Codes

6.1 Definitions and Examples

In this chapter we discuss a class of extremely useful and beautiful linear codes called generalized Reed-Solomon codes. In fact, many linear codes in use today can be expressed as a generalized Reed-Solomon code. For example, generalized Reed-Solomon codes serve as the backbone for the error-correction scheme used by compact disk and DVD players. This chapter will serve as a brief introduction to the subject and is intended to be very basic.[1]

We begin with several definitions.

Definition. Let F be a field. We define the set of polynomials $F[x]$ as

$$F[x] = \{r_0 + r_1 x + r_2 x^2 + \cdots + r_n x^n | r_i \in F, n \in \mathbb{N}\}.$$

Notice that we have a natural addition and multiplication of the polynomials in the set $F[x]$ using "usual" polynomial addition and multiplication and the operations from the field F. We illustrate with several examples.

Example 6.1.1. Let $F = \mathbb{Z}_7$. Then, $\mathbb{Z}_7[x]$ is the set of all polynomials with coefficients from the field $\mathbb{Z}_7$. Now,

$$(5 + 2x + 3x^2 + 6x^3) + (3 + 2x + 6x^2) = 1 + 4x + 2x^2 + 6x^3.$$

---

[1] The reader interested in learning more should consult other sources such as Pless and Huffman (1998).

Notice that all the addition is being done modulo 7 since that is the addition used in the field $\mathbb{Z}_7$. Also,

$$3(5 + 2x + 3x^2 + 6x^3) = 1 + 6x + 2x^2 + 4x^3$$

and

$$(5 + x)(2 + 2x) = 3 + 5x + 2x^2.$$

Definition. The set $F[x]$ together with the addition and multiplication described above is called the *polynomial ring* in the indeterminate x over the field F.

Definition. Let k be a nonnegative integer and F a field. Then $F[x]_k$ denotes all polynomials of $F[x]$ of degree less than k with the convention that the zero polynomial has degree -1.

Notice that $F[x]$ is an infinite dimensional vector space over F and that $F[x]_k$ is a subspace of $F[x]$ of dimension k.

We are now in a position to define a generalized Reed-Solomon code.

Definition. Let F be a field and $0 \le k \le n$ where k and n are integers. Suppose $v_1, v_2, \ldots, v_n$ are nonzero elements of F and $\alpha_1, \alpha_2, \ldots, \alpha_n$ are elements of F satisfying $\alpha_i = \alpha_j$ if and only if $i = j$. Let $\vec{\alpha} = (\alpha_1, \alpha_2, \ldots, \alpha_n) \in F^n$ and $\vec{v} = (v_1, v_2, \ldots, v_n) \in F^n$. Then we define the generalized Reed-Solomon code with respect to $F, n, k, \vec{\alpha}$, and $\vec{v}$ to be

$$GRS_{n,k}(\vec{\alpha}, \vec{v}) = \{(v_1 f(\alpha_1), v_2 f(\alpha_2), \ldots, v_n f(\alpha_n)) | f(x) \in F[x]_k\} \subseteq F^n.$$

Sometimes we will write $\vec{f}$ for $(v_1 f(\alpha_1), v_2 f(\alpha_2), \ldots, v_n f(\alpha_n))$. As the definition of a generalized Reed-Solomon code is a bit complicated, we illustrate with an example.

Example 6.1.2. Let $F = \mathbb{Z}_3, n = 3, k = 2, \vec{v} = (111)$, and $\vec{\alpha} = (012)$. Then

$$GRS_{3,2}(\vec{\alpha}, \vec{v}) = \{(f(0), f(1), f(2)) | f(x) \in \mathbb{Z}_3[x]_2\}.$$

Now, we have that

$$\mathbb{Z}_3[x]_2 = \{0, 1, 2, x, x + 1, x + 2, 2x, 2x + 1, 2x + 2\}$$

so

$$GRS_{3,2}(\vec{\alpha}, \vec{v}) = \{(000), (111), (222), (012), (120), (201),$$
$$(021), (102), (210)\} \subset \mathbb{Z}_3^3.$$

Notice that the size of the field F forces certain constraints on the code $GRS_{n,k}(\vec{\alpha}, \vec{v})$. In particular, since the elements of the vector $\vec{\alpha}$ must be distinct, n cannot be larger than the number of elements of F. For example, if $F = \mathbb{Z}_2$, then the largest that n can be is 2. Of course, codes of length 2 are not particularly interesting, so we will rarely use $F = \mathbb{Z}_2$ for generalized Reed-Solomon codes.

Notice that the code in Example 6.1.2 is linear. It turns out that $GRS_{n,k}(\vec{\alpha}, \vec{v})$ is always linear. (See Problem 1 at the end of this section.) Also notice that for Example 6.1.2 the number of elements in the code is equal to the number of elements in $\mathbb{Z}_3[x]_2$. In other words, all polynomials in $\mathbb{Z}_3[x]_2$ give us *distinct* codewords. Is this true in general? What is the minimum distance of $GRS_{n,k}(\vec{\alpha}, \vec{v})$? In other words, how good are these codes for error correction? These are questions we will discuss and answer in the following sections.

EXERCISES

Problem 1. Show that $GRS_{n,k}(\vec{\alpha}, \vec{v})$ is linear.

Problem 2. Let $n = 4$, $k = 2$, $F = \mathbb{Z}_5$, $\vec{v} = (1111)$, $\vec{\alpha} = (1234)$, and $C = GRS_{n,k}(\vec{\alpha}, \vec{v})$.
  (a) List the elements of C.
  (b) Find a generator matrix for C.
  (c) Find $d_{\min}(C)$.
  (d) How many errors will C correct?

6.2 A Finite Field with Eight Elements

As mentioned in the previous section, it is impractical to use $F = \mathbb{Z}_2$ for generalized Reed-Solomon codes. However, it turns out that generalized Reed-Solomon codes using fields with 2^n elements where $n > 1$ are very useful. We describe such a field here – namely a field with eight elements.

For those of you who have had Abstract Algebra, you will recognize this field as $\frac{\mathbb{Z}_2[x]}{(x^3+x+1)}$.

We let

$$\mathbb{F}_8 = \{0, 1, \gamma, \gamma + 1, \gamma^2, \gamma^2 + \gamma, \gamma^2 + 1, \gamma^2 + \gamma + 1\}$$

with addition and multiplication defined modulo 2 and with the rule that $\gamma^3 = \gamma + 1$. So, for example,

$$
\begin{aligned}
(\gamma^2 + \gamma)(\gamma + 1) &= \gamma^3 + \gamma^2 + \gamma^2 + \gamma \\
&= \gamma^3 + \gamma \\
&= \gamma + 1 + \gamma \\
&= 1.
\end{aligned}
$$

Note that with the arithmetic described above, $\mathbb{F}_8$ is closed under addition and multiplication.

We also have the following equalities.

$$
\begin{aligned}
0 &= 0 \\
1 &= 1 \\
\gamma &= \gamma \\
\gamma^2 &= \gamma^2 \\
\gamma^3 &= \gamma + 1 \\
\gamma^4 &= \gamma(\gamma + 1) = \gamma^2 + \gamma \\
\gamma^5 &= \gamma^2(\gamma + 1) = \gamma^2 + \gamma + 1 \\
\gamma^6 &= (\gamma + 1)^2 = \gamma^2 + 1 \\
\gamma^7 &= \gamma(\gamma^2 + 1) = \gamma^3 + \gamma = \gamma + 1 + \gamma = 1.
\end{aligned}
$$

So we can also think of $\mathbb{F}_8$ as the set $\{0, 1, \gamma, \gamma^2, \gamma^3, \gamma^4, \gamma^5, \gamma^6\}$ with the rule that $\gamma^7 = 1$. It is sometimes useful to think of $\mathbb{F}_8$ in this way.

It turns out that $\mathbb{F}_8$ is a field (see Problem 2 at the end of this section) and so we can use it to construct generalized Reed-Solomon codes.

EXERCISES

Problem 1. Write out a multiplication table for $\mathbb{F}_8$.

Problem 2. Show that $\mathbb{F}_8$ is a field.

Problem 3. How many elements are there in $\mathbb{F}_8[x]_2$?

6.3 General Theorems

Recall from Chapter 4 that the number of errors that a code can detect and correct depends on the minimum distance of the code. In fact, if d is the minimum distance of the code, then it can detect $d - 1$ errors and correct $\lfloor \frac{d-1}{2} \rfloor$ errors, where $\lfloor \frac{d-1}{2} \rfloor$ represents the largest integer less than or equal to $\frac{d-1}{2}$. So the larger the minimum distance, the more errors a code can detect and correct. Because of this, we would like to determine the minimum distance of generalized Reed-Solomon codes. We do so in this section. We begin with the Singleton Bound Theorem.

Theorem 6.3.1. (Singleton Bound). If C is an $[n, k]$ linear code, then $d_{\min}(C) \leq n - k + 1$.

Proof. Let G be a systematic generator matrix for C. So all columns of the identity matrix appear in G. Every row of G has weight at most n. But in every row, at least $k - 1$ entries are zero. So the weight of the codewords in each row is at most $n - (k - 1) = n - k + 1$. It follows that $d_{\min}(C) \leq n - k + 1$. ❑

Theorem 6.3.1 says that the minimum distance cannot be "too big." No matter how hard we try, we cannot construct an $[n, k]$ linear code with minimum distance larger than $n - k + 1$. In light of this theorem, the "best" we can hope for is to have the minimum distance *equal* to $n - k + 1$. This motivates the following definition.

Definition. An $[n, k]$ linear code satisfying $d_{\min}(C) = n - k + 1$ is called *maximum distance separable* or simply MDS.

It turns out that generalized Reed-Solomon codes belong to this nice class of codes. We will prove this fact, but to do so, we need the following lemma.

Lemma 6.3.2. Let F be a field, k a positive integer, and $h(x)$ a nonzero polynomial in $F[x]_k$. Then $h(x)$ has at most $k - 1$ roots in F.

The proof of this lemma will be omitted, but can be found in any standard Abstract Algebra book.

We note here that if F is not a field, Lemma 6.3.2 need not hold. For example, consider

$$f(x) = (x - 2)(x - 3) \in \mathbb{Z}_6[x].$$

The degree of $f(x)$ is 2, but notice that $f(0) = 0$, $f(2) = 0$, $f(3) = 0$, and $f(5) = 0$ (remember, all arithmetic is done modulo 6), so $f(x)$ has four roots in $\mathbb{Z}_6$.

We are now in a position to show that $GRS_{n,k}(\vec{\alpha}, \vec{v})$ has dimension k and is, in fact, MDS.

Theorem 6.3.3. Let F be a finite field and $0 \le k \le n$. Then $GRS_{n,k}(\vec{\alpha}, \vec{v})$ is an $[n, k]$ linear code. Moreover, if $k \ne 0$, then $GRS_{n,k}(\vec{\alpha}, \vec{v})$ is MDS.

Proof. Let $C = GRS_{n,k}(\vec{\alpha}, \vec{v})$. By Problem 1 of Section 6.1, C is linear.

We now show that the dimension of C is k. To do this, we first show that $|C| = |F|^k$ where $|C|$ denotes the number of elements in C and $|F|$ the number of elements in F. Now, the number of elements in $F[x]_k$ is $|F|^k$, so we have that $|C| \le |F|^k$. Assume that $|C| < |F|^k$. Then there exist polynomials $f(x), g(x) \in F[x]_k$ such that $f(x) \ne g(x)$ but $\vec{f} = \vec{g}$. Let $h(x) = f(x) - g(x) \in F[x]_k$ and note that $h(x)$ is not the zero polynomial. Now,

$$\begin{aligned}
\vec{h} &= (v_1 h(\alpha_1), \dots, v_n h(\alpha_n)) \\
&= (v_1 f(\alpha_1), \dots, v_n f(\alpha_n)) - (v_1 g(\alpha_1), \dots, v_n g(\alpha_n)) \\
&= \vec{f} - \vec{g} \\
&= \vec{0}
\end{aligned}$$

so $v_i h(\alpha_i) = 0$ for $i = 1, 2, \dots, n$. But $v_i \ne 0$ for all i, and so we must have that $h(\alpha_i) = 0$ for $i = 1, 2, \dots, n$. Recall that the α_i's are distinct, so $h(x)$ has n distinct roots in F. But by Lemma 6.3.2, we know $h(x)$ has at most $k - 1 < n$ roots, a contradiction. It follows that $|C| = |F|^k$.

Now, we claim that since $|C| = |F|^k$, it must be that the dimension of C is k. Clearly the dimension of C is at least k (or else C would have fewer than $|F|^k$ elements). Suppose the dimension of C is l where $l > k$. Then, there exist $\vec{v}_1, \dots, \vec{v}_l \in C$ such that $\vec{v}_1, \dots, \vec{v}_l$ are linearly independent and so that if G is the matrix where the ith row is $\vec{v}_i$, then $C = RS(G)$. In other words, G is a generator matrix for C. Consider codewords of the form $c_1\vec{v}_1 + c_2\vec{v}_2 + \cdots + c_l\vec{v}_l \in C$ where $c_i \in F$ for all i. If all codewords of this form were distinct, then C would have $|F|^l > |F|^k$ elements, contradicting that $|C| = |F|^k$. Hence, there exists $c_i, d_i \in F$ for $i = 1, 2, \ldots, l$ such that $c_j \neq d_j$ for some j and such that

$$c_1\vec{v}_1 + c_2\vec{v}_2 + \cdots + c_l\vec{v}_l = d_1\vec{v}_1 + d_2\vec{v}_2 + \cdots + d_l\vec{v}_l.$$

It follows that

$$(c_1 - d_1)\vec{v}_1 + \cdots + (c_j - d_j)\vec{v}_j + \cdots + (c_l - d_l)\vec{v}_l = \vec{0}.$$

But $c_j - d_j \neq 0$ and so we have that $\vec{v}_1, \ldots, \vec{v}_l$ are not linearly independent, a contradiction. It follows that the dimension of C is k.

We have left to show that if $k \neq 0$, C is MDS. Recall that by the Singleton Bound, we have $d_{\min}(C) \leq n - k + 1$. We must show that $d_{\min}(C) \geq n - k + 1$. Let $\vec{h} \in C$ with $\vec{h} \neq \vec{0}$. Note that such a codeword exists since $k \neq 0$. Then, by Lemma 6.3.2, $h(x) \in F[x]_k$ has at most $k - 1$ roots. It follows that $\vec{h}$ has at most $k - 1$ entries that are 0. So $w_H(\vec{h}) \geq n - (k - 1) = n - k + 1$. It follows that $d_{\min}(C) \geq n - k + 1$ and so C is MDS.   ❑

Theorem 6.3.3 states that generalized Reed-Solomon codes are very good for error correction. In addition, notice that within the proof of the theorem, we showed that $|C| = |F|^k$. It follows that distinct elements of $F[x]_k$ give us distinct codewords in C. In other words, if $f(x), g(x) \in F[x]_k$ with $f(x) \neq g(x)$, then $\vec{f} \neq \vec{g}$.

EXERCISES

Problem 1. Find an element $\vec{f}$ of $GRS_{n,k}(\vec{\alpha}, \vec{v})$ that satisfies $w_H(\vec{f}) = n - k + 1$.

Problem 2. Let $F = \mathbb{F}_8$ as defined in Section 6.2. Let $\vec{v} = (1, 1, 1, 1, 1, 1, 1)$ and $\vec{\alpha} = (1, \gamma, \gamma^2, \gamma^3, \gamma^4, \gamma^5, \gamma^6)$.

(a) How many elements are there in $GRS_{7,2}(\vec{\alpha}, \vec{v})$? Optional: List them.

(b) How many errors will $GRS_{7,2}(\vec{\alpha}, \vec{v})$ detect? How many will it correct?

(c) List the elements of $GRS_{7,2}(\vec{\alpha}, \vec{v})$ whose entries consist only of zeros and ones. Be sure to explain why your answer is correct.

Problem 3

(a) Let F be a field. Suppose $f(x)$, $H(x) \in F[x]_k$ so that there exist distinct elements $\alpha_1, \alpha_2, \ldots, \alpha_k$ of F satisfying $f(\alpha_i) = H(\alpha_i)$ for all $i = 1, 2, \ldots, k$. Show that $f(x) = H(x)$.

(b) Define

$$L(x) = \prod_{i=1}^{n}(x - \alpha_i)$$

and

$$L_j(x) = \prod_{i=1, i \neq j}^{n} (x - \alpha_i).$$

Use part (a) to show that if
$\vec{f} \in GRS_{n,k}(\vec{\alpha}, \vec{v})$ with
$\vec{f} = (v_1 f(\alpha_1), v_2 f(\alpha_2), \ldots, v_n f(\alpha_n))$ and

$$H(x) = \sum_{j=1}^{n} \frac{L_j(x)}{L_j(\alpha_j)} f(\alpha_j),$$

then $f(x) = H(x)$.

This shows how to find $f(x)$ if we are given $\vec{f} \in GRS_{n,k}(\vec{\alpha}, \vec{v})$. We just use the above problem and observe that if we know $(v_1 f(\alpha_1), v_2 f(\alpha_2), \ldots, v_n f(\alpha_n))$ and all the $v_i's$, which we do, we can find $(f(\alpha_1), f(\alpha_2), \ldots, f(\alpha_n))$. So we know $f(\alpha_i)$ for every $i = 1, 2, \ldots, n$.

6.4　A Generator Matrix for a GRS Code

Since $GRS_{n,k}(\vec{\alpha}, \vec{v})$ is an $[n, k]$ linear code, it must have a generator matrix. We now show that we can easily write one down.

Theorem 6.4.1. The matrix

$$
G = \begin{pmatrix}
v_1 & v_2 & \cdots & v_n \\
v_1\alpha_1 & v_2\alpha_2 & \cdots & v_n\alpha_n \\
\vdots & \vdots & & \vdots \\
v_1\alpha_1^i & v_2\alpha_2^i & \cdots & v_n\alpha_n^i \\
\vdots & \vdots & & \vdots \\
v_1\alpha_1^{k-1} & v_2\alpha_2^{k-1} & \cdots & v_n\alpha_n^{k-1}
\end{pmatrix}
$$

is a generator matrix for $GRS_{n,k}(\vec{\alpha}, \vec{v})$.

Proof. We must show that the rows of G are linearly independent and that $GRS_{n,k}(\vec{\alpha}, \vec{v}) = RS(G)$. Suppose

$$
c_0(v_1, \ldots, v_n) + c_1(v_1\alpha_1, \ldots, v_n\alpha_n) + \cdots + c_{k-1}\left(v_1\alpha_1^{k-1}, \ldots, v_n\alpha_n^{k-1}\right)
$$
$$
= (0, 0, \ldots, 0).
$$

Then the following equalities must hold.

$$
v_1\left(c_0 + c_1\alpha_1 + c_2\alpha_1^2 + \cdots + c_{k-1}\alpha_1^{k-1}\right) = 0
$$
$$
v_2\left(c_0 + c_1\alpha_2 + c_2\alpha_2^2 + \cdots + c_{k-1}\alpha_2^{k-1}\right) = 0
$$
$$
\vdots
$$
$$
v_n\left(c_0 + c_1\alpha_n + c_2\alpha_n^2 + \cdots + c_{k-1}\alpha_n^{k-1}\right) = 0
$$

But $v_i \neq 0$ for all i, so α_i is a root of the polynomial $f(x) = c_0 + c_1 x + c_2 x^2 + \cdots + c_{k-1}x^{k-1} \in F[x]_k$ for all $i = 1, 2, \ldots, n$. But $k \leq n$ and if $f(x)$ is not the zero polynomial, then by Lemma 6.3.2 it can have at most $k - 1$ distinct roots. It follows that $f(x)$ must be the zero polynomial. So $c_0 = 0$, $c_1 = 0$, $\ldots$, $c_{k-1} = 0$. Hence, the rows of G are linearly independent.

Now, we show that $GRS_{n,k}(\vec{\alpha}, \vec{v}) = RS(G)$. Let $\vec{f} \in GRS_{n,k}(\vec{\alpha}, \vec{v})$. Then there exists $f(x) \in F[x]_k$ such that $\vec{f} = (v_1 f(\alpha_1), v_2 f(\alpha_2), \ldots, v_n f(\alpha_n))$. Let $f(x) = c_0 + c_1 x + c_2 x^2 + \cdots + c_{k-1}x^{k-1}$. Then

$$
\vec{f} = \left(v_1\left(c_0 + c_1\alpha_1 + c_2\alpha_1^2 + \cdots + c_{k-1}\alpha_1^{k-1}\right),\right.
$$
$$
v_2\left(c_0 + c_1\alpha_2 + c_2\alpha_2^2 + \cdots + c_{k-1}\alpha_2^{k-1}\right),
$$
$$
\left.\ldots, v_n\left(c_0 + c_1\alpha_n + c_2\alpha_n^2 + \cdots + c_{k-1}\alpha_n^{k-1}\right)\right).
$$

Rearranging this, we get that

$$\vec{f} = (v_1c_0, v_2c_0, \ldots, v_nc_0) + (v_1c_1\alpha_1, v_2c_1\alpha_2, \ldots, v_nc_1\alpha_n)$$
$$+ \cdots + (v_1c_{k-1}\alpha_1^{k-1}, v_2c_{k-1}\alpha_2^{k-1}, \ldots, v_nc_{k-1}\alpha_n^{k-1}).$$

So,

$$\vec{f} = c_0(v_1, \ldots, v_n) + c_1(v_1\alpha_1, \ldots, v_n\alpha_n) + \cdots + c_{k-1}(v_1\alpha_1^{k-1}, \ldots, v_n\alpha_n^{k-1}).$$

It follows that $GRS_{n,k}(\vec{\alpha}, \vec{v}) = RS(G)$.   ❑

EXERCISES

Problem 1. Let p be a prime number. Recall that if $a \in \mathbb{Z}_p$ is nonzero, then there is a $b \in \mathbb{Z}_p$ such that $ab = 1$. We will denote b by a^{-1}. Let $F = \mathbb{Z}_p$ and $C = GRS_{n,k}(\vec{\alpha}, \vec{v})$ where, as usual, $\vec{\alpha} = (\alpha_1, \alpha_2, \ldots, \alpha_n)$. Assume that $\alpha_i \neq 0$ for all $i = 1, 2, \ldots, n$. Define $\vec{\beta} = (\alpha_1^{-1}, \alpha_2^{-1}, \ldots, \alpha_n^{-1})$. Find a vector $\vec{w}$ such that $C = GRS_{n,k}(\vec{\beta}, \vec{w})$.
Note: This shows that if C is a generalized Reed-Solomon code, $\vec{\alpha}$ and $\vec{v}$ are not unique.

6.5   The Dual of a GRS Code

In Section 6.3, we showed that GRS codes are $[n, k]$ linear codes. So we know that the dual of a particular GRS code of length n and dimension k is an $[n, n - k]$ linear code. The natural question to ask, then, is whether or not the dual of a GRS code is again a GRS code. In other words, if $C = GRS_{n,k}(\vec{\alpha}, \vec{v})$, can $C^\perp$ be expressed as $GRS_{n,n-k}(\vec{\beta}, \vec{u})$ for some vectors $\vec{\beta}$ and $\vec{u}$? The following theorem answers this question.

Theorem 6.5.1. $GRS_{n,k}(\vec{\alpha}, \vec{v})^\perp = GRS_{n,n-k}(\vec{\alpha}, \vec{u})$ where $\vec{u} = (u_1, u_2, \ldots, u_n)$ and

$$u_j = v_j^{-1}\left(\prod_{i=1,i\neq j}^{n}(\alpha_j - \alpha_i)\right)^{-1}$$

Proof. Define

$$L(x) = \prod_{i=1}^{n}(x - \alpha_i)$$

and

$$L_j(x) = \prod_{i=1, i \neq j}^{n}(x - \alpha_i).$$

We want to show that if $\vec{f} \in GRS_{n,k}(\vec{\alpha}, \vec{v})$ and $\vec{g} \in GRS_{n,n-k}(\vec{\alpha}, \vec{u})$, then the dot product of $\vec{f}$ and $\vec{g}$ is zero. Let $f(x) \in F[x]_k$ be the polynomial corresponding to $\vec{f}$ and $g(x) \in F[x]_{n-k}$ the polynomial corresponding to $\vec{g}$. Note that the product $f(x)g(x)$ has degree at most $n - 2$. Now, we have

$$\sum_{j=1}^{n} \frac{L_j(\alpha_i)}{L_j(\alpha_j)} f(\alpha_j)g(\alpha_j) = \frac{L_i(\alpha_i)}{L_i(\alpha_i)} f(\alpha_i)g(\alpha_i) = f(\alpha_i)g(\alpha_i)$$

for every $i = 1, 2, \ldots, n$. It follows by Problem 3 from Section 6.3 that

$$f(x)g(x) = \sum_{j=1}^{n} \frac{L_j(x)}{L_j(\alpha_j)} f(\alpha_j)g(\alpha_j).$$

The degree of $f(x)g(x)$ is less than or equal to $n - 2$, so the coefficient of x^{n-1} on the left-hand side of the equation is zero. Hence, the coefficient of x^{n-1} on the right-hand side of the equation is also zero. So,

$$0 = \sum_{j=1}^{n} \frac{1}{L_j(\alpha_j)} f(\alpha_j)g(\alpha_j) = \sum_{j=1}^{n}(v_j f(\alpha_j))(u_j g(\alpha_j))$$

and this is just the dot product of $\vec{f}$ and $\vec{g}$. Hence, the dot product is zero. It follows that $GRS_{n,n-k}(\vec{\alpha}, \vec{u}) \subseteq GRS_{n,k}(\vec{\alpha}, \vec{v})^{\perp}$. But since these are both linear codes of dimension $n - k$, it follows from Theorem A.2.3 that we have equality. $\qquad \square$

Note that we can now easily write down a check matrix for $GRS_{n,k}(\vec{\alpha}, \vec{v})$. We know that a check matrix for a linear code is a generator matrix for the dual of that code. But in the last section we discovered how to find generator matrices for GRS codes. It follows that the following matrix is a check matrix for $GRS_{n,k}(\vec{\alpha}, \vec{v})$.

$$H = \begin{pmatrix} u_1 & u_2 & \cdots & u_n \\ u_1\alpha_1 & u_2\alpha_2 & \cdots & u_n\alpha_n \\ \vdots & \vdots & & \vdots \\ u_1\alpha_1^i & u_2\alpha_2^i & \cdots & u_n\alpha_n^i \\ \vdots & \vdots & & \vdots \\ u_1\alpha_1^{n-k-1} & u_2\alpha_2^{n-k-1} & \cdots & u_n\alpha_n^{n-k-1} \end{pmatrix}$$

EXERCISES

Problem 1. Find a check matrix for the code described in Problem 2 of Section 6.1.

Problem 2. Find a check matrix for the code described in Problem 2 of Section 6.3.

7 Quantum Computing

7.1 Introduction

In an ordinary computer, information is stored in a collection of tiny circuits each of which is designed to have two stable and easily distinguishable configurations: each represents a *bit*. In our study of quantum cryptography, we have seen how it can be useful to express information not in ordinary bits but in *qubits*. Whereas a bit can have only two values, say 0 and 1, a qubit can be in any quantum superposition of $|0\rangle$ and $|1\rangle$. Moreover, a qubit can be *entangled* with other qubits. Thus one might wonder whether a *quantum* computer, in which the basic elements for storing and processing information are qubits, can outperform an ordinary (classical) computer in certain ways. This question was addressed by researchers starting in the 1980s.[1] In terms of practical consequences, perhaps the most dramatic answer has been given by Peter Shor in his 1994 factoring algorithm for a quantum computer, an algorithm that is exponentially faster than any known classical algorithm. As we have seen in Chapter 1, the difficulty of factoring a product of two large primes is the basis of the security of the RSA cryptosystem. So if one could build a large enough quantum computer – and there is no reason in principle why this could not be done – the RSA system would be rendered ineffective. In this chapter we present the basics of quantum computation and then focus on Shor's factoring algorithm.[2]

---

[1] Especially important is the pioneering work of Deutsch (1985).
[2] Over the last several years many books have been written that include chapters on quantum computation. A few such sources are Nielsen and Chuang (2000), Bouwmeester,

How should we picture a quantum computer? In our discussion of quantum cryptography we have usually thought of a qubit as being manifested physically as the polarization of a photon. It is conceivable that one could similarly build a quantum computer using photons as the basic qubits: each photon could either be trapped (temporarily) between two curved mirrors or allowed to fly around at the speed of light. However, most current proposals for building a quantum computer use less ethereal objects as qubits.

One model that is easy to visualize uses ions (i.e., electrically charged atoms) to manifest the basic qubits. The electrons in an ion can arrange themselves in any of a large number of orthogonal quantum states – the dimension of the ion's state space is in fact infinite in principle – but under certain circumstances one can limit the set of *likely* states to a two-dimensional subspace, so that the ion can represent a qubit. For example, a singly ionized beryllium atom contains three electrons, and two of the lowest-energy quantum states of this ion differ from each other only in the orientation of the *spin* of the outermost electron relative to the spin of the nucleus. (Recall the introduction of electron spin in Examples 2.2.1 and 2.2.2.) One can use lasers to prepare and control the ion in such a way that its state is mostly confined to the two-dimensional subspace spanned by these two orthogonal states; these states can then play the roles of $|0\rangle$ and $|1\rangle$. A quantum computer might consist of a collection of these carefully prepared ions, arranged in a line and evenly spaced – they repel each other electrically – the whole array being held in place by an electromagnetic trap. In order to carry out a quantum computation, one could manipulate the states of the ions with laser pulses. We will return to this model of a quantum computer in the following section.

Many other possible designs have been proposed, some of them based on potential refinements, albeit difficult refinements, of the semiconductor technology that underlies present-day computers. For example, in a layer

Ekert, and Zeilinger (2000), Lo, Popescu, and Spiller (2001), Pittenger (2000), Benenti, Casati, and Strini (2004), and Preskill (2004). Three review articles focusing specifically on Shor's algorithm are Ekert and Jozsa (1996), Gerjuoy (2005), and Rieffel and Polak (2000), the last of these being explicitly addressed to nonphysicists. The original paper is Shor (1994); an expanded version is Shor (1997).

of silicon, individual electrons could be localized at special sites forming a regular array, and the spins of these electrons could be taken as the basic qubits.

All potential designs for a quantum computer have to face the same difficulty, namely, how to keep the qubits from interacting too strongly with other objects that they might happen to come into contact with, while at the same time allowing them to interact sufficiently strongly with each other when necessary. Accidental interactions with the outside world could, for example, create entanglement between the qubits of the computer and extraneous quantum variables, and too much of this entanglement would make quantum computation impossible. (We often *do* want the computer's qubits to become entangled with *each other*, but not with the outside world.) The problem of designing a quantum computer is the focus of much ongoing research, and most researchers agree that a full-scale quantum computer is at least decades away. But this problem is beyond the scope of this book. Here we only want to indicate what one could do with a quantum computer if such a computer were available.

One way of representing a *classical* computation is as a sequence of simple *gates*. Each gate is a function, implemented as a physical operation, that takes the state of a small number of bits to another state, possibly of a different number of bits. A simple example of a classical gate is the NOT gate, which acts on a single bit as follows:

$$0 \rightarrow 1$$
$$1 \rightarrow 0 \tag{7.1}$$

Another is the AND gate, which takes as input a pair of bits and produces one bit of output (it is equivalent to multiplication of the bit values):

$$00 \rightarrow 0$$
$$01 \rightarrow 0$$
$$10 \rightarrow 0 \tag{7.2}$$
$$11 \rightarrow 1$$

Finally we mention the XOR (exclusive OR) gate, which is the same as addition in $\mathbb{Z}_2$:

$$00 \to 0$$
$$01 \to 1$$
$$10 \to 1 \qquad \qquad (7.3)$$
$$11 \to 0$$

One can show that, as long as one is given arbitrarily many bits to start with, all in a standard state (say, 0), and as long as one can freely copy a bit or exchange the values of two bits, then the three gates just described are sufficient to perform any calculation that a computer can perform. That is, including additional, more complicated gates does not extend the range of problems the computer can solve.

We begin our study of *quantum* computation by exploring the concept of a quantum gate.

7.2 Quantum Gates

Let us try to express the AND operation [Eq. (7.2)] as an operation on qubits. At the outset we have a problem: the AND operation takes two bits to one bit, but the only operations we know how to perform on qubits are unitary transformations, and these always take one state of a quantum system to another state of the *same* quantum system, not to a state of a *smaller* one. Of course we can always throw away one of the qubits after the operation; so for now let us try to put the output of the AND gate into the second qubit, figuring that we can always throw away the first qubit. Thus we might try to find a transformation that has the following effect, in which the first qubit, which will be thrown away, is always brought to the state $|0\rangle$ at the end of the operation:

$$|00\rangle \to |00\rangle$$
$$|01\rangle \to |00\rangle$$
$$|10\rangle \to |00\rangle \qquad \qquad (7.4)$$
$$|11\rangle \to |01\rangle$$

Is there a single unitary matrix that accomplishes all four of these transformations? It is easy to see that the answer is no. A unitary matrix always has an inverse – the inverse of U is $U^\dagger$ – but the above transformations are not invertible, since three distinct initial states yield the same final state $|00\rangle$.

So let us try to be more clever. Rather than setting the first qubit to the state $|0\rangle$ in each case, let us use three distinct states $|a\rangle$, $|b\rangle$, and $|c\rangle$ to make sure that each initial state has a distinct final state:

$$
\begin{aligned}
|00\rangle &\rightarrow |a0\rangle \\
|01\rangle &\rightarrow |b0\rangle \\
|10\rangle &\rightarrow |c0\rangle \\
|11\rangle &\rightarrow |01\rangle
\end{aligned}
\tag{7.5}
$$

For example, the state $|a\rangle$ might be $|0\rangle$, $|b\rangle$ might be $|1\rangle$, and $|c\rangle$ might be $(1/\sqrt{2})(|0\rangle + |1\rangle)$. But no such scheme will work, for the following reason. A unitary transformation always takes orthogonal states to orthogonal states. (We showed in Section 3.2 that a unitary transformation always preserves inner products. Orthogonality is a special case in which the inner product is zero.) The four initial states in Eq. (7.5) are orthogonal, but the first three of the final states cannot all be orthogonal: the orthogonality would have to come from the first qubit, and it is impossible to find three mutually orthogonal states $|a\rangle$, $|b\rangle$, and $|c\rangle$ in a two-dimensional state space.

At this point we give up on realizing the AND operation as an operation on just two qubits. Let us try to express it as an operation on *three* qubits: the first two are the ones on which the AND gate is acting, and the last one is the one in which the result of the operation is to be expressed. Let us imagine starting this third qubit in the state $|0\rangle$; this will be the "ready" state. Thus we want our operation to effect the following changes:

$$
\begin{aligned}
|000\rangle &\rightarrow |000\rangle \\
|010\rangle &\rightarrow |010\rangle \\
|100\rangle &\rightarrow |100\rangle \\
|110\rangle &\rightarrow |111\rangle
\end{aligned}
\tag{7.6}
$$

Note that Eq. (7.6) *is* consistent with a unitary transformation. The four given initial states, which are mutually orthogonal, are mapped into four mutually orthogonal final states. In fact there are *many* different unitary transformations that will accomplish these transformations. To see this, consider the following orthogonal basis for the three-qubit state space:

$$\{|000\rangle, |001\rangle, |010\rangle, |011\rangle, |100\rangle, |101\rangle, |110\rangle, |111\rangle\} \tag{7.7}$$

Equation (7.6) tells us how four of these basis vectors transform, but it does not tell us what happens to the other four.

How shall we finish defining our transformation? It is sufficient to define it on the basis vectors; then its action on all other vectors can be determined by linearity. (How linearity is used in this way is made explicit in Eq. (7.11) below.) Let us try the following definition:

$$|x_1, x_2, y\rangle \rightarrow |x_1, x_2, x_1 \wedge x_2\rangle \tag{7.8}$$

Here x_1, x_2, and y each takes the values 0 and 1, and $x_1 \wedge x_2$ is the result of applying the classical AND gate to x_1 and x_2. This formulation is consistent with Eq. (7.6), but it cannot be realized as a unitary transformation since the two orthogonal states $|000\rangle$ and $|001\rangle$ both get mapped to the same final state $|000\rangle$. A simple formulation that *does* work is given as follows:

$$U_{\text{AND}}|x_1, x_2, y\rangle = |x_1, x_2, y \oplus (x_1 \wedge x_2)\rangle, \tag{7.9}$$

where $\oplus$ indicates addition mod 2. This transformation has the following effect on the four basis vectors not covered by Eq. (7.6):

$$
\begin{aligned}
|001\rangle &\rightarrow |001\rangle \\
|011\rangle &\rightarrow |011\rangle \\
|101\rangle &\rightarrow |101\rangle \\
|111\rangle &\rightarrow |110\rangle
\end{aligned} \tag{7.10}
$$

Equation (7.9) defines U_{AND} only as it acts on the eight basis states $|x_1, x_2, y\rangle$. We define its action on other states by linearity: that is, for any two states $|s\rangle$ and $|t\rangle$ and complex numbers α and β, we insist that

$$U_{\text{AND}}(\alpha|s\rangle + \beta|t\rangle) = \alpha(U_{\text{AND}}|s\rangle) + \beta(U_{\text{AND}}|t\rangle). \tag{7.11}$$

One can show that the operator U_{AND} defined in this way is indeed unitary. (See problem 1.)

Here, then, is a way to perform the AND operation on two bits x_1 and x_2 using a quantum computer: (i) set two qubits to the state $|x_1, x_2\rangle$, (ii) set a third qubit (playing the role of y) to the state $|0\rangle$, (iii) perform U_{AND} on $|x_1, x_2, y\rangle$, (iv) perform the measurement ($|0\rangle, |1\rangle$) on the third qubit: the outcome of this measurement gives the desired result of the AND operation. By an extension of this strategy, one can see that a quantum computer can perform any ordinary classical operation, though in a rather more cumbersome way.[3]

To get a hint of the potential power of a quantum computer, let us imagine performing the operation U_{AND} on a more interesting quantum state. We begin by defining a new one-qubit operation called the Hadamard gate, whose effect on the basis states is given by $H|0\rangle = (1/\sqrt{2})(|0\rangle + |1\rangle)$ and $H|1\rangle = (1/\sqrt{2})(|0\rangle - |1\rangle)$. As before, let $|0\rangle$ and $|1\rangle$ be represented explicitly by the vectors

$$|0\rangle = \begin{pmatrix} 1 \\ 0 \end{pmatrix} \quad \text{and} \quad |1\rangle = \begin{pmatrix} 0 \\ 1 \end{pmatrix}.$$

Then we can write H in matrix form:

$$H = \frac{1}{\sqrt{2}} \begin{pmatrix} 1 & 1 \\ 1 & -1 \end{pmatrix}. \tag{7.12}$$

Now let us imagine starting a three-qubit quantum computer in the state $|000\rangle = |0\rangle_A \otimes |0\rangle_B \otimes |0\rangle_C$ and then performing the operation $H_A \otimes H_B \otimes I_C$, where I is the identity operation. The resulting state is

$$\frac{1}{2}(|0\rangle + |1\rangle) \otimes (|0\rangle + |1\rangle) \otimes |0\rangle = \frac{1}{2}(|000\rangle + |010\rangle + |100\rangle + |110\rangle). \tag{7.13}$$

On this state let us perform the operation U_{AND}. The result is

$$\frac{1}{2}(|000\rangle + |010\rangle + |100\rangle + |111\rangle). \tag{7.14}$$

Note that in each term of this quantum superposition, the value expressed in the last qubit is the result of applying the classical AND operation to the values of the first two qubits. Moreover, all four possible values of the first two qubits are contained in this state. Thus there is a sense in which the computer has, in a single application of the transformation U_{AND}, performed the AND operation simultaneously on *all* possible inputs. It is the recognition of this "quantum parallelism" that led researchers to wonder whether a quantum computer could outperform a classical computer.

---

[3] Quantum gates such as U_{AND} are *reversible* gates. The study of reversible computation preceded the study of quantum computation. See, for example, Bennett (1973).

One might raise the following objection: In order to write down Eq. (7.14), we had to consider each of the four possible values of (x_1, x_2), that is, 00, 01, 10, and 11, and we had to perform the AND operation on each of these. It must therefore also be harder, or take longer, for a quantum computer to carry out the operation U_{AND} starting with the state Eq. (7.13) than starting with a simple state such as $|000\rangle$. But this is not true. The quantum computer does not "know" what state it is acting on. It goes through the same physical process whether it is acting on the simple state $|000\rangle$ or on the more complicated state given in Eq. (7.13). It is true that it is harder for *us* to write down what the quantum computer is doing when the input state is complicated, but it is not harder for the computer itself.

Even though there is a sense in which the quantum computer can carry out many computations simultaneously, it is no mean feat to take advantage of this quantum parallelism. One may be able to arrive at the state (7.14) in a single application of U_{AND}, but one cannot simply *read out* all the information that appears in the mathematical expression of this state: as we have seen in Chapter 2, it is impossible to ascertain the state of a single quantum system by measurement. We could perform the measurement $(|0\rangle, |1\rangle)$ on each of our three qubits. But the effect of this measurement would be to tell us (i) for which of four possible inputs we will obtain the result of the AND operation, and (ii) the result of the AND operation for that particular input. This is worse than using an ordinary classical AND gate: in that case we at least get to choose our own input, rather than having a quantum measurement choose it for us randomly! We will see in later sections how one can take advantage of quantum parallelism, but for now we continue our discussion of quantum gates.

As in the above examples, the operations that we refer to as quantum gates will always be unitary transformations. Though in the example of the AND gate it was useful to consider a transformation on three qubits, the most basic gates that are typically used in discussions of quantum computation are gates that act on just one or two qubits. Here we present some of the most commonly used gates, expressed as matrices. It will be clear from the size of the matrix whether each gate acts on one or two qubits: recall that a 2×2 matrix acts on a single qubit and a 4×4 matrix acts on a pair of qubits. For completeness we include the Hadamard gate defined above.

1. The T gate: $T = \begin{pmatrix} 1 & 0 \\ 0 & e^{i\pi/4} \end{pmatrix}$
2. The Hadamard gate: $H = \frac{1}{\sqrt{2}} \begin{pmatrix} 1 & 1 \\ 1 & -1 \end{pmatrix}$
3. The X gate: $X = \begin{pmatrix} 0 & 1 \\ 1 & 0 \end{pmatrix}$
4. The Z gate: $Z = \begin{pmatrix} 1 & 0 \\ 0 & -1 \end{pmatrix}$
5. The controlled-not gate: $\text{CNOT} = \begin{pmatrix} 1 & 0 & 0 & 0 \\ 0 & 1 & 0 & 0 \\ 0 & 0 & 0 & 1 \\ 0 & 0 & 1 & 0 \end{pmatrix}$

In writing this last gate as a matrix, we are using the representation

$$|00\rangle = \begin{pmatrix} 1 \\ 0 \\ 0 \\ 0 \end{pmatrix}, \quad |01\rangle = \begin{pmatrix} 0 \\ 1 \\ 0 \\ 0 \end{pmatrix}, \quad |10\rangle = \begin{pmatrix} 0 \\ 0 \\ 1 \\ 0 \end{pmatrix}, \quad |11\rangle = \begin{pmatrix} 0 \\ 0 \\ 0 \\ 1 \end{pmatrix}.$$

Thus the CNOT gate has the following effect on a pair of qubits: $|00\rangle \rightarrow |00\rangle$, $|01\rangle \rightarrow |01\rangle$, $|10\rangle \rightarrow |11\rangle$, $|11\rangle \rightarrow |10\rangle$. That is, when we consider the effect of this gate on the standard basis states, the value of the first qubit is unchanged, and the value of the second is flipped if and only if the value of the first is 1. In this sense the second qubit is controlled by the first one. We call the first qubit the "control qubit," and the second is called the "target qubit."

A quantum program can be regarded as a sequence of quantum gates and measurements, as in the following example.

Example 7.2.1. Consider the following simple program for a three-qubit quantum computer.

1. Start with all three qubits in the state $|0\rangle$; so the whole computer is in the state $|000\rangle$.
2. Perform on the second qubit the operation X, defined above. (Note that $X|0\rangle = |1\rangle$ and $X|1\rangle = |0\rangle$. You may recall this operation from Chapter 3, where it was used in quantum teleportation.)
3. Perform the CNOT gate, with the second qubit as the control and the third qubit as the target.
4. Perform the CNOT gate, with the first qubit as control and the third qubit as target.
5. Finally, measure the third qubit in the basis $(|0\rangle, |1\rangle)$.

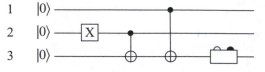

Figure 7.1: A circuit diagram illustrating Example 7.2.1. In each CNOT gate, the symbol • is placed on the control qubit and ⊕ is placed on the target qubit. The symbol for the final measurement is supposed to be a box with two light bulbs on it, one for each possible outcome.

The whole sequence of gates can be expressed as follows:

$$(\text{CNOT})_{13}(\text{CNOT})_{23}\, X_2 |000\rangle \tag{7.15}$$

Here the subscripts indicate, in the case of the single-qubit gate X, which qubit is being acting upon, and in the case of the two-qubit gate CNOT, which qubit is the control and which is the target.

We can interpret our sample program as follows. First, you can convince yourself that the two CNOT gates, acting on a state of the form $|x_1, x_2, 0\rangle$, have the effect of adding (mod 2) the bits x_1 and x_2 and placing the result in the third qubit. That is,

$$(\text{CNOT})_{13}(\text{CNOT})_{23}|x_1, x_2, 0\rangle = |x_1, x_2, x_1 \oplus x_2\rangle,$$

where we again use $\oplus$ to indicate addition mod 2. The initial X gate, acting on the second qubit, has the effect of giving (x_1, x_2) the values $(0, 1)$. So the program evaluates $0 \oplus 1$ and finds that the answer is 1. We extract the answer by measuring the third qubit. With a different use of X gates, we could have prepared any of the four possible combinations of (x_1, x_2) and in this way could have computed $x_1 \oplus x_2$ for any of these cases.

It is often helpful to visualize a quantum program, and there is an easy way to do this: let each qubit be represented by a horizontal line, and each gate or measurement by an appropriate symbol, the whole diagram being read from left to right. In this way the above program can be represented by the diagram shown in Fig. 7.1. A diagram of this sort is traditionally called a *circuit diagram*.

Returning to the ion-trap model of a quantum computer, we can interpret a circuit diagram in very physical terms. Each line in the diagram represents an ion. Each single-qubit gate represents a carefully constructed laser pulse literally focused on the particular ion on which the gate is supposed to act.[4] To realize a two-qubit gate, one method is to hit both of the relevant ions with laser pulses, one at a time, and to use the possibility of an overall vibration of the whole line of ions as a vehicle for conveying quantum information from one ion to the other. Thus we arrive at one possible physical image of a quantum computation: there is a line of ions prepared in a special state, and the computation proceeds as a programmed sequence of laser pulses, each pulse targeting a specific ion. Measuring an ion's state is also accomplished with a laser: one sends in a specific frequency and polarization of laser light that will cause the ion to fluoresce if it is, say, in the $|0\rangle$ state but not if it is in the $|1\rangle$ state.

The general model of quantum computation that we have presented here, that is, a sequence of gates and measurements, is not the only possible model. An alternative model that shows considerable promise is one in which the computation consists *only* of measurements. In this alternative model, one starts by preparing a large collection of qubits in a particular entangled state. The computation is then expressed as a sequence of measurements, each measurement usually being performed on just one or two qubits. The choice of what measurement to perform at each step might depend on the outcomes of earlier measurements. Though there may be advantages to such measurement-based models, we will focus here on the model based on gates, which has been the focus of most of the research so far on quantum computation.

We have not yet presented an example of a problem for which a quantum algorithm can do better than any classical algorithm. In other words, we have not yet shown how, despite the fact that one cannot simply read out a quantum state, one can nevertheless take advantage of quantum parallelism. The following section provides a simple example demonstrating the quantum advantage.

EXERCISES

Problem 1. Show that the operator U_{AND} defined in Eqs. (7.9) and (7.11) is indeed unitary.

---

[4] Actually, because the energy difference between the states $|0\rangle$ and $|1\rangle$ of the ion is much smaller than the energy scale associated with visible light, one uses not a single laser pulse but rather a *pair* of pulses with slightly different frequencies. The *difference* between the two frequencies is tuned to the small energy difference between the qubit states.

Problem 2. Consider the single-qubit operations X and Z that we used for teleportation in Chapter 3 and included in our list of gates in this section:

$$X = \begin{pmatrix} 0 & 1 \\ 1 & 0 \end{pmatrix} \quad Z = \begin{pmatrix} 1 & 0 \\ 0 & -1 \end{pmatrix}$$

Suppose we have a device that can perform the operations $H = \frac{1}{\sqrt{2}}\begin{pmatrix} 1 & 1 \\ 1 & -1 \end{pmatrix}$ and $T^2 = \begin{pmatrix} 1 & 0 \\ 0 & i \end{pmatrix}$. By a sequence of such operations, is it possible to perform X and Z, at least up to an overall phase factor (which is physically irrelevant)? If so, what sequence gives X, and what sequence gives Z?

Problem 3. Suppose that three qubits ABC start out in the state $(1/\sqrt{3})(|000\rangle + |100\rangle + |101\rangle)$. Is it possible by any sequence of single-qubit operations (not necessarily just the ones listed in this section) to bring the qubits to the state $(1/\sqrt{3})(|100\rangle + |010\rangle + |001\rangle)$? If so, find such a sequence. If not, prove that no such sequence exists. (Here, applying a single-qubit gate U to the first qubit, for example, means applying the transformation $U \otimes I \otimes I$ to the whole system.)

Problem 4. The "controlled-Z" gate is defined by the matrix

$$\text{controlled-}Z = \begin{pmatrix} 1 & 0 & 0 & 0 \\ 0 & 1 & 0 & 0 \\ 0 & 0 & 1 & 0 \\ 0 & 0 & 0 & -1 \end{pmatrix}.$$

Show how to perform the controlled-Z gate as a sequence of gates containing only H and CNOT. (Here the H can act on either qubit; that is, the operation on the pair of qubits can be either $H \otimes I$ or $I \otimes H$.)

Problem 5. Consider the single-qubit states $|+\rangle = (1/\sqrt{2})(|0\rangle + |1\rangle)$ and $|-\rangle = (1/\sqrt{2})(|0\rangle - |1\rangle)$. These two states constitute an orthonormal basis for a single qubit.

(a) Find the result of applying the CNOT gate to each of the following two-qubit states: $|++\rangle, |+-\rangle, |-+\rangle, |--\rangle$. (Here "$|++\rangle$," for example, is short for $|+\rangle \otimes |+\rangle$.)

(b) In terms of the basis states $|+\rangle$ and $|-\rangle$, can the action of the CNOT gate be reasonably described as "controlled-not"? In what important way does this action differ from the action of CNOT on the standard basis states?

7.3 The Deutsch Algorithm

In 1985 David Deutsch presented a simple example showing how a quantum computer can in principle outperform a classical computer.[5] The example involves the evaluation of a simple function. So we begin by discussing the general problem of evaluating a function with a quantum computer.

We have already considered one such function, namely, the classical AND gate. This gate can be thought of as the function f from $\mathbb{Z}_2^2$ to $\mathbb{Z}_2$ defined by

$$
\begin{aligned}
f(00) &= 0 \\
f(01) &= 0 \\
f(10) &= 0 \\
f(11) &= 1
\end{aligned}
$$

In the preceding section we arrived at a method of evaluating this function: let U_f be the unitary transformation having the following effect on the basis states of three qubits.

$$ U_f|x_1, x_2, y\rangle = |x_1, x_2, y \oplus f(x_1, x_2)\rangle, \tag{7.16} $$

where $\oplus$ is addition mod 2. The effect of U_f on all other states of three qubits is defined by linearity. To evaluate $f(x_1, x_2)$, we bring our quantum computer, consisting of three qubits, to the state $|x_1, x_2, 0\rangle$, then apply U_f, and finally measure the third qubit. The result of this measurement will be $f(x_1, x_2)$.

In the same way, if we want to evaluate a function $\vec{g}$ from $\mathbb{Z}_2^n$ to $\mathbb{Z}_2^m$, we arrange for our quantum computer to carry out the unitary transformation defined by

$$ U_g|\vec{x}, \vec{y}\rangle = |\vec{x}, \vec{y} \oplus \vec{g}(\vec{x})\rangle, \tag{7.17} $$

---

[5] Deutsch (1985).

where $\vec{y} \oplus \vec{g}(\vec{x})$ is an *m*-component vector whose *k*th component is the sum, mod 2, of the *k*th component of $\vec{y}$ and the *k*th component of $\vec{g}(\vec{x})$. Now, depending on the function, implementing the transformation U_g physically might be quite complicated, but the laws of quantum mechanics tell us that such a transformation, being unitary, is allowed in principle. (You will prove in the exercises that U_g is indeed unitary.)

We are now ready to describe the Deutsch algorithm. Fortunately it requires the evaluation of the simplest sort of function, namely, a function from $\mathbb{Z}_2$ to $\mathbb{Z}_2$. There are only four such functions, which we label $f_1, \ldots, f_4$:

$$f_1(0) = 0; \quad f_1(1) = 0$$
$$f_2(0) = 0; \quad f_2(1) = 1$$
$$f_3(0) = 1; \quad f_3(1) = 0$$
$$f_4(0) = 1; \quad f_4(1) = 1$$

Suppose that we are given a piece of hardware that computes one of the functions f_k, but we are not told the value of k; that is, we are not told which function our device computes. (The problem is going to be to find out something about this function.) Actually let us suppose that we are given *two* such pieces of hardware, each of which computes the same f_k. One of them is classical and can be inserted into a classical computer; the other is quantum – it executes the unitary transformation U_{f_k} – and can be inserted into a quantum computer. We have a choice about which piece of hardware to use – we will use one or the other exclusively – and we need to decide which one is better for our purpose.

Now, what exactly is our purpose? We are asked to figure out, not the whole function f_k, but only the value of $f(0) \oplus f(1)$ (the addition is mod 2). And we are trying to minimize the number of times that we use our piece of hardware.

If we choose the classical device, it is clear that we will have to use the device *twice*: we use it once to evaluate $f(0)$, and we use it again to evaluate $f(1)$. Then we can compute $f(0) \oplus f(1)$. If we have not found both $f(0)$ and $f(1)$, then there is no way we can know the value of the sum.

On the other hand, if we choose the quantum device (imbedded in a quantum computer), it turns out that we need to use it only *once*. In

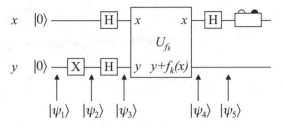

Figure 7.2: A circuit diagram illustrating the Deutsch algorithm.

this sense it is better to use a quantum computer. Let us now see how to accomplish this feat.

Figure 7.2 shows the whole algorithm in diagrammatic form. Our quantum computer consists of two qubits, whose basis states are labeled by the bits x and y. Here are the steps of the algorithm.

1. Start the computer in the state $|00\rangle$. Let us call this state $|\psi_1\rangle$.
2. Apply the X gate to the second qubit. The result is $|\psi_2\rangle = X_2|\psi_1\rangle = |01\rangle$.
3. Apply the Hadamard gate H to each qubit. The result is

$$|\psi_3\rangle = H_1 H_2 |\psi_2\rangle = (H|0\rangle) \otimes (H|1\rangle)$$
$$= \left[\frac{1}{\sqrt{2}}(|0\rangle + |1\rangle) \right] \otimes \left[\frac{1}{\sqrt{2}}(|0\rangle - |1\rangle) \right].$$

4. Apply the device that implements U_{f_k}. To figure out the effect of this device on $|\psi_3\rangle$, let us first think about what happens when we apply it to the simpler state $|x\rangle \otimes [(1/\sqrt{2})(|0\rangle - |1\rangle)]$. The transformation U_{f_k} has the effect of adding $f_k(x)$ to the bit expressed in the second qubit. If $f_k(x) = 0$, then the second qubit is unchanged, and so the whole state is unchanged. But if $f_k(x) = 1$, the state of the second qubit changes from $(1/\sqrt{2})(|0\rangle - |1\rangle)$ to $(1/\sqrt{2})(|1\rangle - |0\rangle)$, which is the negative of the original state. (If the state of the system actually *were* $|x\rangle \otimes [(1/\sqrt{2})(|0\rangle - |1\rangle)]$, this negative sign would be irrelevant – it would be an overall phase factor – but the actual state is a superposition of two states of this form, so the negative sign might make a difference, since it might affect one component of the superposition but not the other.) Putting these observations together, we have

$$U_{f_k}|x\rangle \otimes \left[\frac{1}{\sqrt{2}}(|0\rangle - |1\rangle) \right] = (-1)^{f_k(x)}|x\rangle \otimes \left[\frac{1}{\sqrt{2}}(|0\rangle - |1\rangle) \right].$$

Now applying U_{f_k} to the *actual* state $|\psi_3\rangle$, we have

$$|\psi_4\rangle = U_{f_k}|\psi_3\rangle = \frac{1}{\sqrt{2}}\left[(-1)^{f_k(0)}|0\rangle + (-1)^{f_k(1)}|1\rangle\right] \otimes \frac{1}{\sqrt{2}}(|0\rangle - |1\rangle).$$

Notice that if $f_k(0) \oplus f_k(1) = 0$, that is, if $f_k(0) = f_k(1)$, then $|\psi_4\rangle$ can be written as

$$|\psi_4\rangle = \pm\frac{1}{\sqrt{2}}(|0\rangle + |1\rangle) \otimes \frac{1}{\sqrt{2}}(|0\rangle - |1\rangle) \quad (f_k(0) \oplus f_k(1) = 0).$$

On the other hand, if $f_k(0) \oplus f_k(1) = 1$, so that $f_k(0) \neq f_k(1)$, then we have

$$|\psi_4\rangle = \pm\frac{1}{\sqrt{2}}(|0\rangle - |1\rangle) \otimes \frac{1}{\sqrt{2}}(|0\rangle - |1\rangle) \quad (f_k(0) \oplus f_k(1) = 1).$$

We see, then, that the value of $f_k(0) \oplus f_k(1)$ is expressed in the first qubit. Moreover, the two possible states of that qubit are *orthogonal* to each other. So it should be possible for us to extract that information. We could, in fact, perform at this point a measurement on the first qubit, using the measurement states $((1/\sqrt{2})(|0\rangle + |1\rangle), (1/\sqrt{2})(|0\rangle - |1\rangle))$. The next two steps offer an alternative approach.

5. Apply the Hadamard gate H to the first qubit. Note that $H(1/\sqrt{2})(|0\rangle + |1\rangle) = |0\rangle$ and $H(1/\sqrt{2})(|0\rangle - |1\rangle) = |1\rangle$. So the state of our quantum computer is now

$$|\psi_5\rangle = H_1|\psi_4\rangle = \begin{cases} \pm|0\rangle \otimes \frac{1}{\sqrt{2}}(|0\rangle - |1\rangle) & \text{if } f_k(0) \oplus f_k(1) = 0 \\ \pm|1\rangle \otimes \frac{1}{\sqrt{2}}(|0\rangle - |1\rangle) & \text{if } f_k(0) \oplus f_k(1) = 1 \end{cases}$$

6. Measure the first qubit in the basis $(|0\rangle, |1\rangle)$. The bit labeling the outcome of this measurement is the value of $f_k(0) \oplus f_k(1)$.

We have thus been able to figure out the value of $f_k(0) \oplus f_k(1)$ with only one application of the device that evaluates f_k. (We applied U_{f_k} in step 4 and nowhere else.) We were able to do this because we applied this device to a state that involved *both* of the possible values of x. The result therefore involved both $f_k(0)$ and $f_k(1)$. Notice that this algorithm does not tell us the value of either $f_k(0)$ or $f_k(1)$. We could not have extracted either of these values from $|\psi_4\rangle$, for example. But the algorithm cleverly arranges that the desired combination of these two values can be extracted. Something very similar will happen in Shor's factoring algorithm. The quantum computer will appear to compute many different values in one step, but we will not be able to extract these values from the quantum state. Rather, we will be able to extract the one combination of these values that we need for factoring the given integer.

Though the Deutsch algorithm indicates how a quantum computer can be more efficient than a classical one, there is a sense in which the comparison is not fair. If we choose to use a quantum computer, then we are allowed to use the quantum device that implements U_{f_k}. This is a different sort of resource than the *classical* device that computes f_k. So one could argue that the quantum problem is not the same as the classical problem. A real test of the value of a quantum computer would be to pose a problem that is independent of hardware. The factoring problem will provide such a test.

EXERCISES

Problem 1. (a) Let $|x\rangle$, $x = 0, 1, \ldots, N$, denote the basis states of an N-dimensional state space. Show that if $f(x)$ is any permutation of the integers $0, 1, \ldots, N$, then the linear transformation defined by $U|x\rangle = |f(x)\rangle$ is unitary.

(b) Show that any transformation of the form given in Eq. (7.17) permutes the basis states $|x, y\rangle$ and therefore, by part (a), is unitary.

Problem 2. Why was the initial X gate necessary for the Deutsch algorithm? Go through the remaining steps of the algorithm with the X gate omitted to see what happens in that case.

7.4 A Universal Set of Quantum Gates

Let us summarize again the model of quantum computation that we are considering. First, the computer is placed in a standard state, which we will always take to be $|0\rangle \otimes |0\rangle \otimes \cdots \otimes |0\rangle$. Then one executes a series of steps, each step consisting either of a gate (that is, a unitary transformation) acting on a small number of qubits, or a measurement performed on some of the qubits. At the end, the results of these measurements provide the output of the computation. One can show that any quantum computation of this form can be converted into another quantum computation in which all the measuring happens at the very end. In that case, we have a particularly simple conception of the process: start the computer in its standard state, execute a sequence of gates, and make a measurement. Each gate acts on a limited number of qubits, but we will assume that at each step, one can choose which qubits the gate is to act on. For example, we may choose to let the CNOT gate act on qubits 3 and 17.

Because each of the gates is simply a unitary transformation, the whole sequence of gates that one finds in a quantum computation can together be thought of as constituting a single, usually very complicated unitary transformation performed on the whole computer. A set of gates is called *universal* if, by combining them in a sequence, one can approximate to any desired precision an arbitrary unitary transformation on a quantum computer of arbitrary size. In the following paragraphs we will offer a rough outline of the proof of the following important theorem.[6]

Theorem 7.4.1. The CNOT gate, together with all conceivable single-qubit gates, constitutes a universal set. In fact, for this set of gates one can drop the qualification, "to any desired precision": these gates can generate any unitary transformation *exactly*. (In building an arbitrary unitary transformation out of these basic gates, one will sometimes want to let the CNOT gate act on, say, qubits 4 and 6, sometimes on qubits 71 and 5, and so on. Similarly, in any given step, a single-qubit gate can be applied to any of the n qubits.)

To get a sense of how one might prove this claim of universality, we begin with an easier problem. Let U be an arbitrary 3×3 unitary matrix. (This U does not act on a collection of qubits, since the dimension of the state space of a collection of qubits is always a power of 2. But it is nevertheless helpful to start here.) It is a fact, which you will confirm in Problem 2, that any such U can be written in the form $U = U_1 U_2 U_3$, where

---

[6] DiVincenzo (1995); Barenco et al. (1995). Our treatment follows that of Nielsen and Chuang (2000), Section 4.5.

the U_i have the following forms.

$$U_1 = \begin{pmatrix} a & b & 0 \\ \bar{b} & -\bar{a} & 0 \\ 0 & 0 & 1 \end{pmatrix}, \quad U_2 = \begin{pmatrix} c & 0 & d \\ 0 & 1 & 0 \\ \bar{d} & 0 & -\bar{c} \end{pmatrix}, \quad U_3 = \begin{pmatrix} 1 & 0 & 0 \\ 0 & e & f \\ 0 & \bar{f} & -\bar{e} \end{pmatrix}.$$

(7.18)

Here $|a|^2 + |b|^2 = |c|^2 + |d|^2 = |e|^2 + |f|^2 = 1$. One can verify that each of the U_i is unitary.

Of course if our computer consists of n qubits, the dimension of the state space is $N = 2^n$, but one can similarly show that any $N \times N$ unitary matrix can be written as a product of simple unitary matrices, each of which acts only on two dimensions like the three U_i's in Eq. (7.18). Now, "two dimensions" may sound like it refers to the state space of a single qubit. So it may seem that we have reduced any unitary transformation into a sequence of single-qubit operations. But this is not the case. A unitary transformation acting on two dimensions is more like a *controlled* operation on a single qubit. Consider, for example, a unitary transformation of the form

$$U = \begin{pmatrix} 1 & 0 & 0 & 0 \\ 0 & a & 0 & b \\ 0 & 0 & 1 & 0 \\ 0 & c & 0 & d \end{pmatrix},$$

(7.19)

which acts only on two dimensions, namely, the second and fourth dimensions. That is, only the second and fourth components of a vector are affected by U. Note that this transformation performs the operation $\begin{pmatrix} a & b \\ c & d \end{pmatrix}$ on the first qubit if the state of the second qubit is $|1\rangle$, and leaves the first qubit unchanged if the state of the second qubit is $|0\rangle$. In this sense the operation is controlled by the second qubit.

But what about a unitary matrix of the form

$$V = \begin{pmatrix} 1 & 0 & 0 & 0 \\ 0 & a & b & 0 \\ 0 & c & d & 0 \\ 0 & 0 & 0 & 1 \end{pmatrix},$$

(7.20)

which likewise acts only on two dimensions? This matrix does not represent a controlled operation on a single qubit; rather, it connects the two states $|01\rangle$ and $|10\rangle$, which differ in the states of *both* qubits. Nevertheless, we can express V as a sequence of controlled single-qubit operations. Specifically, one can work out that $V = (\text{CNOT})U(\text{CNOT})$, where U is given by Eq. (7.19). In a similar way, one can show that any unitary transformation that acts only on two dimensions can be written as a sequence of controlled single-qubit operations. It follows, then, that any unitary transformation on n qubits, acting on arbitrarily many dimensions, can likewise be written as a sequence of controlled single-qubit operations.

Finally, one can show that any controlled single-qubit operation can be written as a sequence of ordinary (not controlled) single-qubit operations and the CNOT gate. In this way one sees that the set of gates consisting of the CNOT and all single-qubit gates is universal.

Though it is comforting to have in hand a universal set of reasonably simple gates, the set that we have is *infinite*, since there are infinitely many single-qubit gates. In order to evaluate the efficiency of a quantum computation, it is necessary to work with a *finite* set of basic gates. Then if one asks, for example, how the number of steps in a computation grows with the size of the problem to be solved, one can be confident that the answer has a practical meaning. (For example, one would like to know how the number of steps in a factoring algorithm grows with the length of the number to be factored.) If an infinite number of basic gates were allowed, one expects that it would take an infinite amount of time to home in on the exact gate to be used in a typical step.

Now, we can convert our infinite set of gates into a finite set if we can find a finite set of *single-qubit* gates that, when combined in sequences, are sufficient to generate an arbitrary single-qubit gate. Let $\mathcal{G} = \{G_1, \ldots, G_m\}$ be some finite set of gates that we want to take as basic. It will certainly *not* be possible to express every single-qubit gate as a finite sequence of gates chosen from $\mathcal{G}$, simply because there are uncountably many single-qubit gates and only countably many finite sequences of elements chosen from a finite set. However, we can hope to *approximate* each single-qubit gate with arbitrary precision using such sequences.

In fact one can show that any single-qubit gate can be approximated arbitrarily well by a sequence consisting only of the gates $\{H, T\}$ in some order, where H and T are the Hadamard and T gates defined in

Section 7.2.[7] Since any unitary transformation can be expressed as a sequence of CNOTs and single-qubit gates, it follows that any unitary transformation can be approximated arbitrarily closely by a sequence of gates chosen from the finite set $\{$CNOT, H, $T\}$.

Of course it is conceivable that an algorithm that appears to be quite efficient when expressed as a sequence of CNOTs and arbitrary single-qubit gates might be extremely inefficient once each of the single-qubit gates is expanded out into a sequence of gates chosen from the set $\{H, T\}$. Fortunately it has been proven that in the translation of an arbitrary single-qubit gate into a sequence of H's and T's, the length of the sequence grows quite slowly with increasing precision of the approximation.[8] So the translation from an infinite set of basic gates to a finite set ultimately does not cause any problems for the efficiency of quantum computation.

It turns out that a *typical* unitary transformation on a collection of qubits, when expressed as a sequence of gates chosen from any finite set, requires a sequence whose length grows *exponentially* with the number of qubits. Fortunately, however, some very interesting computational problems require unitary transformations that are very *atypical* in this respect. A prime example is Shor's factoring algorithm, which we begin to study in the following section.

EXERCISES

Problem 1. Show that the transformation V of Eq. (7.20) can indeed be written as $V = (\text{CNOT})U(\text{CNOT})$, with U given by Eq. (7.19).

Problem 2. This problem aims to show that any 3×3 unitary matrix can be expressed as in Eq. (7.18). Let the unitary transformation we are trying to express be

$$U = \begin{pmatrix} r & s & t \\ u & v & w \\ x & y & z \end{pmatrix}.$$

[7] Boykin et al. (1999).
[8] This result is due to Solovay (1995, unpublished) and Kitaev (1997). For a review, see Dawson and Nielsen (2006).

Our strategy is to multiply this matrix on the left by a succession of simple matrices, so that the result is the identity matrix. Reversing the process then produces U.

(a) In terms of the components of U, find a matrix U_1 of the form given in Eq. (7.18), such that $U_1^\dagger U$ has a 0 in the first position of the second row.

(b) Let $U_1^\dagger U$ be written as

$$U_1^\dagger U = \begin{pmatrix} r' & s' & t' \\ 0 & v' & w' \\ x' & y' & z' \end{pmatrix}.$$

In terms of these components, find a matrix U_2 of the form given in Eq. (7.18), such that $U_2^\dagger U_1^\dagger U$ has a 0 in the first position of the third row and a 1 in the upper left-hand corner.

(c) The matrix $U_2^\dagger U_1^\dagger U$ now must have the form

$$U_2^\dagger U_1^\dagger U = \begin{pmatrix} 1 & 0 & 0 \\ 0 & v'' & w'' \\ 0 & y'' & z'' \end{pmatrix}.$$

The zeros in the first row are a consequence of the fact that $U_2^\dagger U_1^\dagger U$ is itself unitary: any other values would make the sum of the squared magnitudes of the first-row elements too large. In terms of the remaining nonzero components, find U_3 of the form given in Eq. (7.18), such that $U_3^\dagger U_2^\dagger U_1^\dagger U = I$. It follows, then, that $U = U_1 U_2 U_3$.

7.5   Number Theory for Shor's Algorithm

Before we start discussing Shor's factoring algorithm in detail, we should note that it is a *probabilistic algorithm*. As we will see shortly, the very first step is to make a random choice. And later we will see that the algorithm involves a quantum measurement whose outcome is probabilistic. As is usually the case with a probabilistic algorithm, there is no absolute guarantee that the algorithm will be successful. Rather, there will be some *probability* of success. For practical purposes this is just fine, as long as one can place a reasonable lower bound on this probability. Even if the probability of failure is, say, 90%, one can run several independent trials, thereby making the overall probability of failure smaller and smaller: for example, the probability of failure in each of 50 successive trials would be $(0.90)^{50} = 0.005$.

The algorithm is based on a mathematical approach to factoring that has been known for some time. In this section we present the basic mathematics; the quantum mechanics will come into our analysis in the following section. It is the quantum part that is usually called "Shor's algorithm."

Let M be the composite integer we are trying to factor. Let us choose at random an integer a, with $1 < a < M$, and find $\gcd(a, M)$. Recall that the greatest common divisor can be found via the Euclidean algorithm, which is quite efficient. If this greatest common divisor is not 1, then we have found a nontrivial factor of M. If $\gcd(a, M) = 1$, then a and M are relatively prime, and we proceed as follows.

Consider the function $f(x) = a^x \pmod M$ for $x = 0, 1, 2, \ldots$. We claim that this function is periodic with period $r \leq M$. (See Problem 1.) Here by "period" we mean the smallest positive integer r such that $f(x + r) = f(x)$ for all x. The period r is called the "order" of a modulo M.

Now suppose that we can find this period. (This is what the quantum computer will do for us.) And suppose that r happens to be even. Then since

$$a^r - 1 = 0 \pmod M,$$

we have

$$(a^{r/2} + 1)(a^{r/2} - 1) = 0 \pmod M,$$

which means that $(a^{r/2} + 1)(a^{r/2} - 1)$, which is a positive integer, is a multiple of M. This in turn implies that all the prime factors of M must be present in $(a^{r/2} + 1)$ and $(a^{r/2} - 1)$ combined. Therefore either $\gcd(a^{r/2} + 1, M)$ or $\gcd(a^{r/2} - 1, M)$, or both, must be a factor of M that is greater than 1. If this factor is not equal to M itself – it could equal M if *all* the prime factors of M were located in $(a^{r/2} + 1)$ – then we have found a nontrivial factor.

There are two ways in which this simple algorithm can fail: (i) r might turn out not to be even, or (ii) the factor we find might turn out to be M itself. We state the following comforting theorem without proof.[9]

---

[9] The proof is in Ekert and Jozsa (1996), Appendix B.

Theorem 7.5.1. As long as M is not even and not a power of a prime, then if a is chosen at random from those integers in $\{2, 3, \ldots, M-1\}$ that are relatively prime to M, the probability of this method giving a nontrivial factor of M is at least $1/2$.

Thus by repeating the algorithm several times, we can quickly increase the odds of succeeding. By the way, it is easy to recognize success when it happens: finding factors is difficult, but checking that one has found a factor is a quick calculation. Note that in the RSA cryptosystem, the integer M, which the eavesdropper would like to factor, is indeed odd and not a power of a prime. (We called this integer n in Section 1.9.)

Example 7.5.1. Let $M = 39$ and $a = 5$. We list the first few values of the function $f(x) = a^x \pmod{39}$.

$$f(0) = 1 \quad f(1) = 5 \quad f(2) = 25 \quad f(3) = 8 \quad f(4) = 1$$

We see, then, that the period r is equal to 4. Since r is even, we can proceed with the algorithm. So we look at $a^{r/2} + 1$ and $a^{r/2} - 1$:

$$a^{r/2} - 1 = 5^2 - 1 = 24 \quad a^{r/2} + 1 = 5^2 + 1 = 26$$
$$\gcd(a^{r/2} - 1, M) = \gcd(24, 39) = 3 \quad \gcd(a^{r/2} + 1, M) = \gcd(26, 39) = 13$$

So in fact we have found both nontrivial factors of 39.

In this example it was easy to find the period r because the integer M was so small. If the number we are trying to factor has several hundred digits, finding the period by a straightforward evaluation of the function $f(x)$ is out of the question, even on a computer (that is, a classical computer). Other factoring algorithms are much more efficient. A quantum computer, however, can do the job, but not by what one would call a straightforward evaluation.

EXERCISES

Problem 1. Let M be any integer greater than 1, let $a < M$ be relatively prime to M, and define $f(x)$ to be $f(x) = a^x \bmod M$. Show that $f(x)$ is periodic with some period $r \leq M$.

Problem 2. Let M, a, and $f(x)$ be as in Problem 1, and let r be the order of a mod M. Show that the integers $f(0), f(1), \ldots, f(r-1)$ are all distinct. That is, show that no value is repeated until one has finished a whole period.

Problem 3. Show how the factoring algorithm presented in this section works out for $M = 85$ and $a = 3$. That is, carry out the steps of Example 7.5.1 but with these numbers.

7.6   Finding the Period of $f(x)$

The basic idea behind Shor's algorithm is this. We will, through a series of operations, bring the quantum computer into a superposition of many distinct quantum states, in which each of the component states expresses (i) a value of x and (ii) the corresponding value of $f(x)$. Moreover, *all* possible values of x up to some chosen maximum will be represented in this superposition. Then we will perform a clever operation, called the "quantum Fourier transform," that will allow us to extract information about the period r. In order to get a sufficiently high probability of obtaining the period in this way, we will need the computer to have computed, in superposition, the values of $f(x)$ over many periods. Since the period r might be of the same order of magnitude as M itself, we want the maximum value of x to be many times M. As we will see later, we can obtain the period with a sufficiently high probability of success if we let this maximum value be approximately M^2. Though we have in mind that this algorithm will be used to factor a product of two large primes, as in the RSA system, we will not assume here that M is such a number. In fact, the algorithm presented here could be used to find the order of a mod M for any integer M greater than 2 and any relatively prime a less than M.

    It is helpful to imagine the quantum computer as containing two "registers." The "x-register" consists of m qubits, with m chosen so that $M^2 \leq 2^m < 2M^2$. In other words, m is the smallest integer greater than or equal to $\log_2(M^2) = 2\log_2 M$. The basis states of this register, such as $|000\ldots0\rangle$, can be read as the binary representations of the integers $0, \ldots, 2^m - 1$. For example, the state $|111\ldots1\rangle$ represents the integer

$2^m - 1$. In this way the register can express values of x at least up to $M^2 - 1$. And the register itself is roughly twice as long as what would be needed to store the number M. The "y-register" will be used to express the value of $f(x) = a^x$ (mod M). This function takes integer values between 0 and $M - 1$, so the number of qubits needed for the y-register is the smallest integer greater than or equal to $\log_2 M$. Thus in the two registers combined, the number of qubits is about three times the length in binary of the number M. Let the basis states of the two registers be labeled $|x, y\rangle$. Here x is an integer whose binary expansion labels a basis state of the x-register, and y similarly labels a basis state of the y-register.

Example 7.6.1. Suppose the number M that we want to factor is a 500-digit number. That is, $M \approx 10^{500}$. Then the number of binary digits it takes to express M is roughly $\log_2(10^{500}) = 500 \log_2(10) = 500(3.32) = 1660$. So the x-register will contain roughly $2(1660) = 3320$ qubits, and the y-register will contain roughly 1660 qubits. This means that in principle, a quantum computer capable of factoring a 500-digit number efficiently would only have to have a few thousand qubits. (In reality many more qubits would be required in order to do the necessary error correction.)

We now go through the steps of Shor's algorithm for finding the period of $f(x)$. For now we will not be concerned with the question of how efficiently each step can be carried out. Rather, we simply assume that any unitary transformation can be realized, and we save questions of efficiency for later. Moreover, while the first four steps in the following sequence are relatively straightforward, the last two involve mathematical claims that we will have to justify. Our approach is to lay out the algorithm in a compact way and to save the justification for the following section. In particular, the quantum Fourier transform appearing in step 5, which is in a sense the heart of the algorithm, will be discussed in some detail in Section 7.7

1. Set the two registers to the initial state $|\Phi_0\rangle = |0, 0\rangle$. That is, each qubit in each register is set to the state $|0\rangle$.
2. Apply the Hadamard gate H to each qubit in the x-register. Recall that $H|0\rangle = (1/\sqrt{2})(|0\rangle + |1\rangle)$. So the x-register is now in the state

$$\frac{1}{\sqrt{2}}(|0\rangle + |1\rangle) \otimes \frac{1}{\sqrt{2}}(|0\rangle + |1\rangle) \otimes \cdots \otimes \frac{1}{\sqrt{2}}(|0\rangle + |1\rangle).$$

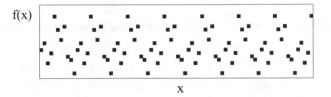

Figure 7.3: A schematic illustration showing which basis states are included in the state $|\Phi_2\rangle$. Note that the periodic function $f(x)$ never repeats itself until it has run through an entire period. The object of the Shor algorithm is to find the period r.

Note that when this product is multiplied out, *every* possible string of m bits is represented, each with the same coefficient. Thus we can write the state of the two registers as

$$|\Phi_1\rangle = \frac{1}{\sqrt{2^m}} \sum_{x=0}^{2^m-1} |x, 0\rangle.$$

3. We now want to evaluate the function $f(x) = a^x \pmod{M}$ and place the result in the y-register. Since the x-register is in a superposition of all values of x that can be expressed in the given number of bits, this operation will simultaneously evaluate $f(x)$ on all such values, an example of quantum parallelism. But how do we represent the operation? It must be represented as a unitary operator, and the operator we use is U_f, defined by $U_f|x, y\rangle = |x, y \oplus f(x)\rangle$, where "$\oplus$" indicates bitwise addition mod 2. (This is similar to what we did to express the AND gate in Section 7.2 and to express the function f_k in Section 7.3.) That U_f is indeed unitary follows from Problem 1 of Section 7.3. Note that $U_f|x, 0\rangle = |x, f(x)\rangle$; so the two registers are now in the state

$$|\Phi_2\rangle = U_f|\Phi_1\rangle = \frac{1}{\sqrt{2^m}} \sum_{x=0}^{2^m-1} |x, f(x)\rangle. \tag{7.21}$$

We can picture this state as in Fig. 7.3. Each possible position within the rectangle represents a basis state $|x, y\rangle$ of the quantum computer, with x plotted horizontally and y plotted vertically. The dots that are shown in the picture indicate those basis states that are actually included in the state $|\Phi_2\rangle$: they are simply a graph of the periodic function $f(x)$. All the basis states that are included have equal weight in the state, as one can see from Eq. (7.21).

4. Now measure the *y*-register in the standard basis. That is, for each qubit, perform the measurement with outcomes corresponding to the states $|0\rangle$ and $|1\rangle$. This is an example of an incomplete measurement of the sort we studied in Section 2.4: we are measuring the *y*-register but leaving the *x*-register unmeasured. The measurement forces each qubit in the *y*-register to be in one of the states $|0\rangle$ or $|1\rangle$. Taken together, these bits constitute the binary expansion of some integer u in the range $0, \ldots, M-1$. Though this measurement "collapses" the *y*-register to the specific value u, it leaves the *x*-register in a superposition of values, namely, all the values of x such that $f(x) = u$. Recall that $f(x)$ is a periodic function with a period no larger than M. The *x*-register holds values up to $M^2 - 1$; so $f(x)$ will take the specific value u for at least M different values of x that can be expressed in the *x*-register. In fact, since $f(x)$ does not repeat itself within a single period,[10] we can write these values as $x_0, x_0 + r, x_0 + 2r$, and so on up to within r of 2^m, where x_0 is a nonnegative integer less than the period r. (This x_0 is the smallest value of x for which $f(x) = u$.) These are the values that are now superposed in the *x*-register. So we can write the state of the two registers after the measurement as

$$|\Phi_3\rangle = \frac{1}{\sqrt{K}} \sum_{x=0}^{2^m-1} g(x)|x, u\rangle,$$

where K is the number of values of x for which $f(x) = u$, and

$$g(x) = \begin{cases} 1, & \text{if } f(x) = u \\ 0, & \text{if } f(x) \neq u. \end{cases}$$

The basis states that are included in $|\Phi_3\rangle$ are illustrated in Fig. 7.4. Notice that the *y*-register is now in the definite state $|u\rangle$ and the *x*-register is in a superposition of all the states $|x\rangle$ for which $f(x) = u$. From now on we will no longer perform any operations on the *y*-register – it has served its purpose – so we will no longer write down its state. (Its state will be $|u\rangle$ for the rest of the computation.)

5. Recall that we are trying to find the period r of $f(x)$. Evidently the function $g(x)$, which is imbedded in the state $|\Phi_3\rangle$, likewise has period r. So we now try to find the period of $g(x)$. We do this by applying

---

[10] See Problem 2 at the end of the preceding section.

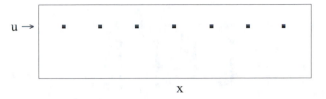

u →

x

Figure 7.4: A schematic illustration of the basis states included in the state $|\Phi_3\rangle$. The period is still r, but the function $g(x)$ is much simpler than $f(x)$.

to the x-register a unitary transformation U_{QFT} – this is the quantum Fourier transform mentioned earlier – defined as follows:

$$U_{\text{QFT}}|x\rangle = \frac{1}{\sqrt{2^m}} \sum_{c=0}^{2^m-1} e^{2\pi i cx/2^m}|c\rangle. \tag{7.22}$$

This transformation can look quite mysterious upon encountering it for the first time. It will seem more familiar after you have done Problems 1 and 2. Applying U_{QFT} to the x part of the state $|\Phi_3\rangle$, we obtain the state

$$|\Phi_4\rangle = \frac{1}{\sqrt{K}} \sum_{c=0}^{2^m-1} G(c)|c\rangle,$$

where

$$G(c) = \frac{1}{\sqrt{2^m}} \sum_{x=0}^{2^m-1} g(x)e^{2\pi i cx/2^m}.$$

The function $G(c)$ is called the discrete Fourier transform of $g(x)$. Because $g(x)$ is a very simple binary function, taking the value 1 only at regular intervals, its discrete Fourier transform $G(c)$ is also fairly simple. We will study its properties in some detail in the following section, and, in particular, we will justify and make precise the following claim: If the integer c is within 1/2 of a multiple of $2^m/r$, that is, if $|c - j(2^m/r)| \leq 1/2$ for some integer j, then $G(c)$ is relatively large; otherwise it is small. Thus the locations of the peaks of the function $G(c)$ tell us something about the desired quantity r. These peaks are regular: they occur near multiples of $2^m/r$. This fact is illustrated schematically in Fig. 7.5.

6. Measure the x-register in the standard basis. The outcome of this measurement will be some integer expressed in binary notation. The

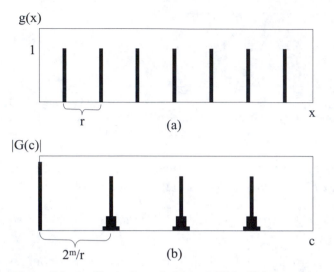

Figure 7.5: An illustration of $g(x)$ and $G(c)$. $G(c)$ determines the likely values of c; so a measurement of c provides information about the original period r. (The peak at $c = 0$ is shown to be higher because this is typically the case in practice. As will become clearer in the following section, this happens because zero is the multiple of $2^m/r$ that is always guaranteed to be an integer.)

probability of getting a specific integer c is $(1/K)|G(c)|^2$. According to what we have just said, this probability tends to be reasonably large for values of c that are within $1/2$ of a multiple of $2^m/r$, that is, for which

$$\left| c - j\left(\frac{2^m}{r}\right) \right| \leq \frac{1}{2}$$

for some integer j. We will refer to such values of c as "good" values. If our measured value of c is a good value (which, again, is reasonably likely), it follows that

$$\left| \frac{c}{2^m} - \frac{j}{r} \right| \leq \frac{1}{2^{m+1}}.$$

From this inequality we can hope to learn the value of r via the next step in the algorithm. (We have now finished the quantum part of the algorithm; the rest is math.)

7. Look for a number j'/r', with j' and r' integers and $r' < M$, such that

$$\left| \frac{c}{2^m} - \frac{j'}{r'} \right| \leq \frac{1}{2^{m+1}}.$$

As we will show in the following section, there will always be at most one such number j'/r'. If our value of c is a "good" value, then there *will be* such a number j'/r' and it will be equal to j/r for some integer j. So our strategy is this: *if* there exists a fraction j'/r' satisfying the above conditions, write this fraction in reduced form and hope that the resulting denominator is r. If there is no such fraction j'/r', start over at step 1, using the same fuction $f(x)$.

8. If the preceding step has produced a candidate value of r, use this value to compute $f(r) = a^r$ (mod M). If $f(r) = 1$, we have almost certainly found the order of a. (If c was "bad," it is still possible, but extremely unlikely, that our candidate value is a *multiple* of the order.) If $f(r) \neq 1$, we run the algorithm again on the same function $f(x)$.

Thus if all has gone well, we will have obtained the period r, which we can then use as in Section 7.5 to try to find a nontrivial factor of M.

You might be wondering why we needed to go through step 5 at all. We already had a quantum state, $|\Psi_3\rangle$, that embodied a periodic function having the period r that we wanted to find. Step 5 replaced this state with another state, $|\Psi_4\rangle$, that is nearly periodic, with a "period" that is not r itself but $2^m/r$. Why is the latter better than the former? Both seem to embody the information that we want to extract. The answer is that in $|\Psi_3\rangle$ the periodic function is not anchored to any particular point on the x-axis, at least no point that we know. So if we were to measure the value of x when the computer is in the state $|\Psi_3\rangle$, we would learn nothing about the period r. If we could measure the same computer several times while it was in the state $|\Psi_3\rangle$, we could extract the period, but such repeated measurements on the same state are not allowed by quantum mechanics: the first measurement would collapse the variable x to a particular value, and subsequent measurements would only produce the same value over and over. Alternatively, we could try repeating the whole algorithm up to that point several times, each time measuring the value of x. But these repetitions would typically produce different values of u in step 4, and the resulting functions $g(x)$ would be shifted relative to each other, so that these measurements of x would tell us nothing about the period r.

In contrast, the function $G(c)$ embodied in $|\Psi_4\rangle$ *is* anchored to the origin, so that measuring the value of c can tell us something about r. This is why step 5 is the crucial step of the algorithm. It is the step that allows us to extract precisely the information we want without asking for more information about the state than quantum mechanics allows.

But there are ways in which the algorithm can fail. Evidently we need to find a good lower bound on the probability of succeeding in a given trial. Moreover, the last two steps involve mathematical claims that clearly need to be justified. These are the jobs of the following section. But first, let us go through the Shor algorithm for the simple case of factoring the number 39.

Example 7.6.2. Let us suppose, as in an earlier example, that the number we are trying to factor is 39. Thus $M = 39$, $M^2 = 1521$, and we therefore choose m to be $\lceil 2 \log_2 39 \rceil$, which equals 11. That is, there are 11 qubits in the x-register. The y-register will consist of 6 qubits, the minimum number required to express all the integers in the range $0, \ldots, 38$.

In our earlier example we used $a = 5$ as the base in the function $f(x) = a^x$ (mod M). For the present purpose it turns out to be more interesting to use $a = 7$. (We will return to $a = 5$ in Example 7.7.1.) So $f(x) = 7^x$ (mod 39). Suppose that we have run the Shor algorithm on our quantum computer and have finally measured the x-register, obtaining the outcome $c = 853$. In theory, this number is likely to be within $1/2$ of a multiple of $2^m/r = 2^{11}/r = 2048/r$. We cannot check this yet because we do not know what r is. But if 853 *is* within $1/2$ of $j(2048/r)$ for some integer j, then the theory guarantees that we can find the fraction j/r, because it will be the *unique* fraction, with denominator less than 39, that is within $1/2^{12}$ of $853/2048$. There is a reasonably small number of likely fractions having denominator less than 39, and one can run through them all with a calculator. One finds, sure enough, that only one of them is within the specified distance of $853/2048$. It is $5/12$:

$$\left| \frac{853}{2048} - \frac{5}{12} \right| = 0.000163 < \frac{1}{2^{12}} = 0.000244.$$

So our candidate for the fraction j/r is $5/12$. This is consistent with $j = 5$ and $r = 12$, but it is also consistent with $j = 10$ and $r = 24$. Now, the algorithm asks us to write the fraction in reduced form, that

is, 5/12, and hope that the denominator is indeed equal to the period r. Does the algorithm succeed in this particular example? One
can check that 7^{12} (mod 39) $= 1$. So we have indeed found the
period.

In this case we were able to find a suitable fraction j'/r' by trial and
error, but if we are trying to factor a 500-digit number, we will not be able
to do this. Toward the end of the following section we will present a more
systematic way of looking for such a fraction.

EXERCISES

Problem 1. This problem explores the discrete Fourier transform for the
case where the variable x can be expressed in just three bits; that is, x
takes the values $0, 1, \ldots, 7$. Define $g(x)$ as

$$g(x) = \begin{cases} 1, & x = 0, 3, 6 \\ 0, & \text{otherwise} \end{cases}.$$

(Such a g could arise in the factoring algorithm if the period r is 3.) The
discrete Fourier transform of g is defined to be

$$G(c) = \frac{1}{8} \sum_{x=0}^{7} g(x)e^{2\pi icx/8}.$$

(a) Find the values of $G(c)$ for $c = 0, 1, \ldots, 7$. (We would strongly
recommend that you do this calculation pictorially. That is, draw eight
equally spaced complex numbers on the unit circle and figure out, for
each value of c, which ones have to be added together. The adding itself
can also be done geometrically.)

(b) In Shor's quantum algorithm, the probability of measuring a spe-
cific value of c is $(1/3)|G(c)|^2$. Check that the probabilities computed from
your answer to part (a) add up to 1.

(c) In order for Shor's algorithm to be successful in a given trial, it is
necessary that the measured value of c be within $1/2$ of a multiple of $2^m/r$,
which in this case is 8/3. Which values of c have this property, and what is
their combined probability? According to the theory (see the following
section), this probability is expected to be at least $4/\pi^2$. Is this prediction
borne out in this example?

Problem 2. In the text, we claimed that the transformation U_{QFT} [Eq. (7.22)] takes the state $|\Phi_3\rangle$ to the state $|\Phi_4\rangle$. Show that this claim is correct.

Problem 3. Consider a modified version of Shor's algorithm in which the y-register is set initially to the binary representation of some fixed integer y_0 rather than to the state $|0\rangle$. Otherwise the algorithm is unchanged. Will this modified algorithm have the same success in factoring as the unmodified algorithm? Explain.

Problem 4. We are using Shor's algorithm to factor the number 35. (In this problem the value of a in $f(x) = a^x \bmod 35$ is not specified.)

(a) How many qubits are in the x-register? How many in the y-register? How does one express the integer 35 in binary notation? Is it true that the number of qubits in the y-register is about the same as the number of bits in the binary expression for 35, and that the number in the x-register is about twice that number?

(b) At the end of the algorithm, we measure the x-register and obtain $c = 341$. We do not yet know whether this is a "good" value of c, that is, whether it is within 1/2 of a multiple of $2^m/r$. Supposing that it *is* a good value, what is the value of the fraction j/r? (Hint: For this problem, it helps to start by trying the smallest possible denominators and working upwards until you find a satisfactory fraction.)

(c) On the basis of your answer to part (b), and still assuming that 341 is a good value of c, what are the possible values of the period r? (Here you are to work only with your answer to part (b). We do not want you to have to go through all the possible values of a to figure out whether some values of r are impossible for $M = 35$.)

7.7   Estimating the Probability of Success

We begin by exploring the properties of the function $G(c)$, which depends on the simple periodic function $g(x)$:

$$G(c) = \frac{1}{\sqrt{2^m}} \sum_{x=0}^{2^m-1} g(x) e^{2\pi i c x/2^m}.$$

We claimed that $G(c)$ has sharp peaks near multiples of $2^m/r$. So our immediate goal is to make this claim precise and to prove it. Because of the way $g(x)$ is produced – that is, by looking for all the integers x for which $f(x)$ has some specific value u – the function $g(x)$ is equal to 1 for the following values of x:

$$x = x_0, x_0 + r, x_0 + 2r, \ldots, x_0 + (K-1)r, \tag{7.23}$$

where x_0 is the smallest integer for which $f(x) = u$ (note that x_0 is in the range $0, \ldots, r-1$), and K is the largest integer for which the sequence does not go beyond $2^m - 1$. We can write K explicitly as $\lceil (2^m - x_0)/r \rceil$, that is, the smallest integer greater than or equal to $(2^m - x_0)/r$. For values of x not listed in Eq. (7.23), $g(x)$ has the value 0. So we can write $G(c)$ as

$$G(c) = \frac{1}{\sqrt{2^m}} \sum_{k=0}^{K-1} e^{2\pi i c(x_0 + kr)/2^m} = \frac{1}{\sqrt{2^m}} e^{2\pi i c x_0/2^m} \sum_{k=0}^{K-1} e^{2\pi i ckr/2^m}. \tag{7.24}$$

The latter sum in Eq. (7.24) is of the form $\sum_{k=0}^{K-1} \alpha^k$, a finite geometric series for which there is an explicit formula. The formula is in fact

$$\sum_{k=0}^{K-1} \alpha^k = \frac{1 - \alpha^K}{1 - \alpha}, \tag{7.25}$$

which holds as long as $\alpha \neq 1$. If $\alpha = 1$, the sum has the value K. In our problem, $\alpha = \exp(2\pi i cr/2^m)$, which equals 1 if and only if $cr/2^m$ happens to be an integer.[11] It turns out that the case $\alpha = 1$ plays a particularly important role when r divides 2^m. Though this case is unlikely, it is also easy to analyze. So we consider this case first.

The case when r divides 2^m (i.e., r is a power of 2)
In this case K is equal to the integer $2^m/r$ – there is no need to subtract x_0 or use the $\lceil \cdots \rceil$ symbol – and the latter sum in Eq. (7.24) has the value K whenever c is a multiple of K. Otherwise the formula (7.25) holds, and the sum has the value 0, since $\alpha^K = \exp(2\pi i c) = 1$. Thus we

---

[11] Here and in several other places in this section we use the common expression "$\exp(\cdots)$" as a substitute for "$e^{(\cdots)}$". We do this only to avoid typographical crowding in the exponent.

have

$$G(c) = \frac{1}{\sqrt{2^m}} e^{2\pi i c x_0 / 2^m} \times \begin{cases} K, & \text{if } c = jK, \text{ for } j = 0, \ldots, r-1 \\ 0, & \text{otherwise} \end{cases}.$$

Recall that the probability of measuring the value c is $(1/K)|G(c)|^2$. Let us evaluate this probability in the case we are now considering. The factor $\exp(2\pi i c x_0 / 2^m)$ has unit magnitude, so it has no effect on the probability. Using the fact that $K/2^m = 1/r$, we get

$$\text{Probability of } c = \frac{1}{K}|G(c)|^2 = \begin{cases} 1/r, & \text{if } c = jK, \text{ for } j = 0, \ldots, r-1 \\ 0, & \text{otherwise} \end{cases}.$$

So in this case the peaks of probability are quite extreme: the *only* possible values of c are multiples of K, that is, multiples of $2^m/r$. In Fig. 7.5 all the peaks would be perfectly sharp in this case. Note that the probabilities add up to 1, as they must.

Suppose we have measured the value of c. Then the above analysis implies that c equals $j(2^m/r)$ for some integer j, so that $c/2^m = j/r$. To find r, we write our known fraction $c/2^m$ in reduced form. As long as c is not 0, the denominator of this fraction is either r itself or a factor of r (since j and r might have a common factor). The value of j is randomly chosen, by the quantum measurement, among the values $0, \ldots, r-1$. In the case we are considering now, j and r will have a common factor if and only if j is even, which happens with probability 1/2. So with probability 1/2, the denominator of the reduced form of $c/2^m$ will in fact be r. Following the Shor prescription, we would now check to see whether this denominator is indeed the period of $f(x)$. (It is easy to check whether $a^r = 1$ (mod M).) If it is, we have found the order of a mod M. If not, we try again, but as we have said before, the probability of failing *every* time diminishes exponentially with the number of trials.

Before we consider the more typical case in which r is not a factor of 2^m, let us illustrate the above considerations in a simple example.

Example 7.7.1. Suppose as always that we are trying to factor the number 39. As we have seen, in this case the number of qubits m in the x-register is 11 (which makes 2^m equal to 2048), and the number of qubits in the y-register is 6. For this example we choose $a = 5$, so that $f(x) = 5^x$ (mod 39).

We saw earlier that the period of this function is $r = 4$. Of course the quantum computer does not know this, but when it goes through the steps of the Shor algorithm, it will produce the state $|\Phi_4\rangle$ of the x-register in which only four values have nonzero probability, namely, the values $c = 0$, 2048/4, 2(2048/4), and 3(2048/4). When we measure the x-register, we will obtain one of these values at random: they are all equally likely. According to the above prescription, we now consider the fraction $c/2^m = c/2048$ in reduced form. This fraction will be 0, 1/4, 1/2, or 3/4. In two of these cases, we obtain the correct value of r by reading off the denominator. We know that we have found the correct answer once we have checked that 5^4 (mod 39) does indeed equal 1.

   In this example, as we predicted above, we have probability 1/2 of finding the period r, since there are two good values of $c/2^m$ out of four possibilities. Notice that even if we fail, we can get some information about r: if we get $c = 2(2048/4)$, so that $c/2048 = 1/2$, we learn that 2 is likely to be a factor of r. (We cannot reach this conclusion with certainty, because we do not know *a priori* that the period divides 2^m. As you will show in Problem 5, when r does not divide 2^m, it is possible for the measured value of c to produce a candidate period that does not divide the actual period r.)

The case when r does not divide 2^m
In this case the quantity $\alpha = \exp(2\pi i cr/2^m)$ takes the value 1 only for very special values of c (indeed only for $c = 0$ if r happens to be odd). Using the formula (7.25), we find that

$$G(c) = \frac{1}{\sqrt{2^m}} e^{2\pi i cx_0/2^m} \times \begin{cases} K, & \text{if } cr = \text{a multiple of } 2^m \\ \frac{1-e^{2\pi i cKr/2^m}}{1-e^{2\pi i cr/2^m}}, & \text{otherwise} \end{cases}.$$

The probability $(1/K)|G(c)|^2$ of obtaining the value c when we make our measurement works out to be

$$\text{Probability of } c = \frac{1}{2^m} \times \begin{cases} K, & \text{if } cr = \text{a multiple of } 2^m \\ \frac{1}{K}\left[\frac{\sin(\pi cKr/2^m)}{\sin(\pi cr/2^m)}\right]^2, & \text{otherwise} \end{cases}.$$

$$(7.26)$$

We claim that this probability, even in the second case, is peaked when $c/2^m$ is near any of the values j/r, where $j = 0, \ldots, r-1$.

   To see this, note first that the spacing between possible values of $c/2^m$ is $1/2^m$, so that each possible value of j/r is within $1/2^{m+1}$ of $c/2^m$ for *some* allowed value of c. That is, for each $j = 0, \ldots, r-1$, there is an integer c in the range $0, \ldots, 2^m - 1$ such that

$$\left| \frac{c}{2^m} - \frac{j}{r} \right| \leq \frac{1}{2^{m+1}}. \tag{7.27}$$

Moreover, this value of c is *unique*, because it is impossible for the fraction j/r to be exactly halfway between two consecutive values of $c/2^m$. (This would require that $j/r = (2c+1)/2^{m+1}$, which is impossible since the fraction on the right cannot be reduced and r is much less than 2^{m+1}.)

Now, let us add up the probabilities of all the c's for which Eq. (7.27) is satisfied for some j. One can show[12] that each of these probabilities is at least $4/\pi^2 r$, except for a very small additive term that is negligible for large M. (See Problem 3.) Moreover, there are exactly r such values of c, since there are r possible values of j. It follows that the sum of the probabilities of the values of c satisfying Eq. (7.27) can be estimated to be at least $4/\pi^2 \approx 0.4$.

We see, then, that there is a reasonable chance that the value of c that we obtain from our quantum measurement will be within $1/2^{m+1}$ of j/r for some $j = 0, \ldots, r-1$. Hoping that our value of c is indeed such a value, how do we go about finding the corresponding fraction j/r? In Example 7.6.2 we did it by trial and error but promised a better method later. Here we present the better method.

First note that given the fraction $c/2^m$, there can be at most one fraction j'/r' with $r' \in \{1, \ldots, M-1\}$ that satisfies the desired inequality,

$$\left| \frac{c}{2^m} - \frac{j'}{r'} \right| \leq \frac{1}{2^{m+1}}. \tag{7.28}$$

(Here we are not insisting that r' be the *actual* period r. It could be any integer in the given range.) For suppose that there were two such fractions. Then the difference between them would be

$$\left| \frac{j'}{r'} - \frac{j''}{r''} \right| = \left| \frac{j'r'' - j''r'}{r'r''} \right| \geq \frac{1}{r'r''} > \frac{1}{M^2}. \tag{7.29}$$

---

[12] See Ekert and Jozsa (1996) or Gerjuoy (2005).

But since both j'/r' and j''/r'' are supposed to be within $1/2^{m+1}$ of the same number, their difference must also satisfy

$$\left| \frac{j'}{r'} - \frac{j''}{r''} \right| \le \frac{1}{2^m} \le \frac{1}{M^2}. \tag{7.30}$$

(We see now why we wanted the x-register to go up to M^2. The size of this register is what determined the constant on the right-hand side of Eq. (7.27).) The contradiction between Eqs. (7.29) and (7.30) shows that there can be at most one such fraction.

Once we have measured the value of c, the algorithm for finding the fraction j'/r', if it exists, is remarkably simple. Any rational number can be expanded as a *continued fraction*, as in the following example.

$$\frac{853}{2048} = \frac{1}{\frac{2048}{853}} = \frac{1}{2 + \frac{342}{853}} = \frac{1}{2 + \frac{1}{\frac{853}{342}}} = \frac{1}{2 + \frac{1}{2 + \frac{169}{342}}} = \frac{1}{2 + \frac{1}{2 + \frac{1}{\frac{342}{169}}}} \tag{7.31}$$

$$= \frac{1}{2 + \frac{1}{2 + \frac{1}{2 + \frac{4}{169}}}} = \frac{1}{2 + \frac{1}{2 + \frac{1}{2 + \frac{1}{\frac{169}{4}}}}} = \frac{1}{2 + \frac{1}{2 + \frac{1}{2 + \frac{1}{42 + \frac{1}{4}}}}}$$

We stop when the numerator of each fraction is 1 (beyond this point the procedure would not produce any new fractions). At each stage, we can drop the final fraction to obtain an approximation to the original number, and the approximation gets better at each stage. In the above example, the approximations are 1/2, 2/5, 5/12, and 212/509, obtained by dropping, respectively, 342/853, 169/342, 4/169, and 1/4. The approximations are called *convergents*. We now invoke without proof a useful theorem.[13]

Theorem 7.7.1. Let z be a rational number and let a and b be integers such that a/b satisfies

$$\left| z - \frac{a}{b} \right| < \frac{1}{2b^2}.$$

Then a/b is one of the convergents in the continued fraction expansion of z.

---

[13] You can find the proof in Hardy and Wright (1965), Section 10.15.

Let us identify $c/2^m$ with the z of this theorem, and j'/r' with the a/b. Then, if there exists a fraction j'/r' satisfying Eq. (7.28), the hypothesis of the theorem is satisfied, since from Eq. (7.28) we have

$$\left| \frac{c}{2^m} - \frac{j'}{r'} \right| \le \frac{1}{2} \cdot \frac{1}{2^m} \le \frac{1}{2} \cdot \frac{1}{M^2} < \frac{1}{2r'^2}.$$

The theorem thus guarantees that if there exists a number j'/r' satisfying Eq. (7.28), we can find this number by finding the convergents generated by $c/2^m$.

What, then, are the possible outcomes of the algorithm? If our measured value of c is "good," then the method of continued fractions will produce a fraction j'/r' that is equal to j/r for some integer j. In this case the algorithm can still fail, in two ways: (i) in its reduced form, the denominator of this fraction might not be r itself but only a factor or r; (ii) the integer j might be 0. If our value of c is *not* good, that is, if Eq. (7.27) is not satisfied for any integers j, then one of two things will happen: (i) every convergent of $c/2^m$ will be unacceptable as a candidate for the fraction j'/r', either because it is not within $1/2^{m+1}$ of $c/2^m$ or because its denominator is not small enough; or (ii) there will be an acceptable j'/r', but r' will not be the actual period r (it need not have any particular relation to r). In the latter case, the discrepancy will almost certainly be revealed when we check to see whether $a^{r'} \bmod M$ is equal to 1.

Example 7.7.2. In Example 7.6.2, we considered the function $f(x) = 7^x$ (mod 39) for factoring the number 39. There, we needed to look for a fraction j'/r' with denominator less than 39 satisfying

$$\left| \frac{853}{2048} - \frac{j'}{r'} \right| \le \frac{1}{4096}. \tag{7.32}$$

To search for such a number more systematically, we expand 853/2048 as a continued fraction and note the successive convergents. In fact we have already carried out this calculation in Eq. (7.31), obtaining the four convergents 1/2, 2/5, 5/12, and 212/509. Plugging these into Eq. (7.32), we find that the first one that is close enough to 853/2048 is 5/12. So 5/12 is our number j'/r'. (And, as must be the case, the denominator of the next convergent, 212/509, is not smaller than 39 and is therefore not an acceptable candidate for j'/r'.)

Let us now bring together various estimates of probabilities. First there is the matter of choosing a good integer $a < M$. Theorem 7.5.1 tells us that as long as M is not even or a power of a prime, then if a is chosen randomly (and is relatively prime to M), the method of finding the period of $f(x) = a^x \pmod{M}$ will produce a nontrivial factor of M with probability at least $1/2$. There are efficient ways to check whether M is even (obviously) or a power of a prime (less obviously). Let us assume that we have done this checking, so that we have a probability at least $1/2$ of choosing a good a. Then, in trying to *find* the order of $f(x)$, we ultimately measure a value of c, which we need to be within $1/2$ of a multiple of $2^m/r$. The probability of this happening[14] is, as we have said, at least $4/\pi^2$.

Finally, if we have obtained such a value of c and therefore have been able to find the corresponding fraction j/r, it is possible that j and r will share a common factor, in which case when we write j/r in reduced form, the denominator[15] will not be r, but will be some factor of r. The conceptually easiest way to deal with this problem is simply to perform the algorithm twice for a given value of a. If each trial does indeed result in a good value of c, then we will get two fractions j/r and j'/r whose reduced forms give us two denominators, each of which is a factor of r. We then take the least common multiple of these two denominators and hope that it equals r. One can show[16] that the probability of succeeding in this way (assuming that each of the two trials has produced a good value of c) is at least $1/4$. Altogether, then, with a random choice of a, and two trials to find the period r, the probability of finding a nontrivial factor of M can be estimated to be at least

$$\left(\frac{4}{\pi^2}\right)^2 \left(\frac{1}{4}\right)\left(\frac{1}{2}\right) = 0.02.$$

This is perhaps not an impressive number! The main point, though, is that the probability is bounded below by a number that does not get smaller as one tries to factor larger and larger numbers. Moreover, the estimate we have given here very much underestimates the actual probability of

---

[14] Again, except for a negligible additive term.

[15] There is a small chance, about $1/r$, that the value of c will be 0, in which case we get no denominator at all by reducing $c/2^m$. The chance of this happening diminishes with increasing M, and we neglect it in this discussion.

[16] See Nielsen and Chuang (2000), p. 231.

success.[17] And in practice, one need not repeat the whole procedure in the case of failure. For example, if the problem is only that the two denominators do not yield the value of r, one can perform a third trial producing a new denominator, which, when combined with the first two, should be much more likely to yield the value of r.

EXERCISES

Problem 1. Suppose we are trying to factor the number 21 using the Shor algorithm. We decide to use $a = 2$, so that we are trying to find the period of the function $f(x) = 2^x \pmod{21}$. We run through the Shor algorithm and finally measure the x-register, getting the outcome $c = 427$.

(a) What is the number m of qubits in the x-register?

(b) Use the continued fraction method to find a fraction j'/r', with denominator less than 21, that is within $1/2^{m+1}$ of the ratio $c/2^m$.

(c) Verify, by considering all possible denominators $11, \ldots, 20$, that there is no other such fraction close enough to $c/2^m$. (For each denominator, it is sufficient to consider just the one fraction that is closest to $c/2^m$. Note that there is no need to include the denominators $1, \ldots, 10$, since any fraction with such a denominator is equal to another fraction with a denominator in the range $11, \ldots, 20$.)

(d) We hope that the denominator in j'/r', when the fraction is in reduced form, is the period of $f(x)$. Check to see that it is indeed the period.

(e) Use your value of r to find the factors of 21.

Problem 2. For $m = 2$, write out U_{QFT} as a matrix and verify that it is unitary.

Problem 3. Consider all "good" values of c, that is, all values that lie within $1/2$ of $j2^m/r$ for some integer $j = 0, \ldots, r - 1$. We claimed that each of these values has a probability at least $4/(\pi^2 r)$ except for a negligible additive term. This problem aims to justify this claim when r is not a power of 2. (When r *is* a power of 2, we have already proved the stronger result that the probability in question is $1/r$.)

---

[17] Improved estimates are given in Gerjuoy (2005). Gerjuoy estimates, for example, that the probability of obtaining a useful value of c in a single run of the algorithm is over 90%.

(a) Let $P(c)$ be the probability of obtaining the value c. When r is not a power of 2, we can write [see Eq. (7.26)]

$$P(c) = \frac{1}{2^m K} \left[\frac{\sin(\pi K r c / 2^m)}{\sin(\pi r c / 2^m)} \right]^2. \tag{7.33}$$

Though c is restricted to integer values, we can make sense of this equation for all real values of c, and when the denominator is 0 we define the function to take its limiting value. Show that, regarded as a function of a real variable, $P(c)$ is periodic with period $2^m/r$. One can also show (but you do not have to) that $P(c)$ takes its maximum value, $K/2^m$, at each of the points $j2^m/r$; moreover, around each of these points, it falls off symmetrically on both sides.

(b) Consider all real values of c satisfying $|c - j2^m/r| \leq 1/2$, for some $j = 0, \ldots, r - 1$. This interval is symmetric around one of the maxima of the function $P(c)$, and within this interval, $P(c)$ takes its smallest value at the two endpoints. (You do not need to prove this fact.) Show that this smallest value can be written as

$$\frac{1}{2^m K} \left[\frac{\sin\left(\frac{\pi}{2} \frac{Kr}{2^m}\right)}{\sin\left(\frac{\pi}{2} \frac{r}{2^m}\right)} \right]^2.$$

(c) Using the fact that $|y| \geq |\sin y|$, show that for each good value of c,

$$P(c) \geq \frac{4}{\pi^2 r} \frac{\sin^2\left(\frac{\pi}{2} x\right)}{x},$$

where $x = Kr/2^m$.

(d) Prove that x defined in part (c) satisfies

$$1 - \frac{1}{M} < x < 1 + \frac{1}{M},$$

where M is the number we are trying to factor.

(e) Another fact you need not prove is that within the interval $1/2 < x < 3/2$, the following inequality holds:

$$\frac{\sin^2\left(\frac{\pi}{2} x\right)}{x} \geq 3x - 2x^2.$$

Use this fact to show that

$$P(c) \geq \frac{4}{\pi^2 r} \left(1 - \frac{1}{M} - \frac{2}{M^2}\right).$$

This is the desired result. Note that in any real-life application, the corrections involving M are quite negligible.

Problem 4. Suppose that someone named Eve is trying to factor the integer 21 using Shor's algorithm. She chooses $a = 5$, so that she is trying to find the period of $f(x) = 5^x$ (mod 21). (It happens that the period is $r = 6$, which actually does not produce any nontrivial factor of 21, but Eve does not know this yet.) Note that the x-register has to hold 512 possible values – that is, $2^m = 512$ – since 512 is the smallest power of 2 that exceeds 21^2.

(a) As usual, let K be the number of values of x for which $f(x)$ is equal to the particular value u measured in the y-register. Show that in this example, there are exactly two possible values of K, depending on the value of u. What are these two possible values of K ?

(b) For each of the two possible values of K, find *all* the values of c (the number measured in the x-register) that have probability *exactly* 0. You should find that there are not many such values of c. This behavior is typical when the period r is not a power of 2 (moreover, the typical value of r is not a power of 2). That is, even though the probability distribution for c is peaked at regular intervals, in a typical example hardly any values of c are absolutely excluded.

Problem 5. Here we consider the same example as in Problem 4; so Eve is trying to find the order of 5 mod 21. Consider each of the following values of c, which she might obtain when she measures the x-register. (None of these values is absolutely excluded.) In each case, say whether the value of c leads Eve to the correct value of r (that is, $r = 6$), and if not, say in which of the following ways the algorithm fails: (i) there exists no fraction j'/r' with $r' < 21$ such that j'/r' is within $1/2^{m+1}$ of $c/2^m$; (ii) there exists such a fraction but the denominator of the reduced form is only a factor of r, not r itself; (iii) there exists such a fraction but the denominator of its reduced from is not even a factor of r.

(a) $c = 85$.
(b) $c = 171$.
(c) $c = 154$.
(d) $c = 112$.

7.8 Efficiency of Factoring

Shor's approach to factoring a large integer is intriguing and original and clearly makes use of the strange behavior of quantum systems – the function $f(x)$ is evaluated for all values of x at the same time in a quantum superposition. But is this method *better* than the best classical methods? The aim of this section is to produce a plausible answer to this question.

First, what is the best that can be done classically? Let M again be the number we are trying to factor, and let $L = \log_2 M$ be the (approximate) length of the binary expansion of M. The best general classical factoring algorithm currently known is called the "number field sieve," and a heuristic argument indicates that the number of basic operations needed to perform this algorithm is

$$\text{Number of basic operations} = e^{(c+\epsilon)L^{1/3}(\log_2 L)^{2/3}}, \qquad (7.34)$$

where $c \approx 1.32$ and ϵ approaches zero as M approaches infinity.[18] It is conceivable that some as yet undiscovered algorithm is considerably more efficient. No one has proved, for example, that there is no classical algorithm that scales as some *power* of L – *any* power of L would, for large enough L, ultimately rise less quickly than the exponential function in Eq. (7.34) – but at present Eq. (7.34) is the formula to beat.

We now need to figure out roughly how many basic operations are needed to carry out Shor's algorithm. There are two operations in the algorithm that could conceivably require a large number of steps: U_{QFT} and U_f. Let us begin by considering U_f. How does the number of steps rise with the length L of the integer we are trying to factor?

Recall that U_f is a quantum version of the computation of an ordinary function, namely, $f(x) = a^x \pmod{M}$. So we can get a sense of the complexity of U_f by asking ourselves how we would go about evaluating $f(x)$. A good strategy is to compute successive squares: that is, we compute in succession

$$a^2, a^4, a^8, a^{16}, \ldots, a^{(\text{some integer close to } x)},$$

---

[18] Coppersmith (1993); Crandall and Pomerance (2005). More precisely, $c = \frac{1}{3}(92 + 26\sqrt{13})^{1/3} \ln 2$.

all mod M. Once the exponent is close to x, we will have to do a few more multiplications to reach x itself, but for large x, the bulk of the computation will be in the sequence of squarings. Now, how many such squarings will we need to do? Roughly $\log_2 x$, since the exponents go up by factors of 2, and $2^{\log_2 x} = x$. The variable x takes many values, the largest of which is around M^2. So the number of squarings the computer will have to do is around $\log_2(M^2)$, which is $2L$.

Each of these squarings in turn requires a number of basic steps which depends on the size of M, since the number being squared in each case might be as large as $M - 1$ and therefore have length L when expressed in binary notation. How many basic steps does it take to square a number consisting of L bits? Here is an example:

$$
\begin{array}{r}
1011 \\
\times \quad 1011 \\
\hline
1011 \\
1011 \\
0000 \\
1011 \\
\hline
1111001
\end{array}
$$

There are exactly L^2 individual multiplications, each being 0×0, 0×1, 1×0, or 1×1. And in the addition part of the process, there are also roughly L^2 basic addition steps in which the summands are 0 and 1. So a single squaring operation takes about $2L^2$ basic multiplication or addition operations. Each of these in turn requires no more than a fixed number of elementary gates. Thus with $2L$ squarings, each requiring a number of basic gates that scales as L^2, we estimate that the number of basic gates required to carry out U_f is $c_1 L^3$, where c_1 is some constant. In fact it turns out that there are more efficient multiplication strategies than the naive one we considered above, and one can show that for large L the number of basic gates required to carry out U_f is bounded by

$$\text{Number of gates for } U_f < c_2 L^2 (\log_2 L)(\log_2 \log_2 L), \qquad (7.35)$$

c_2 being another constant.

We now turn to U_{QFT}, which is more quantum mechanical in the sense that we cannot resort to a classical analogue in order to estimate the number of steps required. To get a handle on the problem, let us consider the operation U_{QFT} acting on just two qubits. Recall the definition given in Eq. (7.22):

$$U_{\text{QFT}}|x\rangle = \frac{1}{\sqrt{2^m}} \sum_{c=0}^{2^m-1} e^{2\pi i c x/2^m} |c\rangle.$$

In the case of two qubits ($m = 2$), with the integer c expressed in binary notation, this becomes

$$U_{\text{QFT}}|x\rangle = \frac{1}{2}\big[|00\rangle + i^x|01\rangle + (-1)^x|10\rangle + (-i)^x|11\rangle\big].$$

More explicitly, writing the integer x on the left-hand side in binary form, we have

$$U_{\text{QFT}}|00\rangle = \frac{1}{2}\big[|00\rangle + |01\rangle + |10\rangle + |11\rangle\big]$$

$$U_{\text{QFT}}|01\rangle = \frac{1}{2}\big[|00\rangle + i|01\rangle - |10\rangle - i|11\rangle\big]$$

$$U_{\text{QFT}}|10\rangle = \frac{1}{2}\big[|00\rangle - |01\rangle + |10\rangle - |11\rangle\big]$$

$$U_{\text{QFT}}|11\rangle = \frac{1}{2}\big[|00\rangle - i|01\rangle - |10\rangle + i|11\rangle\big]$$

This can all be expressed more compactly by giving the matrix form of U_{QFT}:

$$U_{\text{QFT}} = \frac{1}{2}\begin{pmatrix} 1 & 1 & 1 & 1 \\ 1 & i & -1 & -i \\ 1 & -1 & 1 & -1 \\ 1 & -i & -1 & i \end{pmatrix}.$$

We can break this transformation into a few simpler steps, each consisting of one of the following operations: (i) A Hadamard gate acting on a single qubit. (ii) The operation $T^2 = \left(\begin{smallmatrix} 1 & 0 \\ 0 & i \end{smallmatrix}\right)$ acting on the first qubit, but *controlled* by the second qubit, that is, acting only if the second qubit is

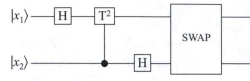

Figure 7.6: A sequence of gates that executes the quantum Fourier transform on two qubits.

in the state $|1\rangle$. The matrix representation of this controlled gate is

$$\text{controlled } T^2 = \begin{pmatrix} 1 & 0 & 0 & 0 \\ 0 & 1 & 0 & 0 \\ 0 & 0 & 1 & 0 \\ 0 & 0 & 0 & i \end{pmatrix}.$$

(Note that we can just as well think of the first qubit as controlling the second.) (iii) The SWAP gate, which interchanges the two qubits. Its matrix expression is

$$\text{SWAP} = \begin{pmatrix} 1 & 0 & 0 & 0 \\ 0 & 0 & 1 & 0 \\ 0 & 1 & 0 & 0 \\ 0 & 0 & 0 & 1 \end{pmatrix}.$$

One can check by direct matrix multiplication that

$$U_{\text{QFT}} = (\text{SWAP})(I \otimes H)(\text{controlled } T^2)(H \otimes I).$$

Figure 7.6 illustrates this method of carrying out the two-qubit quantum Fourier transform.

The problem becomes more complicated when we increase the number of qubits, but one finds that U_{QFT} can still be systematically reduced to simpler operations. We will not attempt to go through the argument leading to such a reduction, but we simply present without proof, in Fig. 7.7, a sequence of operations that realizes U_{QFT}.[19] This sequence includes, in addition to the operations used above, others that multiply the basis state $|11\rangle$ not by the factor i as in T^2 but by different phase factors. The symbol

---

[19] Coppersmith (1994). Figure 7.7 is based on a figure in Nielsen and Chuang (2000), p. 219.

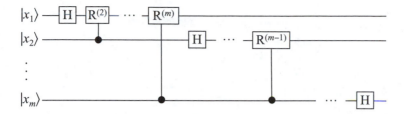

Figure 7.7: A sequence of gates that executes the quantum Fourier transform on *m* qubits. After each Hadamard gate, the qubit on which that gate acted undergoes a series of controlled phase changes, one for each qubit below it in the diagram. Not shown is a sequence of SWAP gates at the end of the computation that reverses the order of the qubits.

$R^{(k)}$ in the figure represents the single-qubit gate

$$R^{(k)} = \begin{pmatrix} 1 & 0 \\ 0 & e^{2\pi i/2^k} \end{pmatrix}$$

Note that the gate T is the same as $R^{(3)}$, and the gate T^2, used above, is the same as $R^{(2)}$.

Let us now estimate the number of steps involved in this implementation of the transformation U_{QFT}. The diagram starts with a sequence of *m* gates acting on the first qubit, followed by $m - 1$ gates acting on the second qubit, and so on, with a single Hadamard gate finally acting on the *m*th qubit. This is a total of $m(m + 1)/2$ gates. The number of SWAP gates at the end, for reversing the order of the qubits, grows linearly with *m*. So the dominant contribution to the number of gates is $m^2/2$. Now, *m* is the number of qubits in the *x* register, which is about twice the length *L* of the number we are trying to factor. So it would seem that the number of gates required to implement U_{QFT} grows roughly as $(2L)^2/2 = 2L^2$. This is not even as quickly growing as the number of gates required to implement U_f, given in Eq. (7.35). Of course the gates used in Fig. 7.7 include many that are not in our set of *basic* gates {H, T, CNOT}. The SWAP is not a problem because each application of the SWAP gate always requires a fixed number of basic gates; so the number of basic gates involved in all the SWAP operations still grows linearly with *L*. The gates $R^{(k)}$ are more problematic since they entail more and more refined phase changes as the number of qubits increases. However for the purpose of factoring, it is not necessary to implement U_{QFT} *exactly*. It is sufficient to implement

number of steps

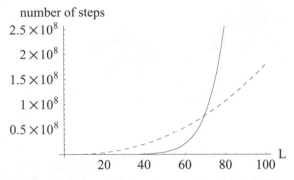

Figure 7.8: A comparison of quantum and classical factoring algorithms, showing the scaling of the number of steps required to factor an integer of length L. The solid curve, growing more quickly for large L, is the classical case given by Eq. (7.34) with $\epsilon = 0$. The dashed quantum curve is the right-hand side of Eq. (7.36) with $c_3 = 1000$.

a good approximation, and for this purpose it turns out that the number of gates required still grows no more rapidly than the number required for U_f.

We have, then, that for sufficiently large L the number of basic quantum gates required to carry out Shor's factoring algorithm is bounded by

$$\text{Gates required for factoring} < c_3 L^2 (\log_2 L)(\log_2 \log_2 L), \qquad (7.36)$$

where c_3 is another constant. The logarithms grow very slowly, so for most purposes we can think of the factoring algorithm as requiring a number of operations that grows as the square of the length of the number to be factored. This is to be contrasted with what is currently the best general factoring algorithm for a classical computer, for which the number of operations grows exponentially in $L^{1/3}$ [Eq. (7.34)].

To give a sense of the difference between the two formulas, we have plotted both of them in Fig. 7.8 as a function of L, choosing c_3 to have the value 1000 and taking ϵ in Eq. (7.34) to have the value 0. One can see that the quantum algorithm wins out dramatically as the length of the number gets very large.

In this chapter we have focused particularly on the factoring problem, but this is by no means the only problem for which a quantum computer would beat a classical computer in efficiency. In the same paper in which Shor presented his factoring algorithm, he also presented a quantum algorithm for computing the discrete logarithm, that is, for finding an integer r such that $g^r = X \pmod{p}$ when the integers g and X and the prime number p are all known.[20] Recall that the Diffie–Hellman protocol for key exchange is secure only because this is a difficult problem to solve. As with the factoring algorithm, Shor's discrete logarithm algorithm is again based on the quantum Fourier transform. And in analogy with the factoring algorithm, the number of basic quantum steps required to compute the discrete logarithm grows roughly as L^2, where L is the number of digits (or the number of bits) in the prime number p. By contrast, the number of steps in the best classical algorithm grows exponentially in L.

A quantum algorithm with a different flavor is Grover's search algorithm.[21] Imagine a mathematical problem of the following type: we are looking for a solution to $f(x) = 0$, where f is a function that is easy to compute but difficult to invert, and x is limited to a fixed range. (The discrete logarithm problem fits this description, with $f(x) = g^x - X \pmod{p}$.) For simplicity, suppose we know that there is one and only one solution in some range $x = 1, 2, \ldots, N$ (an assumption that applies to the discrete logarithm problem if the integer being exponentiated is a *primitive root* of the prime p). Moreover, suppose that our best idea for solving the problem is to use trial and error: we have an f-computing subroutine that we will apply to various allowed values of x, hoping to find the one value for which $f(x) = 0$. How many times will we have to use our subroutine before we find the answer? For classical trial-and-error computing, the answer depends on how lucky we are, but *on average*, we will have to run $N/2$ tests before finding the right answer. Remarkably, the *quantum* algorithm requires running the subroutine only about $\sqrt{N}$ times. So if there are a million potential answers, we will be able to find the correct answer after running only a thousand tests or so. (The underlying idea here is similar to what we saw in the Deutsch algorithm: one applies the test to a quantum register that holds a superposition of many values of x.) Note that the speed-up here is not as dramatic as in the case of factoring: we get a square-root advantage rather than an exponential advantage.

[20] Shor (1994).
[21] Grover (1996, 1997).

Nevertheless, because many different problems can be couched as search problems, this is a very interesting potential application of a quantum computer.

It may be worth reminding ourselves at this point that we are not in possession of any full-scale quantum computers. On the other hand, small quantum computers have been developed, and proof-of-principle tests of the search algorithm[22] and the factoring algorithm[23] have been carried out. So far, the largest number that has been factored by a quantum computer is 15. (The factors turned out to be 3 and 5.) But researchers have been quite creative in identifying physical systems that could potentially be used for quantum computation, and as we have seen, there is much to motivate such research. So it will be quite interesting to follow the progress in quantum computation over the coming years.

EXERCISES

Problem 1. (a) For a general value of m (the number of qubits), find exactly the minimum number of SWAP gates one must execute at the right-hand end of Fig. 7.7 in order to reverse the order of the qubits. For each SWAP gate, you are allowed to specify any pair of qubits for the gate to act on.

(b) Write the SWAP gate as a sequence of the basic gates $\{H, T, \text{CNOT}\}$.

Problem 2. (a) Draw the circuit diagram for the quantum Fourier transform acting on three qubits. (It may contain controlled-$R^{(k)}$ gates and the SWAP gate.)

(b) Starting from Eq. (7.22), write down explicitly the 8×8 matrix that represents U_{QFT} for three qubits. To simplify the notation, it may be helpful to introduce a symbol $\eta = \exp(2\pi i/8)$.

(c) (Optional) Show explicitly that the circuit you drew in part (a) generates the matrix you wrote down in part (b).

[22] Chuang, Gershenfeld, and Kubinec (1998).
[23] Vandersypen et al. (2001).

7.9 Introduction to Quantum Error Correction

In the preceding sections we have talked about preparing each qubit of the quantum computer in the state $|0\rangle$, for example, and performing specific gates on single qubits or pairs of qubits. But the space of states of any quantum system is a continuous space, and the set of unitary transformations is also continuous. It is entirely unrealistic to imagine that in the actual world we will be able to prepare a qubit *precisely* in the state $|0\rangle$, or to perform a unitary transformation that is *exactly* equal to the Hadamard gate. We never have infinite precision in our manipulations of the physical world. Moreover, between gate operations, a qubit will not be perfectly isolated from its environment, so we cannot expect that it will stay precisely in the state that our idealized algorithm assumes it to be in. For example, it will probably become at least partially entangled with some extraneous quantum variable, as we noted in the introduction to this chapter. For all of these reasons, it is crucial that we know how to do error correction on qubits.

The subject of quantum error correction began to be investigated only in the mid-1990s, but the theory is already highly developed.[24] This section will hardly scratch its surface. Our aim here is only to show that it is indeed possible to correct errors in a quantum system. Moreover, we will restrict our discussion in the following three respects: (i) We will consider only the problem of protecting the *state* of a qubit. We will not worry about how to make our quantum gates and measurements free of error. (ii) For simplicity, we will focus on the case in which the qubit to be protected has a quantum state of its own – it is not initially entangled with anything. In an actual quantum computer, a qubit will typically be entangled with other qubits, but this fact turns out not to change the basic strategies of error correction. (iii) We will assume that all the operations that we perform *in order to carry out our error-correction protocols* are themselves perfect. This last assumption is clearly too strong. One needs also to show that quantum computation is possible even when every single measurement, state preparation, and gate is suspect, including those being used to correct

---

[24] For a thorough treatment of quantum error correction, see for example Preskill (1998, 2004) and Nielsen and Chuang (2000). The full theory of quantum error correction uses many ideas from classical error correction, such as those we have introduced in earlier chapters.

errors. A computational design that meets this stronger criterion is called "fault tolerant," and researchers have shown that fault-tolerant quantum computation is indeed possible in principle. But this subject goes beyond the scope of our present discussion.

7.9.1 An *X*-correcting code

Suppose, then, that we are given a single qubit whose state $|s\rangle$ we do not know, and we want to protect the state while it is subject to noise. It may seem at first that this is impossible. We cannot, for example, use a simple repetition code, replacing the single qubit in the state $|s\rangle$ with a triple of qubits in the state $|s\rangle \otimes |s\rangle \otimes |s\rangle$. To do so would violate the no-cloning theorem (recall Section 3.2). However, there is a different way to generalize the repetition code to the quantum setting. Let the state $|s\rangle$ be expressed in the standard basis as

$$|s\rangle = a|0\rangle + b|1\rangle.$$

(Again, we are assuming that we do not know the values of a and b.) We can certainly append two additional qubits in the standard state $|0\rangle$, giving us the three-qubit state $|s, 00\rangle = a|000\rangle + b|100\rangle$. Then we can perform a unitary transformation that leaves $|000\rangle$ unchanged but changes $|100\rangle$ into $|111\rangle$. The result is the three-qubit state

$$|s_C\rangle = a|000\rangle + b|111\rangle, \tag{7.37}$$

in which the subscript C indicates that this is an encoded state. We have encoded the state of a single qubit into three qubits.

In what sense does this simple code protect the qubit's state from errors? Let us suppose that the noise affects at most only one of the three qubits. (This is exactly the sort of assumption we made in the classical case.) Moreover, let us assume for now that the error, if it occurs, flips the qubit from $|0\rangle$ to $|1\rangle$ or from $|1\rangle$ to $|0\rangle$. That is, we assume that the noise source has possibly changed one of the qubits by the action of the operation X, whose matrix representation is

$$X = \begin{pmatrix} 0 & 1 \\ 1 & 0 \end{pmatrix}.$$

There are many other single-qubit errors that we could imagine – for example, the noise source might change one of the qubits by applying the Hadamard gate, or it might rotate the qubit's state by a small angle – but for now we consider only this one kind of error. We can detect and correct an X error as follows. First, we perform a special *incomplete* measurement on the system of three qubits. This measurement will have four outcomes, each associated not with a specific vector in the state space but rather with a two-dimensional subspace, and the subspaces corresponding to different outcomes will be mutually orthogonal. (The state space for three qubits has eight dimensions; so these four mutually orthogonal 2-d subspaces together span the whole space.) As in Section 2.5, each outcome can be represented by a projection operator that projects onto the appropriate 2-d subspace. For the specific measurement we have in mind, the four projection operators are as follows (compare Examples 2.5.2 and 2.5.5):

$$P_1 = |100\rangle\langle100| + |011\rangle\langle011|$$

$$P_2 = |010\rangle\langle010| + |101\rangle\langle101|$$

$$P_3 = |001\rangle\langle001| + |110\rangle\langle110|$$

$$P_4 = |000\rangle\langle000| + |111\rangle\langle111|$$

If there has been no error, then we know that the state, whatever it is, must lie in the subspace picked out by P_4: the state is in the subspace spanned by $|000\rangle$ and $|111\rangle$. Similarly, if there has been an X-type error on the first qubit, then the state will lie in the subspace picked out by P_1, since $|000\rangle$ will have been changed to $|100\rangle$ and $|111\rangle$ to $|011\rangle$. Errors on the other two qubits correspond in the same way to P_2 and P_3. Thus the outcome of this measurement tells us (i) whether an X-type error has occurred and (ii) if so, which qubit was affected. To correct the error, we simply apply X to the affected qubit, since X is its own inverse and will undo the effect of the error.

What is not so clear is whether the above strategy is good for correcting any errors *other* than those corresponding to a simple flip between $|0\rangle$ and $|1\rangle$. In fact it *is* good for correcting at least some other errors, as we now show.

Suppose again that only a single qubit is affected by the noise, but now let the effect be represented by a unitary transformation of the form

$$U = \begin{pmatrix} \cos\theta & i\,\sin\theta \\ i\,\sin\theta & \cos\theta \end{pmatrix}, \tag{7.38}$$

where θ is a real number. For definiteness we suppose that the second qubit is the one that is affected. Then our encoded state $|s_C\rangle$ becomes

$$|s_C'\rangle = U_2|s_C\rangle = a(\cos\theta|000\rangle + i\,\sin\theta|010\rangle) + b(i\,\sin\theta|101\rangle + \cos\theta|111\rangle).$$

(The subscript 2 indicates that U acts on the second qubit.) When we perform the measurement (P_1, P_2, P_3, P_4) on this state, only two of the outcomes have nonzero probabilities, namely, those associated with P_2 (error in the second qubit) and P_4 (no error). We compute these probabilities according to Eq. (2.26):

$$p_2 = \langle s_C'|P_2|s_C'\rangle = \sin^2\theta$$
$$p_4 = \langle s_C'|P_4|s_C'\rangle = \cos^2\theta$$

If we get the outcome P_4, the final state after the measurement is, according to Eq. (2.27),

$$\frac{P_4|s_C'\rangle}{\sqrt{\langle s_C'|P_4|s_C'\rangle}} = a|000\rangle + b|111\rangle. \tag{7.39}$$

That is, in this case the measurement itself, by effecting a projection onto the no-error subspace, has automatically corrected the error! If we get this outcome, we do not need to do any further error correction. On the other hand, if we get the outcome P_2, the resulting state is

$$\frac{P_2|s_C'\rangle}{\sqrt{\langle s_C'|P_2|s_C'\rangle}} = a|010\rangle + b|101\rangle. \tag{7.40}$$

If we get this outcome, we know that we should correct the error by applying the X operator to the second qubit. The result will be the correct state $|s\rangle = a|000\rangle + b|111\rangle$, and we never have to learn the values of a and b. Indeed, we know that it is impossible to learn those values given only a single copy of the state.

Notice what has happened here. When we assumed that the error was a simple flip between $|0\rangle$ and $|1\rangle$, the measurement was used only to inform us about the error; the state was already in one of the subspaces picked out by the measurement. In contrast, when the error was of the type U given by Eq. (7.38), the measurement was an active part of the error-correction process: it placed the state in one of the special subspaces *and* it told us which subspace it had placed it in. We could then finish correcting the error just as in the simpler case. In this way, what might have seemed a very difficult problem – correcting one of a *continuum* of possible errors parameterized by θ – has been turned into a simpler problem of correcting one of a discrete set of errors. This is possible only because a quantum measurement is, as we have emphasized before, not a passive gathering of information; in most cases it actively causes a disturbance in the measured system, and for the purpose of error correction the disturbance is very helpful.

7.9.2 A Z-correcting code

We should not yet be satisfied, though. Errors of the type given in Eq. (7.38) are still very special, and one can show that our X-correcting code does not correct other errors such as the following operation applied to one of the qubits:

$$Z = \begin{pmatrix} 1 & 0 \\ 0 & -1 \end{pmatrix}$$

If this operator acts on *any* of our three qubits, the resulting state is

$$|s'_C\rangle = a|000\rangle - b|111\rangle.$$

As long as neither a nor b is zero, this state is not the state we want, and yet when we perform the measurement (P_1, P_2, P_3, P_4) on this state, we will definitely get the outcome P_4, indicating no error. So we must modify our scheme.

It is helpful to consider a scheme designed precisely for errors of the Z type. It will not correct errors of the X type but later we will combine the two schemes to create a more effective error-correction strategy. Let the states $|+\rangle$ and $|-\rangle$ be defined as

$$|+\rangle = \frac{1}{\sqrt{2}}(|0\rangle + |1\rangle)$$

$$|-\rangle = \frac{1}{\sqrt{2}}(|0\rangle - |1\rangle)$$

One can see that $Z|+\rangle = |-\rangle$ and $Z|-\rangle = |+\rangle$. That is, Z acts on $(|+\rangle, |-\rangle)$ in the same way that X acts on $(|0\rangle, |1\rangle)$. So we can proceed by analogy with the scheme described above. That is, we can protect any single-qubit state from a Z-type error by encoding the state $|+\rangle$ as

$$|+++\rangle = \frac{1}{2\sqrt{2}}(|0\rangle + |1\rangle) \otimes (|0\rangle + |1\rangle) \otimes (|0\rangle + |1\rangle) \tag{7.41}$$

and the state $|-\rangle$ as

$$|---\rangle = \frac{1}{2\sqrt{2}}(|0\rangle - |1\rangle) \otimes (|0\rangle - |1\rangle) \otimes (|0\rangle - |1\rangle), \tag{7.42}$$

again using two additional qubits. To correct such an error, we project onto a different set of four subspaces, defined by the projection operators

$$Q_1 = |-++\rangle\langle-++| + |+--\rangle\langle+--|$$
$$Q_2 = |+-+\rangle\langle+-+| + |-+-\rangle\langle-+-|$$
$$Q_3 = |++-\rangle\langle++-| + |--+\rangle\langle--+|$$
$$Q_4 = |+++\rangle\langle+++| + |---\rangle\langle---|$$

We then apply the operator Z to qubit $1, 2,$ or 3, or not at all, depending on the outcome of the measurement. One can show that this scheme protects not only against Z errors, but also against all single-qubit errors given (in the standard basis) by the unitary transformation

$$V = \begin{pmatrix} 1 & 0 \\ 0 & e^{i\phi} \end{pmatrix}. \tag{7.43}$$

Again, the measurement itself does part of the error correction.

7.9.3 The Shor code

We now put the above two schemes together to create an error-correction protocol that protects against *all* single-qubit errors. Again, we are trying to protect the state

$$|s\rangle = a|0\rangle + b|1\rangle.$$

We begin by appending *eight* additional qubits in a standard state; we then perform a unitary transformation so that the single-qubit state $|0\rangle$

ends up being encoded as

$$|0_C\rangle = \frac{1}{2\sqrt{2}}(|000\rangle + |111\rangle) \otimes (|000\rangle + |111\rangle) \otimes (|000\rangle + |111\rangle), \quad (7.44)$$

and the single-qubit state $|1\rangle$ is encoded as

$$|1_C\rangle = \frac{1}{2\sqrt{2}}(|000\rangle - |111\rangle) \otimes (|000\rangle - |111\rangle) \otimes (|000\rangle - |111\rangle). \quad (7.45)$$

Here we have started with our Z-correcting scheme, defined by Eqs. (7.41) and (7.42), and within this scheme we have replaced each $|0\rangle$ with $|000\rangle$ and each $|1\rangle$ with $|111\rangle$, in accordance with our X-correcting scheme. The initial state $|s\rangle = a|0\rangle + b|1\rangle$ is thus encoded as $|s_C\rangle = a|0_C\rangle + b|1_C\rangle$. This code was discovered by Peter Shor and is known as the Shor code.[25] The process of combining codes as we have just done is called *concatenation* and has been used effectively in proving that fault-tolerant quantum computation can be done in principle.

Let us now ask what happens to the encoded state $|s_C\rangle$ when an error occurs in one of the qubits. We consider for now 27 different single-qubit errors that might occur: $X_1, \ldots, X_9, Z_1, \ldots, Z_9$, and $X_1 Z_1, \ldots, X_9 Z_9$. (We will consider more general errors shortly.) Here the subscript indicates which qubit is affected, and the product XZ is simply the Z operation followed by the X operation. You might think we are about to make the following claim: each of these 27 errors takes the two-dimensional subspace spanned by $|0_C\rangle$ and $|1_C\rangle$ into a different two-dimensional subspace, and all these resulting subspaces are orthogonal not only to the original, uncorrupted subspace, but also to each other. If this were the case, we could perform an incomplete measurement to determine which of these subspaces our state occupies, in order to determine which, if any, of the 27 possible errors occurred. We could then correct the error by applying the appropriate operator (X, Z, or XZ) to the affected qubit.

The actual situation is not quite this simple, but it is not much different. The only subtlety is that the Z errors do not all have distinct effects. For example, if any of the errors Z_1, Z_2, or Z_3 acts on the encoded state $|0_C\rangle$,

---

[25] Shor (1995).

the result is

$$Z_1|0_C\rangle = \frac{1}{2\sqrt{2}}(|000\rangle - |111\rangle) \otimes (|000\rangle + |111\rangle) \otimes (|000\rangle + |111\rangle).$$

(Here we have written Z_1, but we could just as well have written Z_2 or Z_3. The result is the same.) So these three errors cannot be distinguished. But this is not a problem, because all of these errors are corrected in the same way, namely, by applying the Z operator to any of the first three qubits. Similar statements can be made about the other Z_j errors.

Altogether, then, the 27 error operators listed above, along with the identity operator I (associated with the case of no error) define a collection of 22 mutually orthogonal two-dimensional subspaces. Here is a list of the subspace-defining error operators:

$$X_1, X_2, X_3, X_4, X_5, X_6, X_7, X_8, X_9$$
$$\{Z_1, Z_2, \text{ or } Z_3\}, \{Z_4, Z_5, \text{ or } Z_6\}, \{Z_7, Z_8, \text{ or } Z_9\} \qquad (7.46)$$
$$X_1 Z_1, X_2 Z_2, X_3 Z_3, X_4 Z_4, X_5 Z_5, X_6 Z_6, X_7 Z_7, X_8 Z_8, X_9 Z_9$$
$$I \text{ (no error)}$$

Because the subspaces are mutually orthogonal, one can perform a measurement to find out in which subspace the state lies, and then one can correct the error by applying the corresponding operator.[26] As always in quantum error correction, it is important that the measurement is *incomplete*. The measurement is complete enough to tell us how to correct the error, but not so refined as to destroy the subtle quantum superposition that we were trying to protect. A complete measurement might, for example, collapse $a|0\rangle + b|1\rangle$ down to $|0\rangle$, and we would have lost our superposition.

Of course not every single-qubit error is given by one of the 27 operators listed above. Suppose that one of our nine qubits is subjected to a

---

[26] The measurement will have to have more than 22 outcomes, because these 22 subspaces do not span the whole state space of nine qubits. To finish the description of the measurement, it would be sufficient to include just one additional outcome, associated with the entire subspace orthogonal to all 22 of our special subspaces. This last subspace would have $2^9 - 2(22)$ dimensions and would be associated with all the ways in which an error could affect more than one qubit.

general unitary transformation W:

$$W = \begin{pmatrix} w & x \\ y & z \end{pmatrix}.$$

You will show in the exercises that any 2×2 complex matrix such as W, whether or not it is unitary, can be expressed as a linear combination of the four matrices I, X, Z, and XZ. So we can write W as

$$W = tI + uX + vZ + wXZ,$$

where t, u, v, and w are complex numbers. When W acts on, say, the jth qubit of the state $|s_C\rangle$, the resulting state is

$$W_j|s_C\rangle = t|s_C\rangle + uX_j|s_C\rangle + vZ_j|s_C\rangle + wX_jZ_j|s_C\rangle. \tag{7.47}$$

Let us now imagine performing our diagnostic measurement on this state. Notice that the four different terms on the right-hand side of Eq. (7.47) belong to four of the 22 special subspaces defined by our measurement. So when we get a particular outcome, associated with a particular subspace, the measurement will automatically have "collapsed" the state $W_j|s_C\rangle$ into one of the four states

$$|s_C\rangle, \quad X_j|s_C\rangle, \quad Z_j|s_C\rangle, \quad \text{or} \quad X_jZ_j|s_C\rangle.$$

Thus, even though the operation W_j is not one of the error operators we considered above, the measurement *forces* the qubit in question to act as if it had been affected by one of the specific operators I, X, Z, or XZ. We can then correct the error just as before, by applying one of the operators I, X_j, Z_j, or Z_jX_j. (Z_jX_j is the inverse of X_jZ_j.) This is very much like what happened in Eqs. (7.39) and (7.40). Again, the measurement has turned what seemed to be a continuum of possible errors into a discrete set.

The same principle makes it possible to correct errors even in the more realistic case in which *each* of the nine qubits is subjected to some small error. As long as all these errors are small, then when we make our diagnostic measurement, there is a very good chance that we will get an outcome associated with one of our 22 special subspaces. In that case, the measurement will have brought the system to a state in which at most one of the qubits has been affected, and the error can be corrected just as in the above cases.

Actually we still have not considered all possible single-qubit errors. We *have* considered all possible unitary transformations on a single qubit. But what if a qubit in our system becomes entangled with some external quantum variable? Does the code that we have just described also correct this kind of error? It does indeed, and you will work out an example of this sort of error correction in the exercises.

Finally, you may be wondering whether there is a more efficient way of correcting a single-qubit error. In the classical case, we can correct a single bit error by encoding a single bit into three bits. Do we really need nine qubits to correct a single-qubit error? The answer is no, we *can* be more efficient. However, the quantum case cannot be *as* efficient as the classical case, because the complex-vector-space structure of quantum mechanics allows distinct kinds of error (e.g., X and Z), whereas in the classical case there is only one kind. One of the exercises presents the most efficient possible code for correcting a single-qubit error; it encodes one qubit into *five* qubits.

EXERCISES

Problem 1. Show that every 2×2 complex matrix can be written in the form

$$tI + uX + vZ + wXZ,$$

where t, u, v, and w are complex numbers.

Problem 2. Verify that the Z-correcting code presented in this section corrects all single-qubit errors of the type given in Eq. (7.43).

Problem 3. Consider the 22 subspaces defined by applying the operators of Eq. (7.46) to the subspace spanned by the states $|0_C\rangle$ and $|1_C\rangle$ of Eqs. (7.44) and (7.45). Show that these 22 subspaces are all mutually orthogonal. (Hint: You might want to use Eq. (3.9).)

Problem 4. The "five-qubit code" encodes the single-qubit state $|s\rangle = a|0\rangle + b|1\rangle$ into the five-qubit state $|s_C\rangle = a|0_C\rangle + b|1_C\rangle$, where $|0_C\rangle$ and

$|1_C\rangle$ are defined by[27]

$$
\begin{aligned}
|0_C\rangle = \frac{1}{4} \big(& |00000\rangle + |10010\rangle + |01001\rangle + |10100\rangle \\
& + |01010\rangle - |11011\rangle - |00110\rangle - |11000\rangle \\
& - |11101\rangle - |00011\rangle - |11110\rangle - |01111\rangle \\
& - |10001\rangle - |01100\rangle - |10111\rangle + |00101\rangle \big)
\end{aligned}
$$

and

$$
\begin{aligned}
|1_C\rangle = \frac{1}{4} \big(& |11111\rangle + |01101\rangle + |10110\rangle + |01011\rangle \\
& + |10101\rangle - |00100\rangle - |11001\rangle - |00111\rangle \\
& - |00010\rangle - |11100\rangle - |00001\rangle - |10000\rangle \\
& - |01110\rangle - |10011\rangle - |01000\rangle + |11010\rangle \big)
\end{aligned}
$$

There are 15 basic single-qubit errors $X_1, \ldots, X_5, Z_1, \ldots, Z_5$, and $X_1 Z_1, \ldots, X_5 Z_5$. In this problem, consider only $Z_1, \ldots, Z_5$. Show that the five subspaces generated by applying these operators to the subspace spanned by $|0_C\rangle$ and $|1_C\rangle$ are all orthogonal to each other, and are orthogonal to the original uncorrupted subspace. (In fact the subspaces generated by the other error operators also have this property. So this is a good error-correcting code.)

Problem 5. Consider the code defined by Eq. (7.37). Suppose that the last of the three qubits interacts with a *fourth* qubit from outside the quantum computer. This fourth qubit starts out in the state $(1/\sqrt{2})(|0\rangle + |1\rangle)$, and the third and fourth qubits are acted upon by the operation CNOT$_{43}$. (The subscripts indicate that the fourth qubit is the control and the third qubit is the target.) Show that the standard error-correction process for the X-correcting code also corrects this error. (For this problem you will need to use new versions of the projection operators $P_1, \ldots, P_4$, since the space that needs to be acted upon is now a four-qubit state space. This is a straightforward extension, in which the P operators leave the fourth qubit unaffected. For example, whereas the original version of P_1 projects onto the subspace spanned by $|100\rangle$ and $|011\rangle$, the new version will project onto the four-dimensional subspace spanned by $|1000\rangle$, $|1001\rangle$, $|0110\rangle$, and $|0111\rangle$. In other words, the new version of P_1 is $P_1 \otimes I$, where I is the identity operator on the fourth qubit.)

---

[27] Bennett et al. (1996b); Laflamme et al. (1996).

APPENDIX A

A.1 Fields

Fields are important algebraic structures used in almost all branches of mathematics. Here we only cover the definitions and theorems needed for the purposes of this book.[1]

Definition. A *field* F is a set along with two operations (denoted with addition and multiplication notation) on pairs of elements of F such that the following properties are satisfied.

1. For all a and b in F, we have that $a + b \in F$.
2. For all a, b, and c in F, we have that $(a + b) + c = a + (b + c)$.
3. There exists an element 0 in F satisfying $a + 0 = a$ for all $a \in F$.
4. For every $a \in F$ there exists a b in F such that $a + b = 0$.
5. For all a and b in F we have that $a + b = b + a$.
6. For all a and b in F we have that $ab \in F$.
7. For all a, b, and c in F we have that $(ab)c = a(bc)$.
8. There is an element 1 in F satisfying $1a = a$ for all $a \in F$.
9. For every $a \in F$ with $a \neq 0$, there exists a $b \in F$ such that $ab = 1$.
10. For every a and b in F we have that $ab = ba$.
11. For every a, b, and c in F we have that $a(b + c) = ab + ac$.

It is easy to see by the definition that a field F is a group under addition and the set $F - \{0\}$ is a group under multiplication.

---

[1] For an introduction to fields, see Gallian (2006).

The sets of rational numbers, real numbers, and complex numbers are all fields. The set of integers, however, is not. We can easily see that not all integers have multiplicative inverses that are integers. For example, there is no integer we can multiply by 3 to get 1.

Theorem A.1.1. $\mathbb{Z}_n$ is a field under its addition and multiplication if and only if n is a prime number.

To see why the above theorem is true, we suggest reading Section 1.3 and working the exercises following that section.

In Section 6.2 we described a field with eight elements. It turns out that if F is a field with finitely many elements then the number of elements in F must be a power of a prime integer. We can generalize the idea of the construction of the field in Section 6.2 to construct a field with p^n elements, where p is a prime number and n is a positive integer. We briefly describe the method here and leave the details to the reader.

Consider the set of polynomials $\mathbb{Z}_p[x]$ as described in Section 6.1. Now let $f(x)$ be a degree n nonzero irreducible element of $\mathbb{Z}_p[x]$. In other words, $f(x)$ can be written as

$$f(x) = a_n x^n + a_{n-1} x^{n-1} + \cdots + a_1 x + a_0,$$

where $a_n \neq 0$, $a_i \in \mathbb{Z}_p$ for all i, and if $f(x) = g(x)h(x)$ where $g(x)$ and $h(x)$ are elements in $\mathbb{Z}_p[x]$, then $g(x)$ or $h(x)$ is a nonzero constant polynomial. This really means that $f(x)$ is a degree n polynomial that cannot be factored into two polynomials of smaller degree. Now we define $\mathbb{F}_{p^n}$ to be all polynomials in $\mathbb{Z}_p[x]$ with the rule that $f(x) = 0$. In other words,

$$a_n x^n + a_{n-1} x^{n-1} + \cdots + a_1 x + a_0 = 0.$$

This means that

$$x^n = -a_n^{-1} \left(a_{n-1} x^{n-1} + \cdots + a_1 x + a_0 \right).$$

So whenever we see the term x^n, we can replace it with terms of smaller degree. We leave it to the reader to verify that $\mathbb{F}_{p^n}$ is a field with p^n elements.

A.2 A Glossary of Linear Algebra Definitions and Theorems

In this section, we cover only the definitions and theorems from Linear Algebra that we need for the material covered in this book.[2]

Definition. Let V be a set and F a field. Suppose that an operation (called addition) is defined on pairs of elements of V and a scalar multiplication is defined. In other words, we can multiply an element of F by an element of V and we get an element of V. We say that V is a *vector space over F* (or simply a vector space if the field F is obvious) if the following conditions hold.

1. For every $\vec{v}_1, \vec{v}_2 \in V$, we have that $\vec{v}_1 + \vec{v}_2 \in V$.
2. For every $\vec{v}_1, \vec{v}_2, \vec{v}_3 \in V$ we have that $(\vec{v}_1 + \vec{v}_2) + \vec{v}_3 = \vec{v}_1 + (\vec{v}_2 + \vec{v}_3)$.
3. There exists an element $\vec{0} \in V$ such that $\vec{v}_1 + \vec{0} = \vec{0} + \vec{v}_1$ for every $\vec{v}_1 \in V$.
4. For every $\vec{v}_1 \in V$, there exists an element $-\vec{v}_1 \in V$ satisfying $\vec{v}_1 + -\vec{v}_1 = -\vec{v}_1 + \vec{v}_1 = \vec{0}$.
5. For every $\vec{v}_1, \vec{v}_2 \in V$, we have that $\vec{v}_1 + \vec{v}_2 = \vec{v}_2 + \vec{v}_1$.
6. For every $\alpha \in F$ and every $\vec{v}_1 \in V$ we have that $\alpha \vec{v}_1 \in V$.
7. For every $\alpha \in F$ and all $\vec{v}_1, \vec{v}_2 \in V$ we have that $\alpha(\vec{v}_1 + \vec{v}_2) = \alpha \vec{v}_1 + \alpha \vec{v}_2$.
8. For every $\alpha, \beta \in F$ and all $\vec{v}_1 \in V$ we have that $(\alpha + \beta)\vec{v}_1 = \alpha \vec{v}_1 + \beta \vec{v}_1$.
9. For every $\alpha, \beta \in F$ and all $\vec{v}_1 \in V$ we have that $(\alpha\beta)\vec{v}_1 = \alpha(\beta\vec{v}_1)$.
10. For all $\vec{v}_1 \in V$ we have $1\vec{v}_1 = \vec{v}_1$.

Notice that the first four conditions of the definition above could be replaced by the condition that V be a group under addition.

Definition. Let V be a vector space over the field F. Suppose that W is a nonempty subset of V such that W is a vector space over F under the addition and scalar multiplication defined on V. Then W is called a *subspace* of V.

---

[2] For more details see, for example, Leon (2006).

Theorem A.2.1. Let V be a vector space over the field F and W a nonempty subset of of V such that for every $\alpha \in F$ and every $\vec{w}_1, \vec{w}_2 \in W$ we have that $\alpha \vec{w}_1 \in W$ and $\vec{w}_1 + \vec{w}_2 \in W$. Then W is a subspace of V.

Definition. Let V be a vector space over the field F and let $\vec{v}_1, \vec{v}_2, \ldots, \vec{v}_n$ be elements of V. The elements $\vec{v}_1, \vec{v}_2, \ldots, \vec{v}_n$ are said to *span* V if for every $\vec{x} \in V$ there exist elements $\alpha_1, \alpha_2, \ldots, \alpha_n \in F$ such that $\vec{x} = \alpha_1 \vec{v}_1 + \alpha_2 \vec{v}_2 + \cdots + \alpha_n \vec{v}_n$.

Definition. Let V be a vector space over the field F and let $\vec{v}_1, \vec{v}_2, \ldots, \vec{v}_n \in V$. Suppose that the only $\alpha_i \in F$ that satisfy the equation

$$\alpha_1 \vec{v}_1 + \alpha_2 \vec{v}_2 + \cdots + \alpha_n \vec{v}_n = \vec{0}$$

are $\alpha_i = 0$ for $i = 1, 2, \ldots, n$. Then we say that $\vec{v}_1, \vec{v}_2, \ldots, \vec{v}_n$ are *linearly independent*. If $\vec{v}_1, \vec{v}_2, \ldots, \vec{v}_n$ are not linearly independent, we say $\vec{v}_1, \vec{v}_2, \ldots, \vec{v}_n$ are *linearly dependent*.

Definition. Let V be a vector space over the field F. The elements $\vec{v}_1, \vec{v}_2, \ldots, \vec{v}_n$ of V are said to be a *basis* for V if they span V and are linearly independent.

Theorem A.2.2. Let V be a vector space. Suppose that the elements $\vec{v}_1, \vec{v}_2, \ldots, \vec{v}_n$ and $\vec{w}_1, \vec{w}_2, \ldots, \vec{w}_m$ are both a basis for V. Then $n = m$.

Definition. Let V be a vector space. Suppose that the elements $\vec{v}_1, \vec{v}_2, \ldots, \vec{v}_n$ are a basis for V. Then we say that the *dimension* of V is n and we write $\dim V = n$.

Theorem A.2.3. Let V be a vector space with $\dim V = n > 0$ and suppose W is a subspace of V with $\dim W = n$. Then $W = V$.

Definition. The $n \times n$ matrix with ones along the main diagonal (from the upper left to the lower right) and zeros everywhere else is called the $n \times n$ *identity matrix* and is denoted I.

Example A.2.1. The following matrix is the 3×3 identity matrix:

$$I = \begin{pmatrix} 1 & 0 & 0 \\ 0 & 1 & 0 \\ 0 & 0 & 1 \end{pmatrix}$$

Note that for any $n \times n$ matrix A, we have that $AI = IA = A$.

Definition. The *determinant* of the 2×2 matrix

$$A = \begin{pmatrix} a & b \\ c & d \end{pmatrix}$$

is defined to be $ad - bc$.

Definition. The following operations on an $m \times n$ matrix are called *elementary row operations*:

1. Exchanging two rows of the matrix.
2. Multiplying a row of the matrix by a nonzero constant.
3. Replacing a row with the sum of that row and a multiple of another row.

Definition. An $m \times n$ matrix is said to be in *reduced row echelon form* if it satisfies the following properties:

1. The first nonzero entry in every row is 1 and the first nonzero entry in every row is the only nonzero entry in its column.
2. If the ith row is not all zeros, the number of zeros before the first nonzero entry of the ith row is less than the number of zeros before the first nonzero entry of the $(i + 1)$st row.
3. All the rows consisting entirely of zeros are at the bottom of the matrix.

Theorem A.2.4. Let A be an $m \times n$ matrix. Then there is an $m \times n$ matrix U in reduced row echelon form that is obtained by performing elementary row operations on A.

Definition. Let A be an $m \times n$ matrix and U a matrix in reduced row echelon form obtained from A by performing elementary row operations. The number of nonzero rows of U is called the *rank* of A.

Definition. Let A be an $m \times n$ matrix. The *transpose* of A is defined to be the $n \times m$ matrix B such that the entry in the ith row and jth column of B is the same as the entry in the jth row and ith column of A. We denote the transpose of A by A^T.

Definition. Let $\vec{v} = (v_1, v_2, \ldots, v_n)$ and $\vec{w} = (w_1, w_2, \ldots, w_n)$ be elements of F^n where F is any field. The *dot product* of $\vec{v}$ and $\vec{w}$ is defined to be $v_1 w_1 + v_2 w_2 + \cdots + v_n w_n \in F$ and is denoted by $\vec{v} \cdot \vec{w}$.

Definition. Let A be an $m \times n$ matrix with entries from a field F. We define the *nullspace* of A to be the set $\{\vec{v} \in F^n \mid A\vec{v}^T = \vec{0}\}$.

Theorem A.2.5. The nullspace of a matrix A is a subspace of the vector space F^n. (Note that F^n is a vector space over the field F.)

Theorem A.2.6. Let A be an $m \times n$ matrix with entries from a field F. Then the rank of A plus the dimension of the nullspace of A is equal to n.

A.3 Tables for the Alphabet

Letters to Decimal to Binary

Letter	Decimal	Binary
A	0	00000
B	1	00001
C	2	00010
D	3	00011
E	4	00100
F	5	00101
G	6	00110
H	7	00111
I	8	01000
J	9	01001
K	10	01010
L	11	01011
M	12	01100

Letter	Decimal	Binary
N	13	01101
O	14	01110
P	15	01111
Q	16	10000
R	17	10001
S	18	10010
T	19	10011
U	20	10100
V	21	10101
W	22	10110
X	23	10111
Y	24	11000
Z	25	11001

"Addition" Table for the Alphabet

+	A	B	C	D	E	F	G	H	I	J	K	L	M	N	O	P	Q	R	S	T	U	V	W	X	Y	Z
A	A	B	C	D	E	F	G	H	I	J	K	L	M	N	O	P	Q	R	S	T	U	V	W	X	Y	Z
B	B	C	D	E	F	G	H	I	J	K	L	M	N	O	P	Q	R	S	T	U	V	W	X	Y	Z	A
C	C	D	E	F	G	H	I	J	K	L	M	N	O	P	Q	R	S	T	U	V	W	X	Y	Z	A	B
D	D	E	F	G	H	I	J	K	L	M	N	O	P	Q	R	S	T	U	V	W	X	Y	Z	A	B	C
E	E	F	G	H	I	J	K	L	M	N	O	P	Q	R	S	T	U	V	W	X	Y	Z	A	B	C	D
F	F	G	H	I	J	K	L	M	N	O	P	Q	R	S	T	U	V	W	X	Y	Z	A	B	C	D	E
G	G	H	I	J	K	L	M	N	O	P	Q	R	S	T	U	V	W	X	Y	Z	A	B	C	D	E	F
H	H	I	J	K	L	M	N	O	P	Q	R	S	T	U	V	W	X	Y	Z	A	B	C	D	E	F	G
I	I	J	K	L	M	N	O	P	Q	R	S	T	U	V	W	X	Y	Z	A	B	C	D	E	F	G	H
J	J	K	L	M	N	O	P	Q	R	S	T	U	V	W	X	Y	Z	A	B	C	D	E	F	G	H	I
K	K	L	M	N	O	P	Q	R	S	T	U	V	W	X	Y	Z	A	B	C	D	E	F	G	H	I	J
L	L	M	N	O	P	Q	R	S	T	U	V	W	X	Y	Z	A	B	C	D	E	F	G	H	I	J	K
M	M	N	O	P	Q	R	S	T	U	V	W	X	Y	Z	A	B	C	D	E	F	G	H	I	J	K	L
N	N	O	P	Q	R	S	T	U	V	W	X	Y	Z	A	B	C	D	E	F	G	H	I	J	K	L	M
O	O	P	Q	R	S	T	U	V	W	X	Y	Z	A	B	C	D	E	F	G	H	I	J	K	L	M	N
P	P	Q	R	S	T	U	V	W	X	Y	Z	A	B	C	D	E	F	G	H	I	J	K	L	M	N	O
Q	Q	R	S	T	U	V	W	X	Y	Z	A	B	C	D	E	F	G	H	I	J	K	L	M	N	O	P
R	R	S	T	U	V	W	X	Y	Z	A	B	C	D	E	F	G	H	I	J	K	L	M	N	O	P	Q
S	S	T	U	V	W	X	Y	Z	A	B	C	D	E	F	G	H	I	J	K	L	M	N	O	P	Q	R
T	T	U	V	W	X	Y	Z	A	B	C	D	E	F	G	H	I	J	K	L	M	N	O	P	Q	R	S
U	U	V	W	X	Y	Z	A	B	C	D	E	F	G	H	I	J	K	L	M	N	O	P	Q	R	S	T
V	V	W	X	Y	Z	A	B	C	D	E	F	G	H	I	J	K	L	M	N	O	P	Q	R	S	T	U
W	W	X	Y	Z	A	B	C	D	E	F	G	H	I	J	K	L	M	N	O	P	Q	R	S	T	U	V
X	X	Y	Z	A	B	C	D	E	F	G	H	I	J	K	L	M	N	O	P	Q	R	S	T	U	V	W
Y	Y	Z	A	B	C	D	E	F	G	H	I	J	K	L	M	N	O	P	Q	R	S	T	U	V	W	X
Z	Z	A	B	C	D	E	F	G	H	I	J	K	L	M	N	O	P	Q	R	S	T	U	V	W	X	Y

Addition and Multiplication Tables for $\mathbb{Z}_{26}$

+	0	1	2	3	4	5	6	7	8	9	10	11	12	13	14	15	16	17	18	19	20	21	22	23	24	25
0	0	1	2	3	4	5	6	7	8	9	10	11	12	13	14	15	16	17	18	19	20	21	22	23	24	25
1	1	2	3	4	5	6	7	8	9	10	11	12	13	14	15	16	17	18	19	20	21	22	23	24	25	0
2	2	3	4	5	6	7	8	9	10	11	12	13	14	15	16	17	18	19	20	21	22	23	24	25	0	1
3	3	4	5	6	7	8	9	10	11	12	13	14	15	16	17	18	19	20	21	22	23	24	25	0	1	2
4	4	5	6	7	8	9	10	11	12	13	14	15	16	17	18	19	20	21	22	23	24	25	0	1	2	3
5	5	6	7	8	9	10	11	12	13	14	15	16	17	18	19	20	21	22	23	24	25	0	1	2	3	4
6	6	7	8	9	10	11	12	13	14	15	16	17	18	19	20	21	22	23	24	25	0	1	2	3	4	5
7	7	8	9	10	11	12	13	14	15	16	17	18	19	20	21	22	23	24	25	0	1	2	3	4	5	6
8	8	9	10	11	12	13	14	15	16	17	18	19	20	21	22	23	24	25	0	1	2	3	4	5	6	7
9	9	10	11	12	13	14	15	16	17	18	19	20	21	22	23	24	25	0	1	2	3	4	5	6	7	8
10	10	11	12	13	14	15	16	17	18	19	20	21	22	23	24	25	0	1	2	3	4	5	6	7	8	9
11	11	12	13	14	15	16	17	18	19	20	21	22	23	24	25	0	1	2	3	4	5	6	7	8	9	10
12	12	13	14	15	16	17	18	19	20	21	22	23	24	25	0	1	2	3	4	5	6	7	8	9	10	11
13	13	14	15	16	17	18	19	20	21	22	23	24	25	0	1	2	3	4	5	6	7	8	9	10	11	12
14	14	15	16	17	18	19	20	21	22	23	24	25	0	1	2	3	4	5	6	7	8	9	10	11	12	13
15	15	16	17	18	19	20	21	22	23	24	25	0	1	2	3	4	5	6	7	8	9	10	11	12	13	14
16	16	17	18	19	20	21	22	23	24	25	0	1	2	3	4	5	6	7	8	9	10	11	12	13	14	15
17	17	18	19	20	21	22	23	24	25	0	1	2	3	4	5	6	7	8	9	10	11	12	13	14	15	16
18	18	19	20	21	22	23	24	25	0	1	2	3	4	5	6	7	8	9	10	11	12	13	14	15	16	17
19	19	20	21	22	23	24	25	0	1	2	3	4	5	6	7	8	9	10	11	12	13	14	15	16	17	18
20	20	21	22	23	24	25	0	1	2	3	4	5	6	7	8	9	10	11	12	13	14	15	16	17	18	19
21	21	22	23	24	25	0	1	2	3	4	5	6	7	8	9	10	11	12	13	14	15	16	17	18	19	20
22	22	23	24	25	0	1	2	3	4	5	6	7	8	9	10	11	12	13	14	15	16	17	18	19	20	21
23	23	24	25	0	1	2	3	4	5	6	7	8	9	10	11	12	13	14	15	16	17	18	19	20	21	22
24	24	25	0	1	2	3	4	5	6	7	8	9	10	11	12	13	14	15	16	17	18	19	20	21	22	23
25	25	0	1	2	3	4	5	6	7	8	9	10	11	12	13	14	15	16	17	18	19	20	21	22	23	24

×	0	1	2	3	4	5	6	7	8	9	10	11	12	13	14	15	16	17	18	19	20	21	22	23	24	25
0	0	0	0	0	0	0	0	0	0	0	0	0	0	0	0	0	0	0	0	0	0	0	0	0	0	0
1	0	1	2	3	4	5	6	7	8	9	10	11	12	13	14	15	16	17	18	19	20	21	22	23	24	25
2	0	2	4	6	8	10	12	14	16	18	20	22	24	0	2	4	6	8	10	12	14	16	18	20	22	24
3	0	3	6	9	12	15	18	21	24	1	4	7	10	13	16	19	22	25	2	5	8	11	14	17	20	23
4	0	4	8	12	16	20	24	2	6	10	14	18	22	0	4	8	12	16	20	24	2	6	10	14	18	22
5	0	5	10	15	20	25	4	9	14	19	24	3	8	13	18	23	2	7	12	17	22	1	6	11	16	21
6	0	6	12	18	24	4	10	16	22	2	8	14	20	0	6	12	18	24	4	10	16	22	2	8	14	20
7	0	7	14	21	2	9	16	23	4	11	18	25	6	13	20	1	8	15	22	3	10	17	24	5	12	19
8	0	8	16	24	6	14	22	4	12	20	2	10	18	0	8	16	24	6	14	22	4	12	20	2	10	18
9	0	9	18	1	10	19	2	11	20	3	12	21	4	13	22	5	14	23	6	15	24	7	16	25	8	17
10	0	10	20	4	14	24	8	18	2	12	22	6	16	0	10	20	4	14	24	8	18	2	12	22	6	16
11	0	11	22	7	18	3	14	25	10	21	6	17	2	13	24	9	20	5	16	1	12	23	8	19	4	15
12	0	12	24	10	22	8	20	6	18	4	16	2	14	0	12	24	10	22	8	20	6	18	4	16	2	14
13	0	13	0	13	0	13	0	13	0	13	0	13	0	13	0	13	0	13	0	13	0	13	0	13	0	13
14	0	14	2	16	4	18	6	20	8	22	10	24	12	0	14	2	16	4	18	6	20	8	22	10	24	12
15	0	15	4	19	8	23	12	1	16	5	20	9	24	13	2	17	6	21	10	25	14	3	18	7	22	11
16	0	16	6	22	12	2	18	8	24	14	4	20	10	0	16	6	22	12	2	18	8	24	14	4	20	10
17	0	17	8	25	16	7	24	15	6	23	14	5	22	13	4	21	12	3	20	11	2	19	10	1	18	9
18	0	18	10	2	20	12	4	22	14	6	24	16	8	0	18	10	2	20	12	4	22	14	6	24	16	8
19	0	19	12	5	24	17	10	3	22	15	8	1	20	13	6	25	18	11	4	23	16	9	2	21	14	7
20	0	20	14	8	2	22	16	10	4	24	18	12	6	0	20	14	8	2	22	16	10	4	24	18	12	6
21	0	21	16	11	6	1	22	17	12	7	2	23	18	13	8	3	24	19	14	9	4	25	20	15	10	5
22	0	22	18	14	10	6	2	24	20	16	12	8	4	0	22	18	14	10	6	2	24	20	16	12	8	4
23	0	23	20	17	14	11	8	5	2	25	22	19	16	13	10	7	4	1	24	21	18	15	12	9	6	3
24	0	24	22	20	18	16	14	12	10	8	6	4	2	0	24	22	20	18	16	14	12	10	8	6	4	2
25	0	25	24	23	22	21	20	19	18	17	16	15	14	13	12	11	10	9	8	7	6	5	4	3	2	1

References

Barenco, A., C. H. Bennett, R. Cleve, D. P. DiVincenzo, N. Margolus, P. Shor, T. Sleator, J. Smolin, and H. Weinfurter, "Elementary gates for quantum computation," *Phys. Rev. A* **52**, 3457–3467 (1995).

Barrett, M. D., J. Chiaverini, T. Schaetz, J. Britton, W. M. Itano, J. D. Jost, E. Knill, C. Langer, D. Leibfried, R. Ozeri, and D. J. Wineland, "Deterministic quantum teleportation of atomic qubits," *Nature* **429**, 737 (2004).

Benenti, G., G. Casati, and G. Strini, *Principles of Quantum Computation and Information, Volume I: Basic Concepts* (World Scientific, Singapore, 2004).

Bennett, C. H., "Logical reversibility of computation," *IBM J. Res. Develop.* **17**, 525–532 (1973).

Bennett, C. H., F. Bessette, G. Brassard, L. Salvail, and J. Smolin, "Experimental quantum cryptography," *J. Cryptol.* **5**, 3–28 (1992).

Bennett, C. H., and G. Brassard, "Quantum cryptography: Public key distribution and coin tossing," in *Proceedings of the IEEE International Conference on Computers, Systems and Signal Processing*, Bangalore, India, December 1984 (IEEE, New York, 1984), pp. 175–179.

Bennett, C. H., G. Brassard, and J.-M. Robert, "Privacy amplification by public discussion," *SIAM J. Comput.* **17**, 210–229 (1988).

Bennett, C. H., G. Brassard, and A. K. Ekert, "Quantum cryptography," *Sci. Am.* **267**(4), 50 (Oct. 1992).

Bennett, C. H., G. Brassard, C. Crépeau, R. Jozsa, A. Peres, and W. K. Wootters, "Teleporting an unknown quantum state via dual classical and Einstein-Podolsky-Rosen channels," *Phys. Rev. Lett.* **70**, 1895–1899 (1993).

Bennett, C. H., G. Brassard, C. Crépeau, and U. M. Maurer, "Generalized privacy amplification," *IEEE Trans. Inf. Theory*, **41**(6), 1915–1923 (Nov. 1995).

Bennett, C. H., G. Brassard, S. Popescu, B. Schumacher, J. A. Smolin, and W. K. Wootters, "Purification of noisy entanglement and faithful teleportation via noisy channels," *Phys. Rev. Lett.* **76**, 722–725 (1996a).

Bennett, C. H., D. P. DiVincenzo, J. A. Smolin, and W. K. Wootters, "Mixed state entanglement and quantum error correction," *Phys. Rev. A* **54**, 3824 (1996b).

Berrou, C., A. Glavieux, and P. Thitimijashima, "Near Shannon limit error-correction coding and decoding: Turbo codes," in *Proceedings of the 1993 IEEE International Conference on Communications,* Geneva, Switzerland, 1993, pp. 1064–1070.

Biham, E., M. Boyer, P. O. Boykin, T. Mor, and V. Roychowdhury, "A proof of the security of quantum key distribution," in *Proceedings of the 32nd Annual ACM Symposium on Theory of Computing* (ACM Press, New York, 2000).

Bouwmeester, D., A. K. Ekert, and A. Zeilinger, editors, *The Physics of Quantum Information: Quantum Cryptography, Quantum Teleportation, Quantum Computation* (Springer, Berlin, 2000).

Brassard, G., and L. Salvail, "Secret-key reconciliation by public discussion," *Lect. Notes Comput. Sci.* **765**, 410–423 (1993).

Briegel, H.-J., W. Dür, J. I. Cirac, and P. Zoller, "Quantum repeaters: The role of imperfect local operations in quantum communication," *Phys. Rev. Lett.* **81**, 5932–5935 (1998).

Boykin, P. O., T. Mor, M. Pulver, V. Rowchowdhury, and F. Vatan, "On universal and fault-tolerant quantum computing: A novel basis and a new constructive proof of universality for Shor's basis," in *Proceedings of the*

40th Annual Symposium on Foundations of Computer Science (FOCS'99) (IEEE Computer Society Press, Los Alamitos, CA, 1999), pp. 486–494.

Chau, H. F., "Practical scheme to share a secret key through a quantum channel with a 27.6% bit error rate," *Phys. rev. A* **66**, 60302 (2002).

Chor, B., O. Goldreich, J. Hastad, J. Friedmann, S. Rudich, and R. Smolensky, "The bit extraction problem of t-resilient functions," in *Proceedings of the 26th IEEE Symposium on Foundations of Computer Science,* Portland, Oregon, 1985, pp. 396–407.

Chuang, I. L., N. Gershenfeld, and M. Kubinec, "Experimental implementation of fast quantum searching," *Phys. Rev. Lett.* **80**, 3408–3411 (1998).

Coppersmith, D., "Modifications to the number field sieve," *J. Cryptology* **6**, 169–180 (1993).

Coppersmith, D., "An approximate Fourier transform useful in quantum factoring," IBM Research Report RC 19642 (1994).

Crandall, R. and C. Pomerance, *Prime Numbers: A Computational Perspective*, 2nd edition (Springer, New York, 2005).

Dawson, C. M., and M. A. Nielsen, "The Solovay-Kitaev algorithm," *Quantum Inf. Comput.* **6**, 81–95 (2006).

Deutsch, D., A. Ekert, R. Jozsa, C. Macchiavello, S. Popescu, and A. Sanpera, "Quantum privacy amplification and the security of quantum cryptography over noisy channels," *Phys. Rev. Lett.* **77**, 2818–2821 (1996).

Deutsch, D., "Quantum theory, the Church-Turing Principle and the universal quantum computer," *Proc. Roy. Soc. Lond. A* **400**, 97 (1985).

Dieks, D. "Communication by EPR devices" *Phys. Lett. A* **92**, 271–272 (1982).

DiVincenzo, D. P., "Two-bit gates are universal for quantum computation," *Phys. Rev. A* **51**, 1015–1022 (1995).

Dusek, M., N. Lutkenhaus, and M. Hendrych, "Quantum Cryptography," e-print quant-ph/0601207, available at http://www.arXiv. org (2006).

Ekert, A. K., "Quantum cryptography based on Bell's theorem" *Phys. Rev. Lett.* **67**, 661–663 (1991).

Ekert, A., and R. Jozsa, "Quantum computation and Shor's factoring algorithm," *Rev. Mod. Phys.* **68**, 733–753 (1996).

Elliott, C., A. Colvin, D. Pearson, O. Pikalo, J. Schlafer, and H. Yeh, "Current status of the DARPA Quantum Network," e-print quant-ph/0503058, available at http://www.arXiv.org (2005).

Fuchs, C. A., N. Gisin, R. B. Griffiths, C.-S. Niu, and A. Peres, "Optimal eavesdropping in quantum cryptography. I. Information bound and optimal strategy," *Phys. Rev. A* **56**, 1163–1172 (1997).

Gallager, R. G. *Low-Density Parity-Check Codes* (MIT Press, Cambridge, MA, 1963).

Gallian, Joseph A. *Contemporary Abstract Algebra*, 6th ed. (Houghton Mifflin, Boston, 2006).

Gerjuoy, E., "Shor's factoring algorithm and modern cryptography. An illustration of the capabilities inherent in quantum computers," *Am. J. Phys.* **73**, 521 (2005).

Gisin, N., G. Ribordy, W. Tittel, and H. Zbinden, "Quantum cryptography," *Rev. Mod. Phys.* **74**, 145–195 (2002).

Greenstein, George, and Arthur G. Zajonc, *The Quantum Challenge: Modern Research on the Foundations of Quantum Mechanics* (Jones and Bartlett, Sudbury, MA, 1997).

Griffiths, David J. *Introduction to Quantum Mechanics* (Prentice Hall, Englewood Cliffs, NJ, 1995).

Grover, L., "A fast quantum mechanical algorithm for database search," in *Proceedings of the 28th Annual ACM Symposium on the Theory of Computation* (ACM Press, New York, 1996), pp. 212–219.

Grover, L., "Quantum mechanics helps in searching for a needle in a haystack," *Phys. Rev. Lett.* **79**, 325 (1997).

Hamming, R. W., "Error detecting and error correcting codes," *Bell Syst. Tech. J.,* **29**, 147–160 (1950).

Hardy, G. H., and E. M. Wright, *An Introduction to the Theory of Numbers,* 4th ed. (Clarendon, Oxford, 1965).

Kahn, D., *The Codebreakers* (Macmillan, New York, 1967).

Kitaev, A. Y., "Quantum computations: Algorithms and error correction," *Russ. Math. Surv.* **52**, 1191–1249 (1997).

Koblitz, Neal, *A Course in Number Theory and Cryptography* (Springer-Verlag, New York, 1994).

Kraus, B., N. Gisin, and R. Renner, "Lower and upper bounds on the secret-key rate for quantum key distribution protocols using one-way classical communication," *Phys. Rev. Lett.* **95**, 080501 (2005).

Laflamme, R., C. Miquel, J.-P. Paz, and W. H. Zurek, "Perfect quantum error correction code," *Phys. Rev. Lett.* **77**, 198 (1996).

Leon, Steven J., *Linear Algebra with Applications* (Prentice Hall, Upper Saddle River, NJ, 2006).

Levy, Steven, *Crypto: How the Code Rebels Beat the Government–Saving Privacy in the Digital Age* (Viking, New York, 2001).

Lo, H.-K., and H. F. Chau, "Unconditional security of quantum key distribution over arbitrarily long distances," *Science* **283**, 2050 (1999).

Lo, H.-K., S. Popescu, and T. Spiller, editors, *Introduction to Quantum Computation and Information* (World Scientific, Singapore, 2001).

MacKay, D. J. C., and R. M. Neal, "Near Shannon limit performance of low density parity check codes," *Electron. Lett.* **32**(18), 1645–1646 (1996).

Mayers, D., *Lecture Notes in Computer Science*, Vol. **1109** (Springer-Verlag, Berlin, 1996), p. 343.

Mayers, D., "Unconditional security in quantum cryptography," *JACM* **48**, 351–406 (2001).

Mermin, N. D., "From Cbits to Qbits: Teaching computer scientists quantum mechanics," *Am. J. Phys.* **71**, 23–30 (2003).

Nielsen, Michael A., and Isaac L. Chuang, *Quantum Computation and Quantum Information* (Cambridge Univ. Press, Cambridge, 2000).

Park, David, *Introduction to the Quantum Theory*, 3rd ed. (McGraw-Hill, New York, 1992).

Peres, Asher, *Quantum Theory: Concepts and Methods* (Kluwer, Dordrecht, 1995).

Piper, Fred, and Sean Murphy, *Cryptography: A Very Short Introduction* (Oxford Univ. Press, Oxford, 2002).

Pittenger, A. O., *An Introduction to Quantum Computing Algorithms* (Birkhäuser, Boston, 2000).

Pless, Vera, *Introduction to the Theory of Error-Correcting Codes*, 3rd ed. (Wiley, New York, 1998).

Pless, V., Huffman, W. C., editors, *Handbook of Coding Theory*, Vols. I and II (Elsevier, New York, 1998).

Preskill, J., "Fault-tolerant quantum computation," in *Quantum Information and Computation,* edited by H.-K. Lo, T. Spiller, and S. Popescu (World Scientific, Singapore, 1998).

Preskill, J., *Physics 229: Quantum Computation and Information*, California Institute of Technology. URL: http://www.theory.caltech.edu/people/preskill/ph229/(2004).

Rényi, A., "On the foundations of information theory," *Rev. Int. Statist. Inst.* **33**, 1 (1965).

Riebe, M., H. Häffner, C. F. Roos, W. Hänsel, J. Benhelm, G. P. T. Lancaster, T. W. Körber, C. Becher, F. Schmidt-Kaler, D. F. V. James, and R. Blatt, "Deterministic quantum teleportation with atoms," *Nature* **429**, 734 (2004).

Rieffel, E. G., and W. Polak, "An introduction to quantum computing for non-physicists," *ACM Comput. Surv.* **32**, 300–335 (2000).

Sebag-Montefiore, Hugh, *Enigma: The Battle for the Code* (Wiley, New York, 2000).

Shannon, C. E., "A mathematical theory of communication," *Bell Syst. Tech. J.*, **27**, 379–423, 623–656 (1948).

Shannon, C. E., "Communication theory of secrecy systems," *Bell. Sys. Tech. J.* **28**, 656 (1949).

Shor, P. W., "Algorithms for quantum computation: Discrete logarithms and factoring," in *Proceedings of the 35th Annual Symposium on the Foundations of Computer Science*, edited by S. Goldwasser (IEEE Computer Society Press, Los Alamitos, CA, 1994), pp. 124–134.

Shor, P., "Scheme for reducing decoherence in a quantum computer memory," *Phys. Rev. A* **52**, 2493 (1995).

Shor, P. W. "Polynomial-time algorithms for prime factorization and discrete logarithms on a quantum computer," *SIAM J. Comput.* **26**, 1484 (1997).

Shor, P. W., and J. Preskill, "Simple proof of security of the BB84 quantum key distribution protocol," *Phys. Rev. Lett.* **85**, 441 (2000).

Singh, Simon, *The Code Book: The Science of Secrecy from Ancient Egypt to Quantum Cryptography* (Random House, New York, 1999).

Stark, Harold M., *An Introduction to Number Theory* (The MIT Press, Cambridge, 1970).

Stinson, Douglas R., *Cryptography: Theory and Practice*, 2nd ed. (CRC Press, Boca Raton, FL, 2002).

Styer, D. F., *The Strange World of Quantum Mechanics* (Cambridge Univ. Press, Cambridge, 2000).

Tang, X., L. Ma, A. Mink, A. Nakassis, H. Xu, B. Hershman, J. C. Bienfang, D. Su, R. F. Boisvert, C. W. Clark, and C. J. Williams. "Experimental study of high speed polarization-coding quantum key distribution with sifted-key rates over Mbit/s," *Optics Express* **14**, 2062 (2006).

Vandersypen, L. M. K., M. Steffen, G. Breyta, C. S. Yannoni, M. H. Sherwood, and I. L. Chuang, "Experimental realization of Shor's quantum factoring algorithm using nuclear magnetic resonance," *Nature* **414**, 883–887 (2001).

Welsh, Dominic, *Codes and Cryptography* (Oxford Univ. Press, Oxford, 1988).

Wiesner, S., "Conjugate coding," *SIGACT News* **15**, 77 (1983).

Wootters, W. K., and W. H. Zurek, "A single quantum cannot be cloned," *Nature* **299**, 802–803 (1982).

Yurke, B. and D. Stoler, "Bell's-inequality experiments using independent-particle sources," *Phys. Rev. A* **46**, 2229 (1992).

Index